Social Problems: Readings

Social Problems: Readings

IRA SILVER

W · W · Norton & Company

New York   London

Editor: Karl Bakeman
Editorial assistant: Rebecca Arata
Manuscript editor: Philippa Solomon
Project editor: Rebecca A. Homiski
Production manager: Benjamin Reynolds
Composition: Matrix Publishing Services
Design: Margaret Wagner
Manufacturing: The Maple-Vail Book Group, Binghamton

Library of Congress Cataloging-in-Publication Data

Social problems : readings / [edited] by Ira Silver. — 1st ed.
    p. cm.
    Includes bibliographical references and index.

    ISBN 13: 978-0-393-92932-4 (pbk.)

1. Social problems.   I. Silver, Ira.
    HN28.S618 2008
    361.1—dc22

                                    2007024032

W. W. Norton & Company, Inc., 500 Fifth Avenue, New York, N.Y. 10110
                        www.wwnorton.com

W. W. Norton & Company Ltd., Castle House, 75/76 Wells Street, London W1T 3QT

2 3 4 5 6 7 8 9 0

Contents

Preface

You already know a whole lot about social problems—certainly more than you think you do. That is because we talk about social problems all the time. As I write these words in August 2006, a major terrorist plot has just been foiled in London. In the coming days and weeks, there is certain to be an escalation in public dialogue about the terrorism problem. Other social problems similarly occupy people's daily thoughts and conversations, as revealed by comments such as "Did you hear what happened today . . . ?"

Virtually everywhere we turn we encounter experts whose work enables us to gain new information about social problems. Doctors treat different types of disease, social workers help people to find solutions to marital and family problems, and police protect us from the threats that crime poses to social order. These and many other problems are routinely the subject of political discussion and news reports. Therefore, you really do not need to take a course to absorb information about the causes of social problems, the magnitude of the harm, or possible solutions.

This is why the readings that comprise this book offer a different perspective toward social problems than what experts provide. Designed to serve as a companion to Joel Best's *Social Problems*, these readings highlight one of the most interesting themes concerning the study of social problems: that there are a variety of harmful conditions to which our society pays little attention, while there are many other, much smaller harms that consume our everyday thoughts. In reading these selections, you will become familiar with the *social constructionist perspective*, which investigates how and why certain problems elicit more concern and resources from experts, activists, the news media, policymakers, and the public, than do others. This perspective focuses on the activities of *claimsmakers*, those individuals or groups that are involved either in fostering greater awareness about a particular harm or in diverting attention away from that harm.

This book offers tools for acquiring the analytical skills that are so critical to a liberal arts education. The book invites you to explore a series of provocative questions concerning the society we inhabit. Why do some social problems receive substantial attention while others receive comparatively little? How do claimsmakers bring attention to problems in particular ways that galvanize public awareness? How do influential claimsmakers use their power to bring attention to certain problems while diverting attention away from others? What are the impacts of defining, and consequently treating, a problem in a particular way? Addressing these questions provides an introduction to sociology that will enable you to discover for yourself what makes the subject so interesting and often so personally relevant. The readings will afford you the opportunity to look at the social world in ways that may be new to you.

In teaching an introductory undergraduate social problems course for several years, I have found that the best way to get students to use the social constructionist perspective is to foster class discussion and dialogue about specific case studies of social problems that illuminate this perspective. Each of the readings in this book offers such a case study. Just about every major contemporary social problem is addressed in this collection. There are several readings within each of the following broad problem areas: family, health and the environment, drugs, race, disaster, gender, inequality, and violence. I selected the readings with an eye toward those issues that tap student interests and curiosities, and consequently can get students excited about sociology. The questions that follow each selection are the very ones I ask of my own students. I have found that these questions frequently fuel discussions that invite students to think actively and seriously about the topics at hand. Students often find themselves, quite unexpectedly, enjoying the process of thinking in these new ways.

I have organized the table of contents around four themes that are central for understanding and using the social constructionist perspective.

1. The Power to Construct Social Problems

This section exposes the different degrees of power that claimsmakers exercise and specifically how this power manifests itself in claimsmakers' capacity to give greater or lesser visibility to particular problems. This section consequently illustrates why analyzing power is central for understanding how certain problems become matters of greater public and policymaking concern than others.

2. **How Social Problems Are Framed**

   This section focuses on frames, the particular words and phrases that claimsmakers use to portray a problem as a matter of public concern. Frames package particular problems in such ways that audiences can broadly relate to these problems and believe that they are in need of fixing.

3. **Competition among Social Problems**

   Since the social constructionist perspective looks at how and why problems command (or fail to command) scarce resources, this section offers students examples of how problems compete with one another for these resources. For any issue, there is competition among different ways of defining the harm and different strategies for addressing the harm.

4. **Policymaking and Outcomes**

   Finally, the reader will address the larger implications of problems being constructed in particular ways. These selections focus on the policy consequences when a particular framing of a problem has won out over competing frames.

I am very grateful to Karl Bakeman, sociology editor at W. W. Norton & Company, for extending the opportunity to compile this collection of readings. I especially appreciate his consistently thoughtful and friendly comments as I worked on the book. My biggest thanks go to Nancy, Benjamin, and Arielle, who consistently provide me with the love, inspiration, and confidence to pursue sociology with the highest level of passion and vigor.

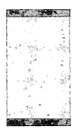

To the Instructor

For those of you using this book alongside Joel Best's *Social Problems*, the following list suggests readings to accompany each chapter of his text.

Chapter 1: The Social Problems Process
   Reading 5. *Making Road Dangers Invisible*, Malcolm Gladwell
   Reading 26. *Black Men as Criminals and as Victims*, Barry Glassner
Chapter 2: Claims
   Reading 3. *Viewing Bodily Imperfection as a Health Problem*, Ken
      Silverstein
   Reading 10. *The Horrors of Child Abuse*, John M. Johnson
   Reading 20. *Compensating for Deficit versus Enhancing Performance*, Kate
      Zernike
   Reading 22. *Babies Having Babies*, Kristin Luker
Chapter 3: Activists as Claimsmakers
   Reading 9. *Random Violence*, Joel Best
   Reading 12. *Injustice Based on Sexual Orientation*, Mitch Berbrier and
      Elaine Pruett
   Reading 19. *Selling Environmental Problems*, Sheldon Ungar
Chapter 4: Experts as Claimsmakers
   Reading 6. *Getting Fat on Misinformation*, The Center for Consumer
      Freedom
   Reading 13. *PMS and the Biological Flaws of Womanhood*, Carol Tavris
Chapter 5: The Media and Claims
   Reading 1. *Spotlighting Disaster*, Eric Klinenberg

Chapter 6: Public Reaction

Chapter 7: Policymaking

Chapter 8: Social Problems Work

Chapter 9: Policy Outcomes

Chapter 10: Claims across Space and Time

For those of you using this book to focus class discussion around particular problems, the following list groups issue areas with the readings that pertain to each of these areas.

Issue Area	Readings
Crime	2, 4, 9, 10, 21, 26, 27, 31
Disaster	1, 25, 31
Drugs	2, 3, 20
Family	7, 10, 11, 20, 22, 23
Gender	13, 17, 20, 28
Health and environment	3, 5, 6, 19, 23
Inequality	8, 12, 14, 15, 24, 28, 29, 32, 33
Race	4, 14, 26, 33
Violence	7, 9, 10, 16, 17, 23, 27

Social Problems: Readings

PART ONE
THE POWER TO CONSTRUCT SOCIAL PROBLEMS

Problems in the world receive greater or lesser visibility based on the efforts of *claimsmakers*—those individuals and organizations that are actively involved either in making the case that resources should be used to fix a particular problem or that a certain problem does not deserve resources. When we begin to look closely at the activities of claimsmakers, we see that it is significant who speaks out on behalf of which problems and how much power these claimsmakers exercise. If we look across the vast spectrum of claimsmakers—a group that includes politicians, activists, corporations, researchers, police, the news media, victims, special-interest groups, and private individuals—we can begin to see some obvious power disparities. For instance, corporate advertisers clearly have a much greater capacity to spread influential messages about how women should feel about their bodies than does any individual woman.

Analyzing the power of claimsmakers enables us to explain why some problems, but not others, are constructed as matters of public and policymaking concern, and why those successfully constructed as social problems receive different amounts of exposure and effort to fix them. Therefore, as students of social problems, we are interested in the different degrees of power possessed by claimsmakers. Certain claimsmakers are influential within a particular field of social problems, such as doctors for health problems, police for crime problems, and therapists for family problems. There are three claimsmakers that exercise extensive claimsmaking power across virtually all issues: large corporations, the government, and mainstream news media. These three claimsmakers use their power to focus public and policymaking attention on certain problems and to divert attention away from other problems.

As an illustration of claimsmaker power, let's take a look at automobile accidents caused by irresponsible drivers. There is considerable public awareness these days that it is unacceptable for a person to drink and drive. News reports give extensive coverage to drunk driving accidents, schools educate students about the multiple impairments that alcohol causes, and even beer ads have started to caution people to drive safely. Moreover, since 1980 the organization MADD (Mothers Against Drunk Driving) has grown from a few mothers who had been traumatized by the deaths of their children in drunk driving accidents and tried to give visibility to this issue to one of the most powerful activist and lobbying groups in the United States.

Why is drunk driving such a visible social problem nowadays? At first glance, the answer seems patently obvious given that people who drink and drive pose a number of obvious hazards on the road. The answer is, in truth, not so obvious if we consider that drunk driving is just one of a number of causes of recklessness on the road. Therefore, we need to look not only at why drunk driving has become such a prominent social problem in recent years, but also at why automobile accidents caused by other kinds of irresponsible behavior on the part of drivers have not.

Take, for example, talking on a cell phone while driving. In 2001, New York became the first state to issue tickets for this behavior, and Washington, D.C. and New Jersey have since followed suit (Radsch, 2005). If this trend continues, it is conceivable that in time the decision to use a cell phone while driving may be viewed as akin to taking the wheel after a night at the bar. However, this is unlikely to happen. The wireless phone industry spends enormous amounts of money lobbying state legislatures not to pass laws prohibiting car usage of cell phones. Moreover, the wireless industry exercises enormous influence over how Americans think about their cell phones. Since cell phones first became available in the early 1990s, the industry has spent billions of advertising dollars on promoting claims that these devices make people's lives better. Central among these claims is that cell phones enable people to do their work more efficiently, since calls can be made from anywhere, including one's car. Therefore, the wireless industry uses its power to present cell phones as a solution, not a problem. This exercise of power diverts attention away from the extent to which cell phones pose a significant road hazard (Gladwell, 1999).

The extensive claimsmaking power of large corporations is similarly illustrated when we look at the welfare problem. Many Americans tend to see it as problematic that the government gives cash assistance to poor single mothers; the reason given is that these women abuse the system in a variety of ways—by not looking for jobs, having more babies, and using the money to buy alcohol or drugs. The public's problem with welfare, therefore, is not that the government helps people but that it should not be helping those who are undeserving of its support. There is, after all, no public sense that those who get laid off from their jobs and become entitled to unemployment insurance are not worthy of the government's help.

But, what about the corporate welfare problem? Over the past decade, a number of critics have tried to raise public awareness of the reasons why large corporations are undeserving of the billions of dollars in assistance they receive from the federal government each year. The chief claim these critics have made is that such assistance, which is supposedly meant to create jobs, has instead led to massive corporate downsizing and the relocation of manufacturing plants from the United States to countries without laws mandating minimum wages or safe working conditions (Bartlett and Steele, 1998; Shields, 2004). The most visible persona behind this perspective has been Michael Moore. His 1997 film *The Big One,* probably the least publicized of his films, documented a series of companies from coast to coast that had downsized while they were recording record profits. Moore highlighted that this downsizing was taking place at the same time that the U.S. Congress was focusing on how to reform welfare so that poor single mothers would no longer abuse the system. Yet, there was silence within Congress and the mainstream news media about the corporate welfare problem.

The key question here is, why has the corporate welfare problem not become perceived as a social problem in the way that poor single mothers receiving cash assistance most definitely has? We can attempt to answer this question in the way that people most often do: by determining whether poor women's abuse of government assistance is objectively more problematic. But going down this road does not take us very far. We quickly see that since claimsmakers establish which harms are most in need of attention, we have to look at various claimsmakers with different levels of power to bring attention to each of these welfare problems.

In order to do this, let's compare a Fortune 500 company that receives tax breaks from the federal government with a poor single mother who receives monthly cash assistance. Each recipient has an interest in doing what it can to prevent being seen as part of a broader welfare problem. The company has several outlets at its disposal for achieving this goal. It can spend money on advertising to promote its public image, so that when people think of the company, they associate it with its wonderful products and charitable work, while not even being aware that it is perhaps an undeserved beneficiary of government assistance. The company can also fund politicians who do not place corporate welfare on their agenda of priorities to tackle while in office (Clawson, Neustadtl, and Weller, 1998). And third, the company might have an ownership stake in a news organization, contributing to the tendency for news reporting to avoid drawing attention to the problems caused by big business and other powerful entities (Bagdikian, 1989).

In contrast, the poor single mother has virtually no means of influencing how the public and policymakers think about and feel about the government assistance she receives. She does not have the money to pay for advertisements that might divert attention away from this assistance and instead focus it on more desirable aspects of her life story, such as her efforts to raise a child as a single parent on very little income. She does not have access to politicians' ears, and therefore cannot exert pressure on them to address other policy questions besides how deserving poor single mothers are of govern-ment support. And finally, she cannot influence how the news media portray her and other poor women.

These examples just discussed—car accidents and welfare—illustrate that claimsmaking power plays an instrumental role in shaping which issues become perceived as social problems and which do not. These examples high-light two broader themes about social problems: (1) The problems that receive significant public or policy attention are caused by individuals or groups that do not exercise much claimsmaking power; and (2) the harms created by pow-erful claimsmakers seldom receive exposure and visibility. While these harms may receive the attention of activists or researchers, they generally remain invisible to wider audiences. This is because powerful claimsmakers use their influence to divert attention away from the problems they cause, and to focus attention instead on problems produced by entities that do not comparably have the capacity to shroud themselves from public scrutiny. It is clear from this discussion that magnitude of harm has little bearing on which problems become social problems. After all, who decides which harms deserve attention and remedy? The answer, like much of history, is written by the powerful.

REFERENCES

Bagdikian, Ben H. (1989). Missing from the news. *The Progressive* 53:32–34.

Bartlett, Donald L., and James B. Steele. (1998, November 9). Corporate welfare. *Time* 160:36–39.

Clawson, Dan, Alan Neustadtl, and Mark Weller. (1998). *Dollars and votes: How business cam-paign contributions subvert democracy*. Philadelphia: Temple University Press.

Gladwell, Malcolm. (1999, March 8). Drunk drivers and other dangers. *New Yorker* 75:23–24.

Radsch, Courtney C. (2005, January 18). Driver-cellphone laws exist, but their value is dis-puted. *New York Times*.

Shields, Janice. (2004). Getting corporations off the public dole. From Jerome H. Skolnick and Elliot Currie (Eds.), *Crisis in American institutions* (12th ed., pp. 21–27). Boston: Allyn & Bacon.

1

Spotlighting Disaster

FROM *The Spectacular City: News Organizations
and the Representation of Catastrophe*

ERIC KLINENBERG

*This case study of the hundreds of deaths that occurred during the 1995 Chicago
heat wave illustrates the enormous power that news organizations have to shape the
public meaning of events. The author goes behind the scenes at the city's leading
newspaper, the* Chicago Tribune, *and documents that the significance given this
disaster had much to do with the conventions that journalists routinely use to capture audience's attention and interest such as jarring photos, dramatic headlines,
and popular storylines. This study illustrates why news accounts of natural disasters typically highlight "acts of God" leading up to the devastation, while obscuring
the social factors explaining why certain people suffer more than others from these
disasters.*

On Wednesday, 12 July, the late-night newscast on Chicago's ABC television affiliate opened with a dramatic close-up of a full moon ablaze in
orange and yellow light. The sweltering city dwellers below could be excused
for mistaking the sight for a second sun. Although it was close to midnight
the heat index was above one hundred degrees, and there was no sign of relief.
It was "a summer sizzler on a moonlit night," anchorman John Drury
announced as the camera panned to shots of people walking the streets. "On
the ground, residents are seeking relief any way they can. . . . The heat is on,
and tomorrow will be the hottest day of all." After a quick series of shots
between the news desk and overloaded air-conditioning units, the cameras
turned to a live view of Marquette Park on the South Side, where a group of
children rejoiced in the shower of a powerful water fountain and defied the
evening heat. Standing before them, reporter John Garcia began to recount

the city's struggle to keep cool. First the screen showed disabled generators at a Commonwealth Edison plant, and then the face of an elderly woman who explained that without power, she "had to go to the basement where it's cool." Next the footage moved to the inside of an appliance store, where anxious Chicagoans clad in shorts and tee shirts scrambled for air conditioners and loaded the heavy units into their cars. "I can't take the heat," a shopper told Garcia, and then a grinning store manager assured the newsman that the customer was not alone. "It's going great. I'm happy to see it," the merchant exclaimed. The store had received a new shipment of air conditioners a few hours before, and already they were selling out.

Garcia's report continued and the camera moved again. Suddenly there was daylight and a panoramic view of bikinied swimmers at North Avenue Beach, where some ninety thousand city dwellers descended to treat themselves to what the reporter called "nature's air conditioner"; then a shot of Human Services Commissioner Daniel Alvarez, who was perched in front of the Chicago city seal, advising people with respiratory problems to stay indoors; finally, back to the newsroom, where meteorologist Jerry Taft summed up the conditions. "It's pretty amazing," he said. "The heat index, right now, makes it feel like one hundred degrees—at ten o'clock at night. . . . Tomorrow will be a dangerous day, actually, for a lot of people, although uncomfortable for most."

The Thursday evening broadcast began similarly. Producers led the news with footage of the sun setting in a smog-filled sky and radiating the number 104 in burnt-orange figures on the screen. Drury, again at the anchor's desk, noted the record temperature and warned that "the heat isn't over yet." The cameras skipped to a public swimming pool crammed with dozens of children, then to a street scene of dozens more dancing in the spray of a fire hydrant, one of three thousand illegally opened that day. The image of young people frolicking in water had already become an emblem for the heat wave coverage. It would recur throughout the week, seamlessly woven into video sequences containing shots of dead bodies, exhausted relief workers, city officials, and weather maps to make a surreal mosaic of the steaming city.

"With the heat," Drury announced, "a serious water problem. . . . Some communities, at times, have lost water pressure completely." The newscast grew somber as coanchor Diann Burns reported that "tonight there's word that the heat wave has now turned deadly in Chicago." Chief Medical Examiner Edmund R. Donoghue said that two men, one eighty-six years of age, the other thirty-two, were the first casualties of the heat; a South Side hospital listed another man in critical condition with a body temperature of 108 degrees. Next Burns introduced reporter Paul Meincke, who narrated footage of irritated African-American residents in two South Side neighborhoods. Open hydrants there had caused water pressure loss serious enough to deplete water supplies, yet the Water Department had not repaired the problem. The contrast between the dry apartment taps and the drenched streets below was striking.

As Chicagoans awaited relief, the national and international news media picked up the story. Cable News Network assigned correspondent Mark Leff to report on the Midwestern casualties, animal and human, and to track the heat storm moving toward the East Coast. On National Public Radio's *All Things Considered,* Chicago-based correspondent Ira Glass reported the air-conditioning crunch story along with an account of two men who tried to sleep outdoors but were driven back inside by police, beggars, and bugs.

As the environment grew more dangerous the two major Chicago newspapers, the *Chicago Tribune* and *Chicago Sun-Times,* organized the most comprehensive efforts to cover and reconstruct the story. When the Chief Medical Examiner announced the rising death rates the journalistic production teams changed gears. The heat wave shifted from a light feature about the weather to a sensational disaster story demanding extensive coverage. There was no shortage of raw material. Dead bodies were piling up at the Cook County Office of the Medical Examiner and police officers were delivering more every hour; political officials were beginning to bicker and City Hall was organizing news conferences to manage the complaints; Com Ed generators were failing and thousands of residents and businesses were stranded in the heat; hospitals were closing their doors to patients seeking emergency care and ambulances were circling the region in search of empty beds; city workers were hosing down children like cattle; concrete roads were buckling. Journalists had all the ingredients to render the heat wave as a spectacle of dramatic proportions.

* * *

WHAT'S NEWS?

What were the professional responsibilities of the reporters and editors who worked on the heat wave stories for various news outlets? According to conventional theories of the news media, and especially those advanced by journalists themselves, "the essence of real journalism . . . is the search for information of use to the public." "Prevailing wisdom," Jay Rosen writes, holds that journalists "give us timely information about matters of common importance; they entertain and enlighten us with compelling stories; they act as our surrogate and watchdog before the high and mighty, asking sharp questions and demanding straight answers; they expose wrong-doing and the abuse of public trust; and they put before us a range of views, through opinion forums marked as such." But in practice, news audiences have always demanded that journalists do more—or maybe less—than provide them with information that will help them act as responsible democratic citizens.

Journalists themselves disagree about the kinds of roles they should play in reporting public events such as the heat wave. During the crisis local newsrooms became the sites of conflicts between editors who wanted to generate large audiences through spectacular human interest stories and those who wanted to produce more substantive news reporting. But even the combatants in these disputes took for granted that the news coverage would employ standard journalistic material such as sensational visual images, provocative headlines, and dramatic story leads that cause little controversy in the newsroom and exert great influence over the content of the coverage. News audiences expect the media to entertain them with spectacles that animate the world. As Daniel Boorstin writes, "we have shifted responsibility for making the world interesting from God to the newspaperman," and most journalistic organizations are designed to serve this role. Yet the major news organizations, particularly reputable and award-winning papers such as the *Chicago Tribune,* are generally committed to a professional ethic that values rigorous and serious journalism. Balancing the market's demand for novelty, drama, and spectacle with the journalistic imperative to produce quality news is one of the great challenges of the news team.

* * *

As the heat wave ran its course, local and national news companies produced hundreds of stories about the disaster, with the Chicago newspapers probing deepest into its nature and causes and integrating the broadest range of editorial content and opinion into their coverage. Relative to local television news, the printed media offer more space for extended and varied treatment of important issues, so it is not surprising that the papers produced more depth, diversity, and detailed reporting in their packages of heat wave stores. Newspapers produce more content than do television or radio, and the multisectioned structure by which they are organized allows editors to present conflicting ideas or opinions in forms that managers in other media do not make available. The *Chicago Tribune,* for example, published roughly 119 news stories, 13 editorials and letters, and 11 news briefs during and immediately after the crisis; the *Chicago Sun-Times* printed 99 news stories, 12 news briefs, 14 editorials and letters, and approximately 30 assorted reports and commentaries. No other news organizations matched the amount of research and reporting that went into the newspaper projects or contributed so much to the public record of the event.

Despite its relative depth and diversity, however, the newspaper accounts of the disaster necessarily focused on the particular sites, issues, and images that made for good copy while marginalizing others. As the newspaper content analyses presented in tables 1 and 2 show, the representations of the heat wave stories in the major local papers emphasized the deaths and scene at Cook County Morgue, the natural or meteorological conditions, the coping strategies of individuals trying to stay cool, and the city's rhetorical and institutional responses to the health emergency. Photographic images of the dead bodies, the morgue, and the use of water to combat the heat were especially prominent. The content analysis also shows that local news organizations deemphasized some of the social conditions that affected the impact of the disaster. There were relatively few stories or images focusing on aging, poverty, isolation, crime and fear, and the ethnoracial or gender distribution of mortality, morbidity, and access to care.

The overall distribution of news stories and images should not imply that the papers neglected to provide any in-depth reporting about the social etiology of the disaster. Indeed, amidst the dominant frames of natural disaster and massive mortality, both the *Tribune* and *Sun-Times* published exemplary

TABLE 1.   Content Analysis of Heat Wave Stories: *Chicago Tribune* (July 1995 to July 1996)

Frame	Text	Title	Image
Deaths and morgue	58	52	35
City government responses	37	28	14
Individuals and coping strategies	36	34	45
Meteorological conditions	29	50	30
Political scandal and death debate	26	24	4
Aging	10	6	12
Isolation	9	8	4
Poverty	3	2	NA
Crime and safety	2	2	NA
Ethnoracial issues	2	2	NA

TABLE 2.   Content Analysis of Heat Wave Stories: *Chicago Sun-Times* (July 1995 to July 1996)

Frame	Text	Title	Image
Deaths and morgue	37	51	23
City government responses	38	36	10
Individuals and coping strategies	42	41	19
Meteorological conditions	23	35	9
Political scandal and death debate	21	20	2
Aging	11	8	7
Isolation	8	8	4
Poverty	4	3	3
Crime and safety	2	2	NA
Ethnoracial issues	0	0	NA

pieces of news reporting about people who died alone and those who managed to make it; neighborhood conditions that made some areas especially vulnerable; and emergency city programs that were not mobilized. These stories were marginal parts of the overall package, though, and often were buried in the back sections and inside pages that fewer readers see. Analyzing the content of newspaper articles helps to establish the general economy of the heat wave coverage, but explaining how and why local journalistic organizations framed and focused their coverage on some issues at the expense of others requires shifting attention from the news stories themselves to the newsrooms where the stories were produced. There is no better place to do this than the *Chicago Tribune,* the city's most renowned and respected news organization, and by many accounts the source of the most thorough and serious heat wave coverage. The story of the *Tribune*'s heat wave reporting, reconstructed from the written record as well as interviews with many of the editors and reporters who worked on the catastrophe, provides a window into the conditions of contemporary news work that helped transform the disaster into a dramatic spectacle and public event.

DISCOVERING DISASTER

On Saturday morning, 15 July, veteran reporter George Papajohn was filling in for an editor on the *Chicago Tribune* Metro desk. By journalistic standards, the amount of newsworthy activity during summer weekends in Chicago is low. Local officials seldom hold weekend news conferences, many businesses are closed, and the public relations teams that feed news organizations with information slow the pace of their work. As Papajohn explained, "generally the Saturday shift is a fairly quiet one. Obviously the government is shut down; the paper has spent all week producing its giant piece of journalism [the Sunday edition] and the stories are generally enterprise stories that you have to play around with. But you're there, editing, to fill in some of the news and update the stories."

Papajohn began his workday by taking up his routine for generating story ideas. He had been following the heat wave coverage closely, watching the television news reports at home and listening to radio while driving to work. In the office he looked over the daily papers, scanned both the national and the City News Bureau wire reports, skimmed the large pile of faxes sent to the *Tribune,* talked with the paper's bureau chief, listened to voice mail, and chatted with fellow reporters. Papajohn soon began to realize that something unusual was happening.

> I was coming in and I had heard on the radio . . . that the Medical Examiners Office was looking into a number of deaths that they thought could be associated with the heat wave. . . . We were still in the mode of gee, it's really hot, you know. What does that mean? . . . However, it seemed to me that, just based on what I heard on news radio, that we ought to make sure we were pursuing the other thing, and that we shouldn't pursue anything else until we made sure we didn't have a major news story on our hands. And then, the other sort of routine thing to do is you sign on the computer and the City News Bureau wires are there, and they're sort of the local AP, they're the people out there who send things out over the wires. You look at that every day. Twice a day they update the Medical Examiner's list of deaths they're investigating. This is normally a list that could be anywhere from five to ten names, but on this day it was just an incredibly thick list that not only was thick, it went on for three thick paragraphs. . . . That was when *I became very certain that we had to just completely shift gears.* . . . And it sort of fell into place after that.

Lou Carlozo, then a suburban reporter who worked the Saturday afternoon shift downtown, was in the newsroom when Papajohn decided to change the focus of the heat wave coverage.

> So I'm on the desk on Saturday and George is looking through the wire reports. And George is shaking his head and he's like, "Something is not

right." There are all these people dying and he says, "I wonder if we have the makings of a catastrophe here. Because it is hot, it has been hot. If this many people are being brought to the morgue, who knows how many people are out there waiting to be discovered?" So immediately . . . he made a couple of us go in pool cars. I was one of the people. He said I want you to go, go to these addresses. Find out everything you can, talk to as many people as you can, learn about these people.

The *Tribune* had originally reported the heat wave exclusively as a meteorological event, describing it with little detail and placing it in the weather section of the paper. On Wednesday, 12 July, though, the temperature matched a Chicago record and the *Tribune* editors were impressed enough to make the heat a front-page feature, the kind that newspapers conventionally publish on days when the climate is extreme enough to affect normal conditions. In the story, which was printed in the Thursday edition, two reporters crafted a light account of residents' coping strategies out of interviews with a number of city visitors and nonnatives who spoke about the heat in their home cities. The article implored Chicagoans to stop complaining about their discomfort. Headlined "If You Can Stand the Heat, You Must be Out-of-Towner" and set beneath a photograph of a park worker hosing herself down, the piece opened, "Stop your whining. So what if it got up to 97 degrees on Wednesday, tying the record. . . . Even though tens of thousands of Chicago-area residents probably suffered through the first day of an anticipated week-long heat wave, for many others, Wednesday's weather was just a walk in the park." Continuing to frame the heat wave event as a humorous feature, the *Tribune* editors next sent a reporter in search of air conditioners, taking up the same theme used by local and national television news reports. The article was also scheduled to make page 1, but when Papajohn and the other editors learned about the ominous death toll on Friday, they realized that they had to change the frame of the story as well as the practical work of producing it. From then until the city cooled down, the *Tribune* would make this coverage its top priority.

George Papajohn had substituted as an editor enough to develop a system for learning about the news on the days in which he "worked the desk," a routine similar to the one he kept as a reporter. He depends heavily on other news media to generate story ideas, with radio broadcasts playing a prominent role because radio reporters can produce fast journalism and late-breaking news by simply reading wire stories as they come into the studio. Little production work or time is necessary for these broadcasts, and although the reports are thinly written, print journalists can use them as points of departure for more-developed accounts. Television news stories, especially now that Chicago and many other cities have local twenty-four-hour news television stations, usually provide the first visual images of events, yet they are seldom longer than a few minutes. Other newspapers suggest additional angles to stories that the *Tribune* staff is likely to have already covered or considered covering. Only occasionally do papers scoop each other on daily news reports in an era when the news cycle has exploded into a twenty-four-hour-a-day news cyclone.

The newsroom itself is saturated with other mainstream news media. Part of the reason that newsmakers in the major media employ conventional frames and themes, such as the story of city residents looking for air conditioners or the image of children playing in water, is that by continuously reading, watching, and listening to their colleagues' reports they internalize a set of routine story types that are easily reproducible in the time constraints that organize journalistic work. The formal and informal training journalists undergo is only a small part of their socialization into the profession. Like other professionals, they are continuously trained on the job and their approaches to the news are regularly reinforced when they consume, critique, and mimic the work of their colleagues. Although journalists write or produce information for the public, they are one another's most important and responsive audience; indeed, several reporters explained that colleagues are their most vigorous critics and supporters. If it is true that, as Manuel Castells argues, members of most contemporary societies "live with the media and by the media," daily journalists live *in* the media, forming a subculture and a "vicious informational cycle" that affirms the importance of issues that interest other journalists but excludes alternative ideas that might otherwise be considered newsworthy.

At the *Tribune,* for example, news stories from other local organizations played a key role in switching the focus of the early heat wave coverage. Hearing the radio reports and reading the other papers helped Papajohn recognize that as the story changed from a weather report to a breaking and continuing feature on a local catastrophe, the *Tribune* had to shift its journalistic strategy and devote more resources to the event. The feature on air conditioners still ran on Sunday, as did a women's fashion piece instructing how to stay cool in the heat and headlined "Gimme Swelter! It's the Height of the Steamy Season, But the Heat Doesn't Have to Sap Your Style. Here's How to Ward Off Wardrobe Wilt and Make-up Meltdown." But neither story made the front section, which featured more serious news reports on the mounting death count.

By Saturday afternoon, 15 July, the editors had decided to increase their coverage of the deaths by sending reporters to the Medical Examiners Office and to the addresses of the deceased, which were included in the mortality lists released by the office. The problem was that the paper generally produces little news on Saturday and Sunday, and some of the weekend staff lacked the experience and the skills that the news editors considered necessary to adequately cover the big story. As one experienced reporter explained, "You have to understand how the *Tribune* works on weekends. There's really not a lot of people here, and a lot of the people who work here on the weekends are the younger staff. So we have a lot of "one-years" [junior reporters hired on one-year contracts] and interns. And they have varying abilities. And most of them don't know the city."

The timing of the disaster on the weekend affected the manner in which the *Tribune* covered it in the first news reports. The shortage of staff was particularly severe on Sunday, the first day that everyone at the paper knew how serious the disaster was, because most of the experienced editors and writers were attending the annual editorial picnic. Yet as a daily procedure, including weekends, the editors on duty have a list of reporters and editors whom they can call if they need additional staffing for a breaking story. During the heat wave they could not have produced the paper without it.

Cindy Schreuder, one of the lead science writers at the *Tribune,* was working on a special project during July and was therefore not involved in production of the daily paper at the time. That Sunday she happened to be heading into the office to work on her series when she was asked to help with the heat wave coverage. The editors had decided that the story needed a medical and environmental perspective, and they wanted a senior science writer to oversee the reporting. Schreuder recalled,

> I was almost walking out the door [when] my telephone rang and it was the Metro editor, and he asked me if I could go downtown and help coordinate the coverage of the heat wave. [He] said, you know, the people we have on this are mostly one-years and he was a little concerned that they just didn't have the experience for what this might turn out to be. When I went down that day I talked to some of the others to find out what they were doing, whom they were calling. Later in the evening there was some sort of discrepancy in the stories we were getting from people in different places. I got a little concerned so I started making some calls. The original lead that I had on that first story was a soft feature. But as the night wore on it was clear that there were a lot of deaths

and that was totally inappropriate. So I started making more calls and I suddenly realized that what we had on our hands was a really large death toll. It became clear that I was going to have to dump [my project] and report on this story.

At the picnic, the editors remained worried about their paper's coverage of the emerging crisis. They were vexed by the reports from the Medical Examiners Office and by the early statements from City Hall that expressed skepticism over the coroner's findings. The situation provoked a conflict among the editors, with some of them sympathetic to Mayor Daley's initial claims that the mortality figures were overstated, while others were convinced that the city was experiencing a genuine catastrophe.

* * *

During the heat wave the initial disputes among the editors, reporters, and producers at several Chicago news organizations were notably acute. Meteorologist Paul Douglas, who was reporting on the crisis for a local television station, newspaper company, and radio station, recalled a conflict he had had with a television producer about whether to frame the coverage as a human interest story or as a public health warning and news story:

> I came in early on the worst of the days, when it got up to 106, and our executive producer came over, and we were very proactive. We went to the producers and we said, "This is going to be a major story. People are going to be dying. This is something you'd better hit very, very hard. What can and should we be doing at other times of the day? Should we be interrupting programs with heat alerts?" And I believe that afternoon we did interrupt programming, even before the news began. We had a couple of cut-ins, where we talked about the extreme heat and the extreme danger. But I'll never forget, [the executive producer] kept coming over to us she kept asking, she wanted to do a live shot with some place in the United States that would be hotter than Chicago. She kept talking about wanting to do a live shot with a meteorologist in Phoenix. . . . You know, basically making it more of a *featury,* lifestyle kind of cutesy—"hey, let's have the dueling meteorologists try to figure out who's hotter"—story. . . . And I kept pleading with her and telling her, "You're missing the point. We should have people at the hospitals, we should have people at City Hall." And it degenerated into a shouting match in the newsroom. She started screaming, "You don't get it, you don't get

it! This is television!" And I said, "I do get it. I understand. This is a dangerous situation for Chicago. We are the hottest spot. People will be dying later today. That's your story."

Douglas was pleased with his producers' decision to clear time for public serv-ice announcements before the news, as well as with the placement of the weather stories early in the news broadcasts. The human interest frames and feature stories seemed inappropriate to him given the danger of the situation, but the television program accommodated the inchoate streams of light images and heavy ideas that blend together to make the news exciting and fresh. The producers, who are ultimately responsible for the broadcast, decided that the human interest stories made better television, and therefore better news.

The early reports of rising heat-related mortality convinced most news organizations to shift the direction of their coverage, but the mayor's public skepticism about the Chief Medical Examiner's scientific methods was another influence on their decision. At the *Tribune,* some editors had been persuaded by the city government's criticisms of the heat-related death measures and the attributions reported by Ed Donoghue, the Chief Medical Examiner. According to Paul Weingarten, the editor at the Metro desk, his colleagues were initially skeptical of the heat wave death reports: "It was a little unclear at first if this was a normal thing, if there was a re-categorizing somehow, or whether this was truly a cataclysmic event. Because, you know, it had been hot in Chicago before, and we were all saying, could one day have killed so many people?" Schreuder felt the tension even from her office. "There was a little disagreement among the editors on the staff. What was going on here? Was this *really real?* Is there really more [mortality] or are people more aware of it? That was the question that was being raised about this. Were deaths that would normally have happened anyway being attributed to the heat wave? Were these people who might have lived only a week longer, or only three days longer, how sick are they?" One key question, reporter Graeme Zielinski explained, was "whether the coverage was being driven by the event or the event was being driven by the coverage. The heat wave had become a cliché almost as soon as it began. Here in the newsroom people were making fun of it, because people make fun of clichés in newsrooms. And 'the heat wave' [he intoned in an anchor's voice] was something that was real present and really real to a lot of people and yet it didn't seem real. It just seemed, it seemed, propped up somehow. There were some editors who were insisting that it was a much bigger deal [in the media] than it was and others who were worried, really worried that we were pushing this thing way too far.

You know, that there was overkill." Zielinski's comments express a reflexive awareness of his own role in constructing the heat wave as a public event. But they also show that the process of transforming the disaster into a news spectacle had confused the same journalists who were in charge of clarifying the nature of the occurrence.

WHOSE NEWS? OFFICIAL SOURCES AND JOURNALISTIC ROUTINES

Some of this confusion stems from the distribution of journalistic labor, because general reporters have to cover such a broad range of events and issues that it would be impossible for them to develop expertise in many of them. Key sources, particularly the local officials and large organizations that employ public relations professionals to generate and manage media interest, play an influential role in helping journalists get the "inside scoop" on political matters and thereby in shaping the substance of the reports. Although not all public officials possess public and media relations skills, media-savvy official sources often cultivate relationships with reporters that heighten their trustworthiness during difficult situations. As communications scholar Phyllis Kaniss notes, journalists are sometimes "reluctant to criticize a source who has provided them with information in the past, for fear of alienating the source and stopping the flow of information." They, too, are embedded in symbiotic relationships of accountability, reliance, and trust with their informants. Journalists learn to understand and gain sympathy for the perspectives of their intimate professional contacts, and when regular sources are also officials, reporters are more likely to present their observations as "facts." Occasional sources they find for specialized stories and issues are unknown and less dependable, though, and consequently reporters are disposed to treat their statements or observations as "allegations" that have to be verified before taken seriously.

The early heat wave reporting was especially difficult because few of the city-beat reporters knew where to turn for reliable information that would clarify their questions or settle the emerging dispute between City Hall and the Medical Examiners Office. They had no choice but to seek reports from city agencies even more than usual because the government offices had unmatched access to morbidity and mortality figures and were the only official information sources capable of centralizing knowledge about the diffuse event. The heat-related death controversy became a major theme in the news coverage in part because journalists depended on the organizations generating the conflicting public statements to produce a unified account of the disaster.

* * *

ALTERNATIVE VOICES AND
THE SPACE FOR DISSENT

. . . Outsider activists and community organizations who criticized the city for failing to secure the health of its most precarious residents, and community leaders who demanded more assistance for their constituencies, received little coverage in the major media; they had no choice but to turn to the smaller, community papers to publicize their positions. A *Tribune* story headlined "Residents Leave Cooling Centers in Cold," for example, quoted Daniel Alvarez, the commissioner of Human Services, Matt Rodriguez, the Police Superintendent, and Mayor Daley as saying that Chicagoans were failing to take advantage of the city's official cooling centers. During the weekend Metro Seniors in Action and other community groups had criticized the city for not providing special transportation to the centers, yet no one other than city officials and a single health care worker was quoted in the article and none of them expressed this position. Other city news agencies treated the story similarly. The *Chicago Sun-Times,* which gave its front-page piece the headline "116 Die; Few Using City Cooling Centers," cited only city officials in its account of the empty centers, but quoted a medical officer from the St. Louis County Health Department who explained that "personal action is the most important thing."

When critics of the city's response to the disaster did appear in the major papers and television news reports they were often relegated to the slot in which journalists, whose professional ethic is to appear objective and neutral and to show both sides of a story, place the dissenting view. Typically, this slot is small enough that the oppositional case is not expressed as completely as are the authoritative views of key sources, which also tend to frame the coverage. On Wednesday, 19 July, for example, the headline for the front-page story in the *Sun-Times* read "The Shocking Toll: 376: Daley Vows to Revise City's Emergency Plan," and Daley provided the lead quotation: "The city did a very good job, but we could have done better." The article, which focused on the city's own effort to assess its emergency response to the heat, outlined several problems that officials had acknowledged. But Daley's spin—

"the city did a very good job"—was not challenged by a dissenting voice until the last column of the six-column story, where state senator Robert Raica called the mayor's promise to evaluate the city emergency plan "totally ludicrous" and a Metro Seniors spokesperson explained that "we expect more from [the city]." Although the criticisms are strongly worded, their placement at the back of the story rendered them not only less prominent, but also less challenging to the frame—responsible reaction to a difficult situation, rather than neglect of vulnerable citizens—that organizes the story.

Other news organizations treated dissident voices similarly. In a *Tribune* article headlined "Daley, Aides Try to Deflect Criticism," John Kass, the City Hall beat reporter at the time, quoted city officials repeatedly and followed the administration through a day of news conferences, giving the mayor and city commissioners the space to explain their positions and define the controversy in their own terms. In the twenty-fourth paragraph of the twenty-eight-paragraph story, Commissioner Alvarez affirmed that the city "did everything possible, everything possible." Only after this, in the twenty-fifth paragraph, did the article state that "Metro Seniors in Action, a politically active seniors group, said City Hall failed to provide transportation for seniors to cooling centers, that some centers were inadvertently closed and that the administration should have done more to stress the physical dangers of excessive heat." Not only was the dissenting position buried in the back of the article; there was also no voice from the oppositional organization, nor from any other nongovernmental agency, appearing in the piece. City officials can speak for themselves in the news report, but those who challenge them are often *spoken for* by the media.

The voices of outsiders and activists received more space in the specialized and less influential city publications, such as the *Chicago Defender,* the city's largest African-American paper, and the *Daily Southtown.* On 23 July, for example, *Daily Southtown* published a story entitled "Experts: Daley Won't Feel the Heat for Long," in which reporter Rick Bryant quoted a political consultant about the fallout from the city's incapacity to manage the crisis. "I don't think this will stick," the consultant explained, because "most of the people who were hurt have no organized spokesman. They were the isolated, the dispossessed, the incommunicado, which is why so many of them died." The same edition of the paper also contained an article reporting that twenty-eight of Chicago's fifty-nine ambulances were idle at some point during the heat crisis, along with an interview with an advocate for local seniors who opined that poverty and fear of unmanageable utility bills left the elderly vulnerable to the heat. Yet relatively few Chicago residents or other journalists read these stories, and the perspectives that the alternative sources offered were unlikely to affect either the local political debates or the national coverage of the event. Most of the local news magazines and weekly papers simply ignored the heat disaster. *The Chicago Reporter,* which is the leading local publication on race and poverty issues and an excellent source for rich investigative reporting on inequality in the city, did not recognize the heat wave as relevant to its concerns. When I asked a staff member whether the magazine had reported on the hundreds of seniors who died alone, she responded plainly, "You know, we don't cover stories like that. We deal mostly with race, poverty, and injustice." The natural framing of the disaster, it seemed, had structured the editors' own perceptions of the crisis.

* * *

FAST THINKING

On breaking news stories, lead writers also face intense time pressure. As Schreuder noted, "It's not a perfect process and in everything we're doing we're dealing with the clock. Bang. Bang. Bang. Bang. Bang. And the clock just goes on all night until the story runs. [The reporter at] the Medical Examiners Office would call in periodically and talk, and I would ask him questions about what I wanted to know to write the story. I would say to him: 'Who are you talking with? How many medical examiners are there? How long are they working? Are they talking to other hospitals?' So there's a lot of back and forth going on between me and the person at the site."

According to Carlozo, there is also a lot of communication among the reporters in the field, even though they, too, have limited time to do their work. Journalists who went out in the pool car spent roughly two hours going to their sites, conducting their interviews and observing the scenes, and reporting to their editors via telephone. This is typically the amount of time budgeted for reporting a breaking city story, Carlozo explained, and sometimes reporters have even less time to scour the streets. The hurried process allows little time for thinking critically or analytically about the interviews or the event, and if reporters revert to conventional frames and story ideas when they write their articles or submit their notes to lead writers it is in part because the system of daily news production constrains their capacity to make sense of the conditions they see. Invoking a journalistic truism, reporter Robert Becker contended that he and his newspaper colleagues do not try to provide definitive answers to difficult questions because "what we do is write rough drafts of history. Someone will come in after us and finish the job." "We didn't do a lot of charts and statistical data," recalled Gerould Kern, an associate managing editor during the heat wave, "because it was not a scientific study and we weren't presenting it as that." Instead, Kern explained, *Tribune* writers tried to depict the heat wave as "a human story and a medical science story," so they were "looking for good storytelling" more than systematic knowledge. Yet in practice, daily news reporters often shift from storytelling to expository writing, and they rarely preface their analyses by reminding their audience that the conclusions presented are provisional or incomplete.

The most common form of slipping from description to explanation involves the journalistic invocation of the official rhetoric and preconstructed folk wisdom that is readily available to account for an event. During the heat wave the frames of natural disaster and climatic causality advocated by city officials and some meteorologists proved particularly appealing to local reporters. One journalist wrote a series of news articles probing the reasons for the heat wave's deadliness, but neglected to consider any social or political causes of the crisis. According to the headlines of a front-page story in the *Tribune*'s Chicagoland section, "Exceptionally High Humidity Proved to Be Real Culprit," in producing the record mortality. "Basically," the article explained, "it all comes down to this: it's not the heat, it's the humidity." A few days later, the lead story of the Chicagoland section elaborated this logic. It is not merely heat, but "humidity, pollution, wind direction and other factors—such as the way the concrete and asphalt turn cities into heat-retaining islands—[that] are now known to be as important as temperature in determining if the weather is dangerous." The articles would have carried different connotations if they had been modestly framed as inquiries into the weather, but instead they were presented as authoritative explanations that the catastrophe was a climatic occurrence and not a social event. Reporting organized entirely around the natural and meteorological frame, which was common during the heat wave, played an important role in naturalizing the disaster.

* * *

HEADLINES AND VISUAL IMAGES

As communications scholars have demonstrated, the central frame for news articles is not established in the stories that reporters write, but in the headlines and graphic or photographic images that draw readers' attention, introduce main issues in the accompanying article, and summarize the article's content. Headlines are important because they both organize the substance of news publications in ways that allow for selective reading and because they suggest which events and issues matter most. Few people have time to read an entire newspaper, but many scan its headlines and photographs as part of their daily routine. Headlines and photographs also serve a marketing function: when used provocatively, they can lure readers to buy a paper they might otherwise ignore, or to pay attention to stories that they might otherwise neglect. At the *Tribune,* as at many other papers, copy editors are responsible for generating most headlines; reporters and editors are seldom involved in the process for stories that do not make the front page. At times this process produces headlines that are not substantiated by the content of the stories, misleading the reader rather than summarizing the articles. When Kiernan and Zielinski submitted their piece for the Tuesday edition, for example, they did not know that the copy editors would title it "Casualties of Heat Just Like Most of Us: Many Rejected Any Kind of Help." The headline, which was the largest and boldest text on the front page that day, is not only manifestly wrong, it is also plainly contradicted by the substance of the reporting as well as by the accompanying graphic. Not far beneath the headline that characterizes victims as "just like most of us," the article text states, "Most of the heat victims were elderly. Many were ill or weak. A number were poor. A few drank or acted a little strange, or otherwise inhabited the dim pockets of society." On the next page, in a caption for the map showing the distribution of heat-related deaths, copy editors—perhaps the same ones who wrote the headline—explained that "[a]lthough the number of heat-related deaths in Cook County increased to 179 Monday, addresses are known for only 60. *Most of those victims were men aged 60 years or older living in Chicago's poorer neighborhoods.*" Why, then, did the copy editors produce a front-page headline claiming that the casualties were typical Chicagoans?

According to one of the copy editors who worked on the heat wave, they had a simple reason for producing the headline. They wanted, he said, "to broaden the appeal of the article to readers and get them into the story." The headline, in other words, was designed to interest readers who are more concerned about people like themselves than they are about poor old men. As one journalist explained, this was a common practice for newspapers and magazines during the 1990s, when market research showed news companies that readers were most likely to pay attention to publications that had the words *you* or *your* on the cover or in article titles. Having reinvented marketing principles as journalistic norms, copy editors could compromise accuracy so long as they gained attention. News reporters and editors had no opportunity to check the work.

Similar pressures shape the journalistic process of illustrating newspapers and other news media with visual images. News editors and producers expect photographers and camera operators to illustrate stories with material representing crucial information that words convey less effectively. But in practice, news agencies use photography and video footage to dramatize their coverage, selecting the images that are the most sensational and unique even though this convention focuses attention on the exceptional rather than the typical features of an issue or event. Extraordinary images are journalistically valuable when the shots capture meaningful social action or unusual occurrences, and news audiences expect to see the highlights rather than the mundane features of newsworthy events. Yet catastrophic situations such as the heat wave offer news organizations so many possibilities for spectacular image making that the news can easily transform crises into visual spectacles concealing the deeper social and political features of events.

When the heat wave first moved into Chicago it posed a visual challenge to photographers and camera operators because heat—unlike hurricanes, tornadoes, blizzards, or floods—cannot be represented directly and contains little dramatic action. The standard solution to this problem—which is apparent in the early television and newspaper images of children playing in open fire hydrants and city residents at the beach—is to express the heat through shots of people cooling down with water. The visual frame of water combating heat, or nature versus nature, dominated the initial reporting of the disaster. When the heat wave became deadly, though, photojournalists could obtain new and even more powerful visual material. News audiences expect to see dramatic images of death and suffering displayed prominently in their television news programs and newspapers. The Cook County Morgue, with hundreds of dead bodies, a parking lot full of refrigerated trucks containing even more corpses, and frenzied emergency workers, was a spectacle waiting to happen. It was also easy to cover, since journalists interested in capturing the image did not have to scour the city in search of the scene. They could simply wait in the morgue parking lot and be confident that a perfect image—shocking, dramatic, morbid, and different—would come to them. Producers and editors, certain that there would be "good color" for their broadcast or publication, sent other staffers into the neighborhoods to capture on photographic or video film police officers carrying dead bodies out of homes and residents coping with the heat. As the content analysis of newspaper graphics for the heat wave coverage shows in tables 1 and 2, after the shots of coping strategies, images of the dead bodies and the morgue were among the most prominent visual features of the news coverage. Photographs depicting the conditions in which the victims had lived and died were not featured in the reporting.

News organizations devote substantial resources to producing and displaying visual images, and the process of planning the look of a segment or story is a fundamental part of journalistic work. Television news, which is the most visual journalistic medium, is most explicitly organized around the production or acquisition of dramatic footage, and reporters working for television are always concerned about making their stories visually rich. Paul Douglas, the meteorologist who covered the heat wave for radio and newspaper as well, explained that even on television weather reports,

> you're constrained by pictures and [the question of] how do you make a heat wave story visual and interesting. I know that we hit the whole "survival tips" hard with special graphics, and so we tried to build graphics that would tell the story. You spend a majority of your time on [planning] what visuals you are going to show. And one of the inherent frustrations with being a television meteorologist is that so much of your day is spent pondering pretty pictures. I don't spend nearly as much time as I'd like actually looking at maps and forecasting, because a majority of my time is spent producing the show.

Douglas has ample support for his belief that the producers' emphasis on planning and arranging graphic images structured the news coverage of the disaster and compromised his time to do conventional reporting. At the *Tribune,* which is relatively less beholden to visual material but still dependent on dramatic shots and powerful graphics to animate its stories, Schreuder summed up her colleagues' positions:

> There's an emphasis [at the paper], much more than ever, on graphics. This [the heat wave] was in many ways a very visual story, and that influences how our editors think we should cover it. . . . So some of the time that you're writing the story has to be spent with the graphics team, talking to them about what we're doing, so that they can add and not simply repeat. But also, as a reporter, you are providing some reporting information for graphics, which is a whole new layer [of production]. And sometimes the information that you provide for graphics isn't necessarily what you would provide for your story. Photography is a whole

other layer. Because generally speaking, at this paper, the reporters fill out the photo assignments. And what this means is that you are responsible for figuring out when a photographer can come, figuring out how to get there, telling them what the story is so that they take pictures that go with the story. You're always supposed to be thinking as a reporter, what can photo do?

The photo editors at the *Tribune* played an active role during their paper's heat wave coverage because it demanded extensive visual material. But news reporters and writers remained involved in the image-making parts of the news production process and looked for the extraordinary sights that might move their story to a more prominent place in the news.

STORIES, IMAGES, AND NEWS PLACEMENT

Photographs and graphics play an even greater role in what is perhaps the most important editorial decision that the news staff makes: the placement of a story or segment within the newspaper or broadcast. Editors and producers are always looking for dramatic images for the front-page or lead story, which is explicitly designed to hook audiences into the coverage. At the *Tribune,* photography and graphic design editors often play a key role in the daily editorial meeting to determine what goes on the front page. If there is no clear choice, dramatic photographs or graphics will often determine the story selection. Sometimes editors place provocative images on the front page even without an accompanying story, or, similarly, delay the publication of an excellent story that has no good visual accompaniment.

Most local and national news organizations that reported on the heat wave displayed prominent images of victims in body bags or the chaotic scene at the morgue. The *Tribune* placed a photograph of autopsy technicians moving corpses from refrigerated trucks into the Medical Examiners Office on the front page of one edition of the 17 July paper, and a shot of Chicago Police Department wagons waiting in line to deliver "freshly discovered casualties" in another. The 18 July front-page photo was similar: an exhausted police officer in the Englewood neighborhood is shown resting against a car after removing a victim's body from an apartment; one pair of gloves remains on his hands, while another lies at his feet. The 19 July front page led with a graphic displaying the record fatalities on a bar chart, and the accompanying story contained a photograph of funeral workers loading into their minivan a body discovered in a Chicago Housing

Authority building. The front page of that day's Chicagoland section was almost identical: four police officers remove a victim from a single room occupancy dwelling on the South Side in one shot, and in another CHA residents look out their window, awaiting the removal of a deceased neighbor. A similar sequence ran in the *Sun-Times*. On 17 July the front page showed an overhead shot of trucks at the morgue alongside a close-up of autopsy technicians loading a body into a vehicle; on 18 July photos of Daley, Commissioner Alvarez, and the unused Chicago Heat Plan made the cover; and on 19 July there was another exhausted morgue worker on page 1. Dramatic images of dead bodies, refrigerated trucks, and wilting emergency workers dominated the heat wave coverage across the media, making for a memorable week of news. But there is little evidence that the photographs helped audiences to understand the sources of the trauma that was happening around them or to establish connections between the social and political conditions in the city and the emerging public health crisis. It is more likely that the sensational accounts and images of death and disaster produced by journalists detracted from the journalistic goals that, in theory, news organizations are designed to achieve.

* * *

THE NEWSWORTHINESS OF DISASTER: THE RISE AND DEMISE OF THE MAJOR STORY

After the heat subsided and the Medical Examiners Office counted the last of the victims, some of the *Tribune* reporters and editors assessed their coverage of the disaster. Bill Recktenwald, one of the paper's revered senior editors and writers, believed that the *Tribune* had failed to tell the human and social side of the story in its reporting. The victims remained mysterious, the conditions of their deaths obscure. As one reporter who had worked on the breaking stories explained,

> The coverage didn't show as much of the life of these people—and these people had really ugly lives. It was just like poor people, crazy people who lived in squalor and had suffered and were in pain for a lot of their lives and died. There is a routinization, there's a routine when you report on poor people dying. There's a tone that's taken and it's almost a cartoonish image of these people. It's journalism shorthand, how you cover poor people, and it's easy. It's hard to write about it without blaming

the victim. You've got very specific things that you describe when you write about poor people. It's very moralistic, but it's not necessarily accurate.

The journalist had good cause for his discomfort with the coverage because his reporting, which he believed to be full of evidence about the hardships and dangers of poverty and isolation, had been used for the story subtitled "Most [victims] Rejected Any Kind of Help." But several of the reporters who had worked on the initial heat wave stories also expressed frustrations with the coverage, and even a few of the editors felt that the paper had treated the heat wave victims superficially when they wanted to do something more.

* * *

Recktenwald assembled his reporters, a group that included Carlozo, Zielinski, Becker, and Kiernan, as well as Michael Martinez, Melita Marie Garza, Janita Poe, Jerry Thomas, and Paul de la Garza. Over a three-week period they produced roughly one hundred hard-won profiles. "I just went to the addresses and knocked on doors," Zielinski explained, "pretty traditional reporting. I ended up in some of the poorer neighborhoods . . . because all of the people that were dying, most, or the majority that we covered, were poor. But I ended up on the West Side [and] in the State Street corridor, some of those [public] housing units there. I was just collecting anecdotes, collecting any stories, you know, trying to put a face on the big story." When the reporting was over, the team had a huge amount of information about the victims and was prepared to write a major piece. Recktenwald also obtained an exhaustive list of the dead from the Medical Examiners Office, which he used to map the deaths. Amidst what one reporter called "a whole lot of numbers and statistics that in themselves reflected certain facets of the heat wave but didn't point to any absolutes," Recktenwald discovered that "the overwhelming numbers of deaths were in the poor areas and the poor areas are normally black or Hispanic." He and his colleagues were ready to produce a powerful and provocative set of stories about the disaster, to make explicit the inequities that the initial coverage had inadequately explored.

But before Recktenwald and the reporters began writing they ran up against a set of substantive commercial considerations that the news team had not expected to see. "By the time we got done [reporting]," Carlozo recalled, "it was September, and it was a very serious decision as to whether people were still interested in this story." Originally supportive of the project, some editors now worried that the story would not work. "There was a perception that our readers didn't care. . . . When it starts to become fall or winter in Chicago, how many people are going to read about a summer thing?" The heat wave had been reframed once again, this time as a "summer story," a particular kind of human interest piece that is appropriate for one season alone.

Ultimately, the top editors concluded that not many readers would care to read a summer story during the fall. Despite the large amount of resources they had committed to the project, they decided that rather than printing the major story Recktenwald had planned, they should run only a brief narrative of the event followed by about eleven short vignettes about individuals who died. The final story was published on 26 November as a front-page story. Headlined "The Heat Wave Victims: Joined in Death" and adorned with a photograph of a North Side rooming house, the article was based on a draft written by Louise Kiernan but never finished because the *Tribune* decided to print it when she was on vacation. Although Kern and Recktenwald had done considerable work to sort out mortality patterns, the story contained no systematic analysis of the deaths and showed little evidence of the extensive reporting that went into it. "I wrote a draft in story form from the information that we gathered. Then I went on vacation for Thanksgiving, and while I was gone they decided to run the story," Kiernan explained.

"It was not a happy project," she remembered, in part because she did not think that the reporters uncovered anything new about the victims, and in part because she never had a chance to finish the article. One editor admitted being "extremely disappointed" with the final product, and some of the journalists who worked on the piece felt that they had wasted their time on the piece. "We could have had a fantastic story," Carlozo lamented, but good reporting and a deadly crisis of historic proportions was not enough to make the news once the city edged toward winter and the disaster receded into the past. In the end, the major story that the editors had planned proved to be as forgettable as the heat wave victims have been themselves.

QUESTIONS

1. Which details of the reporting changed when the *Chicago Tribune*'s coverage shifted from describing the heat wave as a meteorological event to describing it as a human disaster?

2. How did the *Tribune*'s coverage of the heat wave demon-strate journalists' tendency to represent explanations of events given by official sources while marginalizing critics' alternative explanations?

3. How did the *Tribune* represent the heat wave as a visual spectacle? What kind of impact did this visualization have on how audiences understood the event?

4. Why did journalists not regard the social conditions that contributed to the heat wave's devastation—such as poverty, aging, isolation, and access to caring relatives and friends—as particularly newsworthy?

Waging War on Drugs

FROM *The Crack Attack: Politics and Media in the Crack Scare*

CRAIG REINARMAN AND HARRY G. LEVINE

This eye-opening study documents how the significant attention given by the news media and politicians to crack cocaine during the late 1980s and early 1990s greatly exaggerated the magnitude of the problem. The authors argue that constructing crack as a problem out of control and plaguing America's youth justified the government's war on drugs and reinforced the dominant set of explanations for why urban areas were simultaneously experiencing a cluster of social problems such as crime, teenage pregnancy, and school dropout.

America discovered crack and overdosed on oratory.
NEW YORK TIMES (EDITORIAL, OCTOBER 4, 1988)

This *New York Times* editorial had a certain unintended irony, for "America's paper of record" itself had long been one of the leading orators, supplying a steady stream of the stuff on which the nation had, as they put it, "overdosed." Irony aside, the editorial hit the mark. The use of powder cocaine by affluent people in music, film, sports, and business had been common since the 1970s. According to surveys by the National Institute on Drug Abuse (NIDA), by 1985, more than twenty-two million Americans in all social classes and occupations had reported at least trying cocaine. Cocaine smoking originated with "freebasing," which began increasing by the late 1970s. Then (as now) most cocaine users bought cocaine hydrochloride (powder) for intranasal use (snorting). But by the end of the 1970s, some users had begun to "cook" powder cocaine down to crystalline or "base" form for smoking. All phases of freebasing, from selling to smoking, took place most often in the privacy of homes and offices of middle-class or well-to-do users. They typically purchased cocaine in units of a gram or more costing $80 to $100 a gram. These relatively affluent "basers" had been discovering the intense rush of smoking cocaine, as well as the risks, for a number of years before the term "crack" was coined. But most such users had a stake in conventional life. Therefore, when they felt their cocaine use was too heavy or out of control, they had the incentives and resources to cut down, quit, or get private treatment.

There was no orgy of media and political attention in the late 1970s when the prevalence of cocaine use jumped sharply, or even after middle-class and upper-class users began to use heavily, especially when freebasing. Like the crack users who followed them, basers had found that this mode of ingesting cocaine produced a much more intense and far shorter "high" because it delivered more pure cocaine into the brain far more directly and rapidly than by snorting. Many basers had found that crack's intense, brutally brief rush, combined with the painful "low" or "down" that immediately followed, produced a powerful desire immediately to repeat use—to binge.

Crack's pharmacological power alone does not explain the attention it received. In 1986, politicians and the media focused on crack—and the drug scare began—when cocaine smoking became visible among a "dangerous" group. Crack attracted the attention of politicians and the media because of its downward mobility to and increased visibility in ghettos and barrios. The new users were a different social class, race, and status. Crack was sold in smaller, cheaper, precooked units, on ghetto streets, to poorer, younger buyers who were already seen as a threat. Crack spread cocaine smoking into poor populations already beset with a cornucopia of troubles. These people tended to have fewer bonds to conventional society, less to lose, and far fewer resources to cope with or shield themselves from drug-related problems.

The earliest mass media reference to the new form of cocaine may have been a Los Angeles Times article in late 1984 (November 25, p. CC1) on the use of cocaine "rocks" in ghettos and barrios in Los Angeles. By late 1985, the New York Times made the national media's first specific reference to "crack" in a story about three teenagers seeking treatment for cocaine abuse (November 17, p. B12). At the start of 1986, crack was known only in a few impoverished neighborhoods in Los Angeles, New York, Miami, and perhaps a few other large cities.

* * *

THE FRENZY: COCAINE AND CRACK IN THE PUBLIC EYE

When two celebrity athletes died in what news stories called "crack-related deaths" in the spring of 1986, the media seemed to sense a potential bonanza. Coverage skyrocketed and crack became widely known. "Dramatic footage" of black and Latino men being carted off in chains, or of police breaking down crack house doors, became a near nightly news event. In July 1986 alone, the three major TV networks offered seventy-four evening news segments on drugs, half of these about crack. In the months leading up to the November elections, a handful of national newspapers and magazines produced roughly a thousand stories discussing crack. Like the TV networks, leading news magazines such as *Time* and *Newsweek* seemed determined not to be outdone; each devoted five cover stories to crack and the "drug crisis" in 1986 alone.

In the fall of 1986, the CBS news show *48 Hours* aired a heavily promoted documentary called "48 Hours on Crack Street," which Dan Rather previewed on his evening news show: "Tonight, CBS News takes you to the streets, to the war zone, for an unusual two hours of hands on horror." . . .

* * *

The crack scare began in 1986, but it waned somewhat in 1987 (a nonelection year). In 1988, drugs returned to the national stage as stories about the "crack epidemic" again appeared regularly on front pages and TV screens. One politician after another reenlisted in the War on Drugs. In that election year, as in 1986, overwhelming majorities of both houses of Congress voted for new antidrug laws with long mandatory prison terms, death sentences, and large increases in funding for police and prisons. The annual federal budget for antidrug efforts surged from less than $2 billion in 1981 to more than $12 billion in 1993. The budget for the Drug Enforcement Administration (DEA) quadrupled between 1981 and 1992. The Bush administration alone spent $45 billion—more than all other presidents since Nixon combined—mostly for law enforcement.

Democrats and Republicans, liberals and conservatives alike called repeatedly for an "all-out war on drugs." In 1986, President and Nancy Reagan led a string of prominent politicians in asserting that drugs, especially crack, were "tearing our country apart" and "killing . . . a whole generation [of] . . . our children." In the 1988 election season, even more politicians claimed that crack was destroying American youth and causing much of the crime, violence, prostitution, and child abuse in the nation.

An April 1988 ABC News special report termed crack "a plague" that was "eating away at the fabric of America." According to this documentary, Americans spend "$20 billion a year on cocaine," American businesses lose "$60 billion" a year in productivity because their workers use drugs, "the educational system is being undermined" by student drug use, and "the family" is "disintegrating" in the face of this "epidemic." This program did not give its millions of viewers any evidence to support such dramatic claims, but it did give them a powerful *vocabulary of attribution:* "drugs," especially crack, threatened all the central institutions in American life—families, communities, schools, businesses, law enforcement, even national sovereignty.

This media frenzy continued into 1989. Between October 1988 and October 1989, for example, the *Washington Post* alone ran 1565 stories— 28,476 column inches—about the drug crisis. Even Richard Harwood, the *Post's* own ombudsman, editorialized against what he called the loss of "a proper sense of perspective" due to such a "hyperbole epidemic." He said that "politicians are doing a number on people's heads." In the fall of 1989, another major new federal antidrug bill to further increase drug war funding (S-1233) began winding its way through Congress. In September, President Bush's "drug czar," William Bennett, unveiled his comprehensive battle plan, the *National Drug Control Strategy.* His introduction asks, "What . . . accounts for the intensifying drug-related chaos that we see every day in our newspapers and on television? One word explains much of it. That word is *crack.* . . . Crack is responsible for the fact that vast patches of the American urban landscape are rapidly deteriorating."

Bennett's plan proposed yet another $2.2 billion increase in drug war spending, 70% of which was to be allocated to police and prisons, a percentage unchanged since the Nixon administration. The funds were to be used nearly to double prison capacity so that even casual users as well as dealers could be incarcerated. The plan also proposed the sale of drug war bonds (reminiscent of World War II) as a means of financing the $7.9 billion first-year costs. President Bush returned to Washington early from summer vacation at his estate on the Maine coast to rehearse with his media advisors the presentation of the plan.

On September 5, 1989, President Bush, speaking from the presidential desk in the Oval Office, announced his plan for achieving "victory over drugs" in his first major prime-time address to the nation, broadcast on all three national television networks. We want to focus on this incident as an example of the way politicians and the media systematically misinformed and deceived the public in order to promote the War on Drugs. During the address, Bush held up to the cameras a clear plastic bag of crack labeled "EVIDENCE." He announced that it was "seized a few days ago in a park across the street from the White House." Its contents, Bush said, were "turning our cities into battle zones and murdering our children." The president proclaimed that, because of crack and other drugs, he would "more than double" federal assistance to state and local law enforcement. The next morning the picture of the presi-dent holding a bag of crack was on the front pages of newspapers across America.

About two weeks later, the *Washington Post,* and then National Public Radio and other newspapers, discovered how the president of the United States had obtained his bag of crack. According to White House and DEA officials, "the idea of the President holding up crack was [first] included in some drafts" of his speech. Bush enthusiastically approved. A White House aide told the *Post* that the president "liked the prop. . . . It drove the point home." Bush and his advisors also decided that the crack should be seized in Lafayette Park across from the White House so the president could say that crack had become so pervasive that it was being sold "in front of the White House."

This decision set up a complex chain of events. White House Communications Director David Demarst asked Cabinet Affairs Secretary David Bates to instruct the Justice Department "to find some crack that fit the description in the speech." Bates called Richard Weatherbee, special assistant to Attorney General Dick Thornburgh, who then called James Milford, exec-utive assistant to the DEA chief. Finally, Milford phoned William McMullen, special agent in charge of the DEA's Washington office, and told him to arrange an undercover crack buy near the White House be-cause "evidently, the President wants to show it could be bought anywhere."

Despite their best efforts, the top federal drug agents were not able to find anyone selling crack (or any other drug) in Lafayette Park, or anywhere else in the vicinity of the White House. Therefore, in order to carry out their assignment, DEA agents had to entice someone to come to the park to make the sale. Apparently, the only person the DEA could convince was Keith Jackson, an eighteen-year-old African-American high school senior. McMullan reported that it was difficult because Jackson "did not even know where the White House was." The DEA's secret tape recording of the conversation revealed that the teenager seemed baffled by the request: "Where the [exple-tive deleted] is the White House?" he asked. Therefore, McMullan told the *Post,* "we had to manipulate him to get him down there. It wasn't easy."

The undesirability of selling crack in Lafayette Park was confirmed by men from Washington, D.C., imprisoned for drug selling, and interviewed by National Public Radio. All agreed that nobody would sell crack there because, among other reasons, there would be no customers. The crack-using population was in Washington's poor African-American neighborhoods some distance from the White House. The *Washington Post* and other papers also reported that the undercover DEA agents had not, after all, actually seized the crack, as Bush had claimed in his speech. Rather, the DEA agents purchased it from Jackson for $2400 and then let him go.

This incident illustrates how a drug scare distorts and perverts public knowledge and policy. The claim that crack was threatening every neighborhood in America was not based on evidence; after three years of the scare, crack remained predominantly in the inner cities where it began. Instead, this claim appears to have been based on the symbolic political value seen by Bush's speech writers. When they sought, after the fact, to purchase their own crack to prove this point, they found that reality did not match their script. Instead of changing the script to reflect reality, a series of high-level officials instructed federal drug agents to *create* a reality that would fit the script. Finally, the president of the United States displayed the procured prop on national television. Yet, when all this was revealed, neither politicians nor the media were led to question the president's policies or his claims about crack's pervasiveness.

As a result of Bush's performance and all the other antidrug publicity and propaganda, in 1988 and 1989, the drug war commanded more public attention than any other issue. The media and politicians' antidrug crusade succeeded in making many Americans even more fearful of crack and other illicit drugs. A *New York Times/CBS News* poll has periodically asked Americans to identify "the most important problem facing this country today." In January 1985, 23% answered war or nuclear war; less than 1% believed the most important problem was drugs. In September 1989, shortly after the president's speech and the blizzard of drug stories that followed, 64% of those polled believed that drugs were now the most important problem, and only 1% thought that war or nuclear war was most important. Even the *New York Times* declared in a lead editorial that this reversal was "incredible" and then gently suggested that problems like war, "homelessness and the need to give poor children a chance in life" should perhaps be given more attention.

A year later, during a lull in antidrug speeches and coverage, the percentage citing "drugs" as the nation's top problem had dropped to 10%. Noting this "precipitous fall from a remarkable height," the *Times* observed that an "alliance of Presidents and news directors" shaped public opinion about drugs. Indeed, once the White House let it be known that the president would be giving a prime-time address on the subject, all three networks tripled their coverage of drugs in the two weeks prior to his speech and quadrupled it for a week afterward. All this occurred while nearly every index of drug use was dropping.

The crack scare continued in 1990 and 1991, although with somewhat less media and political attention. By the beginning of 1992—the last year of the Bush administration—the War on Drugs in general, and the crack scare in particular, had begun to decline significantly in prominence and importance. However, even as the drug war was receiving less notice from politicians and the media, it remained institutionalized, bureaucratically powerful, and extremely well funded (especially police, military, and education/propaganda activities).

From the opening shots in 1986 to President Bush's national address in 1989, and through all the stories about "crack babies" in 1990 and 1991, politicians and the media depicted crack as supremely evil—*the* most important cause of America's problems. As recently as February of 1994, a prominent *New York Times* journalist repeated the claim that "An entire generation is being sacrificed to [crack]." As in all drug scares since the nineteenth-century crusade against alcohol, a core feature of drug war discourse is the *routinization of caricature*—worst cases framed as typical cases, the episodic rhetorically recrafted into the epidemic.

* * *

CRACK AS AN EPIDEMIC AND PLAGUE

The empirical evidence on crack use suggests that politicians and journalists have routinely used the words "epidemic" and "plague" imprecisely and rhetorically as words of warning, alarm, and danger. Therefore, on the basis of press reports, it is difficult to determine if there was any legitimacy at all in the description of crack use as an epidemic or plague. Like most other drug researchers and epidemiologists, we have concluded that crack addiction has never been anything but relatively rare across the great middle strata of the U.S. population. If the word "epidemic" is used to mean a disease or diseaselike condition that is "widespread" or "prevalent," then there has never been an epidemic of crack addiction (or even crack use) among the vast majority of Americans. Among the urban poor, however, especially African-American and Latino youth, heavy crack use has been more common. An "epidemic of crack *use*" might be a description of what happened among a distinct minority of teenagers and young adults from impoverished urban neighborhoods in the mid to late 1980s. However, many more people use tobacco and alcohol heavily than use cocaine in any form. Alcohol drinking and tobacco smoking each kills far more people than all forms of cocaine and heroin use combined. Therefore, "epidemic" would be more appropriate to describe tobacco and alcohol use. But politicians and the media have not talked about tobacco and alcohol use as epidemics or plagues. The word "epidemic" also can mean a rapidly spreading disease. In this precise sense as well, in inner-city neighborhoods, crack use may have been epidemic (spreading rapidly) for a few years among impoverished young African-Americans and Latinos. However, crack use was never spreading fast or far enough among the general population to be termed an epidemic there.

"Plague" is even a stronger word than epidemic. Plague can mean a "deadly contagious disease," an epidemic "with great mortality," or it can refer to a "pestilence," an "infestation of a pest, [e.g.,] a plague of caterpillars." Crack is a central nervous system stimulant. Continuous and frequent use of crack often burns people out and does them substantial psychological and physical harm. But even very heavy use does not usually directly kill users. In this sense, crack use is not a plague. One could say that drug dealers were "infesting" some blocks of some poor neighborhoods in some cities, that there were pockets of plague in some specific areas; but that was not how "crack plague" was used.

When evaluating whether the extent and dangers of crack use match the claims of politicians and the media, it is instructive to compare how other drug use patterns are discussed. For example, an unusually balanced *New York Times* story (October 7, 1989, p. 26) compared crack and alcohol use among suburban teenagers and focused on the middle class. The *Times* reported that, except for a few "urban pockets" in suburban counties, "crack and other narcotics are rarely seen in the suburbs, whether modest or wealthy." As the *Times* explained:

> Unlike crack, which is confined mainly to poor urban neighborhoods, alcohol seems to cut across Westchester's socio-economic lines. . . . Westchester is not unusual. Across the United States, alcohol eclipses all other drugs tried by high school students. According to a survey by the Institute for Social Research at the University of Michigan, 64 percent of 16,300 high school seniors surveyed in 1988 had drunk alcohol in the last month, compared with 18 percent who had smoked marijuana and 1.6 percent who had smoked crack.

The *Times* also reported that high school seniors were outdrinking the general adult population. Compared to the 64% of teenagers, only 55% of adults had consumed alcohol in the last month. Furthermore, teenagers have been drinking more than adults since at least 1972, when the surveys began. Even more significant is the *kind* of drinking teenagers do—what the *Times* called "excessive 'binge' drinking": "More than a third of the high school seniors had said that in the last two weeks they had had five or more drinks in a row." Drinking is, of course, the most widespread form of illicit drug use among high school students. As the *Times* explained, on the weekend, "practically every town has at least one underage party, indoors or out" and that "fake identification cards, older siblings, friends, and even parents all help teenagers obtain" alcohol.

The point we wish to emphasize is that even though illicit alcohol use was far more prevalent than cocaine or crack use, and even though it held substantial risk for alcohol dependence, addiction, drinking-driving deaths, and other alcohol-related problems, the media and politicians have not campaigned against teen drunkenness. Used as a descriptive term meaning "prevalent," the word "epidemic" fits teenage drinking far better than it does teenage crack use. Although many organizations have campaigned against drinking and driving by teenagers, the politicians and media have not used terms like "epidemic" or "plague" to call attention to illicit teenage drinking and drunkenness. Unlike the *Times* articles on crack, often on the front page, this article on teen drunkenness was placed in the second section on a Saturday.

It is also worth noting the unintentionally ironic mixing of metaphors, or of diagnoses and remedies, when advocates for the War on Drugs described crack use as an epidemic or plague. Although such disease terminology was used to call attention to the consequences of crack use, most of the federal government's domestic responses have centered on using police to arrest users. Treatment and prevention have always received a far smaller proportion of total federal antidrug funding than police and prisons do as a means of handling the "epidemic." If crack use is primarily a crime problem, then terms like "wave" (as in crime wave) would be more fitting. But if this truly is an "epidemic"—a widespread disease—then police and prisons are the wrong remedy, and the victims of the epidemic should be offered treatment, public health programs, and social services.

Finally, we wish to call attention to one particularly flagrant example of a prominent journalist misinforming millions of readers. . . . [I]n 1986, the editor in chief of *Newsweek*, Richard M. Smith, began a full-page editorial with the assertion that "An epidemic [of illicit drugs] is abroad in America, as pervasive and dangerous in its way as the plagues of medieval times." The claim that the effect of illicit drug use in America is comparable in destruction to medieval plagues is an easy one to check. Any good encyclopedia explains that the plague is a bacterial disease that kills people, often very quickly. The bubonic plague killed roughly one hundred million people in the Middle East, Europe, and Asia during the sixth century. In the fourteenth century, the so-called "Black Death" killed one-fourth to one-half the entire population of Europe, about seventy-five million people, *in a few years*. In the United States, perhaps seven to ten thousand deaths a year are "related" to all forms of illicit drug use combined. It is simply untrue that in America the effects of illicit drug use are "as pervasive and dangerous" as medieval plagues. *Newsweek's* statement offers falsehoods as facts. Yet it was a high-profile, well-thought-out statement, a model, given by the editor of a top news magazine, of the way reporters should write about drug issues. And reporters and editors certainly seemed to pick up the message. For example, a month later, *U.S. News and World Report* noted that "illicit drugs pervade American life . . . a situation that experts compare to medieval plagues—the No. 1 problem we face."

THE POLITICAL CONTEXT OF THE "CRACK CRISIS"

If the many claims about an "epidemic" or "plague" endangering "a whole generation" of youth were at odds with the best official data, then what else was animating the new War on Drugs? In fact, even if all the exaggerated claims about crack had been true, it would not explain all the attention crack received. Poverty, homelessness, auto accidents, handgun deaths, and environmental hazards are also widespread, costly, even deadly, but most politicians and journalists never speak of them in terms of crisis or plague. Indeed, far more people were (and still are) injured and killed every year by domestic violence than by illicit drugs, but one would never know this from media reports or political speeches. The existence of government studies suggesting that crack contributed to the deaths of a small proportion of its users, that an unknown but somewhat larger minority of users became addicted to it, that its use was related to some forms of crime, and so on were neither necessary nor sufficient conditions for all the attention crack received.

Like other sociologists, historians, and students of drug law and public policy, we suggest that understanding antidrug campaigns requires more than evidence of drug abuse and drug-related problems, which can be found in almost any period. It requires analyzing these crusades and scares as phenomena in their own right and understanding the broader social, political, and economic circumstances under which they occur. The crack scare also must be understood in terms of its political context and its appeal to important groups within American society. The mass media and politicians, however, did not talk about drugs this way. Rather, they decontextualized the drama, making it appear as if the story had no authors aside from dealers and addicts. Their writing of the crack drama kept abusers, dealers, crimes, and casualties under spotlights while hiding other important factors in the shadows. We suggest that over and above the very real problems some users suffered with crack, the rise of the New Right and the competition between political parties in a conservative context contributed significantly to the making of the crack scare.

THE NEW RIGHT AND ITS MORAL IDEOLOGY

* * *

Once he became president in 1981, Reagan and his appointees attempted to restructure public policy according to a radically conservative ideology. Through the lens of this ideology, most social problems appeared to be simply the consequences of *individual moral choices*. Programs and research that had for many years been directed at the social and structural sources of social problems were systematically defunded in budgets and delegitimated in discourse. Unemployment, poverty, urban decay, school crises, crime, and all their attendant forms of human troubles were spoken of and acted upon as if they were the result of *individual* deviance, immorality, or weakness. The most basic premise of social science—that individual choices are influenced by social circumstances—was rejected as left-wing ideology. . . .

With regard to drug problems, this conservative ideology is a form of *sociological denial*. For the New Right, people did not so much abuse drugs because they were jobless, homeless, poor, depressed, or alienated; they were jobless, homeless, poor, depressed, or alienated because they were weak, immoral, or foolish enough to use illicit drugs. For the right wing, American business productivity was not lagging because investors spent their capital on mergers and stock speculation instead of on new plants and equipment, or for any number of other economic reasons routinely mentioned in the *Wall Street Journal* or *Business Week*. Rather, conservatives claimed that businesses had difficulty competing partly because many workers were using drugs. In this view, U.S.

education was in trouble not because it had suffered demoralizing budget cuts, but because a "generation" of students was "on drugs" and their teachers did not "get tough" with them. The new drug warriors did not see crime plaguing the ghettos and barrios for all the reasons it always has, but because of the influence of a new chemical bogeyman. Crack was a godsend to the Right. They used it and the drug issue as an ideological fig leaf to place over the unsightly urban ills that had increased markedly under Reagan administration social and economic policies. "The drug problem" served conservative politicians as an all-purpose scapegoat. They could blame an array of problems on the deviant individuals and then expand the nets of social control to imprison those people for causing the problems.

* * *

For the Reagan administration and the Right, America's drug problems functioned as opportunities for the imposition of an old moral agenda in the guise of a new social concern. Moreover, the remedies that followed from this view were in perfect harmony with "traditional family values"—individual moral discipline and abstinence, combined with police and prisons for those who indulged. Such remedies avoided all questions about the economic and political sources of and solutions to America's social problems. The Reagan administration preached this ideology from the highest platforms in the land and transformed public policy in its image. It made a most hospitable context for a new drug scare.

POLITICAL PARTY COMPETITION

The primary political task facing liberals in the 1980s was to recapture some of the electorate that had gone over to the Right. Reagan's shrewdness in symbolically colonizing "middle American" fears put Democrats on the defensive. Most Democrats responded by moving to the right and pouncing upon the drug issue. Part of the early energy for the drug scare in the spring and summer of 1986 came from Democratic candidates trading charges with their Republican opponents about being "soft on drugs." Many candidates challenged each other to take urine tests as a symbol of their commitment to a "drug-free America." One Southern politician even proposed that candidates' spouses be tested. A California senatorial candidate charged his opponent with being "a noncombatant in the war on drugs." By the fall of 1986, increasingly strident calls for a drug war became so much a part of candidates' standard stump speeches that even conservative columnist William Safire complained of antidrug "hysteria" and "narcomania." Politicians demanded everything from death penalties in North América to bombing raids in South America.

Crack could not have appeared at a more opportune political moment. After years of dull debates on budget balancing, a "hot" issue had arrived just in time for a crucial election. In an age of fiscal constraint, when most problems were seen as intractable and most solutions costly, the crack crisis was the one "safe" issue on which all politicians could take "tough stands" without losing a single vote or campaign contribution. The legislative results of the competition to "get tough" included a $2 billion law in 1986, the so-called "Drug-Free America Act," which whizzed through the House (392 to 16) just in time for members of Congress to go home and tell their constituents about it. In the heat of the preelection, antidrug hysteria, the symbolic value of such spending seemed to dwarf the deficit worries that had hamstrung other legislation. According to *Newsweek,* what occurred was "a can-you-top-this competition" among "election-bound members of both parties" seeking tough antidrug amendments. The 1986 drug bill, as Representative David McCurdy (D-Okla) put it, was "out of control," adding through a wry smile, "but of course I'm for it."

* * *

As we mentioned earlier, in opinion polls in 1986, 1988, and 1989, more people picked "drugs" as the "most important problem facing the country" than any other public issue. Politicians and the press frequently cited such poll results as the reason for their speeches and stories. For example, the *New York Times* titled one story "The People's Concern: Illegal Drugs Are an Issue No Politician Can Resist" (May 22, 1988, p. E4). That title got it half right; politicians couldn't resist playing the drug issue, but the drug issue wasn't so much "The People's Concern" until they did. The reporter rightly noted that the 1988 election campaign would "resemble a shoving match" over "who can take a tougher line on drugs" and that "those who counsel reason are vulnerable to accusations of being 'soft.' " But then he falsely attributed this phenomenon to the citizenry: "The politicians were reflecting the concerns of their constituents." He also quoted an aide to then–Vice President Bush saying the same thing: "Voters have made this an issue."

Politicians and the media were *forging,* not following, public opinion. The speeches and stories *led* the oft-cited poll results, not the other way around. In 1987, between elections—when drug problems persisted in the ghettos and barrios but when the drug scare was not so enflamed by election rhetoric and media coverage—only 3 to 5% of those surveyed picked drugs as our most important problem (*New York Times,* May 24, 1988, p. A14). But then again in 1989, immediately following President Bush's speech escalating the drug war, nearly two-thirds of the people polled identified drugs as America's most important problem. When the media and politicians invoked "public opinion" as the driving force behind their actions against crack, they inverted the actual causal sequence.

* * *

THE END OF THE CRACK SCARE

In the 1980s, the conservative drive to reduce social spending exacerbated the enduring problems of impoverished African-American and Latino city residents. Partly in response, a minority of the young urban poor turned either to crack sales as their best shot at the American Dream and/or to the crack high as their best shot at a fleeting moment of pleasure. Inner-city churches, community organizations, and parent groups then tried to defend their children and neighborhoods from drug dealing and use on the one hand and to lobby for services and jobs on the other hand. But the crack scare did not inspire politicians of either party to address the worsening conditions and growing needs of the inner-city poor and working class or to launch a "Marshall Plan for cities." In the meantime, the white middle-class majority viewed with alarm the growing numbers, visibility, and desperation of the urban poor. And for years many Americans believed the central fiction of the crack scare: that drug use was not a symptom of urban decay but one of its most important causes.

All this gave federal and local authorities justification for widening the nets of social control. Of course, the new drug squads did not reduce the dangerousness of impoverished urban neighborhoods. But the crack scare did increase criminal justice system supervision of the underclass. By 1992, one in four young African-American males was in jail or prison or on probation or parole—more than were in higher education. During the crack scare, the prison population more than doubled, largely because of the arrests of drug users and small dealers. This gave the U.S. the highest incarceration rate in the world.

By the end of 1992, however, the crack scare seemed spent. There are a number of overlapping reasons for this. Most important was the failure of the

War on Drugs itself. Democrats as well as Republicans supported the War on Drugs, but the Reagan and Bush administrations initiated and led it, and the drug war required support from the White House. George Bush appointed William Bennett to be a "tough" and extremely high profile "drug czar" to lead the campaign against drugs. But Bennett, criticized for his bombastic style, quit after only eighteen months (some press accounts referred to it as the "czar's abdication"). After that, the Bush administration downplayed the drug war, and it hardly figured at all in the presidential primaries or campaign in 1992. Bill Clinton said during the campaign that there were no easy solutions to drug problems and that programs that work only on reducing supply were doomed to fail. The Clinton administration eschewed the phrase "War on Drugs," and Lee Brown, Clinton's first top drug official, explicitly rejected the title of drug czar. After billions of tax dollars had been spent and millions of young Americans had been imprisoned, hard-core drug problems remained. With so little to show for years of drug war, politicians seemed to discover the limits of the drug issue as a political weapon. Moreover, with both parties firmly in favor of the "get tough" approach, there was no longer any partisan political advantage to be had.

The news media probably would have written dramatic stories about the appearance of smokeable cocaine in poor neighborhoods at any time. Television producers have found that drug stories, especially timely, well-advertised, dramatic ones, often receive high ratings. But the context of the Reagan-led drug war encouraged the media to write such pieces. Conservatives had long complained that the media had a liberal bias; in the mid-1980s, drug coverage allowed the media to rebut such criticism and to establish conservative credentials. As we have suggested, news coverage of drugs rose and fell with political initiatives, especially those coming from the president. Therefore, as the White House withdrew from the drug issue, so did the press.

* * *

CONCLUSION

Smoking crack is a risky way to use an already potent drug. Despite all the exaggerations, heavy use of it *has* made life more difficult for many people— most of them from impoverished urban neighborhoods. If we agree that too many families have been touched by drug-related tragedies, why have we bothered criticizing the crack scare and the War on Drugs? If even a few people are saved from crack addiction, why should anyone care if this latest drug scare was in some measure concocted by the press, politicians, and moral entrepreneurs to serve their other agendas? Given the damage that drug abuse can do, what's the harm in a little hysteria? Much of this book addresses that question, but there are a few points that can be mentioned here.

First, we suspect that drug scares do not work very well to reduce drug problems and that they may well promote the behavior they claim to be preventing. For all the repression successive drug wars have wrought (primarily upon the poor and the powerless), they have yet to make a measurable dent in our drug *problems*. For example, prompted by the crack crisis and inspired by the success of patriotic propaganda in World War II, the Partnership for a Drug-Free America ran a massive advertising campaign to "unsell drugs." From 1987 to 1993, the Partnership placed over $1 billion worth of advertising donated by corporations and the advertising industry. The Partnership claims to have had a "measurable impact" by "accelerating intolerance" to drugs and drug users. The Partnership claims it "can legitimately take some of the credit for the 25% decline in illicit drug usage since our program was launched." However, the association between the Partnership's antidrug advertising and the declines in drug use appears to be spurious. Drug use was declining well before the Partnership's founding; taking credit for what was already happening is a bit like jumping in front of a parade and then claiming to have been leading it all along. More important, drug *use* increased in the mid-1990s among precisely those age groups that had been targeted by Partnership ads, while drug *problems* continued throughout their campaign. Furthermore, Partnership ads scrupulously avoided any mention of the two forms of drug use most prevalent among youth: smoking and drinking. This may have something to do with the fact that the Partnership for a Drug-Free America is a partnership between the media and advertising industries, which make millions from alcohol and tobacco advertising each year, and with the fact that alcohol and tobacco companies contribute financially to the Partnership's campaign against illicit drugs. Surely public health education is important, but there is no evidence that selective antidrug propaganda and scare tactics have significantly reduced drug problems.

Indeed, hysterical and exaggerated antidrug campaigns may have increased drug-related harm in the U.S. There is the risk that all of the exaggerated claims made to mobilize the population for war actually arouse interest in drug use. In 1986, the New England Journal of Medicine reported that the frequency of teenage suicides increases after lurid news reports and TV shows about them. Reports about drugs, especially of new and exotic drugs like crack, may work the same way. In his classic . . . "How To Launch a Nation Wide Drug Menace," [Edward] Brecher shows how exaggerated newspaper reports of dramatic police raids in 1960 functioned as advertising for glue sniffing. The arrests of a handful of sniffers led to anti-glue sniffing hysteria that actually spread this hitherto unknown practice across the U.S. In 1986, the media's desire for dramatic drug stories interacted with politicians' desire for partisan advantage and safe election-year issues, so news about crack spread to every nook and cranny of the nation far faster than dealers could have spread word on the street. When the media and politicians claimed that crack is "the most addictive substance known to man," there was some commonsense obligation to explain why. Therefore, alongside all the statements about "instant addiction," the media also reported some very intriguing things about crack: "whole body orgasm," "better than sex," and "cheaper than cocaine." For TV-raised young people in the inner city, faced with a dismal social environment and little economic opportunity, news about such a substance in their neighborhoods may have functioned as a massive advertising campaign for crack.

Further, advocates of the crack scare and the War on Drugs explicitly rejected public health approaches to drug problems that conflicted with their ideology. The most striking and devastating example of this was the total rejection of syringe distribution programs by the Reagan and Bush administrations and by drug warriors such as Congressman Charles Rangel. People can and do recover from drug addiction, but no one recovers from AIDS. By the end of the 1980s, the fastest growing AIDS population was intravenous drug users. Because syringes were hard to get, or their possession criminalized, injectors shared their syringes and infected each other and their sexual partners with AIDS. In the early 1980s, activists in a number of other Western countries had developed syringe distribution and exchange programs to prevent AIDS, and there is by now an enormous body of evidence that such programs are effective. But the U.S. government has consistently rejected such "harm reduction" programs on the grounds that they conflict with the policy of "zero tolerance" for drug use or "send the wrong message." As a result, cities such as Amsterdam, Liverpool, and Sydney, which have needle exchange programs, have very low or almost no transmission of AIDS by intravenous drug users. In New York City, however, roughly half the hundreds of thousands of injection drug users are HIV positive or already have AIDS. In short, the crack scare and the drug war policies it fueled will ultimately contribute to the deaths of tens of thousands of Americans, including the families, children, and sexual partners of the infected drug users.

Another important harm resulting from American drug scares is they have routinely blamed individual immorality and personal behavior for endemic social and structural problems. In so doing, they diverted attention and resources away from the underlying sources of drug abuse and the array of other social ills of which they are part. One necessary condition for the emergence of the crack scare (as in previous drug scares) was the linking of drug use with the problems faced by racial minorities, the poor, and youth. In the logic of the scare, whatever economic and social troubles these people have suffered were due largely to their drug use. Obscured or forgotten during the crack scare were all the social and economic problems that underlie crack abuse—and that are much more widespread—especially poverty, unemployment, racism, and the prospects of life in the permanent underclass.

Democrats denounced the Reagan and Bush administrations' hypocrisy in proclaiming "War on Drugs" while cutting the budgets for drug treatment, prevention, and research. However, the Democrats often neglected to mention an equally important but more politically popular development: the "Just Say No To Drugs" administrations had, with the help of many Democrats in Congress, also "just said no" to virtually every social program aimed at creating alternatives for and improving the lawful life chances of inner-city youth. These black and Latino young people were and are the group with the highest rate of crack abuse. Although, most inner-city youth have always steered clear of drug abuse, they could not "just say no" to poverty and unemployment. Dealing drugs, after all, was (and still is) accurately perceived by many poor city kids as the highest-paying job—straight or criminal—that they are likely to get.

The crack scare, like previous drug scares and antidrug campaigns, promoted misunderstandings of drug use and abuse, blinded people to the social sources of many social problems (including drug problems), and constrained the social policies that might reduce those problems. It routinely used inflated, misleading rhetoric and falsehoods such as Bush's televised account of how he came into possession of a bag of crack. At best, the crack scare was not good for public health. At worst, by manipulating and misinforming citizens about drug use and effects, it perverted social policy and political democracy.

QUESTIONS

1. During the war on drugs, how did the news media and politicians construct the crack problem in the United States? Pay close attention to the particular words and images that these claimsmakers used.

2. In referring to data about alcohol use, how do the authors make the case that the words "epidemic" and "plague" presented an image of the crack problem that went significantly beyond the statistics?

3. According to the authors, how did the social construction of crack as a monumental societal danger reinforce a prevalent set of beliefs about the causes of our society's greatest problems?

4. Why is it significant that the media and politicians portrayed the war on drugs as a *response* to public opinion polls and yet data indicate that the drug war itself was instrumental in shaping the strong public outcry against crack?

5. What do the authors mean when they argue that the media and politicians "decontextualized the [crack attack] drama, making it appear as if the story had no authors aside from dealers and addicts?"

6. Search for a recent news article about a drug that is currently causing public alarm, such as Ecstasy, crystal meth, or heroin. Which claimsmakers are playing leading roles in the construction of this harm? How do their claims compare with the harms attributed to crack during the 1980s?

Viewing Bodily Imperfection as a Health Problem

Millions for Viagra, Pennies for Diseases of the Poor

KEN SILVERSTEIN

This essay highlights the powerful role that drug companies play in influencing the priority given to addressing different kinds of health problems. The pharmaceutical industry spends substantially more money on treatments for lifestyle problems like baldness and impotence, which cause no injury or loss of life, than on drugs for tropical diseases such as malaria and tuberculosis, which kill millions of people each year. The 1998 figures that Silverstein cites at the beginning of this selection remain largely unchanged today. His account suggests that Americans' concerns about bodily perfection drive the pharmaceutical industry to cater to this concern, which in turn leads drug manufacturers to place little priority on developing drugs that might save millions of lives in less-developed countries.

Almost three times as many people, most of them in tropical countries of the Third World, die of preventable, curable diseases as die of AIDS. Malaria, tuberculosis, acute lower-respiratory infections—in 1998, these claimed 6.1 million lives. People died because the drugs to treat those illnesses are nonexistent or are no longer effective. They died because it doesn't pay to keep them alive.

Only 1 percent of all new medicines brought to market by multinational pharmaceutical companies between 1975 and 1997 were designed specifically to treat tropical diseases plaguing the Third World. In numbers, that means thirteen out of 1,223 medications. Only four of those thirteen resulted from research by the industry that was designed specifically to combat tropical ailments. The others, according to a study by the French group Doctors Without Borders, were either updated versions of existing drugs, products of military

51

research, accidental discoveries made during veterinary research or, in one case, a medical breakthrough in China.

Certainly, the majority of the other 1,210 new drugs help relieve suffering and prevent premature death, but some of the hottest preparations, the ones that, as the *New York Times* put it, drug companies "can't seem to roll . . . out fast enough," have absolutely nothing to do with matters of life and death. They are what have come to be called lifestyle drugs—remedies that may one day free the world from the scourge of toenail fungus, obesity, baldness, face wrinkles and impotence. The market for such drugs is worth billions of dollars a year and is one of the fastest-growing product lines in the industry.

The drug industry's calculus in apportioning its resources is cold-blooded, but there's no disputing that one old, fat, bald, fungus-ridden rich man who can't get it up counts for more than half a billion people who are vulnerable to malaria but too poor to buy the remedies they need.

Western interest in tropical diseases was historically linked to colonization and war, specifically the desire to protect settlers and soldiers. Yellow fever became a target of biomedical research only after it began interfering with European attempts to control parts of Africa. "So obvious was this deterrence . . . that it was celebrated in song and verse by people from Sudan to Senegal," Laurie Garrett recounts in her extraordinary book *The Coming Plague*. "Well into the 1980s schoolchildren in Ibo areas of Nigeria still sang the praises of mosquitoes and the diseases they gave to French and British colonialists."

US military researchers have discovered virtually all important malaria drugs. Chloroquine was synthesized in 1941 after quinine, until then the primary drug to treat the disease, became scarce following Japan's occupation of Indonesia. The discovery of Mefloquine, the next advance, came about during the Vietnam War, in which malaria was second only to combat wounds in sending US troops to the hospital. With the end of a ground-based US military strategy came the end of innovation in malaria medicine.

The Pharmaceutical Research and Manufacturers of America (PhRMA) claimed in newspaper ads early this year that its goal is to "set every last disease on the path to extinction." Jeff Trewhitt, a PhRMA spokesman, says US drug companies will spend $24 billion on research this year and that a number of firms are looking for cures for tropical diseases. Some companies also provide existing drugs free to poor countries, he says. "Our members are involved. There's not an absolute void."

The void is certainly at hand. Neither PhRMA nor individual firms will reveal how much money the companies spend on any given disease—that's proprietary information, they say—but on malaria alone, a recent survey of the twenty-four biggest drug companies found that not a single one maintains an in-house research program, and only two expressed even minimal interest in primary research on the disease. "The pipeline of available drugs is almost empty," says Dyann Wirth of the Harvard School of Public Health, who conducted the study. "It takes five to ten years to develop a new drug, so we could soon face [a strain of] malaria resistant to every drug in the world." A 1996 study presented in *Cahiers Santé*, a French scientific journal, found that of forty-one important medicines used to treat major tropical diseases, none were discovered in the nineties and all but six were discovered before 1985.

Contributing to this trend is the wave of mergers that has swept the industry over the past decade. Merck alone now controls almost 10 percent of the world market. "The bigger they grow, the more they decide that their research should be focused on the most profitable diseases and conditions," one industry watcher says. "The only thing the companies think about on a daily basis is the price of their stocks; and announcing that you've discovered a drug [for a tropical disease] won't do much for your share price."

That comment came from a public health advocate, but it's essentially seconded by industry. "A corporation with stockholders can't stoke up a laboratory that will focus on Third World diseases, because it will go broke," says Roy Vagelos, the former head of Merck. "That's a social problem, and industry shouldn't be expected to solve it."

Drug companies, however, are hardly struggling to beat back the wolves of bankruptcy. The pharmaceutical sector racks up the largest legal profits of any industry, and it is expected to grow by an average of 16 to 18 percent over the next four years, about three times more than the average of the Fortune 500. Profits are especially high in the United States, which alone among First World nations does not control drug prices. As a result, prices here are about twice as high as they are in the European Union and nearly four times higher than in Japan.

"It's obvious that some of the industry's surplus profits could be going into research for tropical diseases," says a retired drug company executive, who wishes to remain anonymous. "Instead, it's going to stockholders." Also to promotion: In 1998, the industry unbuckled $10.8 billion on advertising. And to politics: In 1997, American drug companies spent $74.8 million to lobby the federal government, more than any other industry; last year they spent nearly $12 million on campaign contributions.

Just forty-five years ago, the discovery of new drugs and pesticides led the World Health Organization (WHO) to predict that malaria would soon be eradicated. By 1959, Garrett writes in *The Coming Plague,* the Harvard School of Public Health was so certain that the disease was passé that its curriculum didn't offer a single course on the subject.

Resistance to existing medicines—along with cutbacks in healthcare budgets, civil war and the breakdown of the state—has led to a revival of malaria in Africa, Latin America, Southeast Asia and, most recently, Armenia and Tajikistan. The WHO describes the disease as a leading cause of global suffering and says that by "undermining the health and capacity to work of hundreds of millions of people, it is closely linked to poverty and contributes significantly to stunting social and economic development."

Total global expenditures for malaria research in 1993, including government programs, came to $84 million. That's paltry when you consider that one B-2 bomber costs $2 billion, the equivalent of what, at current levels, will be spent on all malaria research over twenty years. In that period, some 40 million Africans alone will die from the disease. In the United States, the Pentagon budgets $9 million per year for malaria programs, about one-fifth the amount it set aside this year to supply the troops with Viagra. For the drug companies, the meager purchasing power of malaria's victims leaves the disease off the radar screen. As Neil Sweig, an industry analyst at Southeast Research Partners, puts it wearily, "It's not worth the effort or the while of the large pharmaceutical companies to get involved in enormously expensive research to conquer the Anopheles mosquito."

The same companies that are indifferent to malaria are enormously troubled by the plight of dysfunctional First World pets. John Keeling, a spokesman for the Washington, DC–based Animal Health Institute, says the "companion animal" drug market is exploding, with US sales for 1998 estimated at about $1 billion. On January 5, the FDA approved the use of Clomicalm, produced by Novartis, to treat dogs that suffer from separation anxiety (warning signs: barking or whining, "excessive greeting" and chewing on furniture). "At Last, Hope for Millions of Suffering Canines Worldwide," reads the company's press release announcing the drug's rollout. "I can't emphasize enough how dogs are suffering and that their behavior is not tolerable to owners," says Guy Tebbitt, vice president for research and development for Novartis Ani-mal Health.

Also on January 5 the FDA gave the thumbs up to Pfizer's Anipryl, the first drug approved for doggie Alzheimer's. Pfizer sells a canine pain reliever and arthritis treatment as well, and late last year it announced an R&D program for medications that help pets with anxiety and dementia.

Another big player in the companion-animal field is Heska, a biotechnol-
ogy firm based in Colorado that strives to increase the "quality of life" for cats
and dogs. Its products include medicines for allergies and anxiety, as well as
an antibiotic that fights periodontal disease. The company's Web site features
a "spokesdog" named Perio Pooch and, like old "shock" movies from high
school driver's-ed classes, a photograph of a diseased doggie mouth to demonstrate what can happen if teeth and gums are not treated carefully. No one
wants pets to be in pain, and Heska also makes drugs for animal cancer, but
it is a measure of priorities that US companies and their subsidiaries spend
almost nothing on tropical diseases while, according to an industry source,
they spent about half a billion dollars for R&D on animal health.

Although "companion animal" treatments are an extreme case—that half-
billion-dollar figure covers "food animals" as well, and most veterinary drugs
emerge from research on human medications—consider a few examples from
the brave new world of human lifestyle drugs. Here, the pharmaceutical companies are scrambling to eradicate:

- *Impotence.* Pfizer invested vast sums to find a cure for what Bob Dole and
  other industry spokesmen delicately refer to as "erectile dysfunction." The
  company hit the jackpot with Viagra, which racked up more than $1 bil-
  lion in sales in its first year on the market. Two other companies, Schering-
  Plough and Abbott Laboratories, are already rushing out competing drugs.
- *Baldness.* The top two drugs in the field, Merck's Propecia and Pharmacia
  & Upjohn's Rogaine (the latter sold over the counter), had combined sales
  of about $180 million in 1998. "Some lifestyle drugs are used for relatively
  serious problems, but even in the best cases we're talking about very different products from penicillin," says the retired drug company executive.
  "In cases like baldness therapy, we're not even talking about healthcare."
- *Toenail fungus.* With the slogan "Let your feet get naked!" as its battle cry,
  pharmaceutical giant Novartis recently unveiled a lavish advertising campaign for Lamisil, a drug that promises relief for sufferers of this unsightly
  malady. It's a hot one, the war against fungus, pitting Lamisil against Janssen
  Pharmaceutical's Sporanox and Pfizer's Diflucan for shares in a market estimated to be worth hundreds of millions of dollars a year.
- *Face wrinkles.* Allergan earned $90 million in 1997 from sales of its "mir-
  acle" drug Botox. Injected between the eyebrows at a cost of about $1,000

for three annual treatments, Botox makes crow's feet and wrinkles disappear. "Every $7^1/_2$ seconds someone is turning 50," a wrinkle expert told the *Dallas Morning News* in an article about Botox last year. "You're looking at this vast population that doesn't want frown lines."

Meanwhile, acute lower respiratory infections go untreated, claiming about 3.5 million victims per year, overwhelmingly children in poor nations. Such infections are third on the chart of the biggest killers in the world; the number of lives they take is almost half the total reaped by the number-one killer, heart disease, which usually strikes the elderly. "The development of new antibiotics," wrote drug company researcher A.J. Slater in a 1989 paper published in the Royal Society of Tropical Medicine and Hygiene's *Transactions,* "is very costly and their provision to Third World countries alone can never be financially rewarding."

In some cases, older medications thought to be unnecessary in the First World and commercially unviable in the Third have simply been pulled from the market. This created a crisis recently when TB re-emerged with a vengeance in US inner cities, since not a single company was still manufacturing Streptomycin after mid-1991. The FDA set up a task force to deal with the situation, but it was two years before it prodded Pfizer back into the field.

In 1990 Marion Merrell Dow (which was bought by German giant Hoechst in 1995) announced that it would manufacture Ornidyl, the first new medicine in forty years that was effective in treating African sleeping sickness. Despite the benign sounding name, the disease leads to coma and death, and kills about 40,000 people a year. Unlike earlier remedies for sleeping sickness, Ornidyl had few side effects. In field trials, it saved the lives of more than 600 patients, most of whom were near death. Yet Ornidyl was pulled from production; apparently company bean-counters determined that saving lives offered no return.

Because AIDS also plagues the First World, it is the one disease ravaging Third World countries that is the object of substantial drug company research. In many African countries, AIDS has wiped out a half-century of gains in child survival rates. In Botswana—a country that is not at war and has a relatively stable society—life expectancy rates fell by twenty years over a period of just five. In South Africa, the Health Ministry recently issued a report saying that 1,500 of the country's people are infected with HIV every day and predicting that the annual death rate will climb to 500,000 within the next decade.

Yet available treatments and research initiatives offer little hope for poor people. A year's supply of the highly recommended multidrug cocktail of three AIDS medicines costs about $15,000 a year. That's exorbitant in any part of the world, but prohibitive in countries like Uganda, where per capita income stands at $330. Moreover, different viral "families" of AIDS, with distinct immunological properties, appear in different parts of the world. About 85 percent of people with HIV live in the Third World, but industry research to develop an AIDS vaccine focuses only on the First World. "Without research dedicated to the specific viral strains that are prevalent in developing countries, vaccines for those countries will be very slow in coming," says Dr. Amir Attaran, an international expert who directs the Washington-based Malaria Project.

All the blame for the neglect of tropical diseases can't be laid at the feet of industry. Many Third World governments invest little in healthcare, and First World countries have slashed both foreign aid and domestic research programs. Meanwhile, the US government aggressively champions the interests of the drug industry abroad, a stance that often undermines healthcare needs in developing countries.

In one case where a drug company put Third World health before profit— Merck's manufacture of Ivermectin—governmental inertia nearly scuttled the good deed. It was the early eighties, and a Pakistani researcher at Merck discovered that the drug, until then used only in veterinary medicine, performed miracles in combating river blindness disease. With one dose per year of Ivermectin, people were fully protected from river blindness, which is carried by flies and, at the time, threatened hundreds of millions of people in West Africa.

Merck soon found that it would be impossible to market Ivermectin profitably, so in an unprecedented action the company decided to provide it free of charge to the WHO. (Vagelos, then chairman of Merck, said the company was worried about taking the step, "as we feared it would discourage companies from doing research relevant to the Third World, since they might be expected to follow suit.") Even then, the program nearly failed. The WHO claimed it didn't have the money needed to cover distribution costs, and Vagelos was unable to win financial support from the Reagan Administration. A decade after Ivermectin's discovery, only 3 million of 120 million people at risk of river blindness had received the drug. During the past few years, the WHO, the World Bank and private philanthropists have finally put up the money for the program, and it now appears that river blindness will become the second disease, after smallpox, to be eradicated.

Given the industry's profitability, it's clear that the companies could do far more. It's equally clear that they won't unless they are forced to. The success of ACT UP in pushing drug companies to respond to the AIDS crisis in America is emblematic of how crucial but also how difficult it is to get the industry to budge. In late 1997, a coalition of public health organizations approached a group of major drug companies, including Glaxo-Wellcome and Roche, and asked them to fund a project that would dedicate itself to developing new treatments for major tropical diseases. Although the companies would have been required to put up no more than $2 million a year, they walked away from the table. Since there's no organized pressure—either from the grass-roots or from governments—they haven't come back. "There [were] a number of problems at the business level," Harvey Bale, director of the Geneva-based International Federation of Pharmaceutical Manufacturers' Association, told *Science* magazine. "The cost of the project is high for some companies."

While the industry's political clout currently insures against any radical government action, even minor reforms could go a long way. The retired drug company executive points to public hospitals, which historically were guaranteed relatively high profit margins but were obligated to provide free care to the poor in return. There's also the example of phone companies, which charge businesses higher rates in order to subsidize universal service. "Society has tolerated high profit levels up until now, but society has the right to expect something back," he says. "Right now, it's not getting it."

The US government already lavishly subsidizes industry research and allows companies to market discoveries made by the National Institutes of Health and other federal agencies. "All the government needs to do is start attaching some strings," says the Malaria Project's Attaran. "If a company wants to market another billion-dollar blockbuster, fine, but in exchange it will have to push through a new malaria drug. It will cost them some money, but it's not going to bankrupt them."

Another type of "string" would be a "reasonable pricing" provision for drugs developed at federal laboratories. By way of explanation, Attaran recounted that the vaccine for hepatitis A was largely developed by researchers at the Walter Reed Army Institute. At the end of the day, the government gave the marketing rights to SmithKline Beecham and Merck. The current market for the vaccine, which sells for about $60 per person, is $300 million a year. The only thing Walter Reed's researchers got in exchange for their efforts was a plaque that hangs in their offices. "I'll say one thing for the companies," says Attaran. "They didn't skimp on the plaque; it's a nice one. But either the companies should have paid for part of the government's research, or they should have been required to sell the vaccine at a much lower price."

At the beginning of this year, Doctors Without Borders unveiled a campaign calling for increased access to drugs needed in Third World countries. The group is exploring ideas ranging from tax breaks for smaller firms engaged in research in the field, to creative use of international trade agreements, to increased donations of drugs from the multinational companies. Dr. Bernard Pécoul, an organizer of the campaign, says that different approaches are required for different diseases. In the case of those plaguing only the Southern Hemisphere—sleeping sickness, for example—market mechanisms won't work because there simply is no market to speak of. Hence, he suggests that if multinational firms are not willing to manufacture a given drug, they transfer the relevant technology to a Third World producer that is.

Drugs already exist for diseases that ravage the North as well as the South— AIDS and TB, for example—but they are often too expensive for people in the Third World. For twenty-five years, the WHO has used funding from member governments to purchase and distribute vaccines to poor countries; Pécoul proposes a similar model for drugs for tropical diseases. Another solution he points to: In the event of a major health emergency, state or private producers in the South would be allowed to produce generic versions of needed medications in exchange for a small royalty paid to the multinational license holder. "If we can't change the markets, we have to humanize them," Pécoul says. "Drugs save lives. They can't be treated as normal products."

QUESTIONS

1. How do pharmaceutical companies justify spending substantially more money on developing drugs to remedy Western lifestyle problems than on drugs to fight Third World tropical diseases?

2. Why was there greater pharmaceutical interest in fighting tropical diseases during the period of Western colonization than there is now?

3. Look through the past week's news coverage to see whether there is evidence to support the author's inference that Americans are more preoccupied with finding remedies for their own lifestyle problems than with the fate of millions of people dying of tropical diseases each year in the Third World. Count the number of news stories about Third World tropical dis-

eases compared to First World lifestyle problems. If indeed lifestyle problems got greater coverage, why do you think these health problems are of
greater interest to Americans?

4. How does the pharmaceutical industry's continuous development of new
lifestyle-enhancing drugs contribute to Americans' views that their bodies
are imperfect and in need of drugs to fix them?

4

Seeing Police Mistreatment of Blacks as a Necessary Evil

Behind Police Brutality: Public Assent

FRANK BRUNI

The police exercise tremendous influence over the level of importance that people place on reducing crime. This influence was particularly pronounced through the war on drugs carried out during the 1980s and '90s. The public and political mandate to get tough on drugs and drug-related crimes elevated these social problems to a level where whites may have inadvertently failed to regard police mistreatment of African Americans as a problem deserving significant attention in its own right.

To the extent that language provides cues for behavior, the orders that American governors, mayors, police chiefs and block association presidents have been giving cops on the beat in big cities over the past few years are unambiguous.

As James Alan Fox, dean of the College of Criminal Justice at Northeastern University, notes, these officers have been told that they form the front line in a "war" on crime and a "war" on drugs, that they have been enlisted in special "operations" and drafted for bold new "offensives."

"We use all these paramilitary terms," Mr. Fox said, "and we have promoted somewhat of a siege mentality among police: The enemy is out there, and there are more of them than we thought."

Mr. Fox paused, sighed and added, "When you have this sort of mentality, excessive brutality and improper actions are more likely to occur."

Mr. Fox's comments root out what is indisputably a dirty little secret embedded in the public angst over police brutality: many Americans have come not only to tolerate a degree of it from their police officers but also, in ways subtle and unsubtle, to encourage it.

That is not to say that Americans are untroubled by such glaring examples of excessive force as the beating of Rodney King by police officers in Los Angeles; the torture of Abner Louima by police officers in a Brooklyn station house or, most recently, the killing of Amadou Diallo, an unarmed African immigrant, in a fusillade of police fire this month in the Bronx. In each case race became an issue.

Just about everybody would agree that if these flagrant episodes were the unintended outgrowths of aggressive policing—and it is by no means certain that they were—then the price for such a modus operandi is exorbitant in the extreme.

But too frequently omitted from discussions of police brutality that attend these cases is the fact that many Americans have tacitly blessed a more vigorous, invasive, belligerent brand of policing. And the line between law enforcement that is aptly forceful and law enforcement that is unduly brutal or abusive can be thin indeed.

"Sometimes, it's in the eye of the beholder," acknowledged William J. Bratton, former Police Commissioner of New York City. "That's part of the dilemma that police find themselves in."

The problem is not confined to the nation's police departments. It also confronts the politicians who help supervise them and the taxpayers who fund them. Underlying it is the age-old tension between public safety and civil liberties. The question now is, can the "zero tolerance" crime policies that have come into vogue over the last decade be executed and achieved without the trampling of innocent people's rights?

The "zero tolerance" policy, which has been given a showcase in New York City, holds that no crime—not the breaking of a window, not the jumping of a turnstile—is too insignificant to capture the swift, decisive attention of the police. Prosecute more petty offenders and offenses today, goes the reasoning, and you will have fewer hard-core criminals and crimes tomorrow.

But as the police were being schooled in this new religion, Mr. Bratton said, they were also being taught a new zealousness.

"In wartime, which we were engaged in for a few years in this city, it required certain strategies," Mr. Bratton said. Among those strategies, he said, was to be less timid in the investigation of crimes and the use of force, so long as the force was justified by the circumstances.

Those sorts of instructions, however, call for judgments that are bound to be imperfect. Take, for example, the statistics concerning the activities of the department's street crimes unit. In 1997 and 1998, officers with the unit frisked more than 45,000 people thought to be carrying guns, but they arrested fewer than 10,000. The rest—the vast majority—were mistakenly detained.

Is that acceptable? The answer depends not only on the sensibilities of the person answering the question but also, in many cases, the race. Black leaders and civil libertarians said that when the police put more emphasis on preventive strategies, they invariably lean on broad profiles in stopping and interrogating possible criminals, and those profiles are racist.

"When you rely on hunches, you rely on prejudices, and the people most likely to be stopped are black or Hispanic," said Ira Glasser, executive director of the American Civil Liberties Union. "When you start throwing around phrases like zero tolerance, you get these kinds of excesses. And if the cops can stop you at will, where's the public safety in that?"

David N. Dinkins, Mayor Rudolph W. Giuliani's predecessor in New York, said that there was a certain blindness among white people who respond to the reduction in crime simply by cheering the ends without scrutinizing the means.

"That's what they'll say," Mr. Dinkins said, "until one day, this white middle-class family has a son who comes home from Harvard or Princeton or whatever university, and he comes home with his black classmate. And they, dressed as young people will dress, get into some altercation with cops"— and become victims of police brutality.

When it comes to force, there is not a police department in the country that expressly commands its officers to use it indiscriminately. Mayor Giuliani told police academy graduates last week that "in a very special sense, you are civil rights workers" whose job of public protection entails an "equal emphasis on treating everyone with respect."

But the broader goals that officers are asked to pursue, the fire instilled in them and the messages that the culture outside of police departments broadcast can easily coax them toward unjustified violence.

The heroes in televised police dramas like "N.Y.P.D. Blue," "Law and Order," and "Homicide: Life on the Street" regularly slam suspects against concrete walls, twists their arms behind their backs, even bloody their noses.

And yet there has not been a popular protest of the possible danger of such examples to match the outcry over, say, the chastely rendered longings of a lesbian who owns a bookstore in the situation comedy "Ellen."

Some experts say that if Americans want to glorify violence, ratchet up the mandates of police officers and cut crime rates to ever lower levels, they must own up to the trade-offs they are bound to be making.

"The more aggressive the police get, the safer the streets can be," Mr. Fox said, "but there's a price in terms of individual freedoms, civil liberties, civil rights."

"The essence of freedom is tolerance, not zero tolerance," Richard D. Emery, a civil rights lawyer, wrote in an Op-Ed article in The New York Times on Friday.

Thomas Reppetto, president of the Citizens Crime Commission of New York City, a watchdog group, said he did not want to believe that the equation was that tidy.

"I see no inherent conflict between good crime control and respect for people's rights," he said.

But, he added with a note of pessimism, "it's very hard to apply in practice."

QUESTIONS

1. What are the various reasons why, during the 1980s and '90s, politicians defined drugs and drug-related crimes as social problems of sufficient magnitude to justify giving the police the mandate to fight a war on drugs?

2. How can being at war against drugs lead police officers to cross the fragile line between law enforcement practices that are justifiably forceful and practices that are excessively brutal and abusive?

3. According to the author, how do whites' attitudes about the importance of getting tough on drugs and drug-related crimes inadvertently encourage police officers to mistreat black crime suspects?

4. In what ways is the tension between public safety and civil liberties described in this article currently manifesting itself in the war on terror? In other words, to what degree is there public sentiment nowadays that restricting the civil rights of people who fit a terrorist profile (people who appear to be of Middle Eastern descent) is necessary for public safety in the post-9/11 era?

5

Making Road Dangers Invisible

Drunk Drivers and Other Dangers

MALCOLM GLADWELL

This essay describes a law passed in New York City in the late 1990s that charac-terizes the tough stance shared by lawmakers and the American public toward peo-ple who drink and drive. After acknowledging the serious dangers of drunk driving, Gladwell discusses the arbitrariness of the New York City law, given that there are a variety of causes of recklessness on the road besides drinking and driving. He high-lights two particular behaviors—driving a sport-utility vehicle and talking on a cell phone while driving—that pose perhaps greater road hazards than drunk driving and yet receive much less public and policymaking attention. And indeed it is no accident that the behaviors that produce these other road hazards are not regarded as irresponsible in the way that drunk driving is. The manufacturers of sport-utility vehicles and cell phones play a powerful role in de-emphasizing the magni-tude of the road dangers they pose.

L ast week, New York City began confiscating the automobiles of people caught drinking and driving. On the first day of the crackdown, the police seized three cars, including one from a man who had been arrested for drunk driving on eight previous occasions. The tabloids cheered. Mothers Against Drunk Driving nodded in approval. After a recent series of brutal incidents involving the police tarnished the Giuliani administration, the Mayor's anti-crime crusade appeared to right itself. The city now has the toughest anti-drunk-driving policy in the country, and the public was given a welcome reminder that the vast majority of the city's thirty-eight thousand cops are neither racist nor reckless and that the justice they mete out is largely deserved. "There's a very simple way to stay out of this problem, for you, your family, and anyone else," a triumphant Giuliani said. "Do not drink and get behind the wheel of a car."

Let's leave aside, for a moment, the question of whether the new policy is constitutional. That is a matter for the courts. A more interesting issue is what the willing acceptance of such a hard-line stance on drunk driving says about the sometimes contradictory way we discuss traffic safety. Suppose, for example, that I was stopped by the police for running a red light on Madison Avenue. I would get points on my license and receive a fine. If I did the same thing while my blood-alcohol level was above the prescribed limit, however, I would be charged with drunk driving and lose my car. The behavior is the same in both cases, but the consequences are very different. We believe, as a society, that the combination of alcohol and driving deserves particular punishment. And that punishment isn't necessarily based on what you have actually done. It's often based on what you could do—or, to be more precise, on the extra potential for harm that your drinking poses.

There is nothing wrong with this approach. We have laws against threatening people with guns for the same reason. It hardly makes sense to wait for drunks or people waving guns to kill someone before we arrest them. But if merely posing a threat to others on the road is the threshold for something as drastic as civil forfeiture, then why are we stopping with drunks?

Fifty per cent of all car accidents in the United States are attributed to driver inattention, for example. Some of that inattention is caused by inebriation, but there are other common and obvious distractions. Two studies made in the past three years—the first conducted at the Rochester Institute of Technology and the second published in *The New England Journal of Medicine*— suggest that the use of car phones is associated with a four-to-fivefold increase in the risk of accidents, and that hands-free phones may not be any safer than conventional ones. The driver on the phone is a potential risk to others, just as the driver who has been drinking is.

It is also now abundantly clear that sport-utility vehicles and pickup trucks can—by virtue of their weight, high clearance, and structural rigidity—do far more damage in an accident than conventional automobiles can. S.U.V.s and light trucks account for about a third of the vehicles on the road. But a hugely disproportionate number of the fatalities in two-vehicle crashes are caused by collisions between those bigger vehicles and conventional automobiles, and the people riding in the cars make up a stunning eighty-one per cent of those killed.

The reason we don't like drunk drivers is that by making the decision to drink and drive an individual deliberately increases his or her chance of killing someone else with a vehicle. But how is the moral culpability of the count-less Americans who have walked into a dealership and made a decision to buy a fifty-six-hundred-pound sport utility any different? Of course, there are careful S.U.V. drivers and careful car-phone users. Careful people can get drunk, too, and overcompensate for their impairment by creeping along at twenty-five miles an hour, and in New York City we won't hesitate to take away *their* vehicles.

Obviously, Giuliani, even in his most crusading moments, isn't about to confiscate all the car phones and S.U.V.s on the streets of New York. States should, however, stop drivers from using car phones while the car is in motion, as some countries, including England, do. And a prohibitive weight tax on sport utilities would probably be a good idea. The moneys collected could be used to pay the medical bills and compensate the family of anyone hit by some cell-phone-wielding yuppie in a four-wheeled behemoth.

QUESTIONS

1. According to Gladwell, what kinds of road hazards are caused by talking on a cell phone while driving? What kinds of road hazards do sport-utility vehicles pose? How extensive are these hazards compared to the dangers of drunk driving?

2. Most people tend to view cell phones and sport-utility vehicles as adding a variety of advantages to their lives, *not* as menacing sources of danger. Let's take a moment to recognize how favorable impressions toward cell phones and sport-utility vehicles are reflected through advertising. Flip through a magazine and find an ad for a cell phone and an ad for a sport-utility vehicle. Then list the various benefits that the ads ascribe to each of these products.

3. Now spend a few minutes thinking more broadly about these ads. How do the wireless phone and automobile industries respectively advertise their products so that consumers are inclined to see the road hazards caused by talking on a cell phone while driving or driving a sport-utility vehicle as *less* in need of fixing than the road dangers caused by drunk driving?

4. Identify some of the ways that the manufacturers of cell phones and sport-utility vehicles can influence the level and kind of attention that lawmakers give to each of these consumer products.

Getting Fat on Misinformation

FROM *An Epidemic of Obesity Myths*
THE CENTER FOR CONSUMER FREEDOM

Why is the United States currently experiencing an obesity epidemic? While experts frequently cite how much people eat or how little they exercise, in this report the Center for Consumer Freedom presents a very different perspective on this epidemic. The report indicates that the data pointing to an obesity epidemic are grossly exaggerated, and it goes on to pinpoint who is responsible for this exaggeration and why. The report highlights those groups that stand to benefit from the public perception that there is an obesity epidemic and points out how these groups exercise the power to construct an epidemic out of data that do not convincingly point to such a conclusion.

Overblown rhetoric about the "obesity epidemic" has itself reached epidemic proportions. Trial lawyers increasingly see dollar signs where the rest of us see dinner. Activists and bureaucrats are proposing radical "solutions" like zoning restrictions on restaurants and convenience stores, as well as extra taxes and warning labels on certain foods.

Relying on peer-reviewed publications and esteemed health experts, this booklet documents the extent to which many researchers and academics are actively questioning the obesity hype. Have you heard that obesity kills 400,000 Americans a year? That it costs $117 billion? That 64 percent of Americans are overweight or obese? It turns out that these statistics are wildly exaggerated, and that most of the increased risks from excess weight actually result from physical inactivity.

The $40 billion weight loss industry is also fueling obesity hysteria. As the former Editor in Chief of *The New England Journal of Medicine* points out:

Physicians have been extensively involved with the pharmaceutical industry, especially opinion leaders and those in the high ranks of academia. The involvement was in many instances quite deep. It involved consulting, service on speaker's bureaus, and service on advisory boards. And at the same time some of these financially conflicted individuals were producing obesity materials, lectures, and obesity articles in major journals.

The pharmaceutical industry in particular is putting its enormous resources behind research that grossly exaggerates the health risks and costs of being overweight. And of course, once they convince us of the problem, drug manufacturers will peddle the cure. "In short," says Paul Ernsberger, a Professor of Medicine, Pharmacology and Neuroscience at Case Western Reserve University, "economic factors encourage a systematic exaggeration of the health risks of obesity."

* * *

On March 9, 2004, the heads of the National Institutes of Health, the Centers for Disease Control and Prevention, and the Department of Health and Human Services held a press conference to announce that "overweight and obesity are literally killing us." *USA Today* typified the press coverage the next day with a lead story titled: "Obesity on Track as No. 1 Killer." The press conference was timed to coincide with the publication of "Actual Causes of Death in the United States" in *JAMA*. Using the risk associated with excess weight that had been calculated in a 1999 study—which blamed obesity for 300,000 deaths a year—the more recent finding reported the number as 400,000 deaths each year. The 400,000 figure (like the 300,000 figure, upon which it was based) has become a fixture of obesity politics. But in reviewing the 400,000 study, *Science* magazine concluded:

Some researchers, including a few at CDC, dismiss this prediction, saying the underlying data are weak. They argue that the paper's compatibility with a new antiobesity theme in government public health pronouncements—rather than sound analysis—propelled it into print. . . . [Some argue that] the new numbers on obesity are weak—or as one critic in CDC says, "loosey-goosey." . . . Several epidemiologists at CDC and the National Institutes of Health (NIH) echoed [concerns about statistical biases that inflated the deaths associated with obesity] but declined to speak on the record. "I don't want to lose my job," said one

CDC staffer who does research in the area. Critics also object the authors added an arbitrary number of deaths from poor nutrition (15,000) to the obesity category. A CDC scientist says internal discussions on these issues got "very contentious" months before publication and left some feeling that the conclusions were not debatable.

The 400,000 study has several other flaws, each of which inflates the number of deaths attributable to obesity:

1. The study uses data from as far back as 1948. The 300,000 paper (which, again, was the basis for the estimate of 400,000 deaths) relied on six observational studies to calculate the mortality risk from excess weight. The average start date of these studies was 1963 (more than 40 years ago) and the average end date was 1983. Consequently, the 400,000 figure assumes that our ability to treat high blood pressure, diabetes, heart disease, and other illnesses linked to obesity has not improved in a generation. The authors admit this is a problem. "When most of the cohort studies used were initiated," they write, "there were fewer intervention strategies to reduce risk factors associated with obesity and fewer medical therapies for postponing death from obesity-related diseases." Yet no adjustment was made.

2. Only one of the six observational studies used to calculate the likelihood of death from excess weight was nationally representative. The others over-represented whites and upper socioeconomic classes. If the authors had included only nationally representative data, they would have reported 47,171—or 13 percent—fewer deaths. It may seem counterintuitive that over-representing whites and upper socioeconomic classes would increase the number of deaths. But there's a simple explanation: Most studies show that African Americans have little, if any, increased mortality risk from obesity.

3. While most of the 400,000 deaths derive from the "obese" (Body-Mass Index, or BMI 30 or higher), a substantial minority derive from the "over-weight" (BMI 25 to 29.9). But the study's own data show no statistically significant relationship between being merely "overweight" and increased risk of death. If the overweight deaths had been excluded—as they undoubtedly should have been—the study would have reported 57,698—or 17 percent—fewer deaths. The failure to report a significant relationship between overweight and increased mortality is not surprising. Most studies find no correlation (much less causation) between the two.

4. The 400,000 figure presumes that any increased rate of death in overweight or obese people is the result of their excess weight—a very unlikely assump-

tion. Those without a high school diploma are nearly twice as likely to be obese as those with a four-year degree. They are also much less likely to have health insurance and to receive quality health care. Other factors that could increase the risk of death among obese people include sedentary lifestyles, genetic ailments, and the negative effects of diet pills—including amphetamines, the weight loss drug of choice for much of the last half century. In 1970, 8 percent of all U.S. prescriptions were for weight loss amphetamines.

The authors of the 300,000 study admit that their calculations assume "all excess mortality in obese people is due to obesity," and that such an assumption would have the effect of overestimating the total number of deaths due to obesity. They continue: "Our estimates may be biased toward higher numbers due to confounding by unknown variables." Of course, access to health care and physical activity levels are known variables. The authors simply chose not to account for them. And as *The New England Journal of Medicine* pointed out in a 1998 editorial: "Mortality among obese people may be misleadingly high because overweight people are more likely to be sedentary and of low socio-economic status."

As Case Western's Paul Ernsberger notes: "Obesity-associated diseases are not necessarily caused by increased body weight. There is evidence to support a number of alternative explanations: (1) A disease or its treatment may itself promote obesity. (2) Lifestyle factors which cause disease may independently promote obesity. (3) The obese may be unhealthy as a group because they are more likely to be older, to have a low socioeconomic status, and to belong to an ethnic minority. (4) Hazardous weight loss methods and the dangers of repeated loss and regaining of weight may be major contributors to obesity-related diseases."

5. Ernsberger points to another factor that results in the exaggeration of obesity-mortality statistics: "Age is the strongest risk factor for nearly all diseases, and it greatly confounds the relationship between obesity and disease. Because most people steadily gain weight as they age, fatter people often appear unhealthy because they are older. Most studies control for age simply by dividing subjects into 10-year age groups. This fails to eliminate the relationship between weight and age; persons in their 40s who are obese are more likely to be 49 than to be 40. Because morbidity and mortality increase exponentially with age, even a small error in correcting for age can drastically overestimate the hazard of obesity."

* * *

Medical organizations have universally embraced the notion that obesity is an "epidemic." The term "epidemic" traditionally refers to disease. But for those who might be tempted to think that obesity is no more a disease than couch potato-itis, the CDC provides a helpful clarification: "Epidemic—a word typically used for outbreaks of infectious disease is now being used by medical professionals to describe the prevalence and rapid rise of obesity in the United States." How does the CDC justify this linguistic mutation? "The numbers alone support the use of the word." But the studies that generate these numbers, as demonstrated throughout, are deeply flawed. Dr. Glenn Gaesser notes that millions of "so-called obese people in the United States have no health problems linked to weight."

There are many reasons why medical authorities have so thoroughly embraced exaggerated claims of obesity health risks, but the most important is the corrupting influence of the $40 billion weight loss industry. According to the promotional material for the upcoming "World Obesity Congress and Expo," the big question for the pharmaceutical industry is: "What kind of obesity outcomes research is needed to make a compelling case for the 'value' of a therapeutic?" The conference will cover crucial topics like, "What studies are needed to persuade managed care [to cover an anti-obesity drug] and how should drug developers prepare to build the case?" The pharmaceutical industry has already spent millions building that case—primarily by funding research that exaggerates the risks of obesity.

The Washington, DC–based American Obesity Association (AOA) is the primary advocate of the "obesity-as-disease" theory. It lobbies to have insurance companies and government programs cover weight loss drugs and weight loss programs. AOA freely discloses: "Our financial support comes principally from pharmaceutical research and development companies as well as other companies in the weight management field such as Weight Watchers Inc., Jenny Craig, Inc. and SlimFast Foods."

In its efforts to have obesity classified as a disease, AOA is prone to exaggerate the threat of obesity. "If we don't try something new," AOA's vice president and co-founder argues, "in about 10 years everyone in the country will be overweight or obese." Everyone? Despite AOA's clear bias, its president and co-founder, Richard Atkinson, is the co-editor of the influential *International Journal of Obesity*.

David Allison is another extremely influential obesity researcher heavily funded by the weight loss industry. Allison was the lead author of the *JAMA* study reporting that obesity caused 300,000 deaths a year, which became the basis of the recently announced 400,000 figure. Allison has consulted for at least nine companies that make anti-obesity drugs, as well as law firms involved in litigation over weight loss pharmaceuticals. As *JAMA* itself noted when it published his 300,000 figure: "Dr. Allison has received grants, honoraria, monetary and product donations, was a consultant to, and has contracts or other commitments with numerous organizations involving weight control products and services."

Allison co-authored an otherwise official-looking study published in the April 2004 issue of *Obesity Research*. The fine print of this study reveals that a drug company and a company that makes body-fat measuring devices actually paid to have it published. The study was, in their own words, an "advertisement."

Five of the six other co-authors of this "advertisement" work under Dr. F. Xavier Pi-Sunyer, one of the most influential U.S. obesity researchers. Among many other high-profile positions, Pi-Sunyer is a past president of the North American Association for the Study of Obesity, and chairman of an influential NIH task force on the treatment of obesity. At the NIH, he was responsible for a definitional change that caused 39 million Americans to go to bed one night a normal weight and wake up the next morning classified as "overweight." Pi-Sunyer serves on the editorial board of *The International Journal of Obesity*; as Editor in Chief of *Obesity Research* from 1997 to 2002, he published the flawed study concluding that obesity imposes a $117 billion annual cost on the U.S. economy.

According to the Center for Science in the Public Interest, Pi-Sunyer has "served on the advisory boards of American Home Products' Wyeth-Ayerst labs, and Knoll Pharmaceuticals; been a consultant to Lilly Pharmaceuticals, Genentech, Hoffman-LaRoche, Knoll, Weight-Watchers International, and Neurogen; served on Knoll Pharmaceutical's Weight Risk Investigation Study Council; [and] has accepted grants or fees from Warner-Lambert." All these companies—many of which fund AOA—have a financial stake in making obesity look terrifyingly dangerous. And as it happens, Pi-Sunyer also serves on the advisory council of AOA.

Perhaps Pi-Sunyer's most obvious conflict of interest is his work with Weight Watchers, a company that benefits from exaggerated notions of the health risks posed by obesity. Pi-Sunyer was executive director of the Weight Watchers Foundation from 1991 to 1995, and he still serves on its board of directors. The primary function of the Weight Watchers Foundation is to fund studies that present obesity as a health disaster, and that offer Weight Watchers as the solution.

To sum up, Pi-Sunyer reclassified millions of Americans as "overweight," published a study that insists obesity is tremendously costly, and played a crucial role in funding, supervising, reviewing and editing a wealth of obesity-related research—all while he was working for Weight Watchers. Most egregiously, he conducted a study on the efficacy of Weight Watchers—funded by his very own Weight Watchers Foundation—which *JAMA* published in 2003.

In 1996, *The New England Journal of Medicine* published a study disclosing the health risks of appetite-suppressant drugs. As the respected medical journal subsequently admitted, an accompanying review—which emphasized the threat from obesity and downplayed the risks of pharmaceutical treatment— was written by consultants for the very companies that made the drugs in question. Their review argued that the "risk of pulmonary hypertension associated with [appetite-suppressant drug] dexfenfluramine is small and appears to be outweighed by benefits." *The New England Journal of Medicine* conceded two months later: "When considered as the conclusion of people who were paid consultants for companies that sell dexfenfluramine, it raises troubling questions."

QUESTIONS

1. List the various groups that have an interest in fostering the public perception that there is an obesity epidemic in the United States. In what ways do these groups benefit from the construction of this epidemic?

2. What evidence does this report offer to suggest that the diet industry, which profits enormously from this epidemic, has played a hand in influencing how scientific research about obesity has been conducted?

3. Why does the word "epidemic" give such urgency to figuring out ways to address the obesity problem, regardless of whether credible scientific data indicate that the use of this word is appropriate?

4. Which industries stand to benefit from the central claim made in this report: that the obesity problem has been grossly exaggerated? What relationship do these industries have to the organization that produced this report, the Center for Consumer Freedom? Go to www.consumerfreedom.com to learn more about this organization and the interests it represents.

Making School Shootings
More Thinkable

Dying to Be Famous

LIONEL SHRIVER

That the news media play a powerful role in influencing how audiences understand a problem and the urgency of addressing it is beyond question. But might news reporting also indirectly increase the likelihood that a problem will manifest itself again in the future? In discussing the March 2005 school massacre on the Red Lake Indian Reservation in Minnesota, Lionel Shriver makes the case that the very publicity given to school shootings is an important contributor to the probability of future school shootings. He argues, moreover, that the role of the news media in making school shootings more thinkable in kids' minds is made invisible by the reporting itself, which is concentrated on highlighting a variety of other explanations for why a particular school shooting has taken place—such as the availability of guns, teenage alienation, absent parents, or inciting musical lyrics.

Adolescents don't conceive the notion of strafing their classmates in a vacuum; they get the idea from cable TV. Bad news in itself, the 10-fatality reprise of the American school shooting last week at the Red Lake Indian Reservation in Minnesota bolsters the archetype. It makes a trend that had seemed to subside since Columbine in 1999 seem current again, and prospectively gives more boys big ideas.

The lessons we've been meant to learn from school shootings have been legion. We need better gun control. We need to be more understanding of misfits. We need to stop bullying. We need to curtail violent films and video games. So far, the suicide of 16-year-old Jeff Weise and his murder of nine people, including his grandfather, has fostered another familiar homily: We need to recognize the "warning signs."

Jeff Weise's "warning signs" have been widely publicized. He drew ghoulish cartoons and wrote gory short stories. He aped his predecessors in Colorado by wearing a black trench coat. On the Internet, heartbreakingly, he admired Hitler and flirted with eugenics—although the Nazis would hardly have championed the pure genetic line of Mr. Weise's Chippewa tribe. Predictably, all this dark ideation took place against the backdrop of a broken family and a forlorn personal life.

But Monday-morning quarterbacking has a reputation as cheap for good reason. A host of teenagers have morbid inclinations that they express through art and schoolwork. The very fact that the style that Mr. Weise adopted has a name—Goth—implies that thousands of other youths don the same dour garb. Many adolescents try on outrageous, painfully incoherent ideologies to set themselves apart. In her book "Rampage," Katherine S. Newman cites factors like access to "cultural scripts" from violent media, victimization from bullying and social marginalization. But such broad characteristics apply to half the children in the country.

I, too, researched school shootings for my seventh novel, about a fictional version of same. But the more I read, the more disparate these stories appeared. The boys had in common what they did, but not who they were or why they did it. If another school is shot up again, rest assured that the culprit will have exhibited his own eccentric set of "warning signs," like Mr. Weise's constantly changing hairstyles, that if plugged into a computer would finger 10,000 other innocents as murderous time-bombs.

But I did identify one universal. The genre is now sufficiently entrenched that any adolescent who guns down his classmates aims to join a specific elect. Like Red Lake's, the public shootings are often a cover for suicide, or for the private settling of scores with a parent or guardian. But a school shooting is reliably a bid for celebrity. As for murder-suicides like Jeff Weise's, even posthumous notoriety must seem enthralling to someone who feels sufficiently miserable and neglected.

Whether we care to admit it, the calculation these boys are making is culturally astute. You do not make headlines by getting an A on your report card. So long as we make a minimal distinction between fame and infamy—and consistently accord infamy a measure more fascination—any smart teenager is going to take the easier, more spectacular route to glory and opt for ignominy over achievement. Far more Americans now know the name Jeff Weise than the winner of last year's Nobel Peace Prize. Only two days after the shooting, a Google search of "Jeff Weise" and "Red Lake" scored more than 8,000 hits. If our boy wanted attention, he got it.

Am I the only one to find those thousands of hits shocking? Am I the only one to feel queasy over the painstaking examination of this boy's psyche—perhaps including this very article?

The Star Tribune of Minneapolis: "Jeff Weise: A Mystery in a Life Full of Hardship." Minnesota Public Radio: "Who Was Jeff Weise?" There's hardly a teenage boy who wouldn't covet those headlines for himself. Are we not dangling a prize of outsized pity for boys with the guts to compete for it? Are we in danger of being too sympathetic?

Surely no single factor explains the perniciousness of school shootings more than the intense news media focus they draw. Too late, we are now combing Mr. Weise's reactionary Internet postings, grisly drawings and gruesome short stories. We are rightly wrenched by his fractured family life—his mother's brain damage, his father's suicide.

But I grew up in North Carolina alongside any number of anguished young men, a few of whom likewise chose to leave the building with a shot in the head. Most humble suicides, however, don't take nine unwilling people with them on the way out the door.

Sympathy, of course, is not zero-sum. We can afford to lavish it unsparingly on all parties in tragedies like this one. But one might make a case for ordinal sympathy. That list should be topped by nine dead people who should have been eating breakfast this morning. Next, their grieving families. The seven wounded. Jeff Weise's extended family, living with shame and perplexity hereon. The Red Lake reservation, now receiving the kind of attention it doesn't want. The nation at large, in which extravagant media response to this killing has once more raised the likelihood that it will happen again. Jeff Weise—overweight, politically confused lonely guy, but also a killer—belongs on the list, but last.

Otherwise, reserve a special compassion for any folks in Mr. Weise's orbit, like the doctor said to have dismissed the boy's cutting himself as "a fad," implicitly being made to feel that by not reading the "warning signs" they are in some way at fault. The hurling of blame constitutes a secondary wave of violence that leaves a second set of scars. Still coping with gratuitous murder, counselors and teachers, parents or guardians, friends and neighbors of the gunman grapple with an equally gratuitous guilt.

For no one should have seen this coming. Screwed-up comes in as many flavors as ice cream, and the merest fraction of troubled boys go literally ballistic at their schools. If occasionally fatal, the combination of despair and grandiosity is as common—and American—as apple and pie.

QUESTIONS

1. According to Shriver, why don't the reasons for school shootings commonly cited in news reports add up to an adequate explanation for why these shootings take place?

2. Why are we culturally more fascinated with people who commit acts of infamy, such as opening fire in a classroom, than those who follow the rules and behave in ways that are socially appropriate?

3. Watch a half hour of local TV news to see whether there is evidence to support the author's inference that news reports tend to highlight infamous acts. Do a count of the headline stories. How many of these stories are about violence or other deviant acts? How many are about great achievements like kids getting an A on their report cards?

4. Shriver argues, "Surely no single factor explains the perniciousness of school shootings more than the intense news media focus they draw." How could we sociologically study whether there is validity to this argument?

The Problem with Welfare
as We Know It

FROM *Why Do Stereotypes and Lies Persist?*

DERRICK JACKSON

Ask most people to describe what is wrong with welfare and they will have no trouble coming up with a laundry list of reasons why poor single mothers should not receive handouts from the government. But, what most people are not aware of and therefore will not tell you is that they are familiar with just one kind of welfare problem, and quite possibly not the one that ought to concern us the most. In this selection, Derrick Jackson outlines another welfare problem: corporate welfare. He argues that despite the fact that there are some good reasons for viewing large corporations as undeserving of the massive government assistance they receive, the corporate welfare problem receives little news coverage or policy debate. In discussing why this problem receives so little attention, Jackson urges readers to analyze the different kinds of power exercised by claimsmakers, and to see how these differences are instrumental in explaining the level of media exposure and public scrutiny given to different welfare problems.

One of my favorite exercises in speeches and college journalism classes is to ask my audience, "What percentage of the federal budget do you think is spent on welfare?"

The answers almost always range between 15 and 50 percent. They are shocked when I tell them that Aid to Families with Dependent Children is only one percent of the federal budget, and even adding other benefits also used by the working poor, such as food stamps and disability, the figure is still no more than six percent. I tell them that spending on welfare, in real dollars, is 20 percent less than 20 years ago.

"So why do you think welfare takes up so much of the budget?" I ask.

Their answer: they learned it from television and newspapers.

* * *

Welfare for the poor has dominated the news for 30 years, beginning with Senator Patrick Moynihan's "discovery" of what he called "welfare dependency." It picked up particular steam in the mid-1980s with the double whammy of Charles Murray's book "Losing Ground" and President Ronald Reagan's mantra of "Welfare queens." Welfare has become a bipartisan devotion on Capital Hill, with Republicans like Rep. Clay Shaw of Florida saying it has "destroyed responsibility," and President Clinton declaring that the biggest problem facing the nation is teenage pregnancy.

In comparison, welfare for the rich has received relatively little notice. In their 1994 book, "America: Who Really Pays the Taxes," Pulitzer Prize–winning reporters Donald Barlett and James Steele laid out a corporate tax break structure that—at the same time welfare was actually shrinking in real dollars—deprives the Treasury of $250 billion a year.

That figure was seven times the figure for welfare for the poor. But can any mainstream media outlet claim to have investigated tax breaks and CEOs with seven times the resources of investigating welfare and poor women? Of course not. In The Boston Globe's newspaper data base, the phrase "welfare reform" for the poor appeared 14 times more than the phrase "corporate welfare."

We in the media find poor folks on stoops, street corners and cacophonic welfare offices far more easy and colorful prey for our notebooks and cameras than executives who can throw up a gauntlet of elevators, secretaries, security guards, insomnia-producing public relations staffs and intimidating lawyers. In explaining in 1990 why African Americans, who consume 13 percent of illegal drugs, make up 74 percent of those sentenced to prison for drug offenses while white Americans consume 80 percent of illegal drugs with little fear of jail, Charles Ramsey, head of the Chicago police narcotics division, said:

> There's as much cocaine in the Sears Tower or in the Stock Exchange as there is in the black community. But those deals are harder to catch. Those deals are done in office buildings, in somebody's home, and there's not the violence associated with it that there is in the black community. But the guy standing on the corner, he's almost got a sign on his back. These guys are just arrestable.

In the same spirit, poor women, particularly low-income African American women, are far more easy to blame for the growing gap between rich and poor than influence-peddlers in the White House and corporations who have either sent overseas many of the jobs that many of the poor's fathers and mothers used to have or shrunk blue-collar payrolls with technology. While politicians justify draconian cuts in welfare by making examples of the deficient character of recipients, the media did not question, with the same veracity, the notion that it was ludicrous for a Louis Gerstner of IBM to chair a national education summit after his prior mission of dealing death for R.J. Reynolds cigarettes.

While welfare recipients bear the public responsibility for destroying responsibility, news organizations give comfort to CEOs who fire thousands of workers by buying into the sanitized corporate-speak of "downsizing." Diane Sawyer of ABC all but prejudged teen welfare mothers by asking them "Why should taxpayers pay for your mistake? . . . Answer their question." No CEO faces that kind of barrage.

While politicians demand that welfare recipients get a job, the media did precious little during the heat of the debate on the welfare bill to tell the public that in reality, the jobs are currently not there. A university study in Chicago found that four percent of entry level jobs in Illinois pay a livable wage for a family of three, while the pay for nearly 40 percent of the jobs is below the poverty line. The media was too late to use ample university-based evidence that the best way to get off or avoid welfare is to get an education. Instead, New York City Mayor Rudolph Giuliani went ahead with welfare cuts so severe that he is forcing college students to leave school to take any job they can find, or lose their benefits.

While every news reporter surely knows who Charles Murray is, how many know the name of an actual researcher on welfare? In a look at welfare reporting, the watchdog organization Fairness and Accuracy in Reporting found that in a three-month period in late 1994–95, 71 percent of the sources for stories on cutting welfare for women were male. Only nine percent of the sources were researchers and advocates for women on welfare. One Sunday in which all three network talk shows discussed welfare, no woman on welfare and no person of color was showed to provide a counterpoint to a George Will or a Gov. Pete Wilson of California.

A media that relies almost exclusively on a steady diet of Shaw, Murray, Newt Gingrich, Clinton, Robert Rector of the conservative Heritage Foundation and welfare-slashing governors like Tommy Thompson of Wisconsin and John Engler of Michigan is consigned to plow ahead with apocalyptic visions of teen mothers having babies to get a check. Ignored are researchers who point out that there is no universal correlation between welfare and pregnancy. In her book, "Teen Mothers," North Carolina Sociology Professor Kathleen Mullen Harris wrote how European countries have far more generous social welfare benefits for single mothers "and yet their rates of teen childbearing are only one-eighth to about one-half of the U.S. rates."

The comparative failure to quote researchers and advocates meant that few Americans were made aware that the so-called rise in teen pregnancy has less to do with unmarried teens having babies than married women having far fewer babies. The failure to look up simple statistics helps fuel stereotypes.

Last year The New Republic, in urging Clinton to end welfare as we know it, used the photo of an African American woman smoking a cigarette and holding a baby. When Clinton signed the welfare bill, the woman closest to him in photographs was a large African American woman. While it is true that African American women are disproportionately on welfare, the majority of women on welfare are white.

* * *

In welfare, women are painted black so they can be removed from the rolls and forgotten about. It is early in the welfare "reform" games and Massachusetts and New York both admitted last year that they have no idea where the majority of the people dropped from the welfare roles have gone. The media would do a much better service if it reported on the stereotypes and lies about welfare before they become permanent truth.

QUESTIONS

1. List all of the problems associated with government assistance to poor single mothers and all of the problems associated with government assistance to large corporations. Which set of welfare problems seems to you to be more harmful to our society? Why?

2. How does the power that large corporations exercise in shaping the social construction of welfare compare with the power exercised by poor single women?

3. What are the various ways that large corporations use their power to divert attention away from the corporate welfare problem and to focus this attention instead on social problems caused by other populations, including poor single mothers?

4. Make a list of all the other claimsmakers besides large corporations and poor single women that are involved in bringing public attention to each type of welfare problem.

a. Which group of claimsmakers has more power and which has less?

b. Why are these power differences important in explaining the unequal attention given to the two welfare problems?

5. Why do you think politicians are so much more interested in creating policies, like the 1996 welfare reform law, that reduce welfare dependency among the poor than in creating policies that limit corporate welfare?

PART TWO
HOW SOCIAL
PROBLEMS ARE FRAMED

Whether a harmful condition becomes perceived as a social problem depends on the language claimsmakers use to describe the harm. Words are powerful in influencing the level of attention a problem receives, since words frame the very ways that people think about the problem. *Frames* give visibility to a problem by packaging it in ways that audiences can readily understand. Frames highlight certain aspects of the problem and how it should be addressed, in the same way that a picture frame draws attention to the photo displayed within it.

Frames are important because they illustrate just how deeply the language used to construct a social problem contributes to our understanding of the problem. Words have meanings that we often take for granted when a particular problem is being discussed by an activist, a politician, a journalist, or any other claimsmaker. Consider the word *danger*. Because we are so familiar with this word, and because danger is something we actively seek to avoid, *danger* is a powerful way of framing a social problem. The word compels the giving of public and policymaking attention to any of a number of dangers lurking within our society, such as violent neighborhoods (Best, 1999) and popular music marketed toward youth (Binder, 1993).

Two factors give frames enormous power to construct social problems: They have meanings with which we are already familiar, and they are used repeatedly to construct different social problems. Thus, when claimsmakers describe the dangers of popular music, no explanation is needed about why claims about *danger* should compel a high level of emotional response among parents because this idea is clearly understood. Claimsmakers have drawn on this frame before in reference to neighborhood violence, as well as in regard to an array of other social problems.

This is true of any frame. To regard people sleeping on the street in the dead of winter as an *emergency* that must be addressed right now is a way of understanding homelessness that is also used to frame the urgency of addressing other social problems, such as hunger and domestic violence (Lipsky and Smith, 1989). Indeed, frames have broader significance than the particular problem at hand: for example, child abuse is constructed as a *horror* (Johnson, 1995); violence as *random* (Best, 1999); and terrorism as justifying the waging of *war*, which has been a historically powerful frame for defining a problem as a society's top concern (Best, 2002).

Since the framing of a particular problem is really a way of conveying to policymakers and to the general public that broader societal values are at stake, frames enable audiences to quickly become familiar with newly emerging issues. When Rachel Carson wrote during the early 1960s about the environmental dangers of chemical pesticides, she was describing a problem that few people at the time knew or cared very much about. But the power of her landmark book lay in the very title she chose to frame the issue: *Silent Spring*. People did not need to have a deep understanding of what pesticides were, why they were being used extensively by farmers, or the science behind the harms they posed. What the book so powerfully conveyed was a daunting image audiences could easily connect with: that nature was no longer able to undergo its annual spring rejuvenation—with birds feathering new nests and singing harmoniously—because of the damage that humans had done to the environment (Gunter, 2005).

Multiple claimsmakers are typically involved in the framing of a social problem. These may include activists, researchers, victims, police, politicians, corporations, special-interest groups, and of course the news media. Since most of what people know about social problems comes either directly from the news or indirectly from what someone hears based on a news story, the news media play the leading role in framing social problems. Given that news is a consumer product, importance is placed on presenting visually dramatic and interesting story angles that will attract audiences and keep their attention (Bogart, 1995). This explains the tendency journalists have to draw on a limited, recurring set of frames, even though the frame used may not accurately represent the social problem being covered. So, for example, news reports highlight the horror stories of child abuse involving significant injury or death, while giving little attention to the variety of less physical, but more mental and emotional, ways that children are abused (Johnson, 1995).

In simplifying a problem, the news media and other claimsmakers often can *statistically misrepresent* it as well, meaning that the claimsmaking presents the problem as more pervasive than it actually is. For child abuse, news reports present the exceptional horror stories as if they were the norm; in truth, the most common manifestations of child abuse are cases of long-term psychological abuse, which are not terribly newsworthy because they evoke little drama that can be captured through pictures (Johnson, 1995). In a similar way, dramatic accounts of the grisly and heinous acts committed by serial killers during the 1980s and '90s validated exaggerated statistics about the number of active killers there were at the time and their total number of victims (Jenkins, 1994). Another example of statistical misrepresentation is the news media's portrayal of the majority of poor people as black, when in truth blacks comprised just 24.5 percent of America's poor between 2003 and 2005 (U.S. Census Bureau, 2006). This statistical misrepresentation feeds public sentiment that poor people are undeserving of government assistance since it reinforces stereotypes about lazy, poor, black people (Gilens, 1996).

Thus, analyzing frames is useful in exposing how problems can be statistically misrepresented, and consequently in enabling students to recognize the danger of investing blind faith in numbers and what they supposedly tell us about social problems. Furthermore, such analysis can highlight the possible alternative frames that might have been used to construct the problem but were not. It is important to underscore that problems do not have pre-defined frames attached to them. Rather, claimsmakers actively draw on certain frames, and not others, in constructing social problems. For example, Martin (2004) reports that the news media framed the 1993 American Airlines flight attendants strike as a problem primarily because consumers were being inconvenienced during the Thanksgiving holiday. He shows that this was just one possible way of framing the issue, and it diverted attention away from another frame that would have constructed the problem quite differently. This frame would have focused on the labor issue itself and would have involved dissecting the complicated relationship at American Airlines between management and flight attendants. Martin's study suggests that claimsmakers' tendency to draw on a limited set of recurring frames impedes audiences' capacity to gain multiple perspectives on an issue.

Although frames can statistically misrepresent a problem or divert attention away from useful alternative ways of understanding it, the consequences of framing are not necessarily negative. Indeed, frames can help people to better understand aspects of their own lives. For example, Tavris (1992) argues that viewing their mood swings throughout the month as attributable to premenstrual syndrome enables women to make sense of what is going on inside their bodies and gives them a medical basis for seeing these mood swings as normal. The larger point to emphasize here is that frames provide particular and powerful ways of understanding social problems by giving audiences the capacity to make sense of problems that would otherwise be difficult to understand. Frames are vital to the construction of social problems since they provide people with a set of categories through which they can understand particular harms in the world and what should be done to address them.

REFERENCES

Best, Joel. (1999). *Random violence: How we talk about new crimes and new victims*. Berkeley: University of California Press.

———. (2002). What's wrong with declaring war on social problems? From *Social problems: Readings with four questions* (pp. 19–29). Belmont, CA: Wadsworth.

Binder, Amy. (1993). Constructing racial rhetoric: Media depictions of harm in heavy metal and rap music. *American Sociological Review* 58: 753–767.

Bogart, Leo. (1995). *Commercial Culture: The media system and the public interest.* New York: Oxford University Press.

Gilens, Martin. (1996). Race and poverty in America: Public misperceptions and the American news media. *Public Opinion Quarterly* 60: 515–541.

Gunter, Valerie J. (2005). News media and technological risks: The case of pesticides after *Silent Spring. Sociological Quarterly* 46: 671–698.

Jenkins, Philip. (1994). *Using murder: The social construction of serial homicide.* Hawthorne, NY: De Gruyter.

Johnson, John M. (1995). Horror stories and the construction of child abuse. From J. Best (Ed.), *Images of issues: Typifying contemporary social problems* (2nd ed., pp. 17–32). Hawthorne, NY: De Gruyter.

Lipsky, Michael, and Steven Rathgeb Smith. (1989). When social problems are treated as emergencies. *Social Service Review* 63(1): 5–25.

Martin, Christopher R. (2004). *Framed! Labor and the corporate media.* Ithaca: Cornell University Press.

Tavris, Carol. (1992). Misdiagnosing the body: Premenstrual syndrome, postmenstrual syndrome, and other normal "diseases." From *The Mismeasure of Woman* (pp. 131–169). New York: Simon & Schuster.

U.S. Census Bureau. (2006). Number in poverty and poverty rates by race and Hispanic origin using 2- and 3-year averages: 2003 to 2005. www.census.gov/hhes/www/poverty/poverty05/table5.html

Random Violence

FROM *Random Violence: How We Talk about
New Crimes and New Victims*

JOEL BEST

*Joel Best uncovers the dominant way that people have come to view violence within
American society over the past couple of decades: as behavior that can only be explained
as occurring randomly. He argues that people rarely question three core assumptions
upon which the randomness frame rests because these assumptions offer familiar and
simplistic ways for people to understand the source of their fears of becoming victimized by violent crime. Upon closer scrutiny, Best illustrates that none of these assumptions prove to be valid. Moreover, how violence is typically framed diverts public
attention away from available information about violent crime that, if framed more
accurately, would provide a clearer and more realistic picture of the violence problem
in the United States.*

* * *

Tales of gang members driving around, planning to kill whoever flashed
headlights at them, spread from coast to coast during the fall of 1993.
Concerned citizens passed along the story via photocopies, faxes, and, of
course, word of mouth. Employers warned their employees, law-enforcement
agencies alerted one another, and the press cautioned the public. It seemed
a plausible story: everybody knew that there were gang members out there;
the notion that gang "initiation rites" required members to commit terrible
crimes was well ingrained; and cars and guns seemed easy to come by. *It could
happen*, people told themselves. *That's just the kind of thing gangs do.*

The previous year's gang-initiation story had been about ankle grabbers at
shopping malls. It involved gang members who crawled beneath parked vehicles, waiting for the drivers to return. When a driver paused to open the car

91

door, the gang member would reach out and grab the victim's ankles. There were different versions of what happened next: in one, when the victim reached down to pry the assailant's hands loose, the gang member chopped off a finger as a souvenir; in others, the gang member slashed the victim's Achilles tendon, dropping the victim to the ground—the first step in a robbery, rape, or murder. People believed the ankle-grabbing story, in spite of its improbable elements (e.g., gang members positioning themselves for criminal attacks by crawling under cars, overpowering victims by grabbing their ankles, easily slicing through the tough Achilles tendon, etc.). After all, it was just the kind of thing gang members do.

There is no evidence that either gang-initiation tale was true. Neither seems especially plausible, yet both were widely believed. What explains this credulity? Concern about random, senseless violence has become a central theme in contemporary culture. In addition to gang initiation rites, we worry about serial murders, carjackings, freeway shootings, sexual predators, wilding, hate crimes, kids with guns, stalking, drive-by shootings, copycat criminals, workplace violence, shootings in schools, and other unpredictable threats. Why shouldn't we also worry about ankle-grabbing attacks and lights-out killings?

The notion that our society is plagued by random violence has surprisingly broad appeal. Consider two recent quotations invoking the concept:

> Our greatest fear is of violence from a nameless, faceless stranger. . . . Citizens of all races who are fearful of random violence have good reason for their concern. Storekeepers, utility workers, police officers, and ordinary citizens out for a carton of milk or a family dinner are all increasingly at risk.

* * *

> We are terrified by the prospect of innocent people being gunned down at random, without warning and almost without motive, by youngsters who afterward show us the blank, unremorseful faces of seemingly feral, presocial beings.

The first quotation is from the liberal attorney Adam Walinsky, the second from the conservative political scientist James Q. Wilson. Although they bring different ideological assumptions to social analysis, and although they recommend different sorts of solutions for society's problems, both Walinsky and Wilson define random violence as a major social crisis.

Similar warnings abound. The Federal Bureau of Investigation warns: "Every American now has a realistic chance of murder victimization in view of the random nature the crime has assumed." Senator Daniel Patrick Moynihan charges: "Violent killings, often random, go on unabated. Peaks continue to attract some notice. But these are peaks above 'average' levels that thirty years ago would have been thought epidemic." The criminologist Jerome H. Skolnick notes the intense media coverage given a few violent crimes:

> The message seemed to be that random violence is everywhere and you are no longer safe—not in your suburban home, commuter train, or automobile—and the police and the courts cannot or will not help you. . . . It is random violent crime, like a shooting in a fast-food restaurant, that is driving fear.

A sociologist conducting focus groups of women talking about crime finds that they describe "predatory, extremely violent, criminals who attack at random." A reader writes to *Time* magazine about "the latest episode in the drama of random violence that airs almost every day in America," calling it a "spiraling epidemic." And a commentator for *U.S. News & World Report* reacts to President Clinton's suggestion that schools begin the day with a moment of silence:

> Silence is a small, fragile thing. It cannot cure teen pregnancy or stop random violence. It cannot banish gangs or drugs. It cannot rebuild families or restore faith. But it can, at times, replenish the spirit.

In short, references to random violence have become commonplace, indicating a widespread sense that random violence is a signifi-cant problem.

In part, this concern with random violence seems grounded in a general sense that crime is both out of control and on the rise. But this generalized sense of dread is heightened by specific fears, fostered by what sociologists call "moral panics"—exaggerated, heavily publicized reports of sudden increases in particular sorts of criminal violence, such as the stories that gangs had begun holding lights-out initiations. And, unlike the lights-out story, which was not true, there is at least some basis for many of the claims that bring new crime problems into the spotlight of public attention.

Consider, for example, the focus on freeway shootings in Los Angeles in the summer of 1987. The story began when reporters juxtaposed stories of two shootings on L.A. freeways during the same June weekend. When a third shooting occurred a few weeks later, the press declared that they had spotted a trend, and, for three weeks in late July and early August, news stories about L.A.'s "road warriors" riding "hair-trigger highways" attracted national attention. These reports emphasized the randomness of freeway violence: anyone in a vehicle could become the target of an unprovoked attack. However, it soon became obvious that freeway violence was not spreading across the country or increasing in southern California; it was not even all that common in L.A. There simply weren't enough serious freeway shootings to justify continued media coverage, and the moral panic faded almost as quickly as it arose.

Concern over freeway violence was an intense but brief episode. In contrast, other crime problems prove to have greater staying power once they gain our attention. Serial murder, for example, achieved high visibility in the early 1980s. Whereas the press had always viewed reports of multiple murders as good news stories, it traditionally treated such killings as unrelated, aberrant episodes. However, after several notorious cases emerged in the late 1970s and early 1980s, people began to view serial murder as a distinct type of crime, and there were claims about an epidemic of serial murders. One sensational book on the topic began with the words "America is caught up in the midst of what one expert calls 'an epidemic of homicidal mania,' plagued by ruthless predators—lately dubbed serial murderers or 'recreational killers'—who stalk their human prey at random, often for the sheer joy of killing," while the feminist Jane Caputi characterized serial sexual murder as "sexually political murder, . . . functional phallic terrorism," and "male torturing and killing of women at random." Interest in the topic remains high: dozens of nonfiction books approach the topic from various angles, ranging from popular accounts to academic studies from disciplines as diverse as history, criminology, anthropology, psychiatry, and women's studies; and the diabolical serial murderer, striking at random, is a standard pop-culture icon in novels and movies.

* * *

THE NATURE OF RANDOM VIOLENCE

Considering our readiness to talk and worry about random violence, we give surprisingly little thought to what the term implies. Warnings about the threat of random violence rarely define the term; instead, they illustrate the problem's nature with typifying examples. These examples can be highly melodramatic: there is an "ideal victim"—usually a respectable person engaged in some innocent activity—who suffers a sudden, unexpected, unprovoked, violent attack by an assailant with no connection to the victim, no good reason to hurt this person in this way. Often the particular example chosen to illustrate the problem is especially horrifying. Consider the first paragraph in a *Newsweek* story on carjackings:

> Pamela Basu had no reason to believe she was in danger. The 34-year-old research chemist was driving her daughter, Sarina, to preschool on a warm morning last September when two young men approached her gold BMW at a stop sign one block from her suburban Maryland home. They forced her from the car and sped away, but Basu's left arm became ensnared in the harness strap of her seat belt. She was dragged for nearly two miles as her assailants swerved into a barbed-wire fence in an apparent attempt to dislodge her. Before finally ridding themselves of the fatally injured woman, they stopped to toss her 22-month-old daughter from the car. She was found, miraculously unhurt, still strapped in her car seat.

This grotesque story offers high melodrama—an upper-middle-class mother attacked and murdered, and her young child endangered, by callous strangers. It justifies *Newsweek*'s title for the piece: "A New Terror on the Road: Carjacking Puts Fear in the Driver's Seat." The example of Pamela Basu suggests that everyone is in danger, that carjacking is random violence; as *Newsweek* warned: "Cars have been commandeered just about anyplace motorists congregate. . . . Routine errands have become a tense exercise in some communities."

Reports of terrible crimes committed by strangers are disturbing, but they do not justify broad generalizations about violence being random. The term "random violence" demands closer inspection. When statisticians speak of randomness, they refer to independent events that occur by chance, in no identifiable pattern. Imagine a set of numbered balls used in a lottery drawing. The balls are stirred into an unpredictable arrangement, then five are drawn. In a random drawing, each ball has an equal chance of being drawn, as does each combination of balls. That is, the number-one ball's chance of being selected is equal to the number-two ball's, and so on, and the combination one-two-three-four-five is just as likely to occur as one-two-three-four-six or any other possible combination. Such is the nature of randomness.

What, then, do we mean by random violence? The term has several implications. Imagine a society within which some number of violent incidents occurs, each incident involving an attacker and a victim. If this violence is truly random, then not only is each individual in that society at risk of being attacked, but all individuals run *equal* risks of victimization, and every individual also is a potential attacker, and everyone is equally likely to attack someone else. Immediately, we recognize that this sort of chaos is not what most people mean when they speak of random violence. Although many claims about random violence imply that everyone is a potential victim, they do not assume that everyone is a potential attacker. Rather, they imagine that attackers are somehow different from their victims, that they are gang members, or psychopaths, or at least males. When most people speak of random violence, they imagine a world in which the general population of potential victims shares the risk of being attacked by these likely attackers. Depending on the crime, the population of victims may be all women (vulnerable to sexual assault), all children (molestation), all gays (homophobic attacks), all drivers (carjacking and freeway violence), and so on. In this sense, we imagine that violence is *patternless:* all potential victims share the risks, so that victimization can happen to anyone: "The list of homicide victims is endless. . . . Grandmothers and college students, prowling street kids and small babies in their walkers, neighbors chatting on city streets, young mothers getting ready for work."

What motivates these random attacks? We may acknowledge that violence can be deliberate and purposeful—what criminologists call "instrumental"— as when a bank robber steals money. But other violence seems pointless, meaningless: the bystander shot in a drive-by; the rape victim selected apparently by chance, and so on. This pointlessness is implied when we talk about random violence: gang members are killing motorists who blink their headlights. Why? Because that's what the gang initiation rite requires. Because it's just the kind of thing gang members do—or might do. The notion of random violence, then, refers to the risk that anyone might be attacked for no good reason. This is possible because the attacks are *pointless,* the victims chosen at random. Again, in a world of random violence, no one is safe.

In addition to patternlessness and pointlessness, there is a third theme that runs through claims about random violence: *deterioration.* Warnings about random violence imply that things are getting worse, that there are ever more violent incidents, that respectable citizens run greater risks of victimization than in the past. There are competing explanations for this deterioration: conservatives tend to blame a deteriorating culture (e.g., "the rising tide of immorality"), while liberals usually point to deterioration in the social structure (e.g., "the growing gap between rich and poor"). But, regardless of which causal explanations they prefer, when people worry about random violence, they assume that things are worse today than they were yesterday, and they fear that things will be even worse tomorrow.

In short, when we use the expression "random violence," we characterize the problem in particular terms: violence is patternless (it can happen to anyone); it is pointless (it happens for no reason at all); and it is becoming increasingly common. This is, of course, a very frightening combination. A society that cannot control the growth of patternless, pointless violence seems on the verge of chaos, anarchy, collapse.

Those who speak of random violence rarely examine these three assumptions. For the most part, they assume—and their listeners take it for granted—that patternless, pointless violence is on the rise. However, even a cursory examination of the most basic, familiar criminological evidence calls all three assumptions into question: most violence is not patternless; nor is it pointless; nor is it increasing in the uncontrolled manner we imagine.

PATTERNLESSNESS

We often have a difficult time thinking about patterns in social behavior. I am reminded of this difficulty at the end of each semester, when my students turn in term papers about such social problems as child abuse, rape, incest, and other forms of victimization. Almost every paper features a passage along these lines:

> What sorts of people suffer this victimization? All sorts. The victims are rich and poor, male and female, black and white, of every age.

These papers always make me feel that I've failed: after spending a semester trying to teach my students to recognize and understand the patterns in social problems, I find their papers cheerfully announcing that there are no patterns to be found.

Yet, in spite of my students' eagerness to deny it, the patterns are there. And, if randomness is the absence of a pattern, then violence isn't random. There are thousands of social-scientific studies, enough to fill a small library, proving that violence is patterned.

Consider one example: homicide in the contemporary United States. According to FBI statistics, the U.S. homicide rate in 1994 was 9.0 per 100,000 population. That is, for every 100,000 Americans, there were nine homicides. But not everyone runs the same risk of being a homicide victim; in fact, the risk of victimization—the homicide rate—varies wildly depending on one's age, sex, and race. Consider the pattern among white males in 1990: during the first fifteen years of life, rates of victimization are low (2.7 or less per 100,000); the figures rises to 12.5 for white males aged fifteen to nineteen, peaks at 18.1 for those twenty to twenty-four, then gradually declines until it reaches about 4.0 for the oldest white males. In other words, the chances of a white male being killed in a homicide are relatively low during childhood, are highest during adolescence and early adulthood, and then decline in middle and old age. This seems reasonable. Few small children become homicide victims: children spend most of their lives under the protection of adults; their greatest risk of homicide is at the hands of an abusive adult caretaker. But adolescents and young adults spend much less time under older adults' supervision, and they take more risks: they experiment with sex and alcohol and illicit drugs; they get into more fights, drive more recklessly, and commit more crimes than older adults; and this independence is more likely to get them killed. As adults mature, they tend to settle down—get married, hold steady jobs, spend more time at home and less on the town—and their risk of becoming a homicide victim falls.

The same general pattern emerges when we add nonwhite males and white and nonwhite females to the graph . . . : for each group, the risk of being a homicide victim is low in childhood, reaches a peak in adolescence and young adulthood, and then declines with age. However, there are striking differences in victimization rates among the four groups. White females have the lowest rates of victimization: through age nine, white males and females run essentially the same risks; but for whites aged ten and older, females are victimized far less often than males. For instance, the peak age of victimization is twenty to twenty-four for both white males and white females, but the victimization rate for white males is 18.1, about four times greater than the rate of 4.5 for white females.

If white females consistently have the lowest homicide victimization rates, nonwhite males have the highest. In every age category, the homicide rates for nonwhite males is three to seven times higher than it is for white males. Again, the age of peak victimization is twenty to twenty-four, but the rate for nonwhite males is 126.8—seven times greater than the rate for white males, and twenty-eight times greater than the rate for white females.

The pattern continues when we look at nonwhite females. Like their white counterparts, nonwhite males and females share similar rates of victimization through age nine; thereafter, females have consistently lower rates of victimization than males. At the same time, nonwhite females run higher risks of victimization—two to five times higher, depending on the age group—than do white females. In most age groups, a nonwhite female's risk of homicide victimization is roughly that of a white male.

Though we can say that everyone runs some risk of being a homicide victim—that homicides kill young and old, male and female, black and white—that broad generalization is fundamentally dishonest, because the risk of victimization varies so markedly. If we were actuaries, writing policies for homicide victimization insurance, we would not charge everyone the same premiums. Rather, we would charge males more than females, nonwhites more than whites, and adolescents and young adults more than children or older adults. To speak of homicide as random violence ignores the clear patterns in these deaths.

* * *

POINTLESSNESS

In October 1994, Susan Smith attracted national attention when she claimed that a carjacker had forced her from her Mazda at gunpoint and then driven away, with her three-year-old and fourteen-month-old sons still strapped in the car. More than a week later, the nationwide hunt for the kidnapper and the two boys ended when Smith confessed to investigators that she had deliberately driven the car into a lake and left her sons to drown. Commentators made much of Smith's claim that the carjacker was a black male; they charged that white racism led people to accept Smith's story. But none of these commentators questioned the readiness of the press and the public to believe a story about a carjacker abducting two little boys and stealing a four-year-old compact car from a small town in South Carolina. Why would a carjacker do that? That's just the kind of thing they do.

The fear of random violence means we no longer expect violence to be purposeful. When we hear about Pamela Basu dragged to her death by carjackers, or an innocent passerby shot in a drive-by, or a teenager killed over a pair of gym shoes, we say the violence is pointless, that it lacks any reasonable motivation. No one should die in a fight over gym shoes. When such tragedies occur—and they do—the very pointlessness of the deaths makes them seem even more tragic.

Precisely because they are horrific, these cases become the subjects of extensive media coverage, coverage that transforms them from terrible tragedies—

remarkable *incidents*—into typical examples—or *instances*—of carjacking, drive-bys, or the larger problem of random violence. These horror stories make powerful examples precisely because they make no sense: "Random violence provides no such mark of intelligibility and moves with a heightened ambiguity. As explanations contest one another, the status of random crime increases to the level of general societal threat." Because horror stories capture moments of seemingly random violence, they exemplify what the media claim is an epidemic of random violence bedeviling the larger society. Some people die in terrible, apparently pointless ways. If, instead of viewing those deaths as extraordinary tragedies, we turn them into typifying examples, then we've given shape to the larger problem of random violence.

Whether violence makes sense, of course, depends upon who is making the evaluation. People who commit violent acts have their reasons. When asked, they may say they attacked their victims because they were angry or because they wanted to maintain their reputation for toughness or because they wanted to intimidate the victim into compliance. Of course, we usually reject the reasons offenders give; we say they are not good reasons, not valid or sensible, that they are senseless from the larger society's perspective. Thus, claims about senseless violence discount offenders' explanations as irrelevant.

There are at least two problems with this line of reasoning. The first is one of perspective. We—the larger society—reject the notion that there is ever a good reason for a drive-by shooting or a lethal fight over gym shoes. This makes violence pointless—but pointless by definition. The logic is circular: violence is pointless because violence is pointless. But from a different perspective, that of the participants in the shootings and fights, the violence may seem sensible—a means of proving oneself or dominating others or getting revenge and so on.

Consider again the very high homicide death rates for young black males in the late 1980s and early 1990s. Criminologists offer a historical account for what happened during that period. When the inner-city trade in crack took off in the mid-1980s, the potentially high profits from dealing drugs created an intense, violent competition for control over the crack marketplace, and competitors spent a portion of their profits to arm themselves, buying more—and more powerful—guns. Gangs sometimes became participants in this struggle. In addition, a growing proportion of youths who were not involved in gangs or the drug trade became concerned for their safety, and they began carrying weapons to protect themselves. Increasingly, minor disputes involved youths who were armed, and who sometimes used their weapons. (According to this explanation, homicide rates began to fall in the mid-1990s as control over the crack market consolidated, reducing the violent competition to control the drug trade.) The net result of these processes was a rising youth homicide rate, particularly in black ghettos. From the view of the larger society, each killing was a pointless tragedy, but for the participants, money, power, and prestige often were at stake.

Of course, it is always possible to identify cases where no one claims that the violence made sense—for example, the uninvolved bystander accidentally killed by a stray bullet fired during a drive-by. There are true, terrible reports of such events. The question is what we should make of these stories. This is the second problem with assertions of pointlessness: when we use, say, the death of an innocent bystander to typify the problem of contemporary violence, we stack the deck. We ignore the killings that occur between rival gangs, between competing drug dealers, between people who have become so angry or ashamed or jealous or frightened of each other that violence escalates. There is a paradox: although we consider homicide to be especially terrible, the most serious crime, most homicides are products of mundane motives; they aren't all that newsworthy and they don't get that much press coverage. In contrast, the press is drawn to the most bizarre, the most frightening, the most pointless killings. Reporters rush to tell these stories, but then convert them into representative instances of contemporary violence. To call violence pointless is to ignore the situations in which it emerges, and the meanings most violence has for the perpetrators and, often, their victims.

DETERIORATION

Warnings about random violence usually imply not only that things are bad, but that they are getting steadily worse. This is one of the great taken-for-granted assumptions about modern life: society is becoming ever more violent. We describe violence in terms of epidemics and plagues—imagery that conveys a sense of devastation, decline, and deterioration.

* * *

. . . [T]he commonplace assumption that violence is escalating out of control can be challenged. Although violent-crime rates have risen considerably since 1960, part of this increase may be due to improved reporting. If more victims report crimes, or if police keep more complete records of the crimes reported, the crime rate will rise, even if the actual incidence of crime goes unchanged. We know that reporting rates have risen and police record keeping has improved, while rates of reported victimization have declined somewhat. This suggests that claims about dramatic increases in the overall level of violence are at least exaggerated. Moreover, the changes in homicide victimization serve as a reminder that different subgroups within the population may experience very different changes in the level of violence.

Warnings about rising random violence rarely incorporate such subtleties. More often, they typify the problem with a horrific example, add a dramatic statistic or two, and mix them with the taken-for-granted notion that violence is on the rise throughout society. The resulting claim—"the random distribution of risk by a society that is fundamentally out of control"—seems so obvious that it needs no close examination. However, the evidence reveals that claims of society-wide deterioration are exaggerated and overly simplistic.

THE APPEAL OF RANDOM VIOLENCE

Although random violence has become a central image in contemporary discussions of crime, the notion of randomness distorts what we know about criminal violence. It exaggerates the degree to which violence is patternless, pointless, and increasing. It is imagery calculated to promote fear rather than understanding.

Then why is this melodramatic imagery so popular? The answer, of course, is that melodrama is powerful. The idea of random. violence is unsettling, disturbing, frightening; it challenges our most basic assumptions about social order. If violence is patternless and pointless, then anyone—women as well as men, children as well as adults, the middle class as well as the poor—might become a victim. If violence is increasing, then everyone is in growing danger:

> Drive-by shootings are particularly distressing . . . because it may appear that the target was chosen at random and that innocent bystanders may be hit. Any person's concern about his vulnerability is heightened. . . . When there is a sense that more murders are being committed against strangers, any person can conceive of himself as a target.

Rhetoric about random violence implies that everyone has a vested interest in supporting efforts to stamp out the problem. If violence is random, then everyone is at risk, and anyone who is at risk—that is, everyone—has reason to be concerned and to demand action. Typifying a problem with frightening examples, and then democratizing the risk—defining the threat as universal—is a recipe for mobilizing maximum social concern.

This widespread concern helps explain why warnings about random violence transcend the obvious ideological divisions within contemporary society. These warnings come from feminists and fundamentalists, liberal Democrats and conservative Republicans. The frightening imagery of random violence can be tailored to fit almost any ideological agenda. But there is another reason why rhetoric about random violence is so popular. By implying that pointless violence is a general, patternless threat to society as a whole, warnings about random violence gloss over the potentially awkward or embarrassing issues of class and race. As we have already noted, there are dramatic racial differences in violence: in particular, African-Americans are far more likely to both commit violent offenses and be victimized by violence than are whites. These racial differences, of course, reflect class differences: rates of violence are highest among the poor, and blacks constitute a disproportionate percentage of the poor. Any discussion of patterns in violence must confront class and race—two of the most awkward topics in American political discourse.

Confronting race and class is awkward for both liberals and conservatives. Liberals fear they will have difficulty arousing sympathy for the poor and minorities, particularly if they propose publicly funded programs to benefit those groups. Opponents of these measures may argue that Middle America has no stake in solving the problems of the poor, saying, in effect, "That's not our problem" or "We've already done enough to help the poor, and we shouldn't have to do more." It is easier to finesse such potential opposition and arouse widespread concern by implying that a problem affects (and the programs to solve it will benefit) everyone. Because references to random violence imply that everyone is at risk, they can help mobilize such general concern. Depicting violence as random, and therefore patternless, also lets liberals circumvent potentially awkward questions about the patterns of violence. In particular, liberals are reluctant to call attention to evidence that blacks commit violent offenses at higher rates than whites. The subject of black criminality may invite all sorts of critiques, ranging from arguments that race somehow biologically fosters criminality to various critiques of black culture and institutions. Moreover, liberals fear both that minority criminality can be used as evidence that social programs don't work, and that focusing on the link between ethnicity and violence will result in a form of "blaming the victim." It is not that liberals lack rejoinders to these arguments—they can respond that social structure, particularly class and racial inequality, should be blamed for crime—but rather that the issue of race is volatile, and it seems easier to ignore it rather than confront it. Talking about essentially patternless random violence offers liberals a way to avoid raising this troublesome subject.

Warnings about random violence serve parallel purposes in conservatives' discussions of crime. For conservatives, it is class, rather than race, that seems awkward to address. Poor people are more likely to both commit violent crimes and be victimized by violence, but acknowledging this seems to invite arguments that more should be done to help the poor by improving job opportunities, increasing social services, and the like. (In an earlier era, conservatives might have found reassurance in the higher rates of criminality among the poor, which could be taken as a sign of the inherent viciousness of the lower orders, but such explanations have lately fallen out of favor.) Most contemporary conservative interpretations locate the causes of criminal violence in culture. In this view, violence is part of a web of interlocking social problems, including broken families, teenage sexuality, premarital pregnancy, welfare dependency, substance abuse, delinquency and criminality, and gangs, all caused by and reflecting a damaged or dysfunctional culture. A potentially embarrassing counter to this argument, of course, is that all of these problems are associated with poverty, with social class: might not these "cultural" problems have their roots in social structure? This is where references to random violence offer conservatives a convenient distraction. Random violence is patternless, and claims about patternless random violence gloss over the links between class and crime. Similarly, random violence is pointless, senseless. And pointless crime need not be understood as an act of frustration, rebellion, or some other more or less comprehensible reaction to the barriers of class. Rather, random violence, in its pointlessness, is just further evidence of the criminals' cultural pathology. In this view, random violence is a symptom of a sick culture, and talking about random violence helps conservatives keep the focus on culture, and play to the fears of the middle class, by invoking the sense that no one is safe from the likes of Willie Horton and other predatory criminals.

* * *

In sum, there are two principal advantages to describing the crime problem in terms of random violence. First, the phrase "random violence" evokes rhetorically powerful imagery: it demands our attention and concern, because it questions the stability of the social order and makes us fear for our own safety, and for the safety of everyone around us. Second, defining the crime problem as one of ever-increasing, patternless, pointless—that is, random—violence eliminates the need to explain the patterns in crime. Focusing attention on random violence allows ideologues to skip over embarrassing or awkward issues: liberals can avoid talking about race and culture, just as conservatives can avoid confronting issues of class and social structure.

It is easy to see the appeal of framing issues in terms of random violence, but it is less clear that this is an effective way to think about crime problems. Defining violence as patternless not only discourages us from searching for and identifying patterns; it keeps us from devising social policies to address those patterns. Defining violence as pointless eliminates any need to consider and address the motivations for violence. Assuming that violence is increasing causes us to ignore patterns in change, and thereby fail to notice which policies are working. Denouncing random violence may work as crowd-pleasing rhetoric, but it does not offer much help in designing effective anti-crime policies.

Obviously, there is an element of chance—randomness—in every social encounter. Incalculable contingencies shape whether we fall in love (and with whom), whether specific investments earn a profit, whether our next automobile trip ends in a fatal accident. We cannot identify, let alone control, many of the factors that shape these outcomes. Still, we know that our individual actions can affect the likelihood of different outcomes: by buckling up, obeying the traffic laws, and not drinking and driving, we can reduce our chances of being killed in a car wreck. And social policy can also influence those outcomes: requiring cars to have seat belts and mandating their use significantly reduced death rates from automobile accidents. As individuals— and as a society—we do not simply throw up our hands in the face of "random traffic accidents." Instead of emphasizing the role of randomness, we search for patterns in risk and devise policies based on the patterns we identify.

In much the same way, if we want to understand criminality and violence, we need to think in terms of their patterns, in terms of the motivations and behaviors of offenders and victims. Random violence is a powerful image, so powerful that it threatens to short-circuit constructive thought about the nature of our society's problems.

THE LANGUAGE OF CRIME

The expression "random violence," then, has become a commonplace in talk about contemporary crime, a sort of cliché of pop criminology, not because it accurately summarizes the nature of crime—it decidedly does not—but because it is rhetorically convenient, arousing intense interest in and concern about crime while diverting attention away from awkward questions of race and class. It is, of course, just one term in the contemporary vocabulary for discussing crime. This vocabulary constantly changes: new crimes (e.g., carjacking) appear and come into vogue, while once familiar expressions (e.g., "garroting" [the nineteenth-century equivalent of mugging] or "soiled dove" [a nineteenth-century euphemism for prostitute]) fall out of favor.

The implications of describing violence as random suggest that the turnover in terms used to talk about crime and other social problems reflects more than a faddish attraction to novel language. People invent new words to describe social problems, sometimes quite deliberately, because those words evoke some connotations and avoid others; consider the different implications of "crippled," "handicapped," "disabled," and "differently abled"; of "drunkard" and "alcoholic"; or of "sexual deviate," "homosexual," and "gay." But it is not enough to create a word; some new words are ignored and soon forgotten. Successful terms get picked up, sometimes self-consciously at first, then used by more and more people, until they seem normal rather than novel. The example of "random violence" suggests that some terms may prove attractive to a broad range of users, and that this broad popularity encourages their adoption and widespread use.

The words we choose when we talk about crime and other social problems are consequential. Describing crime in terms of random violence has implications for how we think about crime, about criminals, and about prospective criminal justice policies. It becomes, therefore, important to stop taking our vocabulary of crime for granted. We need to explore the ways in which this language emerges, spreads, evolves, and influences.

* * *

QUESTIONS

1. Best argues that seeing violence as random involves three assumptions: That violence is patternless, pointless, and on the rise. What is each of these assumptions about specifically?

2. Find a recent newspaper article that discusses a specific violent crime. Some of the types that Best identifies include school shootings, carjackings, rape, and murder. Jot down how the article characterizes each of the three assumptions underlying the randomness frame.

3. According to Best, how does the randomness frame misrepresent the causes of violent crime?

4. Despite its tendency to distort reality, why is this frame so powerful and so popular?

The Horrors of Child Abuse

Horror Stories and the Construction of Child Abuse

JOHN M. JOHNSON

*Since problems that are publicly seen as horrors are those that typically receive sig-
nificant attention from policymakers, it is important to recognize how and why certain problems come to be seen that way in the first place. Johnson's study suggests that
no problem, even one as overtly disturbing as child abuse, speaks for itself. Rather,
his account illustrates that the public association between child abuse and horror is a
product of how news accounts frame the issue. Johnson illustrates that although graphically violent cases of abuse comprise most news coverage of the issue, such cases are
actually only a tiny segment of the child abuse problem. Framing the problem primarily in terms of these atypical horror stories detracts public attention and policymaking resources away from the full range of situations that constitute child abuse.*

Everyone recognizes that the mass media's power extends beyond the mere
transmittal of information. Their power (and some of their mystery) also
derives from their ability to elicit emotions. Eliciting emotions often paves the
way for action. We recognize the importance of this process at a common-
sense level. The Civil Rights Movement of the 1960s, for example, gained
much support and momentum from the publication of emotionally provocative photographs and accounts of the brutalities at Selma and Montgomery,
Alabama. Press coverage helped shape public action, leading to subsequent
civil rights reforms. The Vietnam War—"the first mass media war"—offers
another good example. The pervasive newspaper stories and television
accounts of daily battle scenes were important influences at all stages of the

war, for both its supporters and detractors. More recently, press coverage of the rioting in South Africa is seen as an important influence on U.S. policy.

Sociologists recognize the relevance and importance of emotionally provocative mass media accounts for creating new social problems. Sensationalized mass coverage often is an important aspect of social problems claimsmaking. Examples include the construction of "crime waves," various problems of juvenile justice, foreign policy, corporate homicide, and missing children, among others. This [study] analyzes mass media's use of child abuse horror stories, emotionally provocative stories about violence to children. Such horror stories have played an important role in the political, social, and institutional success of the child maltreatment movement in the United States.

THE EMERGENCE OF CHILD ABUSE AS A SOCIAL PROBLEM

Child battering, child abuse, and child neglect (now commonly subsumed under the term *child maltreatment*) are relatively new terms, even though injuries and fatalities to children are as old as recorded history. Dr. S. West published the first medical documentation of systematic, intentional injuries to children in 1888. Researchers continued reporting important information about nonaccidental childhood traumas to the medical professions long before child abuse emerged as a social problem and political issue in the early 1960s.

In 1962, the research team headed by Dr. C. Henry Kempe and Dr. Ray Helfer published their now-famous article on "The Battered-Child Syndrome" in the *Journal of the American Medical Association*. This study, published in the medical profession's most prestigious and respected journal, was accompanied by an official editorial asserting the seriousness of this new medical problem. The characteristic features of the syndrome included traumatic injuries to the head and long bones, commonly done to children under 3 years of age by parents who were themselves beaten or abused as children. The parents commonly denied mistreatment of their children. The publication of this research article was an important step in legitimizing this problem as one demanding medical intervention.

The first state laws specifically formulated for child abuse intervention were passed in 1963; between 1963 and 1967, 47 of the 50 states passed some form of child abuse and/or neglect legislation. The American Humane Association (AHA) and several professional social work organizations provided expert testimony and played other active roles in advocating legislative initiative.

Technological advances, as well as certain features of pediatric radiology as an occupational specialty, played important roles in these early efforts to establish the child abuse and neglect movement. These developments have increased significantly the number of officially recognized and classified child abuse and neglect cases. In 1963, a study commissioned by the AHA could document only 662 cases of nonaccidental trauma to children for the entire United States but, by 1980, nearly 700,000 cases achieved official recognition and status.

Child abuse began as a relatively esoteric concern of a few medical researchers. But the dramatic article on "The Battered-Child Syndrome" by Kempe et al. attracted the mass media's attention. Barbara Nelson argues that professional and mass media publications offered complementary coverage, which was critical to the early agenda-setting and political successes of the social movement. Initially, the emphasis was on physical abuse or "battering," but as the movement achieved legitimacy, the scope of both media and movement concern expanded to other areas, including child neglect, emotional abuse, and, eventually, incest and sexual abuse of children. The publication of child abuse horror stories has played a prominent role in the social, political, and institutional successes of the child maltreatment movement during the last 25 years. These horror stories are mass media reports of individual cases that involve dramatic or unusual injuries to children and that evoke an emotional response about the problem of child abuse or neglect. This chapter analyzes the formal properties of child abuse horror stories and the role they have played in the emergence and definition of this social problem.

NATURE OF THE RESEARCH

This [study] derives from a larger study of all newspaper stories on child abuse and neglect that appeared for 32 years in the *Arizona Republic* and the *Phoenix Gazette,* the two major newspapers in Arizona. The earliest newspaper files on these topics began in 1948 under the headings cruelty to children, family problems, domestic disturbance, as well as various conventional criminal classifications involving victimized children. Arizona was not one of the 47 states to pass child abuse legislation in the early 1963–1965 period. Arizona passed its first laws in August 1970; they became effective at the beginning of 1971. After the 1970 legislative action, state news organizations began keeping files labeled "child abuse" and "child neglect," as both phenomena were defined in the early legislation. I examined news stories from 1948 to 1980 to study the relations between mass media reporting and legislative action, the role of local versus national wireservice reporting, and the stories' substance. In addition, I collected clippings from many other newspapers, magazines, and other media over a period of more than 10 years.

During 1948–1980, a total of 623 news stories about child abuse and neglect appeared in the Phoenix newspapers. There were 93 stories during 1948–1969, an average of slightly more than 4 per year. Arizona's first child abuse law passed in 1970, producing a 10-fold increase in the news stories about this topic. Between 1971 and 1980, the papers published an additional 490 stories concerning all aspects of child battering, abuse, neglect, and maltreatment, averaging almost 50 per year.

Much of this coverage featured child abuse horror stories. Of the 93 stories published during 1948–1969, 88 (95%) presented facts about an individual case of childhood injury. Most of these were dramatic, horrific stories. While the proportion of child abuse horror stories fell after 1970, they remain the dominant form of newspaper report. Of the 623 stories published during 1948–1980, 436 (70%) placed primary emphasis on reporting the facts of an individual case. Local (Arizona) stories accounted for 350 (80%) horror stories; the remaining 86 (20%) stories came from the AP and UPI national wireservices.

To better understand the nature of these horror stories, I conducted an ethnographic content analysis, which is a method of analyzing documentary evidence, based on the observer's or analyst's insider understanding about a setting or phenomena. In this case, I analyzed the mass media reports on child abuse to identify the formal properties of child abuse horror stories. Formal properties are those analytical features of the newsreporting format that define it as a type. The content analysis of child abuse horror stories reveals five distinct properties of the form: (1) evocation of negative emotionality, which is accomplished by the development of either (a) ironic contrast, or (b) structural incongruity, (2) disembodiment of interaction, (3) decontextualization, (4) use of official sources, and (5) individualization of causal agency.

FORMAL PROPERTIES OF CHILD ABUSE HORROR STORIES

Evoking Negative Emotionality

Ideally, parents love and protect children. Families are the source of intimacy and selfhood, and, even though parents have more power than their children, parents presumably use this power in the child's best interests. Family experience is, for most people, largely favorable and rewarding. For some, it is not, but few view their family experience with emotional neutrality. Thus, stories about violence within the family have a great potential to elicit an emotional response from their audience.

Mass media accounts of domestic violence play upon our common family experience, whether actual or desired, to elicit emotions. The term *child abuse horror story* obviously suggests that such stories evoke feelings of horror, but I use the concept more broadly, referring to stories that elicit strong negative feelings. Whether the specific feelings evoked are horror, shock, revulsion, sadness, anger, tragedy, or some other is less important than the fact that the feelings are strong ones for most individuals. Stories about horrible injuries or gruesome circumstances may produce emotional reaction:

> The Baltimore Police found Patty Saunders, 9, in the 23 × 52 inch closet where she had been locked for half her life. She weighed only 20 pounds, and stood less than three feet tall. Smeared with filth, scarred from parental beatings, Patty had become irreparably mentally retarded. (*Newsweek*, October 10, 1977:31)

The preceding story evokes negative feelings, not only by portraying inhuman treatment, but by specifying the terrible, life-long consequences. Another example:

> Alyssa Dawn Wilson died at the age of six weeks in a Beauford, South Carolina clinic. An autopsy disclosed that the infant had a ruptured liver and spleen and eye injuries, a fractured knee, 14 broken ribs, bite marks on her cheeks, bruises on her stomach and back and alcohol in her bloodstream. Her father was arrested for murder. (*Newsweek*, October 10, 1977:32)

In both examples, the injuries are such that the reader can clearly see that they could not have been either unintentional or accidental. At a common-sense level, we impute moral responsibility or culpability for intentional or willful injuries. We commonly do not hold people blameworthy if it can be shown that their actions were unintentional or accidental. But only the foolhardy could believe that the injuries in these examples could have resulted "from an accident." It is the fact that they are intentionally inflicted, rather than their consequences, that makes these injuries so horrifying. Barbara Nelson observes that one of the ironies of press coverage of child abuse cases is that severe injuries often make "better news copy" than more dramatic acts that result in death, because severe injuries permit a longer follow-up by other reporters and, hence, additional stories. A child's death often precludes such extended coverage.

Negative emotions may be aroused by detailing the gruesome facts of the injury, or the consequences of the abuse, or even the circumstances surrounding the investigation:

> The body of a missing two-month-old boy was found in a pile of rubble Tuesday, hours after the infant's parents were charged in connection with his death. The Marion couple earlier told police that their son was abducted while they completed last minute Christmas shopping. The nude body was found under some dirt, leaves, and cement in the foundation of a torn down house, about four blocks from the parents' home. "The location was given to us by the father," said Detective Larry Connors. Thus far, police do not know if the death was the result of child abuse that went too far, or the result of a deliberate slaying. (*Fort Wayne Journal Gazette,* December 27, 1978:3)

Child abuse horror stories use two journalistic conventions to elicit an emotional response from the reader: ironic contrast and structural incongruity. They are related and similar in some respects, but nevertheless distinct. The press prefers certain kinds of stories because they allow for a better display of the intrinsic properties of the medium. Newspaper reporters have a strong preference for "man bites dog" stories, for example, because the print medium and the linear display allow for a greater exploitation of ironic contrast. "Man bites dog" is a phrase that epitomizes ironic contrast. The phrase creates the image of man, often the unwitting victim of a dog's attack, uncharacteristically turning on the animal alleged to be man's best friend. Presenting the story in print maximizes its ironic possibilities.

Consider the ironic contrast in a 1981 story about Arizona's leading medical expert on virtually all forms of child abuse and neglect. Dr. Larry C. Rork, the 1979 winner of local awards for his expertise and service related to child abuse, was subsequently accused of multiple acts of child abuse and sexual molestation by three boys confined at Camelback Hospital. Even though subsequent investigations completely exonerated Dr. Rork, he committed suicide before the investigation's completion. The juxtaposition of Rork's expertise and the charges against him provides the story's irony.

Another story, from the *Kansas City Star* for Tuesday, August 9, 1977, concerns Herbert Smith, Jr., who faced 5 years to life in prison for the fatal beating of his stepdaughter, whose death he tried to prevent through a law suit. Smith, 31, from Wichita, pleaded no contest to a charge of second-degree murder. His daughter fell into a coma, and Smith filed a civil suit to prevent doctors and the child's mother from unhooking the child's respirator. Smith claimed in the suit that he could face more serious charges if the machine were unhooked. The injunction was denied, and the respirator was unhooked. In this case, the irony comes from the fact that the person responsible for the injuries became the litigant to "save the child's life."

Structural incongruity need not involve a formal irony, but it usually does include some feature that strikes the reader as bizarre, strange, unusual, or "out of place." One well-known example is the now infamous case of the 1984 arrest of the grandmotherly (and 77-year-old) Virginia McMartin, founder and director of the McMartin Preschool in Manhattan Beach, California. Along with six relatives and co-workers, she was charged with nearly 300 counts of sexual abuse and molestation of the children in their care. A second example:

> A nine-year-old girl was sexually molested by her father and uncle, an aunt and her brother's boyfriend over a seven year period without any of the suspects knowing the others were involved. Each suspect had been questioned separately, and then released into the lobby of the police station in this St. Louis suburb. "You should have seen the look on their faces," said Detective Don Gultz. It was "You too?!" The four adults were charged with 53 felony counts. (Overland, Missouri, United Press International, August 16, 1985)

The "shocking" details in such stories elicit negative emotions from readers.

Disembodiment of Interaction

Mass media reports of child abuse never report the interactional sequences leading to abuse. The "facts" of a story are presented as if they "speak for themselves," and reporters make no attempt to give the participant's perspective. This reporting strategy works because reports of statistically rare dramatic injuries or "horror stories" receive disproportionate attention. The typical case of child abuse is not very dramatic: a nonserious injury to a child under 3, committed by a young person (usually the mother), who is under much stress while having few resources to manage the exigent circumstances, and so on. Such cases—*the overwhelming majority of child abuse*—usually are not seen as "good news stories" by the press. Mass media reports disproportionately present the more dramatic cases, with the assumption that "the facts speak for themselves."

> A 40-year-old man has been charged with assaulting his 15-year-old daughter by hanging her upside down by her toes and then beating her. (*Arizona Republic,* March 18, 1979:22)

> A Tucson woman, convicted of dumping her four-year-old daughter into a tub of scalding water for telling a lie, was sentenced to three years in prison. (*Arizona Republic,* March 9, 1978:11)

These stories reflect a common journalistic convention: beginning a story with a shocking or provocative "grabber." A typical grabber presents dramatic details of a specific individual case, intended to grab and retain the reader's attention for the rest of the story. Beginning a story with a "grabber" reflects journalists' "recipe knowledge" used to manufacturer news. In the preceding examples, it seems evident that the abuse could not have been "reasonable," so there is no attempt to place the action described within an interactional or social sequence, no attempt to tell the story from the various participants' points of view, no attempt to place the account into some intelligible, comprehensible context. In this way, abuse is typified as irrational and incomprehensible.

Decontextualization

News reports rip child abuse situations out of their social context. There are some good, understandable reasons for this. First, child abuse almost always occurs within the privacy of the home and is rarely witnessed by outsiders or third parties. So reports invariably reach outside agencies, whether police, social service, or mass media, after the fact. Second, newsworkers place great reliance on institutionalized news sources as their primary source of information on many stories. This makes the original social context of a child abuse incident extremely difficult to recapture, even if reporters were motivated to do so.

> Dianne Devanne, age 11, had a lot to look forward to; high school, perhaps college and a career or raising a family. But she never got the

chance. Police say she was beaten to death by her father and stepmother. A rare case? Hardly. In nearly every state, laws are very loose, accurate models are scarce, and society is restive when faced with terminating parental rights. Dianne Devanne returned home in August to Braintree, Massachusetts, after two years of living in foster homes and institutions. Everyday for two weeks prior to her death, she was beaten for such acts as spilling the salt or not doing the dishes quickly enough. The beatings increased to one an hour on the last day of her life. Her father, claiming she had fallen down the stairs, took her to the local hospital where she was pronounced dead from a blow to the head. A blood clot lodged in her brain. The following day, Dianne's father and stepmother were charged with murder. (*Los Angeles Times,* December 3, 1978:34)

This account displays a common reporting strategy for child abuse horror stories, that is, to describe injuries that could not be "reasonable" by any standard. If there is a counterclaim to the allegations (e.g., Mr. Devanne's claim that she had fallen down stairs), it can be easily neutralized or discredited, usually with a reference to some official source of information (e.g., the hospital's judgment that Dianne died from a blow to the head). This leads to the next property of child abuse horror stories, the reliance on and use of official sources of information.

Reliance on Official Sources

For stories on child abuse, newspapers and television news rely on official sources of information, including police, prosecutors, social welfare departments, hospitals, school officials, and so on. Official sources play prominent roles in many other kinds of stories. The reasons for relying on official sources are clear; official sources can help solve a daily practical problem of newsworkers: the need to generate enough material to fill a paper or news program. But, for stories on child abuse, there is another reason for relying on official sources: It is the official intervention and assessment of the actor's intent that *defines a particular act as abusive or neglectful.* For this reason, it would be implausible (if not impossible) for newsworkers to define some parental act as abusive or neglectful independent of an official assessment of the actor's behavior. News accounts of child abuse invariably rely on official sources of information, and they take the official perspective toward the act being reported. The following story is interesting because it shows the use of four official sources in writing the story (police, social services, courts, and official criminal records):

> Allen Madden was pummeled for perhaps four hours before he died, at times with fists, at times with a wooden club wrapped with gauze and labeled "The Big Stick." He was five years old. Police found his frail body on the living room floor, his blond hair red with blood, his hands bruised from trying to deflect the blows. "Probably, he did something an average little kid does, write on the wall or something. That's all it takes," said a former social worker who had urged that the shy kindergartner not be returned to home because she feared "there's going to be a dead kid." Allen died January 10. His mother and boyfriend are charged with murder. Allen's mother, Pam Berg, quit high school, married a sometime factory worker, Gerald Madden. . . . The Madden marriage ended shortly after Allen was born, each parent accusing the other in court of beating the children. (Quincy, Illinois, Associated Press, January 22, 1979:1)

This is not an example of the routine, ordinary child abuse case that crosses the desk of the average Child Protective Services worker who investigates such matters or that constitutes the overwhelming statistical majority of abuse cases. Most child abuse cases do not involve serious injuries. Few produce death. Few perpetrators have prior criminal records. Few such allegations result in some kind of court proceeding (about 10% nationally). The routine child abuse case does not make very good "copy" for news reporting. What makes good copy is a more dramatic case, such as the example here, and when these are reported on, official sources provide the newsworthy facts, and newsworkers invariably adopt the official perspective in presenting them.

Front line reporters at the local level tend to be young and, unlike seasoned news veterans, unreflective about adopting the official or bureaucratic view about some problem. It often takes years to learn about the deeper realities and meanings of some event or phenomenon, to recognize the hidden organizational interests that lie behind some rational, scientistic rhetoric. This is true in the child abuse field; many local news reporters are seduced by the bureaucratic reporting of a horrific story and rush to news judgment without realizing how the dissemination of these unrepresentative stories promotes vested bureaucratic, agency, or political interests. That two *Denver Post* reporters would win a Pulitzer Prize for exposing the myths and hidden promotive interests in the "missing children" issue is one small indication that the unexamined assumptions of the mass media are changing.

Individualization of Causal Agent

Most reporters and editors have been formally educated; they know the myths and some of the realities of domestic violence. Commonly held beliefs include the following: Abused children grow up to abuse their own children; unemployment places great stresses upon the unemployed individual and the family; drinking problems and alcoholism are frequently involved in domestic disputes; arguments over money and other practical matters are commonplace and frequently severe, etc. Nevertheless, when confronted with the prospect of interpreting the facts of an individual case, reporters rarely refer to such factors. It is much easier to sustain a complicated, mixed sense of social responsibility for other acts, including certain war crimes, employee theft, certain forms of organizational deviance, and some forms of "sexual deviance" (or sexual preference). Despite the fact that virtually all of us have some familial experience, the mass media accounts promote the idea that individuals bear total, absolute responsibility. Whatever the stressful conditions or circumstances that confront the individual, the press treats that individual as responsible for what occurs. Consider the following account:

> "Filth of just about any kind of description" throughout a Huron Street house prompted City County Health officials to charge a woman Thursday morning with neglect of a dependent child. It was the second time this year that Westerman was charged with neglect of the children. Allen Family Relations Court suspended a one-year sentence August 20 after a March 8 arrest because of similar conditions in the two-story house, Holly said. Neglect of a dependent is a felony. Health officials said they found the house filled with rubbish, garbage and excrement. Holly explained that he and Bonnie Rafert, a health inspector, went to the residence Thursday morning with a Board of Works crew to clear rubbish and garbage from the yard. The Health Department has received numerous complaints about the yard, he said. Westerman has been charged at least seven times since 1974 because the condition of the yard violated city ordinances. While Rafert was supervising the removal of the rubbish-filled van from the property, Westerman swung a bat at her, causing a door of the van to slam in front of her, Holly said. When

Holly attempted to arrest her, she ran into the house. Holly said he called the police for assistance. When he and the officers entered the house to make an arrest, the cluttered condition was evident. (*Fort Wayne Journal Gazette,* September 21, 1979: B1,2)

From this account, it seems reasonable to think that Westerman is economically poor (apparently not even having a first name!), having lived in the same residence for at least 5 years, but with few material resources for home repairs or other improvements, having interpersonal skills and a lifestyle that are at variance with middle-class standards and/or the official expectations of police, social workers, health inspectors, etc. And yet, the reporter seems to assume that official suspicions warrant the label "felony," and there is no attempt to assess the relationship between Westerman's material circumstances and their consequences on parental supervision. Whatever these circumstances might be, they apparently do not mitigate the absolute responsibility for maintaining a clean yard. Consider the following story. It asserts that the mother's knowledge was an intentional, willful knowledge, even though the grounds for this judgment are not spelled out to the reader. It concerns the story of a 20-year-old mother charged with neglect of a dependent child in connection with the July 7, 1979 death of her infant, Christopher Swenson, aged 2.

"Mindy Swenson was well aware that Christopher was being mistreated by Timothy Carpenter," the Allen Superior Court affidavit said. Carpenter was charged with murder, an habitual offense in the case, and lived with the mother and the child for several months prior to the death. The mother was booked at the City County lockup Wednesday and is being held at the Allen County jail under $2,000 bond. She had been staying at the home of Carpenter's foster father in rural Auburn, Indiana. (*Fort Wayne Gazette,* July 10, 1979)

There is a general view about child abuse and neglect that pervades all of the mass media accounts. This view holds that child abuse and/or neglect is an entirely individualistic phenomenon, an act for which an individual is solely responsible. Rarely do stories refer to the wide range of stresses that can influence individuals, including such factors as absent partners, alcoholism, unemployment, financial difficulties, drug problems, stigmatization from prior arrests and/or prison records, poor occupational or school preparation, and a wide range of social–psychological difficulties. Even when such factors are cited or alluded to in mass media reports, they are not seen as mitigating personal responsibility. Society and its institutions are not seen as causal agents in producing child abuse and neglect; rather, the press takes the view that society and its institutions represent functional responses to the problem tending to control it. This is, of course, in keeping with larger trends involving the individualization and medicalization of a wide range of social problems.

THE ROLE OF HORROR STORIES IN THE CONSTRUCTION OF CHILD ABUSE AS A SOCIAL PROBLEM

Publishing child abuse horror stories serves a wide range of uses. One of the most obvious is that it fits the organizational needs and interests of news organizations. Barbara Nelson notes that child abuse stories have a great human interest potential, and that human interest stories have become increasingly important to the organizational needs and interests of mass media:

> The reporting of child abuse follows a fairly consistent pattern in which unwholesomely criminal cases where the child survives are preferred to what might be considered the more serious, but somehow more routine cases where the child dies. The titillation of bizarre brutality accounts, in part, for this pattern, but other factors also contribute to the newspapers' preference for this type of story. Part of this preference can be traced to the organizational needs of newspapers. From the perspective of news managers, more information unfolds in a case of brutality than in one where the child victim dies. This fact, in itself, sustains coverage.

More than just new organizations are involved. The publication of child abuse stories also helps many professional and occupational groups, social science and medical researchers, and various private and nonprofit agencies. These agencies establish agendas for the child abuse movement. They are invariably tied to requests for more resources and more public funds. The crowning achievement of this political effort would have to be the passage of "The Mondale Bill," in 1974, which established the National Center for the Treatment and Prevention of Child Abuse and Neglect and infused $80,000,000 into child abuse programs during the ensuing 3-year period.

It would be a mistake to see child abuse as merely a creation of the media. News organizations played a creative role in the process; some would argue a major role. But, just as important, news organizations *responded* to a sense of urgency created by other groups, agencies, and sectors of the public. The press occasionally stimulated government action and legislative initiative, sometimes on their own, but more commonly at the bidding of other parties. Either way, the mass media reports of child abuse and neglect seem to have played a strong role in legitimizing this problem, serving at all phases to present the official conception and definition of child abuse, as well as promoting existing or planned official interventions, policies, programs, and budgetary requests. It is easy to see that the mass media perspective on child abuse is that promulgated by official agencies and their professional supporters. Insofar as the press criticizes official definitions or agencies, its criticism is coupled to the plea that officials do not have the resources they need to do a better job.

It is very important to understand that there is a larger cultural and historical context within which child abuse horror stories have appeared. Many of our contemporary social welfare and criminal justice institutions originated in the Progressive Era of the 1880s to the 1920s, a time of great optimism for institutional solutions to social problems. Today, we seem to have entered a New Progressive Era, characterized by significant cultural optimism about the capabilities of the welfare state to resolve social problems. The mass media organizations that have disseminated child abuse horror stories have, in addition, published many stories on incest, sexual abuse of children, child prostitution, drugs, crime of all sorts, pornography, drunk driving, etc. Such coverage has proliferated to such an extent that psychologist Robert J. Lifton has coined the term "psychological numbing" to refer to the feeling of being overwhelmed or inundated by such problems, even to the point of apathy or cynicism on the part of many citizens.

Educated persons who follow press coverage will feel the "psychological numbing" of which Lifton speaks, and so we will understand the existence of apathy and cynicism. Such feelings, however understandable, are transitory and situational for most people and do not reflect the kind of long range commitment to solving social problems that readers of a book such as this are likely to share. For us, it is important to have a realistic and informed basis of knowledge about modern mass media, definitions of social problems, and welfare state operations to make the best choices we can for a better future.

1. How do news accounts depict horror stories of child abuse as if these were the majority of abuse cases?

2. Which other claimsmakers besides the news media participate in this statistical misrepresentation of the child abuse problem? How specifically?

3. Spend a couple of minutes jotting down the different categories of child abuse that come to mind. Why, despite this range of abuse situations, are news audiences primarily interested in the horror stories?

4. Given the variety of situations of child abuse that exist, in terms of public policy why is it consequential that news reports about abuse tend to concentrate on the tiny percentage of cases that are horror stories?

Dangerous Music in
Black and White

FROM *Constructing Racial Rhetoric: Media Depictions*
of Harm in Heavy Metal and Rap Music

AMY BINDER

This study traces differences in how the news media characterize heavy metal and
rap music as dangerous to youth. Amy Binder identifies key frames used by jour-
nalists during the 1980s and '90s to describe the dangers of each music type in main-
stream newspapers and magazines, and in magazines aimed specifically at black
audiences. Her data show a contrast in how journalists framed the harmfulness of
these two types of popular music based on the perceived racial composition of the
audience for each type—whites for heavy metal and blacks for rap. This study high-
lights why frames are so instrumental in how social problems are constructed. Frames
do not just describe a problem (in this case, dangerous music), but they give audi-
ences lenses for understanding the urgency of addressing that problem by drawing
on ideas people already use to interpret events; in this case, ideas about the con-
nection between race and danger.

In September 1985, a group of politically well-connected "Washington
Wives" calling themselves the Parents' Music Resource Center (PMRC) was
invited to testify before the U.S. Senate Committee on Commerce, Science,
and Transportation. Led by Tipper Gore (wife of then Senator Al Gore of
Tennessee) and Susan Baker (wife of then Treasury Secretary James Baker),
the group's objective was to reveal to committee members the current state
of rock music lyrics—particularly the lyrics of heavy metal music. The PMRC
and its expert witnesses testified that such music filled youthful ears with
pornography and violence, and glorified behaviors ranging from suicide and
drug use to occultism and anti-patriotic activities. The mass media covered
the hearing in great detail, provoking debate in the national press over the

alleged harmfulness of rock music lyrics and whether the proposed labeling of music lyrics constituted censorship.

Almost five years later, another event again focused the nation's attention on music lyrics—the lyrics in rap music. In June 1990, a U.S. District Court judge in Fort Lauderdale, Florida found the 2 Live Crew album *As Nasty as They Wanna Be* to be obscene in the three counties under his jurisdiction. This was the first recording ever declared obscene by a federal court (*New York Times* 17 June, 1990). During the following week, authorities from one of those counties' Sheriff's Department—Broward County—arrested a local record storeowner who had continued to sell the album and took into custody two members of the 2 Live Crew band when they performed material from the album at an adults-only show in the area. The arrest and impending trials again galvanized heated public debate over whether the lyrics in contemporary music harmed listeners and warranted restriction.

These two widely publicized debates about contemporary music, both of which concerned "harmful" lyrics and occurred within five years of each other, provide comparative cases for examining how the mass media serve as an ideological vehicle. In both cases, writers in the mainstream press expressed concern about the harm that could result from exposure to lyrics containing sexual and violent themes, and called for action against such content. Despite these similarities, however, the substance of media arguments changed significantly as the controversy shifted from heavy metal music to rap music. Foremost among these differences was the change in emphasis regarding whom the music was harming: the individual listener or society as a whole.

I suggest that two factors drove the changes in the media discourse surrounding the dangers of heavy metal music versus rap music. One factor is the difference in the content of the lyrics themselves. In general, the controversial rap lyrics were more graphic than their heavy metal counterparts, and discussions in the media reflected this variation.

Second, the broad cultural context in which the "white" music and "black" music were being received also significantly affected changes in the discourse. Rather than asserting a simple reflection model (i.e., the media only mirror "what's out there"), I argue that the pronounced shift in the discourse about lyrics cannot be explained by differences in the cultural objects alone. Instead, the shift reflects opinion writers' perceptions of the populations represented by these two musical genres. Writers who were concerned about heavy metal lyrics and rap lyrics did not address the content of the music alone; embedded in their discussions were reactions to differences in the demographic characteristics of the genres' producers and audiences—music made by and for working and middle-class white youth versus music they perceived as predominantly by and for urban black teenagers.[1] In a cultural landscape marked by divergent perceptions of black youths versus white youths, different concerns emerged in the mainstream media about the impact of each group's form of cultural expression. I show that rap music—with its evocation of angry black rappers and equally angry black audiences—was simultaneously perceived as a more authentic and serious art form than was heavy metal music, and as a more frightening and salient threat to society as a whole than the "white" music genre.

* * *

METHODOLOGY

I examine the national discourse surrounding the harmfulness of music lyrics by analyzing nationally distributed mainstream publications that target a range of audiences. Demographic profiles as of 1991 provided by these publications show that readerships varied along socioeconomic lines: the *New York Times* and *Time* magazine have the wealthiest and most highly educated readers, *Newsweek* and *U.S. News and World Report* represent an intermediate socioeconomic level, and the readership of the *Reader's Digest* has low levels of annual income and education. The publications also vary politically: the *New York Times* is considered one of the most liberal large newspapers, the *Reader's Digest* is considered conservative, and the other three publications fall somewhere in between.

For comparison to this mainstream debate, which was written for a "general" (primarily white) American readership, I also examined the discourse in two popular middle-class publications that serve a predominantly black readership: *Ebony* and *Jet* (hereafter referred to as black or African-American magazines). The articles in these African-American magazines were coded to determine if the race of the readership made a difference in how the music genres were framed.

The articles published in the five mainstream publications and the two black magazines were located in the *Reader's Guide to Periodicals* and the

---

[1]In my data, the vast majority of media writers—particularly those who thought that rap music was dangerous—assume that rap music is produced and consumed exclusively by black youths. The popular assumption about all-black rap audiences was refuted in a cover story in the *New Republic* (11 Nov. 1991), in which the author David Samuels demonstrated that, in absolute numbers, more white suburban youths consume rap music than poor black youths.

TABLE 1.   Distribution of Articles by Type of Music for Mainstream Publications and African-American Publications, 1985–1990

Type of Publication and Year	Type of Music			
	Heavy Metal	Rap	Heavy Metal and Rap	Total
Mainstream Publications[a]				
1985	13	1	1	15
1986	1	5	0	6
1987	4	7	0	11
1988	6	7	0	13
1989	5	5	5	15
1990	5	33	10	48
Total	34	58	16	108
African-American Magazines[b]				
1985	0	0	0	0
1986	0	1	0	1
1987	0	0	0	0
1988	0	2	0	2
1989	0	1	0	1
1990	0	6	0	6
Total	0	10	0	10

[a]The *New York Times, Time* magazine, *Newsweek, U.S. News and World Report,* and *Reader's Digest.*
[b]*Ebony* and *Jet.*

Lexis/Nexis data bank. Between 1985 and 1990, these publications printed more than 1,000 news and opinion articles that concerned heavy metal music or rap music. Of these, 108 of the mainstream articles and 10 of the black magazines' articles were opinion pieces that specifically addressed the lyric content of the music. As shown in Table 1, 34 articles in these five mainstream publications addressed heavy metal music (13 of them written in 1985, the year of the Senate hearing), 58 articles addressed rap music (33 of them written in 1990, the year of the 2 Live Crew arrests), and 16 articles addressed both genres. In the African-American magazines, all 10 articles were written about rap music. Although all of the roughly 1,000 articles were read, for methodological and theoretical reasons I limited coding and analysis to these 118 opinion articles.

The 118 opinion pieces were content-analyzed using coding categories constructed by the author. This first reading generated 68 categories, which were collapsed into nine frames. This set of nine frames accounts for the total discourse surrounding the issue of harm in lyrics in these publications from 1985 to 1990. Each article was then read again to determine which of the nine frames were used in each piece. The mean number of frames per article was 1.6.

The official transcripts of the 1985 Senate Committee hearing and Tipper Gore's 1987 book, *Raising PG Kids in an X-Rated Society,* provided a deeper understanding of the historical narrative concerning this issue.

To address the issue of whether frames were suggested by the cultural objects themselves, I also analyzed the lyrics of a representative sample of the most controversial heavy metal and rap songs. To determine the universe of controversial songs from which to choose a sample, I compared "offensive" songs listed in the Parents' Music Resource Center's press packet with all songs cited in the 118 opinion articles. In these sources, 33 different songs were mentioned a total of 137 times, either by title or by the albums that contained them. I considered these the most controversial songs of the debate.[2] I then randomly selected and coded 20 of the 33 songs.

HARMFUL OR NOT HARMFUL: FRAMING MUSIC LYRICS

Popular music has always been denigrated by adult society. Musical genres like the blues, jazz, and early rock and roll and dances like the jitterbug, samba, and rhumba provoked complaints from the older generation about the perversion and general corruption of its children. Thus, the controversy that made its way into the limelight in the late 1980s to early 1990s was one episode in an ongoing debate.

But to understand the specific nature of the controversy surrounding the lyrics in heavy metal music and rap music, it is necessary to examine the two defining events that shaped this media discourse: the Senate hearing in 1985 and the arrests and trials of rap musicians and record storeowners in Florida in 1990. The data in Table 1 indicate that these events focused the media discourse first on heavy metal music (in 1985, 13 of 15 mainstream articles addressed heavy metal) and later on rap music (in 1990, 33 of 48 mainstream articles addressed rap). In the intervening years, 1986 to 1989, mainstream media attention was more evenly split between the two music genres.

---

[2]For each of the 137 mentions, I noted the year they appeared in the press or the PMRC list and determined how many songs from each year should be represented in the sample.

The Senate Hearing and Its Aftermath

Considered the "hottest ticket in town all year," the 1985 standing-room-only Senate hearing launched a maelstrom of media debate about music lyrics. The competing arguments introduced at the hearing were generally used to discuss heavy metal for the duration of the five-year debate.

One of the most frequent arguments made about heavy metal music throughout the five-year controversy was introduced in 1985 by members of the PMRC and its witnesses. This argument, which I call the *corruption* frame, stated that explicit lyrics—whether glorifying suicide, anti-authority attitudes, or deviant sexual acts—have a negative effect on children's attitudes. This frame emphasized the music's corrupting effect on young listeners rather than on the effects such listeners might have on the society at large. A five-minute speech delivered to the Senate Committee by PMRC witness Joe Steussy illustrates this frame:

> Today's heavy metal music is categorically different from previous forms of popular music. . . . Its principal themes are, as you have already heard, extreme violence, extreme rebellion, substance abuse, sexual promiscuity and perversion, and Satanism. I know personally of no form of popular music before, which has had as one of its central elements the element of hatred.

The *corruption* frame also appeared frequently in the national press. In an article titled "How Shock Rock Harms Our Kids," one writer argued, "lyrics glamorize drug and alcohol use, and glorify death and violent rebellion, ranging from hatred of parents and teachers to suicide—the ultimate act of violence to oneself." The idea that children's values were corrupted by music received considerable play inside and outside the Capitol.

Like *corruption*, the *protection* frame was also introduced around the time of the Senate hearing and was prominent in references to heavy metal music throughout the five-year debate. Similar to the rhetoric found in *corruption*, this frame argued that parents and other adults must shield America's youth from offensive lyrics. Reflecting on her campaign against graphic lyrics, Tipper Gore wrote:

> We feel as we do because we know that children are special gifts, and deserve to be treated with love and respect, gentleness and honesty. They deserve security and guidance about living, loving, and relating to

other people. And they deserve vigilant protection from the excesses of adult society.

While opinions varied over how best to protect children from the dangers of lyrics (some thought that lyrics should be labeled, while others thought laws should be enacted against harmful music), the underlying theme infusing this argument invoked adult responsibility, particularly as exercised by caring parents. In his discussion of heavy metal, William Safire wrote:

> I am a libertarian when it comes to the actions of consenting adults, and hoot at busybodies who try to impose bans on what non-violent grownups can say or read or do. With complete consistency, I am antilibertarian when it comes to minors. Kids get special protections in law . . . and deserve protection from porn-rock profiteers.

Danger to society was a third theme that emerged around the time of the Senate hearing, although arguments containing this frame were used infrequently in relation to the "white" music genre. In contrast to the *corruption* frame, which warned of harm to the individual, the *danger to society* frame warned that when lyrics glorify violence, all of society is at risk. As applied to heavy metal music, the argument focused largely on the satanic influences inherent in some heavy metal music, and warned that vulnerable youths under the music's spell might wreak havoc on innocent citizens. Paul King, a child and adolescent psychiatrist who testified at the Senate hearing on behalf of the PMRC, stated:

> One of the most pathological forms of evil is in the form of the cult killer or deranged person who believes it is OK to hurt others or to kill. The Son of Sam who killed eight people in New York was allegedly into Black Sabbath's music. . . . Most recently, the individual identified in the newspapers as the Night Stalker has been said to be into hard drugs and the music of the heavy metal band AC/DC. . . . Every teenager who listens to heavy metal certainly does not become a killer. [But] young people who are seeking power over others through identification with the power of evil find a close identification. The lyrics become a philosophy of life. It becomes a religion.

In addition to cult-like violence, this frame—when it was used vis-à-vis heavy metal—suggested that violence against parents, teachers, and sometimes women could also result from listening to this music.

Of course, the serious charges brought against music lyrics by the PMRC and supportive media writers did not go unanswered, either at the Senate hearings or in the media. Music industry executives, outraged musicians, and media writers hastened to defend the content of contemporary music and the artistic integrity of its creators. These arguments appeared in the counterframes that were produced in this debate.

Frank Zappa, John Denver, and Dee Snider (of the heavy metal band Twisted Sister) kicked off the attack against PMRC activities and concerns when they served as opposing witnesses at the Senate hearing, where these counterframes first widely appeared. One common argument, termed the *no harm* frame, argued that lyrics were not harmful to young listeners. Covering a variety of ideas around this central theme, this frame claimed that youthful audiences know that the cartoonish lyrics are not meant to be taken seriously, that songs with explicit lyrics represent a small minority of music, that music lyrics are a negligible part of the culture's barrage of sexual and violent images in the media, and that there is no causal connection between music and behavior. This last point was picked up by the media—one writer suggested that "the social impact of a heavy metal concern is belching." The *no harm* frame was often used in this sarcastic manner, where the writer argued that music was safe and belittled the concerns of the opposition.

Opponents of the PMRC also suggested that opposition to heavy metal's lyrics could be explained by the generation gap between Gore and her allies, and the youths they sought to protect. The *generation gap* frame was used at the Senate hearing and subsequently to point out that vulgarity, parental anxiety, and censorship are all perennial concerns. And that outrage expressed about music lyrics bespeaks a generation gap between parents and their children. Although this frame's rhetoric is clearly a subset of the *no harm* frame (e.g., the music isn't harmful, parents just perceive it as harmful), it differs from the *no harm* frame by making explicit the role of parents in the controversy surrounding lyrics. In an article that appeared two weeks after the Senate hearing, Russell Baker picked up the theme of misplaced, but predictable, parental concern:

> Stirred by the [PMRC] alarmed mothers, my mind began playing back the full repertory of bawdy, off-color, and just downright dirty songs it had gathered during years when my mother would have cringed if I let on that I knew a more emphatic way of saying "gosh darn it all to the dickens."

The *threat to authorities* frame, which is closely related to the *generation gap* frame, suggested that people in positions of poli-tical power felt most threatened by contemporary music. Using this argument to ridicule a competing critic's attack on music, one writer complained:

> [Mr. Goldman, a writer for the *National Review*] hallucinates rather luridly: "You needn't go to a slasher film to see a woman being disemboweled in a satanic ritual—just turn on your local music video station." No example is named. Such notions have been a right-wing staple for decades, and they'd be as risible as Mr. Goldman's article if legislators hadn't begun to take them seriously.

Here, the conservative right, which traditionally has caused trouble for youth culture, is blamed for the condemnation of music.

Witnesses at the Senate hearing and media writers frequently disparaged the concerns of the PMRC and its supporters by arguing that they advocated censorship. In one of the most colorful exchanges during the hearing, Frank Zappa charged that "the complete list of PMRC demands reads like an instruction manual for some sinister kind of toilet training program to house-break all composers and performers because of the lyrics of a few." The *freedom of speech* frame maintained that labeling albums, printing lyrics on album covers, and encouraging musicians to use restraint restricted artists' First Amendment right to freedom of speech and created a "chilling effect" on expression. By arguing that "the real danger is presented not by rock music, but by those who want to control what should or should not be heard," this frame minimized the perceived threat of graphic lyrics by focusing on the dangers of abridging musicians' freedom of speech.

In a vivid example of how this discourse about music was a media dialogue, the *freedom of speech* counterframe spawned a counter-counterframe from media supporters of the PMRC, who claimed that they did not favor censorship. Writers sympathetic to the PMRC used the *not censorship* frame to defend their positions against accusations of censorship and presented themselves as providers of consumer information (to parents), not as enemies of free speech. Tipper Gore said:

> We do not and have not advocated restrictions on [freedom of speech]; we have never proposed government action. What we are advocating, and what we have worked hard to encourage, is responsibility.

Rap to the Fore: Framing 2 Live Crew

While most of the frames applied to heavy metal music were also applied to rap music, new concerns emerged as writers turned their attention to the "black" music genre. Some of these concerns were expressed in a frame new to the five-year debate, while others were voiced using frames already developed for heavy metal music.

For example, the *danger to society* frame was frequently used to talk about rap music following the arrests of 2 Live Crew in Florida. However, the concerns about the *types* of danger contained in rap lyrics differed sharply from the concerns about heavy metal. Rather than focusing on the dangers of one-in-a-million devil-worshipping mass killers, the *danger to society* frame as applied to rap much more pointedly emphasized that rap music created legions of misogynistic listeners who posed a danger to women, particularly because rap music depicted rape and other brutality. Providing a short inventory of women-harming abuses, one writer argued, "What we are discussing here is the wild popularity (almost 2 million records sold) of a group that sings about forcing anal sex on a girl and then forcing her to lick excrement. . . . Why are we so sure that tolerance of such attitudes has no consequences?"

One counterframe that was specifically instituted for rap (although it later was occasionally applied to heavy metal) was the *important message/art* frame, which was used most dramatically around the time of the government actions against rap music in Florida.

The *important message/art* frame, which argued against the "harmful" position, asserted that rap lyrics have serious content. The frame includes statements about the important messages and concerns of rap music, the artistic expression contained in the music, the lyrics as a reflection of urban reality, and the fact that rappers were positive role models for young black listeners. Foreshadowing arguments that appeared four months later in the trial over 2 Live Crew lyrics, one media writer stated:

> In its constantly changing slang and shifting concerns—no other pop has so many anti-drug songs—rap's flood of words presents a fictionalized oral history of a brutalized generation.

This frame argued that the music itself is worthy of serious contemplation, and that all people—black, white, young, old—could benefit from its important messages.

With the injection of new concerns in the *danger to society* frame and the emergence of the *important message/art* counterframe largely for rap, the set of frames used to analyze the discourse surrounding these two genres of music in the years 1985 through 1990 is complete.

RACIAL RHETORIC: MAPPING THE SHIFT IN FRAMES

. . . Mainstream media writers used certain frames about equally in their discussions of heavy metal and rap, suggesting that some frames were applicable to both genres. The *freedom of speech* and *not censorship* frames, for example, were about equally frequent in the discourse about both music forms. Both frames were used in 1985 in reference to heavy metal and continued to characterize the discourse about rap. Other frames, however, were applied primarily to one genre and not the other.

"Music Is Harmful" Frames

A pronounced shift occurred in the frames used to construct the "harmful" discourse in the mainstream media: Frames that were used most frequently to describe the dangers of heavy metal—*corruption* and *protection*—were rarely used to describe the harmfulness of rap music; conversely, the *danger to society* frame was prominent for rap music but not for heavy metal music. Thus, the frames used most often to decry heavy metal music were less salient for rap music, while the frames used most often to condemn rap music were less relevant for heavy metal music. The arguments represented by these frames may have been based on different referent images, given their disparate concerns.

The *corruption* frame, which accounted for more than one-third of all frames supporting the harmfulness of heavy metal music, concerned the music's effects on young listeners' values and behavior (e.g., the lyrics may lead some listeners to indulge in "self-destructive" activities). A corollary to this frame, the *protection* frame, urged parents and other adults to care enough about society's youth to get involved in activities that would guarantee their children's welfare. The *corruption* and *protection* frames together accounted for two-thirds of all "music-is-harmful" frames used in the mainstream press' discussion of heavy metal music.

The power of these frames derived from the referent images they evoked.

Articles in which the *corruption* frame appeared often referred to the writers' own children (or children like theirs) being exposed to this dangerous material and the potential suffering because of it. Writer Kathy Stroud reported:

> My 15-year-old daughter unwittingly alerted me to the increasingly explicit nature of rock music. "You've got to hear this, Mom!" she insisted one afternoon . . . , "but don't listen to the words," she added, an instant tip-off to pay attention. The beat was hard and pulsating, the music burlesque in feeling. . . . Unabashedly sexual lyrics like these, augmented by orgasmic moans and howls, compose the musical diet millions of children are now being fed at concerts, on albums, on radio and MTV.

And in another article titled "What Entertainers Are Doing to Your Kids," the following passage was one of many that charged that decent children were being exposed to obscene lyrics so that the music industry could profit:

> President Reagan stepped into the fray in mid-October, venting outrage over music's messages. "I don't believe our Founding Fathers ever intended to create a nation where the rights of pornographers would take precedence over the rights of parents, and the violent and malevolent would be given free rein to prey upon our children," the President told a Republican political meeting. According to growing numbers of critics, irresponsible adults in the entertainment business are bedazzling the vulnerable young with a siren song of the darker sides of life. Violence, the occult, sadomasochism, rebellion, drug abuse, promiscuity, and homosexuality are constant themes.

The frame's implicit message to the reader was that even privileged children from good homes were at risk from the lyrical content of heavy metal music. These arguments contended that *our own kids* were endangered by this music, a message that was absent from the frames used to discuss rap.

While the *corruption* and *protection* frames clearly emphasized the music's harmful effects on individual listeners, writers using these frames expressed little concern that the lyrics would have an unfortunate effect on other members of society. Except for a few references to satanic murders and abusiveness to women, articles using these two frames rarely mentioned the possibility that young listeners might violently direct their new-found rebellion, antiauthority sentiment, and heightened sexuality on the society at large.

The *danger to society* frame argued that changes in attitudes and behaviors stemming from lyrics endangered society as a whole (i.e., listening to lyrics that extol violence and the brutalization of women and police would lead to rape and murder). Nearly two-thirds of the "harmful" frames applied to rap music were the *danger to society* frame, compared to about one-tenth of the frames applied to heavy metal music.

It might be expected that in turning their attention from heavy metal to rap, media writers would have continued using the *corruption* frame and would have argued that rap lyrics harmed young black listeners by spreading messages that would lead to self-destructive behaviors. Because most writers considered rap lyrics to be even more explicit than the heavy metal messages, rap lyrics should have been framed as even more harmful to their young audience. Yet, rather than warning the American public that a generation of young black children was endangered by musical messages, the writers argued that the American public at large would suffer at the hands of these listeners as a result of rap music. Clearly, the listener's welfare was no longer the focus of concern.

Unlike the referent images of "my daughter" and "our own kids" that appeared in articles about heavy metal, the prominent rap frames referred to a very different young listener: a young, urban, black male, or more often a group of urban, black male youths. George Will, drawing on the same images, invoked in the Summer 1990 trial of the alleged Central Park rapists, wrote:

> Fact: some members of a particular age and social cohort—the one making 2 Live Crew rich—stomped and raped [a] jogger to the razor edge of death, for the fun of it. Certainty: the coarsening of a community, the desensitizing of a society will have behavioral consequences.

An article called "Some Reasonings for Wilding," which appeared approximately one year before Will's, used the same referent image of the Central Park rape. In this article, Tipper Gore and Susan Baker stated:

> "Wilding." It's a new word in the vocabulary of teenage violence. The crime that made it the stuff of headlines is so heinous, the details so lurid as to make them almost beyond the understanding of any sane human being. When it was over, a 28-year old woman, an investment banker out for a jog, was left brutally beaten, knifed, and raped by teenagers. . . . "It was fun," one of her suspected teenage attackers told

the Manhattan district attorney's office. In the lockup they were non-chalantly whistling at a policewoman and singing a high-on-the-charts rap song about casual sex: "Wild Thing."

In this passage, the teenagers—who from media accounts were known to be black and Hispanic—"nonchalantly" whistle and sing rap lyrics following their alleged crime spree. The image of listeners here (minority, urban youths) differs dramatically from the listeners portrayed in articles about heavy metal (white, middle-class teenagers). Furthermore, the referent images of the threats posed by these two groups of youths also changed. Whereas "our kids" listening to heavy metal lyrics might stray off their expected social tracks because of their incited disrespect for authority or early interest in sex,[3] listeners to rap music were lamented not because their self-destructive activities were of great importance or concern, but because they would probably travel in packs, rape women, and terrorize society.

"Music Is Not Harmful" Counterframes

The arguments proclaiming that music was not harmful also shifted as the discussion turned from heavy metal to rap. While the *freedom of speech* and *threat to authorities* frame were used about equally for heavy metal and rap, the mainstream press used the three remaining frames (*generation gap, no harm,* and *important message/art*) differently for the two genres. The *generation gap* frame, which derided parents for following the age-old tradition of disliking their children's music, made up 25 percent of the "not harmful" frames applied in the discourse about heavy metal, but only 3 percent of the frames used in the discourse about rap. Thus, writers on the "not harmful" side of the debate also detected the *parental* concerns that infused the debate about heavy metal—concerns that were largely absent in the debate about rap. That mainstream writers on the "not harmful" side rarely used the *generation gap* frame to defend rap against parental assaults is another indication of the invisibility of "parents" and "our kids" in the discourse about rap music.

Just as the *generation gap* frame was used disproportionately to defend heavy metal, so the *important message/art* frame was used asymmetrically by the mainstream press to defend rap. Led by the *New York Times,* 60 percent of the "not

[3]This rhetoric is similar to that used to describe the danger obscenity posed to wealthy children in the late nineteenth century.

harmful" frames used for the "black" genre were the *important message/art* frame, compared to only 14 percent of the frames used for the "white" music form. Mainstream opinion writers described heavy metal music as exaggerated, cartoonish buffoonery that posed no danger to listeners (the *no harm* frame) while they legitimated rap as an authentic political and artistic communication from the streets (the *important message/art* frame). Variously described in the media as "folk art," a "fresh musical structure," a "cultural barometer," and "a communiqué from the underclass," rap was valorized as a serious cultural form by the *New York Times, Newsweek,* and *Time* (but not *U.S. News and World Report* or *Reader's Digest*). As suggested by other authors, elites, such as writers and readers of the *New York Times,* seem to have exerted a pervasive effort to adopt rap as an "authentic" cultural form (just as jazz, country music, and comic books had been adopted previously), but to dismiss heavy metal as inconsequential—the politically empty macho posturing of white males.

. . . [T]he *important message/art* frame also received considerable play in the two African-American magazines, *Ebony* and *Jet*. Of the 10 articles published about music lyrics in these magazines from 1985 to 1990, all were about rap (presumably the "white" genre was not of concern to black readers' children), and all argued that music was not harmful to children or society. Eight of the ten articles contained the *important message/art* frame.

Articles in *Ebony* and *Jet* consistently valorized rap music, assessing its lyrics as harmless and containing only positive and important messages from and for black youths. The African-American magazines also argued that the older black generation could learn something from rap: By listening to the lyrics of the music, black adults could comprehend the daily lives of their own children.

FRAMES SUGGESTED BY AND IMPOSED ON THE CULTURAL OBJECT

What accounts for the shifts in rhetoric about these two music genres, both of which present ostensibly "harmful" messages to listeners? If they are both so explicit, why did the mainstream media frame the two genres differently and use such divergent images to make their claims? One plausible explanation is that the lyrics in heavy metal are radically different from those in rap, and media writers merely reflected those differences. To examine this hypothesis, I looked at the lyrics that writers were responding to.

Content of Lyrics

The content analysis of the lyrics of the 20 controversial songs sampled[4] supports many media writers' claims that rap lyrics are more explicit than the lyrics in heavy metal. Although both genres contain potentially offensive elements, rap songs tend to have a higher frequency of offensive themes and to be more explicit than heavy metal songs. As shown in Table 2, two of the ten heavy metal songs and nine of the ten rap songs included hard swear words (e.g., "fuck," "shit," and "dick"), one heavy metal and seven rap songs depicted graphic sex, and no heavy metal songs and two rap songs portrayed violence against the police. While the lyrics of controversial heavy metal songs dealt primarily with anti-authority statements (against parents and teachers for the most part) and sometimes with violent metaphors for sex (such as "the rod of steel injects"), the majority of rap songs in the sample alluded to violent street scenes and graphic sexual behaviors. While heavy metal songs used double entendres and thinly-veiled symbolic allusions to refer to sexual acts and male domination of women, rap made these acts more graphic and explicit. An example of graphic sex in heavy metal lyrics occurs in the Van Halen song "Black and Blue" from the album *OU812*:

[4]The heavy metal song list included:

"One in a Million"	Guns'n'Roses
"Now It's Dark"	Anthrax
"Black and Blue"	Van Halen
"You're All I Need"	Motley Crue
"Let's Put the X in Sex"	KISS
"Suicide Solution"	Ozzy Osbourne
"We're Not Gonna Take It"	Twisted Sister
"Eat Me Alive"	Judas Priest
"School Daze"	W.A.S.P.
"Necrophobic"	Slayer

The rap song list included:

"Dick Almighty"	2 Live Crew
"Fuck tha Police"	N.W.A
"The Fuck Shop"	2 Live Crew
"Gangster of Love"	Geto Boys
"Girls L.G.B.N.A.F."	Ice-T
"The Iceburg"	Ice-T
"Me So Horny"	2 Live Crew
"Put Her in the Buck"	2 Live Crew
"Straight Outta Compton"	N.W.A
"Wild Thing"	Tone Loc

TABLE 2. Content of Lyrics of a Representative Sample of Controversial Heavy Metal and Rap Songs, 1985–1990

	Type of Song	
Content of Lyrics	Heavy Metal	Rap
Hard swear words	2	9
Sex, graphic	1	7
Violence or murder of police	0	2
Rebellion against teachers/parents	2	0
Degradation and violence to women	3	6
Sex, indirect references (innuendo, double entendre)	2	1
Grisly murder, violence, torture	1	0
Sex, group	2	1
Drugs and/or alcohol	1	0
Incest	1	0
Prejudicial slurs	1	1
Suicide	1	0
Number of songs	10	10

Slip 'n' slide, push it in,
Bitch sure got the rhythm.
I'm holding back, yeah I got control,
Hooked into her system.
Don't draw the line.
Honey, I ain't through with you.

In comparison, 2 Live Crew's rap song, "The Fuck Shop" from *As Nasty as They Wanna Be,* is more explicit:

Please come inside and make yourself at home.
I want to fuck 'cause my dick's on bone.
You little whore behind closed doors,
You would drink my cum and nothing more.
Now spread your wings open for the flight.
Let me fill you up with something milky and white.
'Cause I'm gonna slay you rough and painful.
You innocent bitch, don't be shameful.

As Table 2 shows, lyrics depicting rebellion against authority take crucially different forms in heavy metal and rap. Two of the heavy metal songs in the sample ("We're Not Gonna Take It" by Twisted Sister and "School Daze" by W.A.S.P.) proclaim a strong aversion to and mistrust of the older generation, while no rap songs in the sample state these antipathies. Heavy metal music addresses the frustrations of the child against parental and teacher authority, as the following lyrics from "School Daze" suggest:

> A blackboard jungle, I toed the line the rulers made.
> A whole work hell house screams at me like the grave.
> Tic toc 3 o'clock I'm sittin' here and countin' the days.
> A 5-bell is ringin', hell, and I'd sure love to see it blaze.
> Burn it down!

While heavy metal lyrics stake a claim for the autonomy of the young person against school and adult officials, anti-authoritarian rap asserts independence from the authority of the police and white power structures in general. Two rap songs in the sample by "gangster" rapper Ice Cube and his group at the time N.W.A (Niggers With Attitude) depict graphic scenes of anti-authoritarianism and violence against police. The following lyrics from N.W.A's "Fuck tha Police" pose a striking contrast to W.A.S.P.'s sentiments above:

> Fucking with me 'cause I'm a teenager
> With a little bit of gold and a pager.
> Searchin' my car, looking for the product,
> Thinking every nigger is selling narcota.
> Ice Cube will swarm
> On any mother fucker in a blue uniform.
> Just 'cause I'm from the CPT
> Punk police are afraid of me.
> Young nigger on the warpath,
> And when I'm finished, it's gonna be a bloodbath
> Of cops, dying in LA.
> Yo, Dre, I got something to say: Fuck the Police.

Framing Symbolic Expression

To some extent, then, media writers on both sides of the debate used frames based on the messages in the lyrics of the two genres. Writers on the "harmful" side frequently bemoaned the anti-authority themes in heavy metal music (saying that youths would become corrupted in their attitudes about school, parents, and sex from listening to these songs), and they were generally outraged by the unprecedented explicitness of rap (arguing that rap lyrics would cause listeners to wreak havoc on police and women). Writers on the "not harmful" side, meanwhile, argued that the rebellion in heavy metal music was absurd, exaggerated, puerile fun, while the heightened anti-authoritarian rebellion and graphic sexual activity in rap music indicated a serious political stance and an artistic subversion of the stereotyped sexual images of black men.

Yet the discourse about these cultural objects reflected not only the symbolic meanings residing in the objects themselves, but also the social context in which the objects were produced and received. In applying such markedly different frames to heavy metal and rap, media writers were responding to the cultural and historical currents of the day. On the one hand, the media went out of their way to valorize "black" rap as art and, relative to heavy metal, avoided discussing its negative side (as indicated by the smaller number of "harmful" articles written about rap). Yet when they did address the negative aspects of rap, their framing selection revealed a subtle ideological shift: Mainstream writers were no longer concerned about the detrimental effects of the graphic music on teenaged listeners, as they had been for heavy metal, but were concerned about the dangers these black youths posed to the society at large. The societal belief that black kids pose more of a threat to society than "our kids" was reflected in the arguments about "black" teenagers' cultural objects.

CONCLUSION

I argue that media writers use frames selectively to represent the stories they tell. They choose from a set of social-cultural images to make their accounts convincing, compelling, and familiar to themselves and to their audiences. Although there are many different icons and memories that could be used to catch readers' imaginations, writers choose the same cultural images and memories over and over again to relate their concerns about an issue. This repeated use of certain images produces recognizable patterns of frames, which media writers use to comment on socially important issues.

In the discourse surrounding the harmfulness of music lyrics from 1985 to 1990, media writers in the mainstream press invoked different frames to address the "white" genre of heavy metal music than they used to discuss the "black" genre of rap music. They constructed images of race and adolescence to tell separate stories of the dangers lurking in the cultural expressions of the two distinct social groups. In doing so, they called upon memories of historical events and cultural icons to demonstrate the detrimental effects of these objects on their audiences and on society as a whole. These radically-charged frames were most powerful when they built on the stated or unstated fears and anxieties of readers and tapped into their audience's understandings of what white youths and black youths were like.

Finally, in using these frames, writers provided audiences with a map for understanding what was wrong with the younger generation—whether it was their "own kids" or urban, poor, black kids. This map portrayed a causal relationship between music and behavior and explained phenomena like teen suicide, sex, and violence as consequences of explicit lyrics. These explanatory frames made no reference to such existential conditions as teens' feelings of hopelessness or powerlessness, or to material concerns like diminishing economic prospects. In short, these media accounts made sense of issues that adult readers desperately wanted to comprehend without introducing more nebulous factors. That these frames depended on racial rhetoric to make the explanations comprehensible reflects the degree to which race shapes our understanding of the world.

QUESTIONS

1. What are the messages contained in each of the four media frames the author identifies—*corruption, protection, danger to society,* and *not censorship*?

2. What are the messages contained in each of the five counterframes used by defenders of heavy metal and rap—*no harm, generation gap, threat to authorities, freedom of speech,* and *important message/art*?

3. Why were the *corruption* and *protection* frames used more to describe the harmfulness of heavy metal and the *danger to society* frame used more to describe the harmfulness of rap?

4. In portraying these two types of popular music as harmful to youth but for different reasons, what does this study suggest may be the racist undertones contained in the news media's framing of the dangers of rap music?

Injustice Based on
Sexual Orientation

FROM *When Is Inequality a Problem? Victim Contests, Injustice Frames,*
and the Case of the Office of Gay, Lesbian, and Bisexual Student Support
Services at Indiana University

MITCH BERBRIER AND ELAINE PRUETT

There are innumerable examples of inequality in the world, but only those that
activists can successfully frame as unjust *become perceived as social problems.*
Nowadays there is broad public consensus about the injustices produced by racial
and gender inequalities, largely because the civil rights and feminist movements
respectively worked to frame these inequalities as social problems. The same can-
not be said so clearly about the unequal treatment of gays, lesbians, and bisexu-
als. Whether such inequality will someday be broadly seen as unjust as race and
gender inequalities depends on the ·consequences of current efforts to frame this
inequality as unjust. Berbrier and Pruett discuss these efforts as well as the counter-
efforts of activists vying to deny gays, lesbians, and bisexuals the special protec-
tions typically given to groups victimized by injustice. The authors first discuss a
local controversy during the mid-1990s over Indiana University's creation of an
office to give support services to gay, lesbian, and bisexual students, and then sit-
uate this controversy in relation to the broader national debate at the time con-
cerning gay rights.

One of the biggest questions threading through American political culture
is how to deal with a range of putative inequalities. A closely related
question is precisely which inequalities are worthy of public concern. Activists
of many political, cultural, and social movements on both the Right and Left

are fighting against some perceived injustice or another, with many fighting more specifically against certain perceived unjust inequalities—be they the treatment of poor inner-city blacks or rural white evangelicals. At the same time, across the political spectrum, there are many inequalities regarded as simply irrelevant to political life—for instance, the correlation, among males, between height and economic or political success. Without perceptions of injustice, there can ordinarily be no impetus for activism against inequality, and any social structure upon which it rests may be reproduced with little struggle by the beneficiaries of that arrangement. Therefore, our focus in this article is on those relationships that, while generally agreed to be "unequal," arouse controversy over whether they are justifiably unequal and therefore nonproblematic, or injustices requiring corrective action.

*   *   *

THE OFFICE OF GAY, LESBIAN, AND BISEXUAL STUDENT SUPPORT SERVICES AT INDIANA UNIVERSITY (IU)

Data

The data for this study were originally part of a larger study on the social construction of minority and ethnic groups. In the 1990s, while Berbrier was a graduate student in Bloomington, Indiana, he collected documents relating to a local controversy over efforts to establish an outreach and support office there for lesbian and gay stu-dents. These initial data included many newspaper articles—from *Bloomington Herald-Times* (a mainstream daily), *Bloomington Voice* (an alternative weekly), and *Indiana Daily Student* (the journalism school's student-run daily)—and 200 letters e-mailed to the president of IU, solicited from around the country by local activists. The office continues to operate, and in 2004 we acquired a variety of additional documents that had been reproduced on its Web page. These include the 1993 Final Report of the Indiana University Educational Task Force on Gay, Lesbian, and Bisexual Concerns, many newspaper articles from both the initial period and beyond, and a series of annual reports for the office dating back to 1993. Our presentation here begins with a summary of the story "The Opening of the Office," in order to familiarize readers with the plot and main characters. We then move into an analysis of the framing contest.

The Opening of the Office

The stage had long been set by June 1994, when the trustees of IU voted to establish an office on campus that would support and counsel gay, lesbian, and bisexual students. In 1990, the school's Code of Student Ethics had been revised to include proscriptions against discrimination based on sexual orientation. Also included there was a detailed list of students' individual rights concerning harassment on the basis of sexual orientation and one regarding the specific acts regarded as harassment. Notably, the amendment to the Code of Ethics addressed issues of harassment and discrimination on the basis of sexual orientation as matters of "individual rights."

In September, responding to the IU Board of Aeons and the Student Senate's recommendations for the establishment of a university-funded center for gay, lesbian, and bisexual students, the Office of the Dean of Students established a task force to identify and address "the needs and concerns of the student population as well as to identify and create resources" for the IU community. The group, called the IU Educational Task Force on Gay, Lesbian, and Bisexual Concerns, was composed of 40 members from the faculty, staff, and students.

Two and a half years later, in March 1993, the task force reported on its (several) subcommittees' inquiries and findings. One subcommittee was charged with identifying "challenges as they relate[d] to the recently adopted [revision to the] *Code of Ethics*"—a document that, again, recognized discrimination and harassment of lesbians and gays as matters of individual rights. Under the heading "Assessment of Needs," the subcommittee cited specific policies that distinguished heterosexual from homosexual couples—for example, a campus housing policy that limited family housing to legally married couples and the denial of access to a university chapel for the purpose of same-sex "blessing unions." Throughout its report, the task force deployed language clearly portraying these and other inequalities as unjust violations of rights. For example, regarding the family housing policy, it wrote, "The family housing situation is one of equity. The current family housing policy discriminates against and excludes individuals who are not traditionally married. The proposed family housing policy gives equity to all domestic partners without discriminating against any committed relationship." In June 1994, in response to the many recommendations in this report, the Board of Trustees voted to establish the Office of Gay, Lesbian, and Bisexual Support Services.

While the task force and its efforts had gone essentially unnoticed by the local community, upon the trustees' announcement, an assertive campaign of opposition began. This countermobilization was led by two student organizations and one state legislator. The organizations were the campus branch of Young Americans for Freedom and the IU College Republicans, whose representatives were repeatedly quoted in local newspapers and engaged in ardent exchanges with office supporters via letters to editors. The legislator was Representative Woody Burton, a Republican from the district of Greenwood. Burton became the most polarizing figure in the debate when he threatened to introduce legislation to withhold $500,000 in state funding from the university, retaliating for the $50,000 in taxpayer money that had been earmarked by the university for the office.

Eventually, a compromise was reached. On October 19, 1994, IU's then-president Myles Brand announced that the funding for the office would come from a private donor, not taxpayer money. In addition, Brand announced that unlike the offices for established minority groups, this office would not be independent. Rather, the University's Office of Student Ethics would be renamed as the Office of Student Ethics and Anti-Harassment Programs, and would subsume the Office of Gay, Lesbian, and Bisexual Student Support Services within its structure. In return, Representative Burton agreed to withdraw his threat to cut state funding. Despite an impassioned outcry on the part of the supporters of the office who indicated that these changes would undermine the intended function of the office, the university held firm. The Office of Gay, Lesbian, and Bisexual Student Support Services was officially opened on November 24, 1994.

The Victim Contest

Given that the task force had framed the question as one of individual (rather than group) rights, it is interesting that one of the initial issues in this victim contest was the "minority status" of lesbians and gays, from which were derived other themes for establishing the in/justice of the unequal treatment. These included (a) the relevance of behavior versus orientation, (b) the nature and degree of the discrimination and harassment, (c) the in/justice of discriminating against homosexuals, and (d) the meaning and relevance of "diversity." Since these themes are closely woven together in myriad combinations, we too weave through them in the following analysis; thus, the headings indicate emphases, but the sections are not thematically exclusive.

Opening Salvos: Behavior versus Orientation

As indicated above, the announcement of the planned office generated sustained opposition. An article in *Bloomington Voice* announced that the opponents "see no clear need for the services . . . and object to the use of the term 'minority' in reference to Gays and Lesbians." The article continued by focusing on the disagreement between proponents and opponents of the office over the specific issue of designating "minorities." Jim Holden, president of the IU Republicans, said, "I know a lot of minorities who object to the idea that there is no difference to being a minority and being homosexual. I would personally be offended if that comparison was drawn. I don't think there's a similarity between someone's behavior and the color of their skin. It's a behavior that you willfully choose to participate in." In Holden's view, then, a group's "minority" status is established by "the color of their skin." Being homosexual, on the other hand, is established by "someone's behavior." Carlos Lam, president of the local chapter of Young Americans for Freedom, expanded upon Holden's argument by directly attacking the collective character, denying the group a victim status. "The difference is that the sexual behavior of gays, lesbians, and bisexuals is wrong. . . . The way to correct the wrongs of being gay is by practicing abstinence. With a Hispanic or a white you can see the difference, but the actual gay sex act is the mark that you're gay." For Lam, it is relevant not only that homosexuality is determined by behavior but also that it is "wrong" behavior; the "wrongs of being gay" need to be corrected. Sally Green, president of the IU gay and lesbian organization OUT, responded, "It's not a behavioral choice, it's orientation. The reason they're saying that is because it's easy to pick out an African American or a Latino student, but with gays and lesbians it's a little more difficult, so that makes it harder to appreciate how we actually are a minority." Green distinguishes between "behavioral choice" and "orientation." In her argument, Green asserts that African Americans and Latinos are both minorities, and that they are visible ("they are easy to pick out"), possibly by virtue of skin color or facial features. She concedes that gays and lesbians are less easy to identify but argues that it does not preclude their minority status. Although one cannot see a person's orientation, Green contends that it is no more a behavioral choice than skin color and thus no less a criterion for minority status. That it may be more difficult to discern does nothing to remove gays and lesbians from their status as victims.

The article also indicated that IU trustee Cindy Stone claimed that the opponents' arguments "cut to the very core of diversity issues," calling the distinction between gays and other minorities "ridiculous." "You ask someone who is being harassed, whether they feel like they're in a minority because their skin is different, their gender is different, their orientation is different, they feel like they're in a minority because they're in a potential position to be victims of hate crimes. . . . Hate crimes occur because someone is different in some way. This university is built on inclusiveness, not excluding people because of one or more characteristics that are different." In Stone's construction, minority status is conferred upon those who are "different," on the basis of the nonbehavioral and equivalent characteristics of skin color, gender, and orientation *and* on the basis of the fear of falling victim to hate crimes. This early fight about minority status, behavior, and orientation seemed to set the stage for much of the rest of the debate, which would continue for several months.

Victims versus Villains

Images of homosexuality informed claimants' alternative constructions of people as either victims or villains. . . . A former president of IU's Young Americans for Freedom named Shun Ravago is quoted claiming that there was no need for an office for gay, lesbian, and bisexual support because homosexuality is a "preference rather than something someone is born with" and, moreover, that "IU is saying that being a homosexual is like being black or Asian, but it's not the same at all. It is an immoral lifestyle. The center is going to be a place in which homosexuality is condoned. . . . The gays, lesbians, and bisexuals at IU are a minority group of the population, like pedophiles or masturbators." Here, Ravago presumes two types of minorities—immoral versus moral. He denies that gays embody the victim potential of *oppressed cultural* minorities (blacks and Asians); rather, they comprise a *numerical* minority of villainous sexual deviants. Once again, the question comes down not to inequality but to the question of why people (audiences, "society") should care. If good people are harmed and they are not at fault, our cultural feeling rules call for sympathy: people *should care*. But invoking cultural villains, such as pedophiles, elicits feelings of antipathy and vengeance. Ravago thus denies victim status to gays through an attack on their collective character. "Minorities," in this construction, may be treated unequally, but that is how things ought to be for immoral minorities.

Responding to these sorts of allegations, IU student columnist Matt Oliver asserted that gays do, indeed, constitute an unjustly oppressed group: "homosexuals are clearly a minority group, whether the state wants to officially recognize them or not. Gay bashing is a nationwide pastime. Homosexuals have been kept out of the Army, out of schools, and out of the mainstream of our society. The gay population has been forced to hide in its own bars, in its own cities, and have its own Olympics. It is by the will of the majority that this has occurred." In Oliver's construction, gays are objectively a minority (i.e., whether "officially recognized or not"). Like others, Oliver does not use the word "inequality," choosing instead to dramatize poor treatment ("bashing," "kept out of the mainstream," "forced to hide," and segregated) in which the broader culture becomes the victimizer responsible for the harm; that is, discrimination is the "will of the majority," and harassment is a "nationwide pastime."

Similarly, another student, Raman Nagarajan, asserted that this culture keeps gays closeted. As a result, "it prevents homosexuals from enjoying the same things heterosexuals can. A heterosexual couple can take a walk on a crowded boardwalk at sunset and not have to worry about getting hit with a baseball bat. Homosexual couples can't. This persecution keeps them from the 'pursuit of happiness' that is a cherished American value." Again, without explicitly using the words, Nagarajan claims that homosexuals face both "inequality" and "injustice" because they cannot do and enjoy the same things as heterosexuals. Furthermore, the "pursuit of happiness" evokes constitutional guarantees for the "cherished" inalienable rights of each individual. By claiming that homosexuals are prevented from enjoying this basic right, Nagarajan is claiming that homosexuals suffer an unjust inequality—that it is, indeed, "persecution."

Finally, like so many others, Nagarajan seems to believe that the constitutional frame was not enough and that (at least at that time and place) civil rights framing was particularly appropriate: "if more people realize that homosexuality, like race, is not a characteristic that one can control, then they would see the fundamental similarity between the civil rights movement and the gay rights movement." Again, invoking similarities between homosexuality and race, and between the civil rights movement and the lesbian/gay rights movement, is used to allege that the inequalities homosexuals face are as unjust as those faced by blacks. Or put another way, if you believe that blacks have faced unjust inequality meriting redress, you must also believe this for lesbians and gays.

The Importance of the Minority Designation

Since the case of the Office of Gay, Lesbian, and Bisexual Student Services at Indiana University is not particularly *about* whether gays and lesbians constitute a minority group (like African Americans), that such discourse was generated might indicate something about the potency of "minority" status and the stakes involved in establishing or recognizing a group that way. In the early 1990s, this very "minority" status of gays was being debated politically. The terms of that debate—orientation and minority status versus chosen (and presumably immoral) behavior—were familiar to those who followed gay rights issues in those years, especially the controversy over gays in the military (which we discuss further below).

In the minority-status discourse, the opponents were not arguing about the inequality, but whether it was unjust in the same way as discrimination against blacks and Latinos, whose generally accepted status as "minorities" implied that discrimination against them was both undeserved and illegitimate—that is, emblems of their victimhood. In the context of the debate then, conceding minority status means conceding that there are inequalities that *ought to be* addressed.

The opponents went further, implying not only that the discrimination claims were exaggerated but that they were only to be expected, and even justified, by the deviance of the behaviors. The alleged victimizers were presented in the discourse as provoked by the increased visibility of homosexuality. For example, IU College Republicans' president Jim Holden explained why he saw "no clear need for the services" in this way: "if anything, the center will cause so much tension that it will increase harassment—not that I believe there's an incredible problem with it already." Similarly, Representative Burton—in what some might interpret to be blame-the-victim style—would later attribute any harassment to the activists themselves when he "conceded . . . that there is discrimination," and even that it was wrong, but that lesbians and gays could avoid it by "becoming unknown and invisible." Burton was also quoted as saying that "when people are going to do things that aren't mainstream American, they're going to be discriminated against more." The remedy to injustice was to closet the targets, since their actions (or the actions of their representatives) were responsible for the harassment and attacks. Here Burton parsimoniously illustrates three items from [a] list of counterframing strategies: first, counterattributions—Burton deflected the responsibility to the gay and lesbian activists, thus denying lesbians and gays the status of victim, as "minorities." Second, counterprognoses—Burton's solution is to erase the victims. And third, Burton's attacks on their collective character—the bottom line is that these folks are "not doing the 'mainstream American' things." Thus, once again, the opponents are not arguing about inequality per se, but about whether it can be justified; minority groups can be victims of others, but deviants are only victims of their own behavioral choices.

Equality from Diversity

Throughout, the data also yield frequent references to "diversity." . . . [A] "diversity trope" has developed in our popular discourse that can be (and has been) used in multiple ways, including being co-opted by neoliberals when seen as profitable. For some progressives, the term is invoked with regularity, used as if it were a *universally legitimate symbol mandating equality.* That is, since it is assumed that just about everyone supports diversity, all groups within that diversity who are manifestly subjugated must receive better treatment.

Those supporting the IU office engaged in similar rhetoric. During the height of the victim contest, the university's vice president, Kenneth Gros-Louis, wrote a letter to alumni defending the university's decision:

> A university always has been a place where people of diverse backgrounds gather. . . . What's changed recently is a dramatic increase in . . . violence against people who are perceived as different. Over time, that has included women, African-Americans, Latinos, Jews, foreign students, and increasingly, homosexuals. . . . College campuses across the country are seeing an increase in harassment and other negative acts based on race, religion, and sexual orientation. We are no exception.

Gros-Louis's style here, as well as several other passages presented here (and many more not shown), are examples of . . . "indexical association," wherein a stigmatized group is discursively associated with culturally accepted groups by pointing to putative similarities, thereby equating them. In that article, there was an emphasis on direct comparisons across groups. In contrast, many of the associations here were made less by direct analogy and more indirectly by metaphor. That is, by putting the words side by side, and connecting them, it is implied that "sexual orientation" is akin to "race" and "religion" as a source of unacceptable forms of harassment; "homosexuals" themselves are akin to women, blacks, Latinos, Jews, and foreign students—people who are "different" or have "diverse backgrounds."

In September 1994, IU staff member Duncan Mitchel concluded that Jim Holden and Woody Burton were "unable or unwilling to grasp so simple and basic a concept as equality." This was the last part of a long letter, and the final word in the letter was Mitchel's first use of the word "equality." His conclusion regarding "equality" was built upon two foundations: claims about diversity and indexical associations. Specifically, Mitchel had opened his letter stating that this indicated that Holden had "absolutely no idea what the word 'diversity' is supposed to mean. . . . [He] can only conceive of a world where one sex, race, religion or sexual orientation reigns supreme and all others are suppressed, or at least relegated to the back of the bus." Once again, "diversity" is used here with a metaphorical indexical association; that is, the phrase "the back of the bus" links discrimination against gays with both the oppression of African Americans and one of the civil rights movement's most sympathetic icons, Rosa Parks. Later, Mitchel is still more explicit in turning the diagnosis of the problem from promoting a deviant immoral lifestyle to the justice of opposing discrimination. The office was not promoting anything, but merely "taking gay students, faculty, and staff members under its protection. If the law punishes someone for desecrating a synagogue, it is not 'promoting Judaism.' When the Armed Forces conduct anti-racist training, they are not 'promoting Negritude.'" It is only at this point in his letter that Mitchel finally introduces the issue of "equality."

Mitchel indicated that he had been motivated to write his letter because of a claim, attributed to Holden, that the office would promote "a certain lifestyle above others." Such inversion of putative victims and victimizers is common in anti-gay counterrhetoric: society is presented as the victim of the gay agenda. As Young Americans for Freedom's Carlos Lam put it, "the gay lifestyle has caused demoralization in America." But it was also this point upon which the university bent. Instead of being independent (like recognized minority groups' offices) the office was to be subsumed under the Office of Student Ethics and Anti-Harassment Programs. According to Vice President Gros-Louis, this was because it was intended "to provide a safe educational environment and not to advocate a lifestyle or political agenda." In reaction, two local gay activists, Gary Pool and Daniel Soto, solicited letters from around the country via e-mail; they asked that these letters of support for the office be addressed to President Brand, who subsequently received over 200 such letters. Many of them criticized the university president for "capitulating." A contribution from Jeffery Bass noted that "the original proposal by the Board of Aeons called for a center similar to the Black Culture Center and the Latinos Center." Eric Hinsch-Little wrote and asked President Brand, "If a group calling themselves say, The African-American Student Union formed on the IU campus, would you force them to change their name?" And Martin Meeker, a graduate student in history at the University of Southern California, wrote to the IU president, "Although ignorant and hateful people would like to deny us our identity and community, gay, lesbian, and bisexual people do form an ethnicity, as diverse as any other but also as cohesive. In face of intense discrimination (as a historian I am quite aware of the position of gays in the 1950s) we have formed our own culture, institutions, and even traditions."

To sum up to this point, the literal terms of this debate—"behavior," "orientation," "victim," "villains," "minority," "deviant," "diversity," and "culture"—were not deployed in order to establish or deny inequality or even degrees of inequality. Rather, the claimants were directing their audiences to consider the *meaning* of relationships of power, prestige, and rights. Those relationships appear to have been understood by all parties to be unequal, with the focus on whether those inequalities reflected problematic situations in need of rectification, or not.

Thus far, our analysis has not strayed from Bloomington, Indiana. But while all discourse (like all politics) is inherently local, any discourse that is *only* local, and thus only locally meaningful, is sociologically uninteresting. Hence, we now inquire into how these events may have been related to things beyond the local setting.

CONTEXTUALIZING THE DISCOURSE

* * *

Locally Appropriating from a National Issue:
Status versus Behavior Revisited

The debate over status versus behavior that played out on the national level in 1993 was very familiar to people following the gay rights movement, so much so, we believe, that it seems implausible to suggest that it did not influence the events one year later in Bloomington. We easily found several instances of how that debate played out there. For example, the head of the Joint Chiefs of Staff at the time, Colin Powell, wrote, "Skin-color is a benign, non-behavioral characteristic. Sexual orientation is perhaps the most profound of human behavioral characteristics. Comparison of the two is a convenient but invalid argument." At around the same time, in an article that appeared in the *Los Angeles Times,* Charles Bussey, a black veteran of World War II, was quoted as having said, "I resent people who try to compare our situation with gays. There's no similarity. Blacks couldn't hide their blackness. Gays are able to hide their sexual preference. The issues are nowhere near the same." Similarly, John Watkins wrote a letter to the *Seattle Times* in which he described how he had served in the army while it was being integrated and how, contrary to the rhetoric of those advocating integration of gays into the military, opposition to integration was the (numerical) minority opinion and most soldiers, including the top brass, supported the idea as "a matter of simple justice." He went on: "they backed integration and worked hard to make it work. And it did work. We should remember this when we discuss the homosexual problem. Blackness is a matter of appearance, not behavior. Homosexuality is a matter of behavior, not appearance. Do we want to endorse the behavior?" These claims are remarkably consistent with those made by Jim Holden in the local case described above. Both Holden and these claimants from the national controversy held that homosexuality is distinguished by choice and "preference." "Appearance" is therefore held up as the essence of what makes for a minority group: it is an involuntary and ascribed "status."

Also as with the local Bloomington case, the gays-in-the-military discourse produced claims in which the status-behavior distinction was explained via comparisons with blacks, as in the following letter to the editor: "you can tell when someone is African-American or Asian because it is self-evident. But you know someone is gay only because they express it with words or actions. Regardless of whether its origins are genetic or social, homosexuality manifests itself by behavior—and only by behavior." In this case, the comments echo those of State Representative Burton who argued that you can know a visible "minority"—including Jews but not closeted homosexuals—when you see one.

We use these examples of the national case of gays in the military to direct attention to the fundamentally collective nature of the representations made in the Indiana victim contest. That is, the national controversy generated a public discourse that became accessible for appropriation into other disputes. Since it is unlikely that the claimants in the Indiana case had all just then become interested in or concerned about homosexuals in 1994, we believe it is reasonable to assume that most (on both sides) had keenly followed the "gays in the military" controversy the year before. The terms of that debate about the in/justice of discrimination is thus circumscribed by the prior and larger debate, which provides people in local settings with discursive resources with which to debate the meaning of inequalities.

Appropriating from and Indexically Associating with Blacks and the Civil Rights Movement

In both national and local gay rights victim contests, indexically associating with and invoking "civil rights" themes were common. Again, examples abound. Massachusetts Congressman Gary Studds (who is openly gay) argued that "the American people are just beginning to wrestle with this issue [of gay rights]. Rosa Parks wasn't asking to sit in the middle of the bus." In a separate piece, the *San Francisco Chronicle* reported how Representative John Lewis of Georgia (a civil rights movement icon who was one of the leaders of the Selma-to-Montgomery voting rights march in 1965) said that the claims of opponents of gay rights were "like the words we heard in 1965." These comparisons to the civil rights movement made in the national discourse are remarkably similar to those drawn by IU staff member Duncan Mitchel and student Raman Nagarajan above. Both local- and national-level rhetors were drawing upon a broader cultural discourse that is a legacy of the African American struggle for civil rights—the "civil rights master frame." It seems, therefore, not only that the Indiana case was influenced by discourse produced in the gays-in-the-military controversy but that in both contexts people were influenced by the still broader discourse about minority rights that had developed over several decades.

The national case also resulted in a discourse comparing President Clinton's initiative to allow gays into the military to President Truman's racial integration of the military. Indeed, from the outset, gay rights advocates and supporters of Clinton's initiative made this comparison "the cornerstone of their campaign." Truman's initiative was regularly invoked when comparing the discrimination of gays in the 1990s with that of blacks under Jim Crow. By indexically associating gays and blacks, and by mirroring the discourse of the opposition to racial integration—a practice that by 1993 was widely regarded as ridiculous, if not a national embarrassment—these claimants seek to dramatize the injustice of excluding gays as something that over the decades would be recalled as similarly absurd. Moreover, it is important to note that it was precisely because racial integration was perceived as having been both traumatically difficult and notably successful that it was all the more appropriate. As expressed by Kahne Parsons, "Truman's decision recognized that cultural norms were insufficient grounds for discrimination. He did not exempt the military from standards of fairness and tolerance; instead, he placed the military in the position of racial pioneer, with the result that today the U.S. armed forces exemplify the highest standards of racial tolerance and equality. . . . Let us not kid ourselves that the stakes are not equally high for our gay and lesbian brothers and sisters: Gays and lesbians are the target of physical and psychological violence every bit as cruel as that directed against racial minorities."

* * *

QUESTIONS

1. The authors discuss how the injustice frame is built on claims about minority status. Discuss the various ways that activists at Indiana University made the case that gay, lesbian, and bisexual students constitute a minority group.

2. How did these activists embrace the diversity frame in an effort to legitimize the university's giving gay, lesbian, and bisexual students special support services?

3. Discuss the counter-efforts of activists that sought to deny gays, lesbians, and bisexuals the protections typically given to groups victimized by injustice.

4. Now let's think beyond the local controversy at Indiana University and focus on the broader national debate over the status of gays, lesbians and bisexuals. How have activists drawn on the successes of the civil rights movement in making their case that gays, lesbians, and bisexuals experience injustices deserving of special protection?

5. Discuss the reasons why, prior to the civil rights movement, many non-blacks did not view the unequal treatment of blacks as an injustice. What kinds of claims were made about why this inequality was justified?

6. How is the controversy discussed in this reading concerning Indiana University's creation of an office to give support services to gay, lesbian, and bisexual students similar to the recent debate over gay marriage?

PMS and the Biological Flaws
of Womanhood

FROM *Misdiagnosing the Body: Premenstrual Syndrome, Postmenstrual Syndrome, and Other Normal "Diseases"*

CAROL TAVRIS

Carol Tavris discusses how Premenstrual Syndrome (PMS) came to be seen as a disease afflicting women. She traces the historical construction of this medical category and shows how it has become widely accepted by women as a way to understand changes in their moods and behaviors over the course of their menstrual cycle. While the construction of this category gives visibility to women's feelings of distress that doctors and psychologists had previously marginalized, Tavris argues that these benefits are overshadowed by the ways the PMS category stigmatizes women by legitimizing the notion that women's bodies are deficient and in need of fixing.

> *Conversation overheard in a Hollywood casting office, between a man and a woman angry at being kept waiting by a female casting director:*
> MAN: *"It must be her time of the month."*
> WOMAN: *"And how do we explain the rudeness of male casting directors?"*

In 1975, when I was working for *Psychology Today* magazine, we ran a short article called "A Person Who Menstruates Is Unfit to Be a Mother." The author maintained that women are hypertense and anxious for the week before menstruation, moody and incapacitated for the week of menstruation, and utterly exhausted for the week after menstruation. How, then, could the complex care of children, which requires stamina, intelligence, and several advanced degrees, be entrusted to persons who are erratic and unreliable three weeks out of the month?

This essay poked delighted fun at the then-common argument that women's abilities are limited by their physiology. Edgar Berman, Hubert Humphrey's personal physician, had recently declared that women's "raging hormonal influences" made them unfit for political office. The Canadian anthropologist Lionel Tiger had publicly worried that female hormones were ruining women's entire intellectual lives: "An American girl writing her Graduate Record Examinations over a two-day period or a week-long set of finals during the premenstruum," he wrote, apparently with a straight face, "begins with a disadvantage which almost certainly condemns her to no higher than a second-class grade. A whole career in the educational system can be unfairly jeopardized because of this phenomenon."

So all of the second-class female students I knew were heartened by the burst of new research in the 1970s that was rapidly debunking many old myths and preconceptions about women's alleged physical limitations. Raging-hormone theories were on the way out, as research showed again and again that women were just as able as men to work, play, think, sing, pass exams, and otherwise carry on, even when they were menstruating, premenstruating, postmenstruating, and nonmenstruating.

It was too good to last, and it didn't. Today we are witnessing a rebirth of the belief in the unruly female body. A U.S. District Judge, hearing a recent sex discrimination case, commented that women "have a monthly problem which upsets them emotionally, and we all know that." Every week another story appears about how women's hormones affect women's personalities and behaviors, another research finding about sex differences in hormones and anatomy. On a basis of a single small study, "Female Sex Hormone Is Tied to Ability to Perform Tasks" was a front-page news story coast-to-coast, although no headline appeared to announce, as a much larger study found, "Male Sex Hormone Is Tied to Antisocial Behavior and Crime."

Hormone studies are part of an ongoing tidal wave of biological research in general, and much of this research has benefited women. Women should know that the physiological changes of the menstrual cycle vary enormously, that *normal* women range from having no pain or discomfort to having considerable though temporary pain. It is important for women to know that morning sickness during pregnancy is entirely a hormonal matter, and not, as a male physician once said to a friend of mine, "a woman's way of saying she doesn't want to be pregnant." It is important for women to know that hot flashes and vaginal dryness during menopause are likewise due to temporary hormonal changes, not to a neurotic loss of femininity or sexual inhibitions.

In short, it is beneficial and empowering for women to understand the normal changes of their bodies, and not to have their feelings dismissed as psychosomatic whining. A friend of mine told me that she felt depressed when she stopped breastfeeding her daughter, and, being a psychotherapist, she immediately reached for a psychological explanation. "I thought my depression must signal a pathological inability to 'let go' of my daughter," she said, "until I mentioned my feelings to my female pediatrician. She said, 'Oh, sure, that depression is due to the hormonal adjustment. It'll be gone in a few days.'"

But while there are many dangers to the overpsychologizing of normal biological processes, as my friend learned, there are also dangers of reducing all of our feelings, problems, and conflicts to them. Everywhere we look today, we find that the normal changes of menstruation and menopause are increasingly being regarded as diseases, problems, and causes of women's emotional woes and practical difficulties. In particular, biomedical researchers have taken a set of bodily changes that are normal to women over the menstrual cycle, packaged them into a "Premenstrual Syndrome," and sold them back to women as a disorder, a problem that needs treatment and attention. Of course, the only thing worse for women than menstruating is not menstruating. When women cease having the monthly "disease" of PMS, they suffer the "disease" of Menopausal Estrogen Deficiency.

The biological mismeasurement of women's bodies poses many emotional and intellectual conflicts for women, who are caught between defending their reproductive differences from men and asserting their intellectual equality and competence. The story of "premenstrual syndrome" highlights this conflict perfectly. Research on the menstrual cycle was long overdue, as it were, and feminist scholars had to press for research funds and scientific attention to be given to a bodily process that only women experience. Many women themselves have responded positively to the language of PMS, feeling validated at last by the attention being paid to menstrual changes. But the enthusiastic support for PMS masks the more important fact that the menstrual cycle does not affect a healthy woman's ability to do what she needs to do. It also diverts public attention from other matters, such as the effects of hormones on men and the fact that men's and women's moods and physical symptoms are more alike than different.

The public and scientific fascination with PMS and allied "normal disorders" of the female reproductive system is, in turn, part of a larger medical zeitgeist, reflected in the continuing effort to reduce all human problems and emotions to the correct gene, neurotransmitter, hormone, or disease. I'm getting very grumpy about this. I must be premenstrual.

THE MANUFACTURE OF "PMS"

Let's start by trying to identify the problem. A small percentage of women report having particularly difficult emotional symptoms associated with the premenstrual phase. Some describe severe Jekyll-and-Hyde-like personality changes that recur cyclically and predictably. In my lifetime of knowing hundreds of women, I have never met such a Jekyll-and-Hyde-like female. But there is something compelling about the testimony of women themselves and of researchers who have observed their behavior clinically. A woman in one study described herself this way:

> Something seems to snap in my head. I go from a normal state of mind to anger, when I'm really nasty. Usually I'm very even tempered, but in these times it is as if someone else, not me, is doing all this, and it is very frightening.

A larger percentage of women described premenstrual mood changes, notably depression and irritability, that they swear occur as predictably as ragweed in spring. "Unbeknownst to me, my husband kept track of my irritability days in his office diary," one friend reports, "and he could predict like clockwork when I was within a week of my period."

Which group has the premenstrual syndrome? The Jekyll-and-Hyde phenomenon reflects an abnormality in degree, kind, and severity of symptoms. But many researchers, the media, and women themselves now confuse mood changes that are abnormal and occur in *few* women with mood changes that are normal for *all* women—and, as it turns out, for all men, too.

This confusion is apparent in virtually all contemporary discussions of PMS in the media. Most of the media today regard PMS as if it were a clearly defined disorder that most, if not all, women "suffer." For example, *Science News* called it "the monthly menace," and the *Orange County Register* called it "an internal earthquake." An article in *Psychology Today* began: "Premenstrual Syndrome (PMS) remains as baffling to researchers as it is troublesome to women." *Troublesome?* To *all* women, as implied? The article turns out to be about a study of 188 nursing students and tea factory workers in China. In the tea factory, "almost 80% suffered from PMS." *Suffered?* "Overall, nearly 74% rated their symptoms as mild, 24% as moderate and 3% said they were severe." In other words, for 97 percent of the women the symptoms of this "syndrome" were no big deal.

Likewise, an article in the *Baltimore Sun,* headlined "Why PMS Triggers

Hunger," begins by asking "Why is it so hard to diet when you're suffering from premenstrual syndrome?" (There we are "suffering" again.) The answer turns out to have nothing at all to do with PMS, or, for that matter, with suffering. According to the research, women feel hungrier in the few days before menstruation because their metabolism was increased. This is normal, the article states: "Your body is working as it should, building up the uterine lining . . . " Working as it should? Then why am I suffering from a syndrome?

It's easy to understand the media's confusion, because the list of symptoms thought to characterize "PMS" doesn't leave much out. One popular paperback book offers a "complete checklist" of physical, behavioral, and emotional changes, including weight gain, eye diseases, asthma, nausea, blurred vision, skin disorders and lesions, joint pains, headaches, backaches, general pains, epilepsy, cold sweats and hot flashes, sleeplessness, forgetfulness, confusion, impaired judgment, accidents, difficulty concentrating, lowered school or work performance, lethargy, decreased efficiency, drinking or eating too much, mood swings, crying and depression, anxiety, restlessness, tension, irritability, and loss of sex drive. That's just for starters. Other alleged symptoms include allergies, alcoholism, anemia, low self-esteem, problems with identity, and cravings for chocolate. Some physicians have specified as many as 150 different symptoms.

Mercy! With so many symptoms, accounting for most of the possible range of human experience, who wouldn't have "PMS"? Obviously, the more symptoms that are listed, the more likely that someone will have them, at least sometimes. This likelihood is increased in checklists that include mutually contradictory symptoms (such as "was less interested in sex" *and* "was more sexually active," or "had less energy" *and* "couldn't sit still") and the entire range of negative emotions ("irritable or angry," "sad or lonely," "anxious or nervous"). On these lists, there is no way you can't have some symptoms.

Because researchers themselves don't agree on whether they are talking about a problem that a few women experience or that all women experience, estimates of the prevalence of the syndrome range from 5 percent (women who are severely incapacitated) to 95 percent (the number of women who will experience, as one article put it, "one or more PMS symptoms sometime in their lives"). In one typical conference on "PMS—an important and widespread problem," sponsored by England's Royal Society of Medicine Services, participating physicians tried to determine the scope of the "widespread problem." One thought it affected "between 20% and 40% of women at some stage in their lives." Another said that "a very large proportion of women are aware of cyclical physical and mood changes, but probably fewer than 5% of them are sufficiently moved by these symptoms to seek medical help." A third said that "Probably all women at some time in their lives have disturbing premenstrual symptoms . . . [but only] 5–10% of women have clear-cut PMS."

* * *

In short, everywhere you look, you find agreement that PMS is a real disorder, a disease. There's a widespread sickness among women! Up to half of all women are sick every month! Nearly all of us are sick sometimes! We're slowing down the economy! How fortunate that men are running things!

* * *

. . . The real mover and shaker on behalf of PMS was Katharina Dalton, a British physician, who throughout the 1950s wrote articles on the dangers of menstruation: "Effect of Menstruation on School-girls' Weekly Work," "Menstruation and Crime," "Menstruation and Accidents," "Menstruation and Acute Psychiatric Illness," "The Influence of Mother's Menstruation on Her Child." Reading these articles is enough to make you agree that a person who menstruates is unfit to be a mother.

In the early 1950s, Dalton and a colleague coined the term "premenstrual syndrome" (to include all those women who had more symptoms than simply premenstrual tension), and in 1964 she published a book, *The Premenstrual Syndrome.* The term stuck like lint. In the ensuing decades, PMS became an increasingly hot research topic. . . .

* * *

The move toward the medicalization of PMS was and is actively supported by drug companies, [Mary Brown Parlee, a psychologist who has been conducting excellent menstrual-cycle research for many years] observes, which stand to make a great deal of money if every menstruating woman would take a few pills every month. Drug companies sponsor research conferences and "medical education" seminars on PMS, events, she says, "for which they actively and effectively seek media coverage." It is to the drug companies' interest, she adds, if physicians and the public confuse the small minority of women who have premenstrual or menstrual problems with the majority who have normal, undrugworthy menstrual cycles.

* * *

By 1987, PMS was enshrined as an official psychiatric disorder in the reference manual of the American Psychiatric Association, *The Diagnostic and*

Statistical Manual of Mental Disorders, where it is called Late Luteal Phase Dysphoric Disorder, or LLPDD. LLPDD is supposed to apply to premenstrual symptoms that are severe enough to "seriously interfere with work or with usual social activities or relationships with others." Even for women who have severe symptoms that are unrelated to existing emotional disorders, it is bizarre, and many researchers think detestable, to have such a diagnosis in a manual of *mental disorders.* If LLPDD is a medical condition, why is a psychiatric diagnosis necessary? Thyroid abnormalities cause mood and behavior changes, but we don't consider these physiologically based changes a psychiatric disorder. And if LLPDD reflects a psychological problem, such as depression, why is a medical diagnosis of "late luteal phase disphoric disorder" necessary? We might draw an analogy to a man who suffers from chronic anxiety. Several times a month, he plays racquetball, an exercise that raises his heartbeat and sets off an anxiety attack. The man's problem is anxiety, not racquetball; he does not have Post-Exercising Syndrome.

Because of the evidence of sloppy research and confusion over the prevalence, diversity, and nature of premenstrual changes, LLPDD was relegated to an appendix in the manual, in a section of diagnoses needing "further study." Nevertheless, there it sits, a convenient label for physicians and psychiatrists to use in diagnosing patients and in turn receiving insurance compensation.

In the early 1970s, Parlee published a major review of the research that had been done to date on the effects of the menstrual cycle. She put "PMS" in quotation marks, in order to denote it as an odd or unusual concept that "was purportedly scientific but was not supported by data." In a recent speech she described what happened:

> A copy editor took out all the quotation marks, and with them the meaning I wanted to establish. I lost—was silenced—then in my effort to shape in a small way the scientific discourse about PMS. The processes through which "PMS" has come to mean what it does today are too powerful, too internally and mutually self-sustaining, for that meaning to be affected by the results of good science. . . . People—women, researchers, the media, drug company representatives—now use the term PMS as if it had a clearly understood and shared mean-ing; the only question is how to help women who "have" it. Thus PMS has become real. The quotation marks have been removed.

Many institutions and individuals now benefit from the concept of PMS. Biomedical researchers, medical schools, and drug companies profit financially.

Gynecologists, many of whom have closed their obstetrical services because of malpractice insurance costs, have lost a traditional source of income and are turning to new patient groups and new diagnoses for replenishment. Many psychiatrists have shifted from conducting long-term psychotherapy to prescribing short-term (repeatable) drug treatments. Indeed, obstetricians and psychiatrists are already engaged in turf wars over who is best suited to diagnose and treat all those women with premenstrual symptoms.

But the success of PMS is not entirely a conspiracy of big institutions, although, as Parlee says, if PMS didn't exist as a "psychologically disturbing, socially disruptive, biologically caused disease" they would have needed to invent it. (They did.) We must also ask why so many women have responded so favorably to the term and use it so freely. Parlee suggests that "the language of 'PMS' is a means by which many women can have their experiences of psychological distress, or actions they do not understand, validated as 'real' and taken seriously." In that sense the language of PMS is empowering for women, she believes, because it gives a medical and social reality to experiences that were previously ignored, trivialized, or misunderstood.

Like all psychological diagnoses, then, PMS cuts two ways: It validates women, but it also stigmatizes them. Psychiatrist Leslie Hartley Gise directs a PMS program at Mt. Sinai Hospital in New York, yet she too is worried about the stigmatizing effects of making PMS a psychiatric diagnosis. "If even the rumor that Michael Dukakis had undergone treatment for depression could be held against him," Gise told an interviewer, "think of what a PMS diagnosis would mean for a woman seeking public office." We've come full circle. The ghost of Edgar Berman must be smiling.

OF MENSTRUATION AND MEN: THE STORY BEHIND THE HEADLINES

The research on the physiology and psychology of the menstrual cycle paints a very different picture from the popular impression that PMS is a proven, biomedical syndrome. It is clear that some physical changes normally occur: breast tenderness, water retention, and increased metabolism being the most common. The key word here is *normally*. It is normal for premenstrual women to have some aches and pains, to gain a few pounds (because of temporary water retention), or to crave food (because of increased metabolism). Leslie Gise puts it this way: "Although PMS is used for convenience, *premenstrual changes* is a more accurate term."

You might think, with all the studies trying to document the existence of a "widespread" biological disorder that so many women are "suffering" from, that researchers would have some idea of what causes it. Yet in spite of more than a decade of biomedical research, no biological marker has been found that distinguishes women who have severe premenstrual symptoms from those who do not. There is no support for theories suggesting that premenstrual symptoms are caused by abnormally high (or low) hormones, low magnesium, high sodium, abnormal thyroids, a deficiency of hormonelike substances called prostaglandins, steroid fluctuations, or the like.

Moreover, thus far, no drug or vitamin has been found to be effective. There is no evidence that vitamins help, and megadoses of B-6 supplements, which are commonly recommended, carry significant risks, such as causing nerve damage, for some individuals. In most of the double-blind treatment studies, in which neither the women nor her physician knows whether she is being given an active drug or a placebo, the placebo effect is as strong as the drug. Upward of 60 to 70 percent of the women who are given a placebo report improvement in their symptoms.

For many years, the treatment of choice for PMS was progesterone suppositories, in spite of a lack of clinical evidence demonstrating their effectiveness. Recently, however, Ellen Freeman and her colleagues, who conducted the largest and best-controlled study to date of the effects of progesterone, found that "progesterone suppositories have no clinically significant therapeutic effect greater than that of placebo for premenstrual symptoms." Progesterone did not improve individual symptoms or severity of symptoms in any way. If anything, symptoms remained *higher* in the women given progesterone than in those on the placebo!

So what is going on here? Up to the mid-1970s, researchers kept finding what they called the "classic" menstrual mood pattern: greater happiness and self-esteem during ovulation (mid-cycle), followed by depression, irritability and low self-esteem premenstrually. But as Mary Brown Parlee noticed back in 1973, the professional journals were not publishing negative results—that is, studies that were finding *no* premenstrual differences or mood variations over the menstrual cycle. In the last fifteen years, more of these disconfirming studies have been published, and many errors have been discovered in the earlier research. The new evidence finds that most of the so-called emotional and behavioral symptoms of Premenstrual Syndrome may not have much to do with menstruation, and in any case are not limited to women.

* * *

The Power of Expectations and Circumstances

The belief in PMS has, itself, a powerful influence on a woman's likelihood of noticing some symptoms and ignoring others at different times of the month. This is why even the day-by-day method of tracking symptoms has a problem: For some women, the strong belief that their moods change predictably over the menstrual cycle affects their actual experience of symptoms.

In one fascinating study, for example, two groups of women and a comparable group of men filled out daily inventories of their moods and physical symptoms. Half of the women were aware that menstrual-cycle changes were a focus of the study, and half were unaware. During the premenstrual phase of their cycles, the "aware" women reported a significantly higher level of negative moods and uncomfortable physical changes (such as headaches and muscle tension), and fewer positive feelings, than did either the "unaware" women or the men. The belief in PMS and the expectation of negative symptoms, apparently, influence a woman's likelihood of noticing some symptoms and ignoring others at different times. And it's a big likelihood. In this study, the "aware" women, premenstrually, reported a 76 percent increase in negative emotions (anxiety, depression, anger) and a whopping 193 percent increase in physical complaints. The "unaware" women did not.

Being aware of bodily changes or expecting them to occur can make us more sensitive to them; conversely, distracting influences can override them. This fact may explain why moods have less to do with a woman's time of the month than with her time of the week. Women's positive moods (and men's) peak on the weekends! If you want to predict when a woman will feel happiest, according to several studies, you do better to know when it's a Saturday or Sunday than when she is ovulating.

As this research suggests, the mood effects of the menstrual cycle often depend on whether a woman is paying more attention to her bodily changes or to her immediate situation. A friend of mine put it this way:

If, one day, I'm aware of feeling too easily annoyed by telephone interruptions, or if my threshold for bureaucratic stupidity plummets, I may suddenly realize that I'm "pre-menstrual." This mood can be easily overturned, though, if I do something I enjoy, like taking a hike or going to the movies. It just depends on whether I want to indulge my moods or break them.

The Male Comparison

One of the most misleading consequences of the popular focus on Premenstrual Syndrome is that it omits men as a comparison group. Yet if you give men those same checklists of symptoms (reduced or increased energy, irritability and other negative moods, back pain, sleeplessness, headaches, confusion, etc.), men report having as many "premenstrual symptoms" as women do—when the symptoms aren't called PMS. (You do have to omit the female-specific symptoms, such as breast tenderness.) If the identical checklist is titled "Menstrual Distress Questionnaire," however, men miraculously lose their headaches, food cravings, and insomnia.

When men are included as a comparison group in menstrual-cycle research, it turns out that their moods also change over the course of a month, just as much as women's moods do. Among men, as among women, individuals vary enormously in their moodiness, frequency of mood swings, and general levels of grumpiness. It's just that men can't blame their mood changes on a menstrual cycle, and their mood changes are more unpredictable and idiosyncratic.

Psychologist Jessica McFarlane and her associates, who conducted the "weekend happiness" study, observed mood fluctuations in women and men over a span of seventy days. Their findings reinforce all of the points I have been making here:

> . . . the women in this study did not actually experience the classic menstrual mood pattern but when they were asked to recall their moods, they reported that pattern. . . . [They] were relatively unaffected emotionally by menstrual hormonal fluctuations.
>
> . . . young women's moods fluctuated more over days of the week than across the menstrual cycle, and young men also experienced emotional fluctuations over days of the week. The women were not "moodier" than the men; their moods were not less stable within a day or from day-to-day. Evidence of weekday mood cycles in both sexes suggest that *treating emotional fluctuations as unhealthy symptoms, and assuming that only women usually manifest them, is misleading.* [My emphasis.]

* * *

I do not wish to replace the biological reductionism of women's behavior with a biological reductionism of men's behavior, but rather to highlight the different diagnoses that society favors and to raise some questions. Of course women are influenced by their bodies—by aches, pains, puffiness, water retention, and headaches—but so are men. Why, then, are women's mood changes a "syndrome," but men's mood changes just "normal ups and downs"? Why are women, but not men, considered "moody," and why are mood changes, which are normal, considered undesirable? Why are variations in testosterone not considered a medical and social problem, whereas variations in female hormones are a focus of national concern? Why is the *Wall Street Journal* unruffled about the cost to the economy of men's hormonal changes? Why is there no psychiatric diagnosis of "Excessive Testosterone Syndrome" or "Nonmenstrual Lability Disorder" that reduces male moodiness and antisocial behavior to their hormones?

Compare the following true cases. In Los Angeles in 1988, Sheryl Lynn Massip was accused of murdering her infant son by running over him with her car. Her defense was diminished responsibility resulting from postpartum depression. The jurors found her guilty, but the judge overruled their decision on the grounds that she was, in his legal terminology, "bonkers." Yet in Texas in 1988, Ronnie Shelton pleaded not guilty to twenty-eight counts of rape, on the grounds that he was a victim of "compulsive rape syndrome," due to his high testosterone levels. Shelton failed to convince his jurors, too, but his judge agreed with them.

Regardless of what you believe about the appropriateness of hormone defenses, the issue here is why so many people are more eager to blame women's behavior on their hormones than to blame men's behavior on theirs. Why do experts focus on the possible blip in the female crime rate one week out of the month, when that rate is so much lower than the number of men who have accidents and commit crimes all four weeks of the month? In this respect Harriet Goldhor Lerner puts the matter of women's hormones and behavior into the appropriate perspective:

> Let's face it. Do *you* stay off the streets at night because you fear attack from uncontrolled, irrational women in the throes of their Premenstrual Syndrome? Probably not. We stay home at night because we fear the behavior of men.

READING THE BODY:
THE PSYCHOLOGY OF SYMPTOMS

Many women are highly resistant to the evidence that their beliefs and expectations about PMS might be influencing their symptoms, or that their memories of symptoms might not be entirely accurate. It sounds as if psychologists are refusing to believe them, singing the old refrain that was so patronizing for so long: "It's all in your head." When I've talked to women about this research, many say, "Well, the research is plain wrong; I *know* my body changes and I *know* I become irritable," or "That research may apply to other women, but not to me."

Something is going on, therefore, between the evidence of the research and the private experience of the body. How might women (and men) begin to regard the normal symptoms of the menstrual cycle, without transmogrifying them into a problem or syndrome, yet recognizing their influence in daily life and emotional well-being?

Recall these puzzles of PMS. There is no special biological marker or abnormality that characterizes women who report having PMS from those who do not. The symptoms include contradictory conditions, such as irritability and euphoria, lack of energy and increased energy, and every sort of emotion. Some women feel "impelled" to yell at their husbands when they are premenstrual, but others feel equally impelled to bake bread. Both women and men have hormonal fluctuations and mood changes in the course of a month, but only women's moods are attributed to their hormones. And although women everywhere in the world experience similar physical symptoms along with menstruation (cramps, tender breasts, aches and pains), a World Health Organization survey of hundreds of women in each of ten nations found that "PMS" and its associated mood shifts are a Western phenomenon.

This collection of anomalous facts suggests that the changes associated with the menstrual cycle are "real," are felt physically, and that they provide a fuel for moods and feelings. But the *content* of those moods and wishes often depends on a woman's attitudes, expectations, situation, personal history, and immediate problems and concerns. To try another metaphor, hormone changes provide the clay; the mind and experience shape and mold it into a form. It's real clay, but it's only clay.

Symptoms are therefore not "all in the mind," but they aren't exactly "all in the body," either. No hormone could, by itself, account for yelling *and* bread-baking. But hormonal changes can make a woman feel edgy, bloated, and "not herself." They can create a feeling of fatigue and enervation. A woman then interprets these bodily changes in a particular way: as symptoms to be ignored, as signs of temporary insanity, as a sickness to be medicated, as an opportunity to tell her husband what she is afraid to say otherwise, as a liberating opportunity to write poetry. This is why the same physiological process expresses itself in so many different psychological forms.

In a series of studies, Randi Koeske has found that positive *and* negative emotions are often enhanced premenstrually and that it is the situation a woman is in, more than her hormones, that determines which emotions (if any) she feels. Her reactions also depend on how she explains her feelings. A woman who says to herself "water retention makes my tear ducts feel full" is going to feel different from one who regards the same physical sensation as evidence that "I am about to cry and must be depressed."

Sometimes women are aware of how their attitudes and expectations affect their experience of the menstrual cycle, as in the case of my friend who decides whether she wants to overrule her premenstrual symptoms or indulge them. But usually women are unaware of the combined and invisible impact of their unique package of physical histories, family attitudes, culture's views of menstruation, and individual experiences. They are usually unaware, for example, of the fact that they selectively notice certain physical signs or emotional states and ignore others. (So do men.) As one woman I spoke with said:

> If I feel irritable and then get my period a day or two later, I'll say, "Oh, it was just my period speaking, thank goodness. What a relief; it wasn't important." But if I feel irritable at other times, I don't usually put it down as just being in a bad mood; I try to figure out why.

For women and men, the long and varied process of learning how to interpret and respond to their bodily sensations results in a deeply held belief that "this is just the way I am; I can't help myself." This belief feels like, and is experienced as, a biological inevitability over which the person has no control. But a woman's reaction to menstruation is no different in kind from the man who says, "I can't help losing my temper; I was born angry." No, he wasn't. He was born with a physiological capacity for anger, with the adrenaline that fuels the fight-or-flight response; but he has learned, over a lifetime, what provocations warrant his anger, what he can get away with when he feels angry, and that the belief that he cannot control his temper will get him the results he wants.

* * *

All the talk about the biochemical origins of women's moods, therefore, overlooks the content of those moods. In her studies, Katharina Dalton was remarkably blind to the substance of the stories her interviewees told her. Many of these women spoke of feeling bored to tears by repetitive housework, drudgery, and unsupportive husbands—only premenstrually, of course. So maybe the real question is not why some women become irritable before menstruation, but why they aren't angry the rest of the month, and why they (and others) are so quick to dismiss their irritations as being mere symptoms of PMS. This trend deflects attention away from the real problems that a "PMS sufferer" might have: menstrual-cycle irregularities; chronic depression; or month-long grievances, such as family conflicts, low pay, long hours, or the housework blues. It also deflects attention away from the normal feelings of grumpiness, sadness, weariness, and other mood changes that both sexes can have any day of the month.

* * *

DOCTORING THE FAILED FEMALE

Ultimately, the belief that menstruation and menopause are problems for women is part of a larger assumption that female physiology itself is abnormal, deficient, and diseased. But this view is so pervasive, it is easy to forget that it is not the only one possible.

In fact, the idea that menstruation is a problem for women (and their families) is new to this century. For most of human history, from the ancient Greeks until the late eighteenth century, medical writers assumed that male and female bodies were structurally similar, and that there was nothing inherently pathological or debilitating about menstruation. (They held many misconceptions about the magical powers of menstrual blood, but that's another story.) For example, in seventeenth- and eighteenth-century America, when women were believed to be biologically similar to men, menstruation was considered a natural, unproblematic process.

In the nineteenth century, . . . a major transformation took place in the scientific and popular views of the female body. It was no longer seen as analogous to the male body, but as distinctly opposite, different. Menstruation became a symbol of that difference. Walter Heape, a zoologist at Cambridge University, wrote in his 1913 book *Sex Antagonism* that "the reproductive system is not only structurally but functionally fundamentally different in the Male and the Female; and since all other organs and systems of organs are affected by this system, it is certain that the Male and Female are essentially different throughout." Heape's description of menstruation, a "severe, devastating, periodic action," was, dare I say, hysterical. The menstrual flow, he wrote, leaves behind "a ragged wreck of tissue, torn glands, ruptured vessels, jagged edges of stroma, and masses of blood corpuscles, which it would seem hardly possible to heal satisfactorily without the aid of surgical treatment."

Today, Heape's descriptions seem as outdated as the old brain studies do, and it would surely surprise no one to learn that Heape was a militant anti-suffragist. Yet the legacy of this attitude survives. It is much toned down, to be sure, but no less influential, and just as much a part of the political and social culture in which it occurs.

The view of menstruation as a monthly wound from which women must recover, along with the view of its sister sickness, menopause, are subtly enshrined in our language as processes that involve weaknesses, losses, and debilities. In a dazzling analysis of the language that describes menstruation and menopause in medical textbooks, Emily Martin showed how physicians, anatomists, and the public have come to regard these processes. Menstruation is *failed* conception; menopause is *failed* reproductive functions.

Thus, textbooks describe the process of menstruation in terms of deprivation, deficiency, loss, shedding, and sloughing. The fall in hormones "deprives" the uterine wall of its "hormonal support," "constriction" of blood vessels leads to a "diminished" supply of oxygen and nutrients, and finally "disintegration starts, the entire lining begins to slough, and the menstrual flow begins." The imagery of menstruation that Martin found in textbook after textbook is one of "catastrophic disintegration: 'ceasing,' 'dying,' 'losing,' 'denuding,' and 'expelling.' "

* * *

Martin then casts her observant eye on the way textbooks describe sperm production and ejaculation. She finds not a whisper of information that the ejaculate is composed of shedded cells or any discussion of the processes of deterioration and renewal in the male reproductive system. Instead, there is much celebration of the "remarkable" male reproductive physiology. As one textbook author described it, "Perhaps the most amazing characteristic of spermatogenesis is its sheer magnitude: the normal human male may manufacture several hundred million sperm per day." This gee-whiz, ain't-it-remarkable tone is absent from descriptions of female reproduction. "Although this text sees such massive sperm production as unabashedly positive," Martin observes, "in fact, only about one out of every 100 billion sperm ever makes it to fertilize an egg: from the very same point of view that sees menstruation as a waste product, surely here is something really worth crying about!"

* * *

If the female reproductive process were regarded as the norm (or at least as being normal) in this society, our ways of thinking about and treating the female body would be entirely different. Consider just a few changes that would occur:

Women and men would regard changes in moods, efficiency, and good humor as expected and normal variations, not as abnormal deviations from the (impossible) male ideal of steadiness and implacability. Why must women defend themselves from the charge of having mood changes, anyway? Mood changes are perfectly normal. Everyone has them. Even men.

We would, by understanding the interplay of mind and body, be better able to distinguish emotions that signify something important (such as a family conflict that should be dealt with) from those that are momentary blips on the screen of life. We would travel a clearer path between reducing important problems to biological imperatives ("I'm not mad at you for stealing my inheritance, dear; it's just my PMS speaking") and inflating mild biological changes into serious problems ("I feel puffy and ugly; I want a divorce").

We would regard the changes of menstruation and menopause as normal, not as failures, losses, deficiencies, and weaknesses. Some bodily status or transitions (for both sexes) may not be comfortable one hundred percent of the time, but, under normal circumstances, the best remedies are patience, a moderate diet, exercise, and good humor. Morning sickness, menstrual cramps, and hot flashes are hormonal; they will pass.

We would not confuse normal physical changes with symptoms of a disorder or a disease. We can protest the mindless application of the term "PMS" and speak instead of the variety of premenstrual changes in women *and* of hormonal changes in men. The same applies to menopause; we can try to nip in the bud the forthcoming onslaught of diagnoses that will try to turn this healthy, beneficial, and to most women liberating change into an estrogen-deficiency disease. We can also learn how to live with the normal hormonal effects of menopause without regarding them as major psychological disorders. As one friend of mine, a teacher who is going through menopause, says:

> Occasionally, I'll have a very uncomfortable hot flash when my whole body feels feverish. I no longer try to pretend it isn't happening. I just say to the class: "OK, everybody, this is what a person having a hot flash looks like. Take five while I get a drink of water and mop my brow." Then we all carry on.

We would regard surgical procedures and drugs as treatments of last resort, when medically necessary to save a woman's life or when, on balance, they will significantly improve the quality of a woman's life. We would not resort to them casually, to "cure" normal female processes. Instead, we would regard menstruation and menopause as processes of renewal and change, processes that do not need to be conquered, cured, or altered.

Most of all, we would recognize that if hormones affect one sex, they also affect the other. The current embrace of hormonal diagnoses of women's behavior feeds the belief that women aren't really responsible for their actions—not in the way men are, anyway. Hormones affect behavior, but we must think carefully and critically about whose hormones, and which behaviors, are legitimate legal defenses, let alone personal excuses to use around the house.

I believe that women long to achieve legitimacy for the unique experiences of the normal female body, and that they embrace the biomedical language of PMS and Estrogen Deficiency Disease as a way of getting there. But trusting to a language that proclaims these experiences deficient and diseased is not the solution. The price, for women's psychological well-being and for their status in society, is too great.

QUESTIONS

1. How does the category "Premenstrual Syndrome" depict normal female bodily changes as a disease in need of treatment?

2. How can the PMS label be validating to women?

3. Which institutions and individuals benefit from the PMS category? How so specifically?

4. In what ways can a woman's expectations that she will experience PMS powerfully influence which of her moods and behaviors she does—and does not—pay attention to over the course of her menstrual cycle?

5. How does the prevalent belief that PMS is a biological condition unique to women mask medical evidence indicating that men's and women's moods and behaviors are more similar than distinct?

Black and Undeserving: Exposing Myths about America's Poor

FROM *Race and Poverty in America: Public Misperceptions and the American News Media*

MARTIN GILENS

In this selection, Martin Gilens challenges readers to confront a set of powerful misconceptions about America's poor. He identifies two prevalent and intertwined public misconceptions about the poor. The first is that the majority of poor people are black, and the second is that the majority are working age, able-bodied, and hence undeserving of government support. Gilens shows that these misconceptions are reflected by public opinion surveys and reproduced by news reporting. He discusses a variety of explanations for why media constructions misrepresent the realities of America's poor.

INTRODUCTION

> *The only feeling that anyone can have about an event he does not experience is the feeling aroused by his mental image of that event. That is why until we know what others think they know, we cannot truly understand their acts. ([Walter] Lippman [1922])*

As Walter Lippmann argued 70 years ago, our opinions and behavior are responses not to the world itself but to our perceptions of that world. It is the "pictures in our heads" that shape our feelings and actions, and these pictures only imperfectly reflect the world that surrounds us. Just as important, our experience of the world is largely indirect. "Our opinions," Lippmann wrote, "cover a bigger space, a longer reach of time, a greater number of things, than we can directly observe. They have, therefore, to be pieced together out of what others have reported." Already in Lippmann's time, and even more so in our own, "reports around the world" come primarily through the mass media.

To understand the roots of American public opinion, we need to understand Americans' perceptions of the social and political world they inhabit and the role of the media in shaping those perceptions. Survey data show that public perceptions of poverty are erroneous in at least one crucial respect: Americans substantially exaggerate the degree to which blacks compose the poor. Furthermore, white Americans with the most exaggerated misunderstandings of the racial composition of the poor are the most likely to oppose welfare.

This study investigates the portrayal of poverty in the national news, compares these images with the reality of poverty in America, and offers some preliminary evidence that media coverage of poverty shapes public perceptions—and misperceptions—of the poor. Examining weekly news-magazines and, to a lesser extent, network television news shows, I find that news media distortions coincide with public misperceptions about race and poverty and that both are biased in ways that reflect negatively on the poor in general and on poor African Americans in particular.

I argue in this article that the correspondence of public misunderstandings and media misrepresentations of poverty reflects the influence of each upon the other. On the one hand, the media are subject to many of the same biases and misperceptions that afflict American society at large and therefore reproduce those biases in their portrayals of American social conditions. On the other hand, Americans rely heavily on the mass media for information about the society in which they live, and the media shape Americans' social perceptions and political attitudes in important ways. Media distortions of social conditions are therefore likely to result in public misperceptions that reinforce existing biases and stereotypes.

Public Perceptions of Race and Poverty

African Americans account for 29 percent of America's poor (U.S. Bureau of the Census 1990). But recent national surveys show that the public substantially overestimates the percentage of blacks among the poor. When one survey asked, "What percent of all the poor people in this country would you say are black?" the median response was 50 percent. Another survey simply asked, "Of all the people who are poor in this country, are more of them black or are more of them white?" Fifty-five percent of the respondents chose black compared to 24 percent who chose white, with 31 percent volunteering "about equal."

The public's exaggerated association of race and poverty not only reflects and perpetuates negative racial stereotypes but it also increases white Americans' opposition to welfare. Whites who think the poor are mostly black are more likely to blame welfare recipients for their situation and less likely to support welfare than are those with more accurate perceptions of poverty. In one national survey, 46 percent of the white respondents who thought African Americans make up more than half of the poor wanted to cut welfare spending. In contrast, only 26 percent of those who thought blacks compose less than one-quarter of the poor wanted welfare spending cut.

Americans' views on poverty and welfare are colored by the belief that economic opportunity is widespread and that anyone who tries hard enough can succeed. For example, 70 percent of respondents to one survey agreed that "America is the land of opportunity where everyone who works hard can get ahead." For those who perceive abundant opportunities, poverty itself is presumptive evidence of personal failure. Thus Americans' exaggerated association of race and poverty perpetuates longstanding stereotypes of African Americans as poor and lazy. When social scientists began studying stereotypes in the early twentieth century, they found a widespread belief that blacks are lazy, and this stereotype does not appear to have faded much over the years. In 1990, the General Social Survey asked respondents to place blacks as a group on a 7-point scale with "lazy" at one end and "hard working" at the other. Forty-seven percent of whites placed blacks on the "lazy" side of the scale; only 17 percent chose the "hard working" side.

Negative stereotypes of African Americans as lazy and misperceptions of the poor as predominantly black reinforce each other. If poverty is a black problem, many whites reason, then blacks must not be trying hard enough. And if blacks are lazy in comparison with other Americans, and economic opportunities are plentiful, then it stands to reason that poverty would be a predominantly black problem. In sum, the public rather dramatically misunderstands the racial composition of America's poor, with consequences harmful to both poor people and African Americans.

* * *

DATA AND METHODS

The primary data for this study consist of every story on poverty and related topics appearing between January 1, 1988, and December 31, 1992, in the three leading American newsmagazines, *Time, Newsweek,* and *U.S. News and World Report.* The *Reader's Guide to Periodical Literature* was used to identify stories related to poverty and the poor. In each year the "core categories" of *poor, poverty,* and *public welfare* were examined. . . .

* * *

In addition to newsmagazines, coverage of poverty by network television news was also examined. Stories on poverty and related topics were identified using the *Television News Index and Abstracts,* published by Vanderbilt University. During the 5-year time frame for this study, the three weeknight network television news shows broadcast 534 stories on poverty and related topics, the equivalent of about one story every week and a half per network. Although the differences among networks were not great, ABC broadcast the largest number of poverty stories (207), followed by NBC (173) and CBS (154). Of these 534 stories, 50 stories were randomly chosen for analysis. These 50 stories contained pictures of 1,353 poor people.

* * *

FINDINGS

During the 5-year period examined, *Newsweek* published 82 stories on poverty and related topics, an average of about one story every 3 weeks (table 1). Fewer stories on poverty were found in the other two magazines, with *U.S. News and World Report* publishing 56 poverty stories over this period and *Time* only 44. Overall, African Americans made up 62 percent of the poor people pictured in these stories, over twice their true proportion of 29 percent. . . .

A reader of these newsmagazines is likely to develop the impression that America's poor are predominantly black.[1] This distorted portrait of the American poor cannot help but reinforce negative stereotypes of blacks as mired in poverty and contribute to the belief that poverty is primarily a "black problem." Yet as problematic as this overall racial misrepresentation of the poor is, we shall see

---

[1] For the next stage of this research, the percentage black among the magazine poor has been coded for the period 1950–94. Since 1965, when these magazines began to include large numbers of African Americans in their pictures of the poor, the percent black has averaged 54 percent. Thus it appears that for the period under study in this article—1988–92—the magazine poor are somewhat "more black" than average for the past 3 decades. In future analyses I will attempt to account for variation over time in the racial complexion of poverty in the news media.

TABLE 1. Stories on Poverty in U.S. Newsmagazines, 1988–92

	Number of Stories	Number of Pictures	Number of Poor People Pictured[a]	Percent African American[b]
Time	44	36	86	65
Newsweek	82	103	294	66
U.S. News and World Report	56	67	180	53
Total	182	206	560	62

[a]Excludes 75 people for whom race could not be determined.
[b]Difference in percentage African American across the three magazines is significant at $p < .02$.

that the portrayal of poor African Americans differs from the portrayal of the nonblack poor in ways that further stigmatize blacks.

Age Distribution of the "Magazine Poor"

The public is more sympathetic toward some age-groups of poor people than others. Working-age adults are expected to support themselves, and poverty among this group is viewed by many Americans as indicating a lack of discipline or effort. Children and the elderly are, to a large extent, not held to blame for their poverty, and these groups are looked upon much more favorably for government assistance. In one survey, for example, respondents gave the disabled elderly the highest priority for government financial assistance, followed by the poor elderly and poor children. Respondents were much less sympathetic toward the working-age poor, who were given the lowest priority for government help of the six groups examined. Yet as the authors of this study point out, sympathy toward poor children is often not translated into support for government aid when providing that aid means helping their working-age parents. In terms of public policy, therefore, the elderly are the only unambiguously privileged age-group among the poor.

Given the public's greater willingness to help the elderly poor, and to a lesser degree poor children, public perceptions of the age distribution of the poor are likely to have an impact on overall levels of support for government antipoverty efforts. Although dramatically off base in terms of the racial composition of the poor, newsmagazine portrayals of poverty are fairly accurate in showing large numbers of children among the poor. Forty-three percent of the poor people pictured were coded as under 18 years old, compared with the true figure of 40 percent of America's poor (table 2). And newsmagazines

TABLE 2.   Age Distribution of the American Poor and Age
Distribution of the "Magazine Poor," by Race (Percent)

	Total[a]	African American	Non-African American
True poor:			.
Under 18 years old	40	47	37
18–64 years old	49	45	51
Over 64 years old	11	8	12
Magazine poor:			
Under 18 years old	43	52*	35
18–64 years old	55**	48	60***
Over 64 years old	2***	1***	5***
Number of magazine poor	635	345	215

SOURCE.—U.S. Bureau of the Census 1990.
NOTE.—Significance levels indicate differences between magazine portrayals and census figures for
each category. Percentages may not add to 100 percent due to rounding error.
[a]Includes 75 people for whom race could not be determined.
*$p < .05$.
**$p < .01$.
***$p < .001$.

are also accurate in showing a somewhat larger number of children among
the black poor than among the nonblack poor. The census bureau reports
that 47 percent of poor African Americans are under 18, while newsmagazines
show 52 percent. Similarly, children make up 37 percent of the nonblack
poor, while newsmagazines show 35 percent.

With regard to the elderly, however, the magazine poor and the true poor
differ substantially. In reality, those over 64 years old account for 11 percent
of all poor people, but they are scarcely to be found at all in magazine poverty
stories (table 2). If newsmagazine pictures reflected the true nature of American
poverty, we would expect to find about 70 elderly people among the 635
poor people pictured; instead we find a mere 13 (2 percent). (In coding the
age of the magazine poor, a very lax criterion was applied, so that any poor
person who could at all plausibly be thought to be over 64 years old was so
coded.)

The most sympathetic age-group of poor people—the elderly—while a
small proportion of the true poor, are virtually invisible among the magazine
poor. Furthermore, of the 13 elderly poor shown over the 5-year period under
study, 10 are white and only two are black (the race of one person could not
be determined). According to census data, those over 64 constitute 12 per-

cent of the nonblack poor and 8 percent of poor African Americans (table 2); but in newsmagazines, the elderly represent only 5 percent of poor nonblacks and a scant six-tenths of 1 percent of the black poor. Thus, the most sympathetic age category for the poor is both underrepresented in general and reserved almost exclusively for nonblacks.

Work Status of the "Magazine Poor"

For centuries, Americans have distinguished between the "deserving poor," who are trying to make it on their own, and the "undeserving poor," who are lazy, shiftless, or drunken and prefer to live off the generosity of others. More remarkable than the tenacity of this distinction is the tendency to place a majority of the poor in the "undeserving" category. In one study, for example, 57 percent of the respondents agreed that "most poor people these days would rather take assistance from the government than make it on their own through hard work." While the true preferences of the poor are hard to measure, the fact is that 51 percent of the working-age poor (and 62 percent of poor working-age men) are employed at least part-time (table 3).

The magazine poor are much less likely to be employed than their real-world counterparts. Overall, only 15 percent of the working-age magazine poor hold a paying job (table 3). If we add in all those described as looking for work, or participating in some kind of vocational training program, or even just collecting bottles and cans, the number only increases to 21 percent. Thus the clearest indication of "deservingness"—preparing for or engaging in some form of employment—is rare indeed among the magazine poor. Whatever public sympathy might accompany the perception that the poor are trying to work their way out of poverty is unlikely to emerge from these newsmagazines.

Just as newsmagazines' underrepresentation of the elderly poor is greater for African Americans than for others, so is their underrepresentation of the working poor. In reality, poor African Americans are somewhat less likely to be employed than non-African Ameri-cans, but the difference is modest: 42 percent of poor African Americans work compared with 54 percent of the non-African American poor (table 3). But among the magazine poor, this difference is much greater. While 27 percent of the nonblack poor are shown as working, only 12 percent of the African American poor are portrayed as workers. Thus the true proportion of poor nonblacks who work is twice as high in real life as it is in these newsmagazines (54 percent vs. 27 percent), while the true proportion working among the black poor is three and one-half times that

TABLE 3. Work Status of the Working-Age American Poor and Work Status of the Working-Age "Magazine Poor," by Race (Percent)

	Total[a]	African American	Non-African American
True poor:			
Working	51	42	54
Not working	49	58	46
Magazine poor:			
Working	15***	12***	27***
Not working	85***	88***	73***
Number of working-age magazine poor	351	165	129

SOURCE.—U.S. Bureau of the Census 1990.
NOTE.—Significance levels indicate differences between magazine portrayals and census figures for each category. Working age includes those 18–64 years old.
[a]Includes 57 working-age poor for whom race could not be determined.
***$p < .001$.

shown in *Time, Newsweek,* and *U.S. News and World Report* (42 percent vs. 12 percent). Once again, the misleadingly negative portrait of the poor presented in these news stories is even more misleading and more negative for poor African Americans.

* * *

Race and Poverty in Television News Stories

The three newsmagazines examined here have a combined circulation of over 10 million copies, and 20 percent of American adults claim to be regular readers of "news magazines such as *Time, U.S. News and World Report,* or *Newsweek.*" In addition, these magazines influence how other journalists see the world. In one study, for example, magazine and newspaper journalists were asked what news sources they read most regularly. Among these journalists, *Time* and *Newsweek* were the first and second most frequently cited news sources, far more popular than the *New York Times,* the *Wall Street Journal,* or the *Washington Post.*

Despite the broad reach of these weekly magazines and their role as "background material" for other journalists, there can be little doubt that television is the dominate news source for most Americans. In recent surveys, about 70 percent of the American public identifies television as the source of "most of your news about what's going on in the world today." If TV news coverage of poverty were to differ substantially from that found in newsmagazines, the implications of this study would be severely limited.

Unfortunately, it is difficult to analyze television news in the way that news-magazine coverage of poverty was analyzed here because television news typically provides far less information about the individuals pictured in poverty stories than do newsmagazines. The analysis of television news is therefore limited to the race of the poor people used to illustrate stories on poverty.

During the 5-year period of this study (1988–92), weeknight news shows on ABC, NBC, and CBS broadcast 534 stories on poverty and related topics, of which 50 stories were randomly selected for analysis. Of the 1,100 race-codable poor people in these stories, 65.2 percent were black—a slightly higher figure than the 62 percent black found in newsmagazine stories on poverty. Clearly, then, the overrepresentation of African Americans found in weekly newsmagazines is not unique to this particular medium but is shared by the even more important medium of network television news.

DO MEDIA PORTRAYALS OF POVERTY INFLUENCE PUBLIC PERCEPTIONS?

Although we lack the data to demonstrate directly the impact of media portrayals of poverty on public perceptions, a variety of evidence suggests that such portrayals are likely to be important influences. First, both experimental and nonexperimental studies have demonstrated the power of the media to shape public perceptions and political preferences. Media content can affect the importance viewers attach to different political issues, the standards that they employ in making political evaluations, the causes they attribute to national problems, and their issue positions and perceptions of political candidates.

None of these studies focused on the visual aspect of media content. Other evidence suggests, however, that visual elements of the news—including the race of the people pictured—are highly salient to viewers. . . . [A] study aptly titled "Seeing Is Remembering" found that people were more likely to remember what they saw in a television news story than what they heard. With regard to viewers' use of race as a visual cue, . . . subjects [were presented] with television news stories about unemployment in which the unemployed individual pictured was either black or white. Following the unemployment story (which was included as part of a larger compilation of news stories), subjects were asked to name the three most important problems facing the nation. Of those white viewers who were randomly assigned the story about an unemployed white person, 71 percent said that unemployment was among the three most important national problems. Of those whites who saw a story about an unemployed African American, however, only 53 percent felt that unemployment was a pressing national concern.

Thus past research has shown that the mass media can exert a powerful influence on public perceptions and attitudes, that news pictures convey important information that viewers are comparatively likely to remember, and that the race of people pictured in news stories is a salient aspect of the story for many viewers. While past studies have focused largely on television news, there is no reason to think that the impact of pictures, or the salience of the race of those pictured, would be any less in newsmagazines.

* * *

EXPLAINING NEWS MEDIA MISREPRESENTATIONS

Studies of the news process suggest a number of factors that might help to account for distortions in the news media's coverage of poverty. In his classic study of newsmagazines and network television news [*Deciding What's News*], Herbert Gans identified "availability" and "suitability" as the most significant determinants of news content. By availability, Gans referred to the accessibility of potential news to a journalist facing a variety of logistical constraints and time pressures, while suitability concerns a story's importance and interest to the audience and its fit within the framework of the news medium (whether newspaper, magazine, or television news).

Gans argued that availability is a product of both the news organization and the social world in which it operates. For example, the location of news bureaus in large cities lends an urban slant to the national news, while economically and politically powerful individuals and organizations use their resources to make themselves more easily available to journalists. Thus news "availability" reflects the social structure that exists outside of news organizations as well as decisions made within those organizations.

With regard to the pictorial representation of poverty, the availability of different subgroups of the poor may shape the images captured by news photographers. Because news bureaus and the photographers they employ tend to be found in and around large cities, it should not be surprising that the poverty images produced by these organizations are dominated by the urban poor. And if African Americans make up a larger share of the urban poor than of the country's poor in general, then the "availability" of poor blacks to news photographers might explain their overrepresentation in magazine and television news.

This "geographic" explanation for the overrepresentation of blacks in poverty news sounds plausible, but census data show that it is clearly wrong, at least in this form. Within the nation's 10 largest metropolitan areas, blacks constitute 32.1 percent of the poverty population, only marginally higher than the 29 percent of all poor Americans who are black. Thus the poverty population that urban-based photographers have ready access to does not differ substantially in its racial composition from the American poor as a whole.

Another version of the "geographic" explanation may hold more promise in accounting for the overrepresentation of blacks in newsmagazine pictures of poverty. When an urban-based photographer receives an assignment for pictures of poor people, he or she is likely to look in those neighborhoods in which poor people are most concentrated. It is simply more efficient to look for poor people in neighborhoods with high poverty rates than to seek out the relatively few poor people in more economically heterogenous neighborhoods.

To the extent that photographers look for poor people in poor neighborhoods, the racial mix of their photographs will reflect not the racial composition of poverty in the entire metropolitan area but the composition of poverty in poor neighborhoods within the metropolitan area. Because poor blacks are more geographically concentrated than poor whites, neighborhoods with high poverty rates are likely to be more disproportionately black than the percentage of blacks among the poverty population as a whole would suggest. In other words, poor whites tend to be "spread around" in both poor and nonpoor neighborhoods, while poor African Americans tend to live in neighborhoods with high poverty rates.

To gauge the extent to which the geographic concentration of African American poverty might lead to the misrepresentation of the poor in newsmagazines, I again examined the 10 largest metropolitan areas, this time looking at the racial composition of only those poor people living in poor neighborhoods. . . . "[p]overty areas" [are] census tracts in which at least 20 percent of the population are poor. Using this criterion, about half (50.9 percent) of the poor people in these 10 cities live in "poverty areas," and blacks constitute 46.5 percent of the poor people living in these neighborhoods—substantially higher than the overall proportion of 29 percent, yet still far below the proportion of blacks among portrayals of the poor in newsmagazines and on television news shows. But if photographers were even more selective in the neighborhoods they chose, they would encounter poverty populations with even higher percentages of African Americans. For example, in . . . "high poverty areas" (census tracts with at least a 30 percent poverty rate), blacks comprise 53.2 percent of the poor in these 10 cities. And if photographers were to visit only "extreme poverty areas" (with poverty rates of at least 40 percent), they would find that 60.7 percent of the poor are black.

In the 10 largest metropolitan areas as a whole, then, just over 30 percent of poor people are black, but in the very poorest neighborhoods of these 10 large cities, blacks comprise over 60 percent of the poor. For photographers working under deadline, the easier availability of poor African Americans might skew the images of poverty that appear in the national news. Although Gans focused on the forces that shape the substantive text of the news, the production of news pictures follows the same logic. Social structures outside of the newsroom influence the availability of news content. Because poor blacks are disproportionately available to news photographers, they may be disproportionately represented in the resulting news product.

But the disproportionate availability of poor African Americans cannot explain all of the racial distortions in media images of poverty. First, only the very poorest neighborhoods come close to the extremely large proportions of poor blacks found in news stories on poverty. And by focusing exclusively on these neighborhoods, photographers would have to ignore the vast majority of urban poor, not to mention the millions of poor people living in smaller cities or rural areas. . . . [O]nly 8.9 percent of all poor people live in "extreme poverty areas" as defined above, and as we saw, once the definition of poverty areas is broadened to include a larger percentage of the poor, the proportion of blacks declines significantly.

Furthermore, the residential concentration of black poverty can at best explain the racial mix of photographs that a newsmagazine photo editor has available to choose from. Because a photo editor typically has a vastly larger number of pictures available than will be used for publication, the racial composition of the photographs that ultimately appear in the magazine will reflect the selection criteria of the photo editor. A photographer will typically produce anywhere from 400 to 4,000 photographs for a single newsmagazine story. Thus even if photographers submit, on average, three pictures of poor African Americans for every two pictures of poor whites, magazine photo editors have the ability to determine the racial mix of the few pictures that find their way into print.

The third and perhaps most important limitation of accessibility as an explanation for media portrayals of the poor is that racial distortions are not limited to the overall proportion of African Americans in news stories on poverty. As we saw above, there also exists a pattern of racial misrepresentation, such that blacks are especially overrepresented among the least sympathetic groups of the poor and comparatively underrepresented among the most sympathetic poverty groups. Such a consistent pattern cannot be explained by the differential accessibility of the black and nonblack poor and suggests instead that judgments of "suitability," rather than (or in addition to) accessibility, shape the pictorial representation of poverty in the national news.

Judgments of suitability enter into both the selection of news stories and the content of those stories (and of the pictures used to illustrate them). Perhaps the most fundamental aspect of suitability with regard to story content concerns the veracity of the news story. "Accuracy" and "objectivity" remain primary goals among news professionals, yet as Gans argued, journalists cannot exercise news judgments concerning story accuracy and objectivity without drawing upon their own set of "reality judgments." Such judgments constitute the background understanding of society upon which a news story is built, and journalists' efforts to accurately portray the subject matter of their stories depend not only upon the specific information newly gathered for a particular story but also upon this background understanding. While journalists' understandings of society derive in part from their professional work, they inevitably share as well the popular understandings—and misunderstandings—held by the larger society in which they live.

Most photo editors are as concerned with providing an accurate impression of their subject matter as are the writers they work with. In interviews I conducted with photo editors at *Time, Newsweek,* and *U.S. News and World Report,* most expressed a concern that their selection of photographs should faithfully reflect the subject of the story and, in particular, that the photographs of poor people should provide a fair portrayal of the demographics of poverty in the United States.

Given the professed concern for accuracy of the photo editors I talked with, it is important to know whether these news professionals subscribe to the same stereotypes of the poor as the rest of the American public. If photo editors believe that most poor Americans are black, then their choice of pictures may simply reflect the world as they believe it truly is. To assess whether newsmagazine photo editors share the public's stereotypes of the poor, I asked each of the editors I contacted the same question that the public was asked in the 1991 National Race and Politics Study: What percent of all the poor people in this country would you say are black? As a group, these photo editors did share the public's misperceptions regarding the racial composition of the poor, but not to the same degree. On average, the photo editors estimated that 42 percent of America's poor people are black, somewhat less than the public's estimate of 50 percent but still a good deal higher than the true figure of 29 percent.

Some part of the misrepresentation of poverty found in weekly news-magazines may be attributable to the misperceptions of the photo editors responsible for selecting the pictures. However, a substantial gap still remains between the editors' perception that 42 percent of the American poor are black and the pictures of poor people that appear in their magazines, consisting of 62 percent blacks.

One possible explanation for this remaining discrepancy is that in responding to my explicit query about the racial composition of the poor, these photo editors provided a "reasoned judgment"—a judgment that may differ from the seat-of-the-pants intuition that in fact guides their selection of photographs. That is, given the opportunity to reflect upon the question, these editors conjecture that most poor Americans are nonblack, but in the everyday process of choosing news photographs, the unexamined, subconscious impressions guiding their ideas of "what the poor should look like" reflect a sense that blacks compose a majority of America's poor.

Social psychologists have demonstrated that even people who explicitly reject specific stereotypes often use those same stereotypes subconsciously in evaluating members of the relevant social group. Similarly, photo editors who consciously reject the stereotype of the poor as black may nevertheless subconsciously employ just that stereotype in selecting pictures to illustrate American poverty.

Alternatively, photo editors may be aware that popular perceptions of the poor as largely black are misguided, but may choose to "indulge" these misperceptions in order to present to readers a more readily recognized image of poverty. That is, if an editor wants a picture that is easily identified as a poor person, and believes that readers strongly associate poverty with blacks, he or she may feel that a picture of a poor African American would be more easily recognized as a poor person than a picture of a poor white. (This need not be a conscious process. An editor might sense that one picture is more easily recognized as a poor person than another without being aware of the importance of race in generating that recognition.)

The possibility that photo editors hold unconscious stereotypes, or that editors (consciously or unconsciously) indulge what they perceive to be the public's stereotypes, necessarily remains speculative. Yet it is clear that the other explanations for distortions in the portrayal of poverty cannot fully account for the very high proportions of blacks in news stories about the poor. More important, it is the pattern of racial misrepresentation that most clearly signals the impact of negative racial stereotypes on the portrayal of poverty. The absence of blacks among pictures of the working poor, the elderly poor, and poor people in employment programs; the abundance of blacks among pictures of unemployed working-age adults; and the association of blacks with the least favorable poverty topics indicate the operation of a consistent prejudice against poor African Americans. As one photo editor I talked with acknowledged, it appears that only some kind of "subtle racism" can explain the racial patterning of poverty in American newsmagazines.

SUMMARY AND CONCLUSIONS

If 560 people were selected at random from America's poor, we would expect 162 to be black. But of the 560 poor people of determinable race pictured in newsmagazines between 1988 and 1992, 345 were African American. In reality, two out of three poor Americans are nonblack, but the reader of these magazines would likely come to exactly the opposite conclusion.

Although the newsmagazines examined grossly overrepresent African Americans in their pictures of poor people as a whole, African Americans are seldom found in pictures of the most sympathetic subgroups of the poor. I found that the elderly constitute less than 1 percent of the black poor shown in these magazines (compared with 5 percent of the nonblack poor) and the working poor make up only 12 percent of poor blacks (compared with 27 percent of poor nonblacks).

I also found that stories dealing with aspects of antipoverty policy that are most strongly supported by the public are less likely to contain pictures of African Americans. Although 62 percent of all poor people pictured, African Americans make up only 40 percent of the poor in stories on employment programs and only 17 percent in stories on Medicaid. In contrast, we find far too many African Americans in stories on the least favorable subgroup of the poor: the underclass. Every one of the 36 poor people pictured in stories on the underclass was black.

A number of explanations for the racial misrepresentation of poverty were considered in this article. First, the greater geographic concentration of poor blacks in comparison with poor whites might lead photographers to overrepresent African Americans in their pictures of poor people. Second, photo editors' own misperceptions of the racial composition of American poverty can explain some of the overrepresentation of blacks among published photographs of the poor. But since neither of these factors can fully account for the dramatic distortions of the racial composition of the poor, two additional possibilities were considered. First, editors' conscious or unconscious indulgence of what they perceive to be the public's stereotypes could explain distortions in the portrayal of poverty. Alternatively, editors' own unconscious stereotypes concerning the nature of poverty in America could be at work. Although considerations of unconscious stereotypes must be somewhat speculative, the consistent pattern of racial misrepresentation (along with the consistently liberal nature of these editors' conscious beliefs about racial inequality) strongly suggests that unconscious negative images of blacks are at work.

Perhaps the most disheartening aspect of the situation is that apparently well-meaning, racially liberal news professionals generate images of the social world that consistently misrepresent both black Americans and poor people in destructive ways. Whether these distortions stem from residential patterns, conscious efforts to reflect the public's existing stereotypical expectations, or editors' own unconscious stereotypes, these racial misrepresentations reinforce the public's exaggerated association of blacks with poverty.

Whatever the processes that result in distorted images of poverty, the political consequences of these misrepresentations are clear. First, the poverty population shown in newsmagazines—primarily black, overwhelmingly unemployed, and almost completely nonelderly—is not likely to generate a great deal of support for government antipoverty programs among white Americans. Furthermore, public support for efforts to redress racial inequality is likely to be diminished by the portrait of poverty found in these newsmagazines. Not only do African Americans as a whole suffer from the exaggerated association of race and poverty but poor African Americans (who are often the intended beneficiaries of race-targeted policies) are portrayed in a particularly negative light.

A more accurate portrayal of poverty would still, of course, include a large number of blacks. But rather than portraying poverty as a predominantly black problem, a true reflection of social conditions would show the poverty population to be primarily nonblack. The danger, perhaps, is that a more accurate understanding of current conditions might lead some to feel the problem of racial inequality is less pressing. But current misunderstandings may pose a greater danger: that whites will continue to harbor negative stereotypes of blacks as mired in poverty and unwilling to make the effort needed to work their way out. By implicitly identifying poverty with race, the news media perpetuate stereotypes that work against the interests of both poor people and African Americans.

* * *

QUESTIONS

1. What data does Gilens present to show that the news media frame poverty as primarily a black problem?
2. What data does Gilens present illustrating that the news media frame the poor as largely undeserving of government support?
3. What are the policy consequences of these misrepresented poverty frames?
4. Why do the news media misrepresent America's poor?
5. What are the realities about poor people in the United States that this reading substantiates?

Treating Social Problems
as Emergencies

FROM *When Social Problems Are Treated as Emergencies*

MICHAEL LIPSKY AND STEVEN RATHGEB SMITH

What is an emergency? Since this word is used all the time, its meaning is often taken for granted. In this selection, the authors touch on a variety of issues—including homelessness, hunger, and violence against women—in order to illustrate how claimsmakers frame social problems as emergencies and the implications this framing has for policymaking. The authors highlight the political and popular reasons why the emergency frame carries so much influence, as well as how it can divert attention from important alternative ways of framing problems.

* * *

There are many reasons why public officials might favor treating recent social problems as emergencies, including the straightforward desire to put helpful programs in place quickly. But the long-run consequences are not so straightforward. They include at least temporarily deflecting attention from more deeply probing solutions, substantially surrendering control over admission to client rolls, and a degree of inequity in policy delivery.

The two major social welfare problems that have captured public attention in the 1980s, hunger and homelessness, share distinctive features. They are partly manifestations of the gap between incomes and the costs of acquiring minimal necessities. Both arose and were first recognized and addressed by community organizations operating without public funds. Both seemed to require public response outside the array of established social welfare services.

In light of evidence of a growing demand for supplementary food and shelter, government officials reacted in patterned ways. (1) They accepted the claims of need but defined the need as temporary, responding, particularly at first, with ad hoc, stopgap policies dealing, for the most part, only with manifestations of the problems. This approach was facilitated by labeling the needs "emergencies." (2) The institutional focus of these emergency policies was nonprofit emergency service agencies. Many of these responded to the need before government began to play a role. Now they continue to play a role as service providers under government contracts or through the distribution of government food surpluses and other commodities.

The tendency to respond to social problems as emergencies—the "emergency services solution," it might be called—is also evident in other problem areas. Governmental support for programs dealing with violence against women, such as rape crisis centers and battered women's shelters, is provided primarily in emergency form. The problems are defined as emergencies, and the solutions involve utilization of community organizations to provide temporary relief.

* * *

THE MEANING OF EMERGENCY IN SOCIAL POLICY

It should be axiomatic that social problems do not arise accompanied by some natural or inevitable conceptualization of their essential causes and remedies. Indeed, the most critical moments in the life cycle of an issue may well be the outcome of the contest over how it will be understood. Sociologist Joseph Gusfield illustrates this when he shows that as long as the problem of deaths from drinking and driving was defined as a problem of the drivers' moral character or ignorance, automakers could (and until the 1960s did) avoid pressures to manufacture safer vehicles. It follows that defining problems of hunger, homelessness, and violence against women as emergency matters is likely to be consequential for the ways in which these issues are processed. It follows as well that the definition of problems as emergencies persists in part because the designation meets the needs of various actors in the service delivery system. It is important as well that the emergency designation not contradict popular understanding of these matters.

The assertion that designating these problems "emergencies" is not inevitable or natural may raise certain questions. After all, are not these problems emergencies for the people who experience them? But there are alternate conceptualizations.

One is that hunger and homelessness result from individuals' chronic disorganization and inability to cope. This view leads to criticism of mental health policy, particularly the failures of deinstitutionalization, and leads to calls for improved mental health services. Indeed, as the issue of homelessness matures, a tendency to disaggregate the homeless population has become evident, and this view, to a degree, has taken hold.

An alternate conceptualization is that hunger and homelessness result from systemic inadequacies of income, or the gap between income and living costs. This perspective would lead to dramatic increases in welfare and other benefits, increased provision of supplementary food assistance, and more vigorous low-income housing policies.

These alternative perspectives are articulated concurrently with the views that the problems are temporary and require short-term, immediate responses. They are not incompatible with policies designed to treat short-term need while more lasting solutions are generated. Yet while the advocates for these perspectives compete to determine which views will prevail, the emergency metaphors remain dominant. These metaphors profoundly affect society's responses to the social problems under discussion.

An emergency is a state of affairs recognized by relevant publics and authorities, consisting of a life-threatening or system-threatening condition of recent onset or severity about which there is a general belief that something can and should be done. The presence of all of these conditions is generally necessary to make the case that an emergency exists.

Emergencies have to signal virtually catastrophic problems to distinguish them from the normal catalog of distresses that affect many in the population. They have to be of recent origin, or else they are more properly categorized as chronic, long-lasting problems to which the person suffering the condition has become inured and with which he or she has already coped. The problem must be presumed to be responsive to intervention, or else one has described a chronic rather than an emergent problem, an act of God, or a matter of fate for which the designation "emergency" is pointless. To illustrate, a plague of locusts is only regarded an emergency in a society that has the capacity to control the pests.

The issue of when a condition is an emergency will change as times, circumstances, resources, and technologies change. Before the automobile, good roads, and high-tech hospitals, people with health needs in rural areas were treated at home or by local physicians without thought of receiving aid in alternative settings. Today, the same conditions lead to heroic efforts to rush victims to modern hospital centers.

An additional observation about emergencies clarifies their function in society and social welfare policy: the designation "emergency" mobilizes resources. To call something an emergency is to claim that extraordinary efforts be made to alleviate the condition. Designation of an emergency legitimates the mobilization. It permits functionaries to take claimants out of turn, treat them differently from the rest, and spend money or devote time to them disproportionately.

This characteristic of emergencies is understood by caretakers and policymakers. Doctors call cases emergencies in order to obtain attention for their patients more quickly. Welfare recipients can receive additional benefits if they qualify for "emergency assistance." Federal policy funnels low-cost loans to flood and drought victims when states of emergency are declared. Troubled youth can receive immediate services, including out-of-home shelter, if their situation is defined as an emergency.

Generally, advantages to recipients of emergency services are the ability to claim and receive extraordinary resources. But there are inherent limits to the needy population as a whole in labeling conditions "emergencies." For example, extraordinary resources can only be mobilized if the number of emergency claims is limited. If everyone claims and seeks special treatment, no one can receive it. Emergency police response numbers only work if the public limits its requests for emergency responses. Emergency rooms in hospitals cease to function effectively when people begin to use emergency rooms for routine treatment.

It follows that there are limits to the extent that society will respond to increases in emergency claims by increasing resources. At some point, public agencies will respond to increased claims by routinizing the provision of aid to the claimant population, reducing the per capita costs of providing emergency assistance, and challenging the basis of the claims themselves. Since resources are finite and other claims over resources compete, the fact that emergency designations mobilize resources creates the conditions for developments directed toward curbing expenditures.

Virtually by definition, emergency services are unstable bases on which to ground policy. Claims are expected to disappear or diminish in intensity, or institutions may be expected to routinize interventions. A critical question is whether emergency policies will deteriorate into routine policies with lower levels of service and reduced constituencies or whether public concern for the affected population is high enough to evoke a commitment to deal with the chronic or structural problems from which emergencies arise.

THE CONSEQUENCES OF LABELING SOCIAL PROBLEMS "EMERGENCIES"

* * *

In the struggle to gain issue recognition, advocates deploy various symbolic strategies to advance their causes. They may claim that vital national interests are at stake now (national defense, trade policy) or in the future (funding social security, rebuilding the highways). Or they may claim that individuals will suffer irreversible injury. The threat of severe damage to health is the not-so-hidden rationale for crash programs for some research (on AIDS, for example) and for emergency allocations to relieve life-threatening conditions.

But these symbolic strategies must be pursued in the face of competing demands. When the food stamp program is unable to meet the food needs of the poor across the board, how can one justify special food supplements for only a portion of the needy? When tens of thousands wait for years to get into public housing, how does one justify diverting housing resources to aid new claimants who are not even on the list? The first consequence of labeling problems "emergencies" is to legitimate the allocation of scarce resources to an individual or group at the expense of others who may suffer from similar conditions but who have not been so labeled.

* * *

Social consensus that a presenting situation constitutes an emergency permits resource mobilization directed toward stabilizing conditions but says nothing about long-term problem resolution. Disaster victims, for example, are provided shelter, health services, and food, but their homes are not restored under disaster relief policies. Likewise, people who claim they are hungry may receive a hot meal but are not provided long-term income support. Nor are the homeless provided with long-term shelter arrangements under emergency policies, although the high cost of emergency facilities puts a premium on moving people out of existing shelters and finding more stable solutions that are less costly on a per capita, per day basis. (Even when homeless families are moved out of shelters into permanent housing, this generalization may apply because without long-term income supplements they may fall back into homelessness.) Agencies may provide troubled youth with short-term shelter and services but be unable to provide adequate long-term services or support.

Paradoxically, despite the very high costs of sheltering people on an emergency basis, emergency shelters may actually be cheaper than some plausible alternative policies. Although putting people up in hotels and motels seems scandalously expensive, it is vastly cheaper than addressing the problem of providing adequate living standards, affordable housing, or long-term placement. This is because the only people one has to serve on food lines or in emergency shelters are the people who come forward to accept emergency aid. If one were to provide for peoples' income needs, in fairness, eligibility for relief would have to be available to all people with low incomes. Moreover, emergency designations allow policymakers to avoid or postpone consideration of expen-sive restructuring or expansion of existing services to address long-term needs.

* * *

THE INSTABILITY OF THE EMERGENCY
SERVICES SOLUTION

By definition, emergencies are short-lived phenomena; the designation characterizes situations that appear relatively suddenly and are not likely to be long lasting. The designation "emergency" permits extraordinary mobilization of resources, but at some point these resources must be diverted from other uses. The uses that compete with emergency social problems have their claimants and advocates. Extraordinary resource utilization also attracts critics concerned about overall expenditures and governmental tax burdens. It follows that political pressures will eventually arise to transform emergency activity into more routinized policies.

Routinization has several implications. With respect to the character of service, government is likely to seek imposition of rules and regulations that make the practices of emergency service agencies conform to government standards. For example, such rules may require these agencies to employ norms of equity in the selection and treatment of clients. Many battered-women shelters and rap crisis centers find themselves forced to adjust their programs in response to government requirements that they select clients based on nondiscriminatory principles and consideration of financial status in the duration of client treatment.

At a broader level, routinization can result in reduced public commitments. It can lead to low-level continuation of emergency services in routinized fashion. It can also result in creation of new, heightened public expectations and obligations. The long-term struggle in emergency services is over which of these divergent futures will ultimately prevail.

In struggles over emergency services, some interests will seek initially to reduce or minimize the sense of public urgency or need (just as other interests will seek to maximize the size and sense of urgency of the problem). The insistence of high-ranking federal officials that hunger does not exist in the United States and the report of the Department of Housing and Urban Development that the problem of homelessness is considerably smaller than had been portrayed in the media are characteristic of this sort of reaction.

But social problems are not simply epiphenomena of the media; they are rooted in underlying social realities that are only partially driven by collective perceptions. Sometimes emergencies evaporate because the underlying social reality does not sufficiently support emergency campaigns. For example, the campaign to save missing children has lost support in the face of convincing challenges to the severity of the problem. The number of missing children was originally projected at 2 million each year. Recently critics have observed that most of the 2 million are runaways, children missing but soon found without notifying the police, or children involved in custody disputes.

Some emergencies devolve into a middle ground of routinized treatment, in which they continue to receive support for amelioration, but at modest funding levels. They may have distinct but relatively narrow constituencies, or they may not be very costly to sustain. Shelters for abused women may have suffered (or enjoyed) this fate, having become relatively uncontroversial elements of federal and state service provision plans but with little ability to grow or resist cutbacks at the margins.

Hunger and homelessness, however, have not diminished as emergencies. Public officials such as big city mayors, and advocates at the local and national levels, continue to demonstrate successfully that these problems have not gone away and, if anything, have continued to grow. Moreover, the very provision of emergency food and shelter creates conditions that keep the problems in the public eye. Long lines at soup kitchens, crowding around shelter doors, and police sweeps of the homeless on freezing nights hold society's attention. The visibility of emergency programs, as we have argued, also helps recruit clients.

Faced with the need to continue to fund emergency aid programs at high levels, public officials have few options as long as problems are defined as emergencies. They may seek to narrow eligibility or otherwise reduce the pool of eligible claimants. In the case of surplus commodities, federal officials sought to persuade states to narrow income eligibility for free food in order to reduce demand and minimize the number of unserved needy. Massachusetts officials limited the pool of claimants for spaces in emergency shelters for adolescents by accepting referrals only from state agency personnel. In the case of homelessness, local officials have questioned claimants for emergency housing more closely concerning whether they have other options. They have at times also tried to ensure that publicly supported shelter options are not perceived as excessively attractive, lest people abandon questionable private alternatives for public services.

How long can social problems be treated as emergencies if there is high demand? When, in the early 1970s, the welfare rights movement sought to exploit the availability of emergency assistance by encouraging claims, states met the challenge by "cashing out" emergency aid so that every recipient received some additional benefits. This reform had the effect of preventing individuals from mak-ing extraordinary claims on the system. Yet the more visible and apparent the need for emergency relief, the less will any administrative solution to emergency services expenditures prove politically feasible.

Persistent emergencies eventually focus attention on the need for systemic solutions. City governments have begun to respond to homelessness with proposals for increases in low-income housing and housing appropriate to the needs of the subpopulations of elderly, families, veterans, alcoholics, and mentally ill that combine to make up the homeless population. State governments have begun to examine how to deploy resources to prevent families from becoming homeless. The persistence of emergencies makes it difficult for public officials to ignore the need for long-run answers, however expensive they may be.

Emergency services are inherently unstable. The size and severity of the problem appears to require public responses, while the high cost of providing emergency services suggests the desirability of normalizing service provision. Up to a point, responding to social problems as emergencies serves public officials who, for one reason or another, wish to minimize institutional commitments. But responding in emergency terms can result in costs, issues of fairness, and problem visibility that will soon make it difficult to continue to respond in emergency fashion.

QUESTIONS

1. What are the various characteristics of social problems that claimsmakers frame as emergencies?

2. Whose interests does the emergency frame serve?

3. Identify a problem that has recently been framed as an emergency. Identify some alternative ways that this problem could have been framed.

4. Identify the various reasons why it is more attractive for policymakers to frame social problems as emergencies than to embrace one of these alternative frames.

Killer Tales about Serial Killings

FROM *Using Murder: The Social Construction of Serial Homicide*

PHILIP JENKINS

Philip Jenkins illustrates how, during the 1980s and '90s, law enforcement agencies, the news media, and popular culture each contributed to an over-simplified image of serial murder. The Justice Department and journalists jointly misrepresented the magnitude of the problem, citing statistics about the number of killers and number of victims that did not add up to an accurate picture of what was actually occurring. Moreover, the FBI mythologized "mind-hunters," the people in its Behavioral Sciences Unit investigating serial murders, as crusaders who were uniquely capable of solving these heinous crimes. And finally, news media and popular culture accounts, such as the blockbuster film Silence of the Lambs, *manufactured public fears of serial killers who posed one of the greatest and most barbaric menaces to society, especially to children.*

THE PANIC, 1983–1985

. . . In October 1983, the Justice Department held a news conference on the danger of the growing danger of serial murder. Justice Department experts Roger Depue and Robert Heck confirmed . . . that the number of victims annually might reach several thousand, but they also enunciated another statistic that would enjoy wide notoriety when they stated that there might be thirty-five such killers active in the United States at any given time. . . .

Thirty-five killers, four thousand victims: Both figures were freely quoted and generally accepted, although the juxtaposition of the two presented definite problems. In order to produce four thousand victims, each of the putative killers would have to kill at least a hundred people annually, and there was no case on record where an offender was known to have killed at anything like so high a rate. The only parallels to such activity were to be found in some of the largely speculative figures cited in the Specter committee for individuals like Ted Bundy, but these assumed that each killer claimed a huge "dark figure" of victims. In reality, very few recorded killers have ever claimed more than ten or so victims in a given year, and most were associated with far fewer deaths. It was therefore likely that one of the popular figures was wrong: Either there were more than thirty-five killers at any one time, or there were far fewer than four thousand victims.

Ironically, we know in retrospect from their own figures that the Justice Department officials were actually underestimating the number of killers active at any given time. In any given year in the early 1980s, there were at least fifty individuals who had already killed multiply, and who would kill again. For 1981, we can now trace fifty-eight such cases then active, and there were at least fifty-six in 1982. However, it was years before such information became available. In the short term, the claims-makers faced an apparent contradiction.

The Lucas Case

Fortuitously for the incipient panic, reporting of the Justice Department news conference coincided almost exactly with the national attention paid to a news story from Texas, where convicted killer Henry Lee Lucas was claiming that he had been responsible for several hundred killings in the previous five years. According to his original story, Lucas had traveled the country with a number of friends, including murderer Ottis Toole, and had killed perhaps 360 people in over twenty states. This case seemed to reinforce the images presented in the Specter committee hearings, both of vast numbers of victims and of the roaming killer who wandered freely between jurisdictions. If there were thirty-five such individuals active at one time, then the serial murder problem represented an appalling social crisis, and there really might be four or five thousand victims. . . .

Much remains controversial about the Lucas confessions, and it rapidly became apparent that many of his claims could not be substantiated. By 1985, it was suggested that his confessions were almost entirely spurious, and that his number of victims was in reality closer to the thirteen or so for which he was actually convicted than to 360 (though some credible authorities accept figures far larger than 13). It appeared that law enforcement agencies had been much too quick to accept his confessions, and that some had been anxious to clear unsolved killings in their jurisdictions without due investigation. However, at the time, Lucas seemed to epitomize the worst fears of the serial killer as an itinerant monster from whom no one was safe.

The impact of the story was all the greater because of what appeared to be the killer's lucid and extremely frank discussions of the most grisly crimes, which he recounted in interviews with police and press. During 1984 and 1985, interviews were shown on ABC's "20/20" and "Good Morning America," on CBS' "Nightwatch," and they also aired in the 1985 television documentary *Acts of Violence*. The reports inspired two feature films, *Confessions of a Serial Killer* (1987) and *Henry: Portrait of a Serial Killer* (1986, released in 1990), while there were also a number of true-crime books and detective magazine accounts. In February 1985, a major interview with Lucas appeared in the pages of *Penthouse*.

In 1984 and 1985, concern about serial murder became intense, and the problem was clearly defined according to the model proposed by the BSU [Behavioral Science Unit of the FBI] authorities. Such images were enhanced by other events in 1984, especially the manhunt for a killer named Christopher Wilder. Wilder began his violent career in Florida, but in April he began a nationwide rampage in which he killed at least nine women in eight states in the West and Midwest. Wilder spent months on the FBI's ten most wanted list, prior to committing suicide in New Hampshire. This case regularly made headline news on the television networks, and ABC's "Nightline" used it as a vehicle for a program on the serial murder phenomenon. The story confirmed the Lucas image of the killer as a sexual predator roaming from state to state in pursuit of victims, who snatched innocent prey almost at random; and the *New York Times* reported current efforts at "Stopping Them Before They Kill Again and Again and Again."

At exactly the time of the Wilder case, the Congress once more provided a platform for those warning of a national serial murder menace. In February and March of 1984, the Specter committee held hearings on the Missing Children's Assistance Act, a measure that was to be discussed further that April by the House committee on Human Resources. Major witnesses included John Walsh, who was introduced in reverential tones by the powerful Democrat Senator Paul Simon of Illinois. Walsh claimed, "We found that the number of random unsolved murders of women and children in this country rose from 600 in 1966 to 4,500 in 1981." At this point, he was apparently inflating the July 1983 estimate of 3,600 victims, and further claimed that this corresponded only to the number of women and children victimized, a statement whose warrant is unclear. However, this was consistent with his belief in the high rate of child victimization. Every hour, he stated, 205 children were reported missing in this country, a figure corresponding to 1.8 million cases per annum, and many of these would be found murdered.

The Media Response

Once these ideas were established, they were rapidly disseminated by the media, who virtually never questioned the evidential bases for the assertions. The new problem was presented on the network television news programs, in journals as various as *Time* and *Newsweek, Life* and *OMNI, Psychology Today,* and men's magazines like *Hustler, Penthouse,* and *Playboy.*

A characteristic statement of the problem was presented in a major front-page story published in the *New York Times* in January 1984, on the "rise in killers who roam U.S. for victims." This emphasized that serial murder in contemporary America was a new phenomenon that had exploded since the late 1960s and that was distinctively American in nature. The American murder wave was both qualitatively and quantitatively different from anything recorded in previous history, with vastly more victims, and much greater occurrence of savage torture and mutilation. In short, serial murder had become an *epidemic,* a word attributed to the Justice Department's Robert O. Heck. The term implied widespread social pathology, rapid and uncontrollable growth, and ubiquitous threat, as well as the need for urgent countermeasures.

According to the article, Justice Department officials "assert that history offers nothing to compare with the spate of such murders that has occurred in the United States since the beginning of the 1970s." Heck was quoted for the view "that as many as four thousand Americans a year, at least half of them under the age of eighteen, are murdered in this way. He said he believes that at least 35 such killers are now roaming the country." Many of their victims were to be found among the thousands of bodies that turned up each year unidentified and unexplained. In August, the *Times* followed this with another lengthy story about the psychology of "mass killers," which quoted experts who believed that the serial killer represented an altogether "new personality type." This again confirmed that the scale of serial activity was quite unparalleled in American history, while claiming that of Lucas's 360 claimed victims, "more than 142 have reportedly been verified by police."

Newsweek presented a similar account in "The Random Killers," a story that occupied four full pages and that employed the term *epidemic* in its subtitle. It similarly argued, "Law enforcement experts say as many as two-thirds of the estimated 5000 unsolved homicides in the nation each year may be committed by serial murderers." *Life* suggested that "hundreds" of serial killers might be at large.

Characteristic of the coverage at this time was the television documentary *Murder: No Apparent Motive,* made in 1984 for the HBO series "America Under Cover," though it was often repeated over the next decade on other cable channels. This begins with a photograph of one of Bundy's victims from the Florida sorority house, with the narrator stating, "Four thousand a year—dead. Killed by total strangers. It's an epidemic of murder in America—murder with no motive." The program then turns to a California police officer who remarks, "We have people that commit murders like you might go out and mow the lawn. That's about as much thought as they give. A term that's been used is *recreational murder.* Nothing else to do—they go out and kill." At that point, the screen fades to red.

Neither *stranger* homicide nor *recreational* murder is necessarily synonymous with serial murder, though all these terms are here presented as essentially identical, and the program that followed was based on reconstructions of celebrated serial cases Edmund Kemper, Ted Bundy, and Henry Lee Lucas, all of whom were interviewed. It was further suggested that these individuals were representative of a large social threat, defined in the now familiar terms of the Justice Department's experts. One of the authorities most frequently consulted was Robert Ressler, who remarks, "Serial killing—I think it's at epidemic proportions. The type of crime we're seeing today did not really occur with any known frequency prior to the fifties. An individual taking ten, twelve, fifteen, twenty-five, thirty-five lives is a relatively new phenomenon in the crime picture of the U.S."

* * *

The Myth of the Mind-Hunter

After 1985, the panic over serial murder died away somewhat, due in large part to the various activists having achieved their legislative agendas. However, the figure (and name) of the serial killer had decisively entered the culture, and the second half of the decade witnessed a rapid growth in both scholarly and true-crime publications on the topic. Between 1985 and 1992, there appeared at least fourteen scholarly or professional books on the general phenomenon, apart from the many true-crime contributions.

A serial murder problem had now been established on the lines advocated by the Justice Department; but during the late 1980s, the same agency enjoyed continued success in redefining the issue along lines that provided the maximum benefit and prestige for the FBI and its investigators. Specifically, this meant presenting the FBI's behavioral scientists (the "mind-hunters") as uniquely qualified to deal with the serial murder menace, and this interpretation became very influential. The mind-hunter image of the BSU was initially presented in a series of highly laudatory media accounts, which reinforced the prestige of the unit as the world's leading experts on serial violence.

One of the first such articles appeared in 1983 in the pages of *Psychology Today*, and like its many successors was largely based on interviews with the leading BSU agents Robert Ressler, John Douglas, and Roy Hazelwood. Typically, such a report would describe true life cases in which uncannily accurate profiles led to the apprehension of unknown killers. Among specific achievements, the most frequently cited was the use of FBI profiles to assist prosecutors in the trial of Wayne Williams. This was the format followed in a 1986 article in the highly visible setting of the *New York Times Magazine*, by journalist Stephen Michaud, who had earlier published his interviews with Ted Bundy. The article depicted the achievements of the NCAVC [National Center for the Analysis of Violent Crime] profilers ("The FBI's New Psyche Squad") in straightforward though admiring terms, while the article helped to popularize the FBI jargon then becoming popular, such as the distinction between *organized* and *disorganized* offenders, and the term *Unsub* for *unknown subject*.

Admiring articles were followed by book-length studies, including Paul Jeffers's *Who Killed Precious? How FBI Special Agents Combine High Technology and Psychology to Identify Violent Criminals*. The book's blurb suggested, questionably, that "until now, [serial killers have] been almost impossible to catch," but that now the criminals had met their match in the BSU, "the only thing that stands between us and the country's most deranged psychopaths." FBI agents like Ressler and Douglas consulted extensively on this and other works, while Ressler himself became a visible public spokesman for the new techniques after his retirement from the bureau.

The public triumph of mind-hunting was neither assured nor inevitable. In fact, the adulatory works of the 1980s rarely made mention of the number of cases in which the FBI contribution had been negligible or actively counterproductive, and there were incidents that contributed little positive to the reputation of the BSU. For example, Roy Hazelwood is cited in a study of the Charlie Hatcher case as producing a profile that is justly described as "uncannily accurate"; but the same author also notes that an earlier profile "drawn up by Hazelwood in a Georgia case turned out to be the most inaccurate in the agency's history." In the Green River case, similarly, John Douglas had been involved in offering profiling assistance from the earliest stages of the investigation in 1982–1983, but the case still remained unsolved a decade later. The profiling endeavors of the BSU have been severely criticized within the FBI, and agent Paul Lindsay has denounced the claims made in Ressler's autobiography. Lindsay, an experienced homicide investigator, has also asked, "I mean, how many serial killer cases has the FBI solved—*if any*?" (for Lindsay's critique of the Bureau, see also his 1992 novel *Witness to the Truth*).

* * *

The Image of Jack Crawford

By far the most influential account of the BSU group came from the fictional work of Thomas Harris, author of *Red Dragon* and *The Silence of the Lambs*. Harris's writing[s] were a critical contribution to the renewed upsurge of concern about serial murder in the early 1990s, and also ensured that the problem was defined according to the views of the Justice Department. It was *Red Dragon* above all that established the idea of the detective as mind-hunter, employing scientific crime-fighting skills well beyond the normal level of police procedures, and the book helped to popularize the methods of profiling and other investigative techniques characteristic of the BSU.

In fact, the detectives depicted as interviewing convicted killers are based heavily on real-life agents who had provided information for the book, so inevitably the FBI personnel are depicted as the heroic counterpoint to the villainous killers. The figure of FBI agent Jack Crawford was loosely synthesized from the real-life characters of Ressler, Douglas, and Hazelwood. (The British version of Robert Ressler's autobiography stressed that of all this agent's lifelong investigative accomplishments, the one deserving note was that he had served as adviser to Thomas Harris on *Silence of the Lambs*.) The BSU was portrayed as an elite team of superdetectives called in to assist local agencies facing the threat of savage roaming killers, while there was at least the impression that the unit had a special jurisdiction over serial murder cases wherever they occurred. This was an appealing and influential picture. Intentionally or not, Thomas Harris provided the FBI's violent-crime experts with invaluable publicity and unprecedented visibility. . . . As Ressler has written in his remarkably candid autobiography, "The media have come around to lionizing behavioral science people as supersleuths who put all other police to shame and solve cases where others have failed."

This is suggested by a report broadcast in November 1991 by CBS's "60 Minutes" on the Justice Department's Investigative Support Unit, the "psycho squad" headed by John Douglas. The preamble stated, "It would be comforting to think that the movie *Silence of the Lambs* was pure fiction. It wasn't. It was based on real crimes and a real FBI unit which is known affectionately as the Psycho Squad." The report suggested that this group and the subjects it investigated were in fact the true life equivalents of Harris's fictional creations. Harris's detective Crawford is presented (questionably) as a straightforward depiction of the real-life agent Douglas. An interview with killer Gary Heidnik is introduced with the words, "This is not a scene from *Silence of the Lambs* but it could have been." Such interviews are juxtaposed with clips from the film in which the fictional Hannibal Lecter is interrogated. The overall impression is both that Heidnik represents one of the monsters of fiction, while the Justice Department investigators really were the superdetectives suggested by the film. Agent Douglas even remarked that his aspirations for the unit would be that agents could intervene in a crime and depart suddenly; reminiscent of the Lone Ranger.

The CBS interviewer's questions and remarks were uncritical to the point of being quite reverential. For instance, the accuracy of the unit's profiles and analyses is said to be so uncanny that these are believed to result from mystical means: "The police say that you hold seances, and that you're weird, that you're sorcerers, and that you're the ouija board men . . . witch-doctors." Ironically, many of the occult terms often applied to the profilers were by no means intended to be flattering, and some of the harshest criticisms levied against Ressler and Douglas dismiss their work as "voodoo." However, the news report leaves the disingenuous impression that such words reflect breathless admiration.

It would be difficult to conceive of a more favorable depiction, of brilliant and heroic mind-hunters combating the most savage enemies of society, yet never losing the fundamental humanity that causes them to sympathize deeply with the individuals who are the victims of these atrocities. Moreover, this was a report from "60 Minutes," the program that shortly before had led the assault on the *Iowa* verdict.

THE NEW PANIC, 1990–1992

The factual accuracy of *Silence of the Lambs* has been much criticized by law enforcement officers, including Ressler, Hazelwood, and other Quantico investigators themselves. More hostile critics have denounced the "slavish P.R. the Bureau reaped from *Silence of the Lambs,*" and Paul Lindsay has noted how the bureau's reputation was "vastly puffed up by the hype" from the film. He further describes the film itself as "far fetched, a fabrication . . . *totally* fiction."

But such criticisms were rarely heard in the media, and the Justice Department's specialists earned still more prestige during the renewed concern with serial murder in the early 1990s. Though not as intense or as exaggerated as the panic of 1983–1985, the events of 1990–1992 did substantially reshape perceptions of serial murder, and a concatenation of incidents made serial murder almost as keen a focus of media attention as it had been in the mid-1980s. In addition, there was even more debate about the role of the serial killer as a figure in art and literature. Media reporting constantly reinforced the idea that there was an overwhelming menace to society, and the only hope for combating it lay in Quantico, exactly the linkage that the Justice Department had been trying to establish for a decade. The delineation of the new panic demonstrated the federal agency's complete ownership of the murder problem.

Signs of renewed concern emerged in August 1990 with the reporting of a series of five gruesome mutilation murders on the University of Florida campus in Gainesville. Though technically spree crimes, these attacks were universally construed as serial murders, and so the topic was brought back to the headlines. Within days, ABC's "20/20" estimated that eighty news reporters were covering the case. The impact of these crimes was all the greater because of the "innocent" nature of the victims. These were, after all, students, not people engaged in prostitution or homosexual activities, a distinction that often leads to an undervaluing of victims in other cases. The attacks seemed all the more threatening because they occurred in the apparent safety of the victims' homes; and the location inevitably recalled Ted Bundy's final spree on another Florida campus. In Gainesville, "You've got Jack the Ripper loose at the state's flagship university"; and it was soon recognized that the initial suspect was not in fact involved in the crimes, so that the real killer remained at large. News coverage of Gainesville placed the incident in the context of a number of current and unsolved cases around the country: in New Bedford and San Diego, Philadelphia and New York, Norfolk, Virginia, and Washington D.C., reinforcing the concept of a generalized problem.

Over the next three months, serial murder remained in the news because of the dispute over Bret Easton Ellis's book *American Psycho.* In February 1991, the release of the film version of the *Silence of the Lambs* provided a central point of reference in the renewed concern with serial homicide, and the popular enthusiasm it generated lasted for several months. Just as that interest was beginning to fade, a number of true-life murder cases occurred that reawakened public fears.

In July 1991, the gruesome and cannibalistic elements of the Jeffrey Dahmer case ensured that this would become one of the best known of all serial murder incidents nationwide. In the *New York Times,* for example, there was a major half- or full-page feature on the case for each of the next ten days, and there were interviews and discussions on all the major talk shows and news programs. According to several *Milwaukee Journal* reports, an estimated 450 journalists sought to cover the ensuing trial. The vast impact of the affair was also suggested by the wide popularity of jokes and tales based on the case, and the cannibalistic theme helped to reinforce the connection with the fictional Hannibal.

August 1991 found other serial murder cases in the headlines. For example, it was suggested that there had been a string of almost twenty related murders in Riverside County, California, the victims being mainly female prostitutes. (The following January, William Lester Suff was charged in two of these crimes.) The same August, there was also an abortive revival of the Lucas stereotype, when a drifter named Donald Leroy Evans was widely reported for his claim that he had killed up to sixty people in twenty states, and that he was "actually the worst serial killer in the nation's history." However, police were very anxious to avoid a repetition of "a Henry Lee Lucas kind of thing," and were very cautious about accepting these boasts. The allegations indeed proved difficult to substantiate, and little more was heard of the case, but the denial of the charges received far less publicity than the initial claim. Also during 1991, Aileen Wuornos was arrested for a number of murders in Florida and was promptly billed as "America's first female serial killer." Interest in the phenomenon was maintained into 1992 by the televised trials of both Dahmer and Wuornos on the television cable channel Court TV.

In the spring of 1992, there was also widespread concern about a proposal to issue sets of trading cards depicting serial killers, an idea originally reported in a sensational story on the television program "Entertainment Tonight" in January. The concept appeared especially frightening because of the supposed appeal of such objects to children, and on the television talk show "Larry King Live," it was incorrectly stated that these cards were being sold through Toys 'R Us. By April, there were movements to ban sale of the cards in seven states and Canada, and the Maryland legislature proposed a sweeping measure prohibiting simple possession.

These events gave the news media a new tag for the examination of serial murder on a level unparalleled since 1985, and stories were now likely to be adapted to fit the concerns and emphases of Harris's work, and thus the federal model of the problem. Virtually every feature on the subject included at least one interview on the subject of profiling and crime scene analysis, usually with one of the Quantico investigators; and reporting of the Gainesville murders disseminated awareness of terms like *blitz* attacks and *disorganized* offenders. On several occasions in these years, the present author was approached for interviews by journalists who assumed that anyone with a professional and academic interest in serial murder must automatically be an authority on profiling, which was seen as the chief or only methodology for studying the offense.

Over the next two years, the fictional Hannibal Lecter and his real-life counterparts featured prominently in news and magazine stories on all television networks, as well as in numerous magazines. *People Weekly* used *Silence of the Lambs* as a vehicle to discuss the factors that gave rise to real-life serial murder. In *Village Voice*, director Jonathan Demme was quoted as an authority on the topic of authentic serial murder, and discussed the contributions made by child abuse to the causation of the offense. Such articles were especially likely to appear in periodicals chiefly aimed at younger women, perhaps suggesting the greater fear that this audience would be likely to have in the face of sexually moti-vated attacks.

Television often returned to the theme. Between 1991 and 1993, ABC's main news program "20/20" included segments on the Gainesville murders, Leonard Lake and Charles Ng, Andrei Chikatilo, and Texas serial murderer Kenneth McDuff. In May 1991, CBS's "48 Hours" presented a one-hour special entitled "Serial Killer," which included a case study of the then unsolved Riverside murders, as well as harrowing interviews that first brought the case of child killer Westley Alan Dodd to national attention. In April 1993 the show addressed another full program to the case of Kenneth McDuff. The same network's "60 Minutes" offered a report on the FBI's "Psycho Squad," and in 1992 reported the case of Ray and Faye Copeland. NBC's news program "Dateline" presented two major reports on Aileen Wuornos.

Meanwhile, PBS's "Frontline" series presented two full documentaries during 1992: "Monsters among Us" ostensibly concerned sex offenders and their treatment, but in reality focused on multiple-child killer Westley Alan Dodd. "Nova"'s "The Mind of a Serial Killer" was mainly concerned with the Arthur Shawcross case. The program focused on the achievements of the ISU [Investigative Support Unit], and intercut real-life footage of John Douglas's real-life office with scenes depicting Jack Crawford's desk from *Silence of the Lambs*. In 1993, another "Nova" examined the use of DNA testing to catch a serial sex-killer. In January 1993, CNN presented the five-part series, "Murder by Number," which included interviews with Dodd and other serial killers as well as psychologists and criminological experts. Moreover, this listing of news reports is far from comprehensive, and it does not include programs on related topics such as satanism or child abuse, which might well include accounts of serial killers.

The apparent surge of reported cases led to revived suggestions of a murder epidemic. In May 1991, CBS's "48 Hours" began by noting that "More than twenty-one thousand Americans are murdered each year." There were many motives for such crimes, "but the most horrifying deaths come at the hands of serial murderers, people who actually enjoy making other people suffer and die." Although it could not be quantified, the problem was thus immeasurably grave. It was "a crime against humanity, a race against time." The following April, Robert Ressler was quoted in *Mirabella*: "We're seeing an upward spiraling trend where one week you have Jeffrey Dahmer, the next week Donald Evans. It just never stops. America is going to turn into *A Clockwork Orange*. The sexual psychopath will become the norm."

* * *

QUESTIONS

1. What are some examples of ways that the U.S. Department of Justice and the news media each exaggerated the magnitude of the serial murder problem?

2. How did the fictional depiction Thomas Harris gave of Jack Crawford in *Red Dragon* contribute toward idealizing the *mind-hunters* in the FBI's Behavioral Sciences Unit who worked on serial murder cases?

3. How did news coverage of several high-profile serial murder cases during the early 1990s feed public fears that serial killers posed a monumental and gruesome menace to society?

4. In what sense is serial murder the perfect news story? Discuss by identifying the various characteristics that make certain events particularly newsworthy.

Stalking as a Danger Potentially Menacing All Women

FROM *Stalking Strangers and Lovers: Changing Media Typifications of a New Crime Problem*

KATHLEEN S. LOWNEY AND JOEL BEST

Lowney and Best illustrate how a certain type of behavior got framed and reframed over a fourteen-year period leading to the creation of criminal statutes against a newly defined problem—stalking—and widespread public awareness of this issue. The authors show that the early frames activists used concerning obsession and psychological rape were not, in themselves, very successful in the construction of the problem. Activists' subsequent reframing of the issue as star stalking proved more successful, and their further reframing of it as violence against women enabled the problem to catapult to the top of lawmakers' and the news media's agenda. All of these claimsmaking efforts explain why nowadays stalking is a punishable criminal offense and is widely understood to be a menace that potentially afflicts all women.

* * *

Studies of social problems construction usually examine successful claims, claims that attract media coverage, affect public opinion, and receive policymakers' attention. But successful claims are often the product of a prolonged, largely unsuccessful sequence of claimsmaking. Claimsmakers compete within a social problems marketplace. There are always many claimsmakers trying to testify before Congress, attract press coverage, appear on talk shows, and otherwise bring their causes to the fore. Inevitably, many of these efforts fail, and claimsmakers struggle to develop rhetoric that will draw attention and lead to action. This often requires reframing or repackaging a problem, offering new typifications. Because constructionist research tends to focus on claims that succeed in the social problems marketplace, most analysts neglect the earlier phases of claimsmaking campaigns, when claimsmakers revise and alter their typifications. These early phases may involve dissension and debate among claimsmakers promoting rival typifications and interpretations. Usually, claims that succeed reflect a particular construction of the problem, which becomes seen as authoritative, and those claimsmakers achieve "ownership" of the problem. A successful typification is taken for granted by press, public, policymakers—and all too often constructionist analysts—who lose sight of the earlier, unsuccessful claims. This chapter extends constructionist analysis by exploring how earlier, unsuccessful typifications evolved into the successful construction of stalking as a crime problem.

Stalking—"men and women who are repeatedly followed, harassed, or physically threatened by other persons"—was recently and successfully constructed as a crime problem. California passed the first antistalking law in 1990. Three years later, 48 states and the District of Columbia had such laws, and several states were considering further legislation to expand or toughen their statutes. As one legislator put it:

> Michigan and its sister States are creating a new crime. We are defining it, essentially, one unknown to the common law. We are making conduct illegal which has been legal up until now, and we are using the most serious proscription our society can devise, the deprivation of liberty, through a felony penalty. This is experimental legislation.

Claims that stalking was a large and growing problem led to hearings before the U.S. Senate; the National Institute of Justice developed a Model Anti-Stalking Code for States. By late 1993, claims about stalking had become familiar, and reports of strangers attacking women (e.g., the kidnap/murder of Polly Klaas, or the assault on figure-skater Nancy Kerrigan) often assumed that stalkers committed the crimes. Less than 5 years after the term "stalking" emerged, stalking had widespread recognition as a crime problem.

* * *

Following the discussion of our methods, we first describe early, unsuccessful claims about what would later be called stalking (1980–1988). We next discuss the importance of celebrity victims during the emergence of the stalking problem (1989–1991), and then examine how the definition of stalking changed as the press, legislators, and activists began linking stalking to domestic violence (1992–1994). Our analysis combines qualitative interpretation with quantitative data on changing typifications of stalking. Finally, we explain how a new set of typifying claims mobilized cultural and organizational resources, making possible the successful construction of stalking as a new crime problem.

METHODS

We examined several dozen examples of claimsmaking about stalking, including videotapes and transcripts of television news broadcasts and talk shows; articles from newspapers, popular magazines, law reviews, and scholarly journals; and transcripts of Congressional proceedings. Although we could not examine everything written or broadcast about stalking, we searched several standard indexes for references to this crime problem, and we believe that our sources reflect the range of claims about the stalking problem.

These claims provide our analytic focus: rather than trying to assess the objective nature of stalking, we ask how claimsmakers depicted this crime problem. After collecting and examining claims about stalking, we sought to identify key elements in the typifications of offenders, victims, and the offense (e.g., whether the victim was a celebrity, the relationship between victim and offender prior to the stalking, whether the stalking led to homicide, and so on). As we identified key analytic dimensions, we systematically reexamined our collection of claims along those dimensions. By comparing individual claims with one another, we identified patterns and trends in our data, developing generalizations through this comparative process.

Our analysis includes quantitative data from stalking coverage in 24 U.S. popular magazine articles and 47 nationally televised news and information broadcasts between 1980 and June 1994. We chose these media for quantitative analysis because they reach national audiences and have reasonably thorough indexes. Magazine indexes (e.g., the *Reader's Guide to Periodical Literature*) are a staple source of constructionist data. Although there is no adequate single index of television programming, it has become possible to identify and retrieve broadcasts for news and information programming, ranging from the networks' evening news programs to talk shows. We located most of the magazine articles by searching the *Reader's Guide,* although our sample includes a few articles that appeared in magazines not indexed there. *Television News Index and Abstracts* indexes the evening network news broadcasts; Journal Graphics (a television transcript clearinghouse that began in 1981) listed many other television programs (e.g., talk shows, CNN broadcasts, and morning shows), and we also checked for transcripts of major talk shows (e.g., *Oprah*) not indexed by Journal Graphics. Since "stalking" did not become common parlance until after 1989, we searched the indexes under various headings, including crimes against women, following, harassment, and sexual harassment; of course, many of the stories indexed under these headings were not about stalking and are not included in our analysis. Our data do not provide a perfect measure of magazine and television coverage: we may have missed relevant stories that were not indexed or indexed under other headings; and the indexes' coverage changed over time (in particular, the number of programs indexed by Journal Graphics grew). Still, our analysis includes every relevant magazine story and television program we located. In each article or broadcast, we identified typifying examples—cases used to illustrate the problem of stalking. All but one of the articles and broadcasts featured one or more examples. Some cases, usually involving victims who were either celebrities or active in the movement for antistalking laws, were described two to eight times. Since each description served as a typifying example in a different story or broadcast, we included each in the sample. The full sample contained 215 typifying examples.

BEFORE STALKING: OBSESSION AND PSYCHOLOGICAL RAPE, 1980–1988

Between 1980 and 1986, national magazines published seven articles describing women being followed or harassed with letters, telephone calls, or unwanted gifts. Some of the annoying behaviors continued for years; some women were physically assaulted. Any female could be a victim: although most of the victims knew their harassers as colleagues at work, ex-husbands, or ex-boyfriends, some of the men were strangers.

The articles called these behaviors "a form of sexual harassment," "obsession," or "psychological rape." One psychiatrist, interviewed shortly after John Hinckley tried to assassinate President Reagan, said that psychological rape "has linked such celebrities as Jodie Foster and Caroline Kennedy to ordinary women who've found themselves pursued by men who claim to be in love with them."

The articles described the harassers, all males, as obsessive, compulsive, often passive in nature, with a limited range of sexual expression and low self-esteem. Many had "only protective feelings [toward their victim], and believe that their actions may shield their loved ones from imagined 'enemies' such as the Mafia or CIA." The term psychological rape reflected "the nonviolent nature of the harassment—letters, obscene phone calls and persistent shadowing are its most common forms." Most harassers were "lovesick," although a few might become violent.

The articles held the harasser responsible for his behavior. A female attorney described harassment as "plain male possessiveness." A more psychological explanation held that some men were more susceptible to rejection by women with whom they were romantically linked. The psychological rapist, however, does not acknowledge his problems; rather, he blames his victim. One harasser was quoted: "*I'll* say I have a problem, the woman I love doesn't love me. It's the worst thing that can happen to anyone." Some psychological experts held victims partially responsible for subtly encouraging their harassers:

> [T]hey can often get away with it because their ex-girlfriends unwittingly allow them to. . . . Kate [harassed for over a decade] admits that even while Will [her former boyfriend] was harassing her with phone calls and driving by her house in the middle of the night, she gave him a scarf she had knitted for him.

The articles portrayed victims as confused by the harassers' attention; some women acknowledged partial culpability: "He said I'd provoked him into anger last night and I had the guilty uneasy feeling that maybe that was partially true." The articles warned that common social scripts for ending relationships often do not work with psychological rapists: "It's hard to turn your back on a former lover who's obviously in pain, and it may seem cruel to avoid all contact with him. In the end, however, there's no other way."

The victims in these articles complained of the criminal justice system's failure to protect them. Police often did not treat harassment as serious, even when it involved criminal behavior. But victims reported feeling terrified:

> Basically, the psychological rapist works by gradually reducing the number of places a woman feels safe or functional in her daily life. This is why relatively harmless behavior, repeated over months or years, can inspire real terror.

Victims claimed the criminal justice system did not understand their terror, and that this precluded their cases being handled properly. A Los Angeles prosecutor explained that these cases were hard to prosecute: "A jury will want to know why *emotional* harassment is damaging when the victim is never touched. . . . I see only six prosecutable cases of emotional harassment each year."

Thus, early magazine articles depicted female victims of male harassers. (In 1987, the popular movie *Fatal Attraction* [about a harassing female] inspired an article in *People* describing three men harassed by women). Experts typified the harassers' behaviors as nonviolent, and sometimes portrayed victims as coresponsible for their plight. Victims complained they felt terror, but got little help from the criminal justice system. In retrospect, these articles can be seen as early claims about what would become the stalking problem, although only one article used that word (among others). While occasional press coverage viewed the behavior as problematic, the issue had not yet been packaged and presented so as to command public attention.

STALKING EMERGES: STAR-STALKERS AND CELEBRITY VICTIMS, 1989–1991

Stalking became a visible issue in 1989 following the sensational murder of actress Rebecca Schaeffer, killed by fan Robert Bardo, a stranger who became obsessed with her, attempted to contact her, then shot her. Her murder received widespread publicity as "The case that galvanized the public: the fatal attraction of a disturbed young man for an up-and-coming actress." Schaeffer was not the first celebrity victim; John Hinckley stalked actress Jodie Foster before attempting to assassinate President Reagan in 1981, and a fan stalked and stabbed actress Theresa Saldana in 1982. However, claims about stalking rarely drew on these examples until Schaeffer's murder. The stalking problem did not, then, simply emerge following a well-publicized crime against a celebrity victim. Yet Schaeffer's murder became the typifying example for what the media now termed "star-stalking."

The construction of star-stalking as a crime problem typified victims as celebrities—actors and actresses, television personalities, and political figures. Claimsmakers referred to such celebrity victims as talk show hosts David Letterman and Johnny Carson, author Stephen King, actor Michael J. Fox and actresses Jodie Foster, Theresa Saldana, and Sharon Gless, singers Olivia Newton-John and Sheena Easton, and musician John Lennon. Several of these examples were not current; the harassment had occurred years earlier. During 1989 and 1990, national magazine articles and television broadcasts presented 16 typifying examples of stalking; 11 (69%) involved celebrity victims. In every other year, celebrity victims were a minority among the examples.

* * *

Some discussions of star-stalking referred to the psychiatric disorder "ero-tomania." First described in 1921, erotomania entered the American Psychiatric Association's *DSM-III-R* as "delusional (paranoid) disorder, ero-tomanic type":

> The central theme of an erotic delusion is that one is loved by another. . . . The person about whom this conviction is held is usually of higher status, such as a famous person or a superior at work, and may even be a complete stranger. Efforts to contact the object of the delusion, through telephone calls, letters, gifts, visits, and even surveillance and stalking are common.

Erotomania usually affects women, and discussions of star-stalking often mentioned the women who had harassed David Letterman, Michael J. Fox, and Sharon Gless.

A primary difference between earlier claims about psychological rape and the more successful campaign against star-stalking was the redefinition of the behavior as *violent*. The stalker's behavior, which might be threatening or merely inappropriate, needed to be seen as potentially violent. Some claims-makers suggested that stalkers "deteriorated," becoming increasingly capable of violence. Unpredictable and possibly lethal, stalking was a form of random violence.

While earlier claimsmakers criticized the criminal justice system's failure to halt psychological rape, their claims produced no legislation. However, concern over star-stalking led to California passing an antistalking law; claims-makers linked Schaeffer's murder, the 1982 stabbing of Theresa Saldana (in the news because her attacker was about to be paroled), and the deaths of four Orange County women within a 6-week period (each killed by a man against whom she had a restraining order). These cases became typifying examples, evidence of the need for an antistalking law. Supported by peace officers' associations and the Screen Actors Guild (SAG), California's law passed in 1990. When it took effect, the Los Angeles Police Department established a six-person Threat Management Unit (TMU) to investigate stalking cases. Both SAG's lobbying and the creation of a TMU in Los Angeles (with its many show business celebrities) reveal that concern over star-stalking fostered the initial antistalking law.

STALKING REDEFINED: FAILED RELATIONSHIPS
AND MALE VIOLENCE, 1992–1994

In 1992, other states began following California's example. Often, a highly publicized attack inspired lawmakers: "Behind almost every state stalking bill has been at least one local tragedy." Twenty-nine states passed antistalking laws (many modeled on California's law) in 1992; 18 other states and the District of Columbia followed suit in 1993. Also in 1992, Senator William Cohen (R—Maine) began calling for federal action, and the national media dramatically increased their coverage of stalking. Between 1980 and 1988, national magazines and television broadcasts averaged one story about stalking per year; during 1989–1991 (when star-stalking attracted attention) the average more than doubled to 2.3 stories per year; but there were 22.0 stories per year—another, nearly 10-fold increase—during 1992 through June 1994. Some stories achieved high visibility: *Washington Post* reporter George Lardner received a Pulitzer Prize for reporting on his daughter's murder by a stalker, and the award triggered additional press coverage; in 1993, Kathleen Krueger, wife of U.S. Senator Bob Krueger (D—Texas), used her own experiences as a stalking victim to campaign for a federal antistalking law.

These new claims reframed stalking as a women's issue, a widespread precursor to serious violence, typically committed by men against former spouses or lovers. The term "stalking"—now the consensus replacement for such earlier labels as psychological rape, star-stalking, and erotomania—implied deliberate intent to harm the victim:

> The verb "stalk" is defined as: (1) "to move threateningly or menacingly;" (2) "to pursue by tracking;" and (3) to go stealthily towards an animal "for the purpose of killing or capturing it." These definitions say much about the crime of stalking, suggesting that a stalker is a hunter, is dangerous, and thus should be avoided if at all possible.

In this new construction, stalking was a common problem. An often-repeated estimate suggested that there were 200,000 stalkers. We do not know the origin of this statistic. It first appears in our sample of national media coverage in *U.S. News and World Report*'s February 17, 1992 issue: "researchers suggest that up to 200,000 people exhibit a stalker's traits." Like other statistical estimates of social problem magnitude, this number soon took on a life of its own; it was often repeated, but never examined or explained. Other claimsmakers suggested that 200,000 was an underestimate:

There was an estimated 200,000 stalkers in the United States, and those are only the ones that we have track of.

Some two hundred thousand people in the U.S. pursue the famous. No one knows how many people stalk the rest of us, but the figure is probably higher.

Four million women that we know about—know about each year are beaten and terrorized and stalked by somebody they know.

Claimsmakers variously estimated that lifetime victimization by stalkers would affect one American in 40, or 30, or 20. The numbers varied, but there was agreement that stalking was increasing, "a national epidemic."

Most claimsmakers also agreed that stalking was a form of domestic violence against women. To be sure, occasional claimsmakers asserted that "the violent ending is actually very rare," that "men are stalked just as many times as women," or that the stalker was "often a total stranger." But most claims typified stalking as "almost exclusive to women," and "often preced[ing] violent acts, from assault to rape, child molestation, and murder." In this construction, stalkers were not strangers ("as many as 75 or 80 percent of cases involve people who were once married or dating," and their victims were not celebrities ("38 percent . . . are ordinary Americans").

Linking Stalking to Domestic Violence

This new construction connected stalking to a well-established social problem—domestic battering: " 'the majority of battered women experience stalking in some form,' says Vickie Smith, head of the Illinois Coalition Against Domestic Violence." The battered women's movement had long complained that the criminal justice system failed to protect women trying to escape abusive partners, that restraining orders were ineffective. By reframing these women's problems as stalking, a visible issue with connotations of extreme violence, battered women's claimsmakers could move their concerns to the top of the policy agenda.

During the intense claimsmaking of 1992–1993, there were only two published scholarly studies of stalkers: an examination of LAPD TMU files— "erotomanic and obsessional subjects in a forensic sample," and a typology of "criminal stalkers." Neither offered much original data. However, antistalking claimsmakers routinely borrowed data from research on domestic violence to characterize stalking:

Approximately 50 percent of all females who leave their husbands for reasons of physical abuse are followed, harassed, or further attacked by their former spouses. This phenomenon is known as "separation assault." . . . The broader concept is called "stalking."

Studies in Detroit and Kansas City reveal that 90 percent of those murdered by their intimate partners called police at least once.

Nearly one third of all women killed in America are murdered by their husbands or boyfriends, and, says Ruth Micklem, codirector of Virginians Against Domestic Violence, as many as 90 percent of them have been stalked.

The juxtaposition of the latter two quotes reveals how evidence used in claimsmaking evolves: Senator Cohen cited a finding that 90% of women killed by husbands or lovers had previously called the police; when later claimsmakers repeated that statistic, they equated having called the police with being stalked, ignoring the likelihood that many women called to complain about abuse by partners living in the same residence (and therefore not stalkers). Presumably similar assumptions lay behind U.S. Representative Joseph Kennedy's claim that, "Nine women a day are killed by stalkers in our country." Claimsmakers described antistalking laws as "an effective deterrent to domestic abuse"; West Virginia's original law narrowly defined victims as "those who either cohabitated or had intimate relationships with their stalkers."

Claims that many stalkers were former husbands or boyfriends cast virtually all women as potential victims: "We're not idiots up here that asked to be victims. This happens to anybody period" (former victim Stephanie). Here, as in earlier claims about star-stalking, victims bear no responsibility; claimsmakers emphasized that most victims did nothing to encourage their stalkers. (One exception was a talk show devoted to women harassing former boyfriends; the host repeatedly suggested that the men encouraged stalking.) In most ways, stalking's typification resembled that of domestic violence: "wife abuse is a label for severe, frequent, and continuing violence that escalates over time and is unstoppable. Such violence is that in which unrepentant men intentionally harm women and where women are not the authors of their own experiences which they find terrifying." Once they linked stalking to battering, claimsmakers had little difficulty attributing the same characteristics to both crimes.

This link became apparent in state legislative proceedings. Illinois lawmakers, for example, justified antistalking legislation by pointing to four recent cases of victims murdered by former husbands or boyfriends in Chicago suburbs. . . . [A] *Chicago Tribune* . . . editorial endorsing an antistalking law shared this frame: "Hundreds of women are threatened and harassed and intimidated by ex-boyfriends or ex-husbands. . . . [An antistalking law has] the potential to be a helpful weapon against domestic violence." Supported by the Illinois Coalition Against Domestic Violence, the bill received unanimous support in both legislative houses; mothers of two of the dead victims were on hand when the bill was signed into law. Both state and national branches of the battered women's movement and the victims' rights movement supported antistalking bills. The National Victim Center lobbied in more than a dozen states, and Theresa Saldana (a former stalking victim and the founder of Victims for Victims) campaigned in behalf of the laws. In Nebraska, for instance, both the Nebraska Coalition for Victims of Crime and the Nebraska Domestic Violence-Sexual Assault Coalition supported antistalking legislation. Stalking was now a form of both violent crime and domestic violence.

Patterns in Media Typification

Media coverage of stalking reflected this new construction. Table 1 compares the typifying examples—the cases illustrating the stalking problem—in national magazine articles and television broadcasts from 1980–1988, 1989–1991, and 1992–mid-1994. While stalking was always depicted as something male offenders did to female victims, this characterization intensified over time. Celebrity victims received more attention during 1989–1991, when claimsmakers focused on star-stalking. In 1992–1994, typifying examples were slightly more likely to feature victims who had been engaged or married to their stalkers, and less likely to depict stalkers who were strangers to their victims. And, perhaps most dramatically, later claimsmaking used more examples that ended in homicide. Stalking was reconstructed as a serious, violent crime, often committed against women by former or current husbands or lovers.

Earlier constructions of the stalking problem fell under joint ownership; the media consulted experts from both law and medicine. While lawyers and criminal justice system agents spoke of the law's difficulty in stopping stalkers, psychiatrists and psychologists interpreted stalking as mental disorder. Even after stalking's boundaries expanded to include much domestic abuse, most claims continued to depict stalking as a psychological problem: "Ninety percent of

TABLE 1.   Characteristics of Typifying Examples in Magazine Articles and Television Broadcasts about Stalking, 1980–1994[a]: Percentage of Examples with Different Characteristics[b]

	1980–1988 (%)	1989–1991 (%)	1992–June 1994 (%)	χ^{2c}
Victim is female	86	83	94	n.s.
Victim is a celebrity	18	48	16	0.002
Stalker is male	82	78	90	n.s.
Victim and stalker have been en- gaged or married	14	5	18	n.s.
Victim and stalker were strangers	24	68	19	0.001
Stalking leads to homicide	5	10	30	0.008
	($n = 22$)	($n = 23$)	($n = 170$)	

[a]1994 sources January through June only.
[b]Calculations do not include missing values.
[c]Statistical significance of χ^2 test

stalkers suffer from mental disorders." Oprah Winfrey offered this "profile" of stalkers: "low self-esteem, feelings of dependency, views people as possessions, fears abandonment, severely jealous, easily irritable and 40 percent of them have alcohol problems."

But claimsmakers denied that psychological problems absolved stalkers of responsibility. Some labeled stalkers "essentially evil" or located stalking within a context of male domination of women:

> They're not so much crazy men as slightly exaggerated men. They have a view that women should be controlled. . . . They tend to view women as property. . . . They target women because women are targets of oppor-tunity in our society.

> Another group . . . does this because it has something to do with men's privilege and they think it is OK to do this to women, and while I would-n't call them well-balanced people, I wouldn't call them crazy.

While claimsmakers after 1991 might not agree on a single model of stalkers' psychology, there was no hint—as there had been in some earlier claims about

TABLE 2. Authorities Cited in Magazine Articles and Television Broadcasts about Stalking, 1980–1994[a]: Percentage of Articles or Broadcasts Citing Different Authorities[b]

	1980–1988 (%)	1989–1991 (%)	1992–June 1994 (%)
Medical, mental health experts	44	71	36
Legal, criminal justice experts	44	71	65
Women's, victims' movement experts	11 (n = 9)	0 (n = 7)	22 (n = 55)

[a]1994 sources January through June only.
[b]Because an article or broadcast could cite more than one type of authority, percentages do not total 100%.

psychological rape—that female victims might bear any responsibility for being stalked. Typifying examples featuring children or adolescents as victims made the pedophile/stalker's responsibility especially clear.

After 1991, the medical model became less important in constructing the stalking problem. As Table 2 indicates, during both 1980–1988 and 1989–1991, the media turned to medical authorities as often as legal authorities. In contrast, only one pre-1992 story cited a representative of the battered women's or the victims' movements. After 1992, media discussions of stalking referred to mental health experts less often, while citations to representatives from the legal system remained stable, and references to experts from the battered women's and the victims' rights movements increased. (Because there were few articles and broadcasts before 1992, none of these findings is statistically significant.) This shift reflects the reconstruction of the stalking problem: the media asked legal authorities for assessments of the new antistalking laws, while members of the victims' and battered women's movements became relevant experts once stalking was linked to domestic violence.

The stalking problem, then, was not constructed all at once. After 1992, the press portrayed stalking as a violent crime against women, typically committed by former husbands or lovers. This construction built upon earlier (1989–1991) concern about star-stalking by men and women suffering from erotomania. And the issue of celebrity stalking had precursors in still earlier claims about harassment, obsession, and psychological rape, claims that, in retrospect, resemble the later claims about stalking.

RETYPIFICATION AND THE MOBILIZATION OF
CULTURAL AND ORGANIZATIONAL RESOURCES

* * *

The case of stalking demonstrates the complexity of successfully constructing new social problems. Preceded by earlier, less successful typifications, the successful construction of stalking combined three elements: (1) typifying claims, which mobilized both (2) cultural resources and (3) organizational resources.

Typifying Claims

The raw material for the stalking problem—people who objected to being harassed, harassment sometimes ending in homicide, even well-publicized cases with celebrity victims—existed long before claimsmakers began talking about "stalking." Presumably, the stalking problem might have been constructed much earlier than it was.

A key step in social problems construction is linking a troubling event to a problematic pattern, defining a particular *incident* as an *instance* of some larger problem. In the case of stalking, this juxtaposition of event and pattern occurred at several points, producing various typifications. While some media reports described the harassment of lone individuals, others juxtaposed several cases, suggesting they were all instances of psychological rape or fatal attractions or star-stalking. Of course, the key juxtaposition occurred in Southern California after 1989, when claimsmakers linked Rebecca Schaeffer's murder with the attacks on Theresa Saldana and the four women killed in Orange County.

Table 3 summarizes this sequence of typifications, noting some of the characteristics claimsmakers associated with psychological rape (1980–1988), star-stalking (1989–1991), and stalking (1992–1994). Although our analysis links these different claims, arguing that they dealt with essentially the same phenomenon, it is interesting to note how the typifications differed in their characterizations of the gender of both victim and offender, the victim's responsibility and celebrity, the nature of the offender's psychological problem, the prior relationship between victim and offender, and the prospect of violence.

Claimsmakers rarely offer formal definitions. Rather, they illustrate a problem's nature through typifying examples. We have already noted how typify-

TABLE 3. Elements in the Construction of Stalking as a Crime Problem

Period	Typifying Claims	Cultural Resources	Organizational Resources	Results
1980–1988	Psychological rape: males harass females; usually not violent; victim may share responsibility; obsessed offender	Vulnerability to harassment Women heading households		Occasional media coverage
1989–1991	Star-stalking: celebrity victim; offender can be either gender; offender may suffer from erotomania; offender may deteriorate; violence and homicide as outcomes; victim not responsible	Vulnerability to harassment Random violence	Screen Actors Guild lobbying Celebrity protection services	Increased media coverage California law passed
1992–1994	Stalking: males harass females; often former intimates; form of domestic violence; victim not responsible; statistical claims; homicide as outcome	Vulnerability to harassment Victimization of women Male violence Pedophilia	Crime victims' movement Battered women's movement LAPD TMU	Frequent media coverage Laws in other states Federal attention

ing examples presented in the media changed. By 1992, claimsmakers offered other evidence to support the current typification of stalking, including statistical claims (e.g., the number of stalking cases, the frequency of stalking-related homicides, the proportion of victims whose stalkers were former intimates). This represented domain expansion: stalking claims expanded what had been a relatively narrow focus on star-stalking to include much domestic violence.

Cultural Resources

Not all claims receive ratification from press, public, and policymakers. Constructionist analysts suggest that claims attract notice when they "relate to deep mythic themes," have "cultural resonance," or draw upon "cultural resources." Claims can be packaged in ways more or less likely to elicit favorable responses, and the cultural themes that claims evoke are a key element in this packaging.

Consider a central theme in stalking claims: the victim's inability to make the harasser stop. These claims routinely emphasized the victims' emotions, e.g., their frustration and anxiety over the continuing harassment and their uncertainty and fear over what might happen next. The obsessive pursuit of another is a standard theme in American popular culture; many movies, novels, and popular songs center around obsessive love. The treatment can be comic or romantic (e.g., the would-be lover who won't give up until love is reciprocated, as in *The Graduate*), but it is often central to horror or suspense stories (e.g., *Fatal Attraction, The Bodyguard*). This suggests widespread cultural recognition of the troubling qualities of such pursuit. Of course, the relationship between cultural resources and claimsmaking is not one-way. Claimsmakers draw upon available cultural resources, but their claims also inform and shape popular culture. For example, one 1994 suspense novel borrows heavily from stalking claims: the hero, a police detective in Beverly Hills' TMU, discusses the psychological and social patterns of stalkers.

It is more difficult to prove a link between other, less specific cultural resources and the success of stalking claims. For instance, concern over stalking may have reflected the growing proportion of households headed by women, to the degree that women not living with a man seemed more vulnerable to a stalker's harassment. And concerns expressed in other claimsmaking campaigns seem consistent with the emergence of stalking as a social problem. These include concern over random violence (found in claims about serial murder, freeway shootings, drive-by shootings, carjacking, and other crimes), male violence and the victimization of women (forcible rape, date and acquaintance rape, and domestic violence), and pedophilia. When claims-makers typified stalking as random or unpredictable, violent, or gendered, they drew upon cultural resources that might encourage a favorable response to their claims. If stalking was somehow "like" other, well-established problems, then claims about stalking became more credible.

Organizational Resources

Claims also vary in the degree to which specific organizations promote them. In a competitive social problems marketplace, whether well-publicized claims lead to policy changes depends less on press coverage than upon organized pressure to propose, pass, and implement new policies. During its brief moment in the national spotlight in 1987, freeway violence attracted more intense press coverage than stalking ever received, yet the issue faded within a few weeks. Press coverage drew attention to freeway violence, but when the media's attention shifted, no one continued promoting the problem.

Prior to 1989, claims about psychological rape lacked significant organizational support, and these issues never attracted prolonged attention. Mobilization of organizational resources occurred only after Rebecca Shaeffer's murder and the retypification of the problem as star-stalking. Key actors in promoting star-stalking had ties to the entertainment industry: the media's appetite for dramatic news about celebrities ensured increased coverage; individuals who specialized in providing security services for celebrities (e.g., Gavin de Becker) discussed their work with the media; and the SAG [Screen Actors Guild] lobbied for California's antistalking law.

But antistalking laws spread only when other social movements supported the new legislation. In particular, the battered women's movement and the victims' rights movement campaigned for laws modeled on the California statute. Linking their cause with the visible problem of star-stalking gave the battered women's movement a fresh face. Coupling longstanding complaints about ineffective restraining orders to the lethal menace of stalking turned a tired topic into a hot issue. Antistalking laws put reform of the restraining order process on the public agenda, promising to give an established system of control new teeth. Media coverage of stalking increasingly cited experts from such organizations as Virginians Against Domestic Violence. These statewide groups had links to the National Victim Center, Victims for Victims, and other victims' rights organizations. Like other long-term social movements, the victims' rights movement must continually reframe their claims in fresh ways. Opposition to stalking linked both the battered women's movement and the victims' rights movement to a new, dramatic, highly visible problem. By assuming ownership and using their resources to continue promoting the stalking problem, these movements kept stalking before the public and policymakers.

Mobilizing organizational resources helped pass antistalking legislation, but the absence of organized opposition may have been equally important. Violent, even murderous crimes by vengeful ex-husbands or mentally disturbed fans had few defenders; the campaign for antistalking laws met little opposition. While civil libertarians questioned the laws' constitutionality, the consensus deplored stalking.

* * *

QUESTIONS

1. Why was the *star stalking* frame that was predominant in news reporting between 1989 and 1991 so much more influential than the *obsession and psychological rape* frame that activists had used from 1980 to 1988?

2. Why did the reframing of stalking as *violence against women* between 1992 and 1994 give significantly greater urgency to the problem, as evidenced by the explosion of media coverage and many states' passage of antistalking laws?

3. How did women's rights activists such as the Illinois Coalition Against Domestic Violence piggyback on the visibility of the domestic violence problem in their efforts to bring greater attention to stalking?

4. In depicting stalking as the obsessive pursuit of a woman by a man, how did activists tap into a longstanding theme in American popular culture? Why were activists' efforts to attach their agenda to this theme consequential?

18

A Picture Is Worth a
Thousand Words

IRA SILVER

*Photos are crucial to the construction of social problems since they literally provide
a picture of what a problem looks like and its magnitude, as well as a moral com-
pass guiding how audiences ought to feel about the problem and the urgency of
addressing it. Photos carry tremendous power in framing the importance of addressing specific problems in particular ways because they convey meanings that words
alone rarely can articulate. Without such visibility, social problems do not get the
kind of exposure needed to galvanize broad public awareness and policy reforms.*

Illustration 1 was featured in the extensive news coverage of the devastating Indian Ocean tsunami that occurred on December 26, 2004. The photo
puts a human face on this disaster and the horrors it inflicted. No words can
possibly capture the scene pictured here, as this woman, surrounded by a
morass of dead children, appears utterly devastated as she tries to fathom the
magnitude of the tragedy unfolding all around her.

The tsunami galvanized the largest international humanitarian relief effort
of any human disaster in history. Governments, private institutions, and individuals around the world made charitable contributions that totaled in the billions of dollars. Photos like this one were instrumental in calling forth incredible
compassion on a global scale. For indeed, this photo fostered the image that
the tsunami was first and foremost a *human* tragedy. This was a particularly
powerful image for Americans, given that the disaster took place on the other
side of the world and seemingly did not affect Americans. But who could not
relate to, and have compassion for, a woman crying out in desperation for help
as children lay dying by her side!

Illustration 1. (Bettmann/Corbis)

Terry Schiavo (Illustration 2) is now a household name, symbolizing the battleground in American society over the right to die. If someone did not recognize her as the woman in this photo, that would be a powerful indication of exactly what the photo aimed to convey. For indeed, the photo did not depict a woman who appeared to be in a "persistent vegetative state," as those defending her right to die claimed was her immutable medical condition. Rather, we see a woman who, like millions of other women, looks alert and vibrant. This was, of course, exactly the image that those defending Terry Schiavo's right to life wanted audiences to have.

Illustration 3 shows two scenes of desperation following Hurricane Katrina. The first photo, of a dark-skinned man, was accompanied by the caption: "A young man walks through chest deep floodwater after looting a grocery store in New Orleans." The second photo, of two lighter-skinned people, was captioned: "Two residents wade through chest-deep water after finding bread and soda from a local grocery store after Hurricane Katrina came through the area in New Orleans."

Given how each of these photos was captioned, the two photos present contrasting images about personal responsibility in the wake of this disaster. The first photo suggests that this man was committing a crime by eating food that did not belong to him. He was irresponsible not just for "looting" but

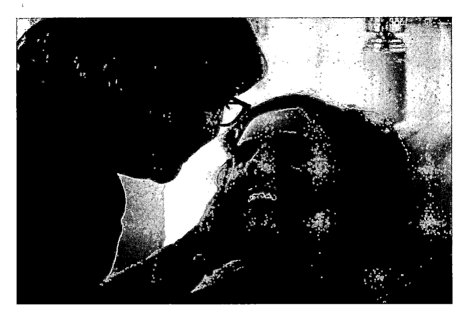

Illustration 2. (*New York Times*, published multiple times during 2004 and 2005)

also, as other post-storm images suggested, for being a holdout who chose not to evacuate the city as the storm neared and was now taking advantage of the free supplies left behind in abandoned stores. This man is portrayed not as a victim of Hurricane Katrina but rather as caught in the act of victimizing those who have already been dealt a serious blow by this storm. The second photo, on the other hand, presents these two people as victims—as people left in ruins by the floodwaters who have luckily "found" some food to help them make do until help arrives. Unlike the first man, these people deserve our sympathy.

The two photos comprising Illustration 4 were part of a *Time* feature entitled "School Shootings: A Deadly Pattern," which chronicled a series of school shootings that took place during the two years prior to the 1999 Columbine massacre and suggested that these incidents were all linked. Shown side by side, these photos suggest a national *pattern* in the occurrence of school shootings. The framing of this pattern was based on an array of similarly grisly events taking place in schools in geographically disparate parts of the United States. The first photo is of the December 1, 1997, shooting at Heath High School in Paducah, Kentucky, where a 14-year-old boy killed three fellow students and wounded five others. The second photo is of the March 21, 1998, shooting at Thurston High School in Springfield, Oregon, where a boy killed two and wounded twenty after killing his parents the previous day.

The pair of photos in Illustration 5 is trying to dramatize a problem that, compared to the others discussed thus far, has been difficult for claimsmakers to portray visually: global warming. Unlike many other issues such as

Illustration 3. (*Associated Press*, August 2005)

Illustration 4. (*Time*, 1999)

school shootings, the harmful consequences of global warming are not easy to discern in the short term. This pairing of photos aims to illustrate that global warming *is* having demonstrable effects, and that people need to start paying attention to this problem and work to address it.

The caption accompanying these photos says: "Some scientists predict that a warmer climate will trigger more violent storms, which will cause increased rates of coastal erosion. This is a section of shoreline at Cape Hatteras in North

Illustration 5. (*BBC News*)

Carolina in the USA, pictured in 1999 and 2004. The southern United States and Caribbean region were battered by a series of powerful hurricanes last year (2005)." These photos are significant because they reflect a growing trend in recent years for claimsmakers to make global warming more visible by linking it to hurricanes, for which there are abundant visible images dramatizing the harm. Claimsmakers especially want audiences to associate global warming with the array of unforgettable images people have of Hurricane Katrina and how it ravaged the Gulf Coast.

QUESTIONS

1. Much of the power that photos have in constructing social problems lies in their ability to convince audiences that the problem affects them directly. Discuss how this claim is conveyed in the photos depicted above.

2. For Illustration 3, how does pairing these two photos side by side reinforce racial stereotypes? Which stereotypes in particular? Use the selection by Gilens (Reading 14) to characterize the depth of these stereotypes.

3. For Illustration 4, what are the implications of using these photos to frame different episodes of school shootings as comprising a *pattern*? What does this frame suggest is the magnitude of the school shootings problem? Why does this frame carry such credibility even though, as the Joel Best selection "When Kids Become Victims of Violence" in Part Three of this volume indicates, no such pattern actually existed during the late 1990s?

4. How successfully does the pair of photos in Illustration 5 counteract the future-orientation obstacles that Sheldon Ungar describes in the selection "Selling Environmental Problems" contained in Part Three of this volume—obstacles that have prevented global warming from attracting significant public and policymaking attention?

PART THREE
COMPETITION AMONG SOCIAL PROBLEMS

There are many more problems in the world than there are resources for addressing them, and people have only so much time, energy, and money. Social problems compete with other matters that preoccupy us, such as school, work, and our relationships with friends and family. During those times when social problems manage to enter into our thinking, most of us can only devote our attention to the one or two issues that seem the most pressing at the time (Loseke, 1999). And as far as money goes, our society simply cannot address all problems with the funds that are available. Although private citizens, foundations, and the government collectively have enormous resources to devote to fixing problems in the world, these problems must continuously compete with one another for a piece of the pie.

How well a particular problem fares against the competition typically has more to do with how it is presented to audiences than with the problem itself. In other words, those harms that inflect the greatest objective danger are not necessarily the ones that get the most attention. Attention depends instead on the following: Who is affected by the problem? Which claimsmakers speak on its behalf? And how sellable is the harm? Looking at social problems in these ways, it becomes clear that problems compete within a marketplace in the same way that consumer products compete against one another. Explaining why, for example, terrorism is a higher national priority nowadays than malnutrition requires the same kinds of investigative tools as explaining why Coca-Cola outsells generic, store-brand colas. Like a successful product that depends on slick marketing, a social problem will beat out the competition if and when claimsmakers pitch the issue in ways that tap into audiences' interests and concerns. Hence, although claimsmakers vary widely in their specific societal roles, they have one thing in common when it comes to social problems. All are involved in the business of marketing particular kinds of problems to wider audiences. ,

Competition between social problems manifests itself most typically within a specific issue area. Take the environment, for example. Nowadays, there are many environmental problems that receive public and policymaking attention. These include acid rain, hazardous waste, pesticides, ozone depletion, and global warming. Yet, there is substantial variation in how much attention these issues receive. The comparison between ozone depletion and global warming is particularly interesting. While both of these issues are familiar to many people, ozone depletion is the issue that more people feel demands immediate attention and can be solved through their own actions. Despite the growing sense of urgency that leading climatologists nowadays attach to halting global warming, this issue still remains one that people have a hard time wrapping their hands around and recognizing as immediately in need of fixing (Ungar, 1998).

The different degree of success that ozone depletion and global warming have had in galvanizing public and policymaking attention has everything to do with claimsmakers' capacity to package these problems. Indeed, winning the competition has had little, if anything, to do with the objective magnitude of the problems themselves. Many environmental scientists see global warming as the *more* pressing issue here in the United States—in part because it simply poses a more pronounced threat, and in part because ozone depletion has successfully attracted responsive action from private citizens and our government has been willing to cooperate with other nations in stopping the production of chemicals that are harmful to the ozone layer.

Another noteworthy example of competition between social problems concerns the victimization of youth by violence. Enormous attention has been given in recent years to school shootings—the 1999 massacre at Columbine High School in Littleton, Colorado, being one of the most infamous casees. Media coverage of school shootings tends to be extensive, with follow-up stories running for days, weeks, or even months on end. School shootings are a highly marketable manifestation of how youth are victimized by violence, since there are so many different kinds of visual images that can provocatively portray the horror taking place. These images collectively construct one of the most effective ways that social problems compete for attention and resources: via ironic contrast. Since schools are places that evoke a variety of benign images, the notion that this safe haven for youth is actually a war zone conveys shock on a massive scale because there are millions of parents who send their children off to school every morning.

The marketability of the school shootings problem explains why there exists a public perception nowadays that there has been an epidemic of school shootings in recent years (Best, 2002). This perception persists in the face of statistical evidence indicating that over the very period that the news media, politicians, school administrators and other claimsmakers constructed this epidemic—the 1990s—violent crime fell by 50% across U.S. schools. Another noteworthy yet unpublicized statistic is that virtually all instances in which youth are victimized by violence take place *away* from school (Butterfield, 2004). Nevertheless, political rhetoric and public policy have been steadfastly directed toward making schools safer through the implementation of a variety of measures. These include stationing police officers in hallways, ending after-school programs, increasing suspensions and expulsions, and prosecuting juveniles as adults (Donohue, Schiraldi, and Ziedenberg, 2005).

Policymakers have worked to implement these kinds of measures because they stand as tangible evidence of their commitment to stopping the school shootings epidemic. Indeed, for any social problem, policies and reforms that *visibly* demonstrate that the problem is being fixed are instrumental in enabling that problem to beat out the competition. This theme helps to explain the unprecedented outpouring of international charity in the aftermath of the December 2004 Indian Ocean tsunami. Certainly the devastating magnitude of this disaster—with estimates as high as 250,000 people dead and millions left without food, water, shelter, or medical supplies—cannot be overstated. Yet, it is instructive to consider why this particular episode of suffering that afflicted several countries in Africa and Asia galvanized such incredible relief efforts, whereas other episodes of suffering in these same places routinely do not.

Soon after the tsunami, United Nations humanitarian chief Jan Egeland publicized the fact that at least 30,000 people die every single day throughout the Third World of preventable causes such as starvation and disease. This means that in little over a week's time more people die from these causes than perished in the tsunami ("Official fears drop in aid for others," 2005). Yet, these everyday tragedies seldom get media coverage, precisely because they occur every day. News reports tend to emphasize events that are both atypical and easily visible to audiences. The tsunami perfectly fit this combination, given the rarity of the calamity and the fact that many tourists who were on their Christmas vacations videotaped the carnage as it was unfolding. Not only did the tsunami receive monumentally more news coverage than do everyday calamities in the very same parts of the world stemming from disease and malnutrition, but the charitable response to the tsunami was, as a result, exponentially greater (Hertzberg, 2005).

As students interested in analyzing competition between social problems, we must recognize that freakish disasters like the tsunami that capture the media spotlight are not necessarily worse than those misfortunes that occur on an everyday basis. For example, we can compare the massive media exposure and charitable response that victims of Hurricane Katrina received with the paltry public and policymaking attention that poor people in New Orleans (and other U.S. cities) got before the hurricane. While news coverage of the hurricane exposed the dark realities of urban poverty to millions of onlookers in ways that journalism rarely has before, this problem was every bit as real before the storm hit and will remain long after the relief funds have been allocated (Shipler, 2005). The fact that natural disasters tend to out-compete everyday calamities for resources illustrates that natural disasters are more marketable, but not necessarily more harmful or deserving of resources. Indeed, given the billions of dollars in humanitarian relief that the Indian

Ocean tsunami and Hurricane Katrina collectively amassed, these disasters arguably became *less* deserving of charitable funds than are the everyday suffering that poor people experience, both in the United States and throughout the world.

Attempting to understand why the Indian Ocean tsunami and Hurricane Katrina were more marketable than the everyday calamities poor people experience brings us back to looking at public policies aimed at mitigating the victimization of youth by violence. Just as a case can be made that putting police officers in schools makes them visibly safer, sending $50 to an international relief organization such as Doctors Without Borders after the tsunami was a way that a donor could visibly help a person left homeless by the disaster. It would be much less clear to that donor how sending the same $50 one week prior to the tsunami to help distribute tuberculosis vaccines would have been of significant help, since the victims of tuberculosis were not visible to the donor via the news media in the ways that the tsunami victims were. This point underscores a more general theme: that a social problem will win out over the competition if claimsmakers can successfully make both the harm and the remedy visible to audiences. Competition is won based on marketability, not on the objective severity of the problems competing for resources.

REFERENCES

Best, Joel. (2002, Summer). Monster hype: How a few isolated tragedies—and their supposed causes—were turned into a national epidemic. *Education Next* 2(2): 51–55.

Blasi, Gary. (1994). And we are not seen: Ideological and political barriers to understanding homelessness. *American Behavioral Scientist* 37: 563–586.

Butterfield, Fox. (2004, November 30). Crime in schools fell sharply over the ten years ended '02. *New York Times*, p. A19.

Donohue, Elizabeth, Vincent Schiraldi, and Jason Ziedenberg. (2005). School house hype: School shootings and the real risks kids face in America. From Leonard Cargan and Jeanne H. Ballantine (Eds.), *Sociological footprints: Introductory readings in sociology* (pp. 225–231). Belmont, CA: Thomson Wadsworth.

Hertzberg, Hendrik. (2005, January 17). Flood tide. *New Yorker* 81: 35–36.

Loseke, Donileen. (1999). The people and the tasks in constructing social problems. From *Thinking about social problems: An introduction to constructionist perspectives* (pp. 25–44). New York: De Gruyter.

Official fears drop in aid for others. (2005, January 1). *Boston Globe*, p. A18.

Shipler, David. (2005, November/December). If polls ignore poverty, the press does too. *Columbia Journalism Review* 44(4): 11–12.

Ungar, Sheldon. (1998). Bringing the issue back in: Comparing the marketability of the ozone hole and global warming. *Social Problems* 45: 510–527.

19

Selling Environmental Problems

FROM *Bringing the Issue Back In: Comparing the Marketability of the Ozone Hole and Global Warming*

SHELDON UNGAR

Sheldon Ungar explores how different environmental problems compete with one another for public attention by comparing ozone depletion and global warming. Although these are both issues that large segments of the American public have heard about and have a basic familiarity with, ozone depletion has been more successfully constructed as an issue that people feel must be addressed in a timely fashion. Ungar shows that this discrepancy is not due to the fact that the ozone hole has gotten greater claimsmaking attention; to the contrary, global warming has been more widely publicized. Rather, the issues themselves have different degrees of marketability. Marketing global warming is challenging because audiences see it as a future-oriented problem without a solution that can produce visible short-term reductions in harm. In contrast, the ozone hole can be neatly packaged as a problem that people believe can be meaningfully addressed through their own individual actions—namely reducing the use of products that contain chemicals harmful to the ozone layer.

* * *

. . . Scientists customarily define global warming as a future-oriented problem, with effects predominately predicted for the middle or end of the next century. From the start of concerted scientific claimsmaking in the late 1970s, a future orientation became a definitive characteristic of this problem for numerous and often overlapping reasons. First, the doubling of pre-industrial CO_2 levels will not occur until about 2060. Doubling can be considered a benchmark measure, a binary that is more intuitively clear than claiming that levels have increased by (for instance) 40 percent. Doubling was also significant because scientists held that their computer models of the climate system were

243

too primitive to deal with smaller changes on a shorter-term basis. At the time, scientists were only beginning to collect the long-term observations that could be used to document climate changes over time. In order to generate concern, the size of impacts delineated in scientific scenarios had to be sufficiently large or visible on a human scale (e.g., a meter of sea-level rise, rather than a few centimeters) that they would take decades to occur on a natural scale. Finally, since computer models only predict general tendencies, particular extreme weather events cannot be directly attributed to climate change.

* * *

This discussion suggests that a future-orientation is a "sticky" element of the scientific trajectory of global warming. That is, the idea recurs so regularly that it is a definitive, unavoidable, undeniable definitional feature of the problem. It is a resource that anyone making claims about the problem can securely draw on. Yet, from the point of view of selling the problem, a future-orientation creates a clear discursive liability. Specifically, concern about the future is discounted in institutional thinking and in virtually every public arena. Since people are apparently unwilling to sacrifice much for future generations, selling a future-oriented—and by implication somewhat uncertain—threat is extremely difficult. So stable and recurrent is this effect that economists routinely devalue the future in their calculations. Given its wide purview, future discounting can be regarded as a stable discursive formation or cultural given that results in *expectable* limitations on the marketability of a future-oriented social problem. Certainly the distant nature of the threat is routinely referenced by climate activists who bemoan its existence even as they search for ways to render the envisioned fate of our grandchildren real and vivid.

* * *

THE PRESENT STUDY

* * *

The Differential Outcomes Attained by the Two Problems

.   * * *

The threat of ozone depletion has twice attained celebrity standing among social problems. In the 1970s, there were concerns about ozone loss due to supersonic aircraft and aerosol cans. However, a National Research Council Report (NRC) concluded in 1984 that the threat was greatly exaggerated. Still, major Northern nations agreed in 1985 to the Vienna Convention, that provided a framework without controls. That year also brought the "surprise" discovery of an ozone hole over Antarctica, which culminated in the 1987 Montreal Protocols. This was not only the first international treaty on a global ecological problem, but is widely regarded as a landmark regime and prototype for future negotiations. Its significant innovations include automatic provisions for review and funding by rich nations for adaptations by the poorer nations. Reviews have led to expedited schedules for complete phase outs of most chemicals suspected of causing ozone damage. The United Nations reports general compliance with treaty provisions (with some black marketing of CFCs) and measurable reductions of depleting emissions.

In recent times, the threat of global warming was announced at the First World Climate Conference in 1979. The first scientific consensus emerged in 1985 in Villach, Austria. However, it was the concatenating weather impacts of the summer of 1988 that rendered it a celebrity issue. This "greenhouse summer" underwrote the reaction of the Intergovernmental Panel on Climate Change (IPCC) and the 1992 Framework Convention on Climate Change signed at the Rio Earth Summit. Commentary on the Convention broadly agrees that it creates weak commitments, asking that the industrialized nations "aim" to stabilize CO_2 emissions at 1990 levels by 2000. This non-binding target falls far short of the recommendations made by the IPCC (which called for a worldwide 60–80 percent reduction of greenhouse gas emissions), and most nations will overshoot even the modest stabilization target. The 1997 Kyoto agreement on climate change requires industrial nations to reduce their greenhouse gas emissions by amounts varying between 6 and 8 percent by 2010.

There are often gaps between signed international commitments and national responses. Domestic policy also tends to be more changeable than international agreements, since the anarchical international system affords little leeway for revisions. With ozone depletion, the U.S. took the leading role in negotiations and provided the incentives that moved other nations. Du Pont, the largest producer of CFCs, was the first to announce that it would cease all production of suspect chemicals. Despite earlier opposition, other U.S. companies promptly announced similar actions and initiated an "energetic pursuit" of substitutes.

In international negotiations on global warming, the U.S. played the opposite role. It was steadfast in opposing a stabilization target. That President Bush even went to Rio was attributed to domestic pressures; Rio occurred during an election year, and all five potential Democratic Presidential candidates criticized the administration for refusing to accept a quantified target. Candidate Clinton said he would give "serious consideration" to cuts of 20–30 percent by 2005. The Clinton/Gore administration subsequently signed the Convention, but only established "voluntary" controls. Clinton's effort to impose an energy tax was beaten back by an array of opposition. As a result, the U.S., which ranks first in greenhouse gas emissions, will overshoot the Rio target by about 10 percent.

With the Kyoto meetings, the U.S. played a less obstructive role, though it is not clear that its climate policy has significantly changed. In July 1997, and in direct contrast with the ozone protocols, the Senate passed the Byrd-Hagel resolution prohibiting the government from entering any commitments to restrict emissions unless developing countries accept some limitations on their own emissions. A proposed research and tax incentive package to comply with Kyoto worth $6.3 billion over five years has been killed by Republicans in the Senate. Even if these recommendations were implemented, spending on energy alternatives would remain at historically low levels (a proposed $2.7 billion versus a 1978 peak of $10 billion, in current dollars).

At the level of public concern, poll data is gathered too infrequently and questions are too broad to differentiate between the two problems. However, studies of public understanding of these problems reveal significant differences. Using diverse but nonrandom samples, this research reveals that people have limited scientific knowledge about global warming and tend to confound it with ozone depletion. . . . " . . . [R]esults are consistent with . . . [the] claim that 'the ozone hole has arrived as a concept in the U.S. public's consciousness, but the greenhouse effect is entering primarily as a subset of the ozone hole phenomenon, the closest model available.' " . . . "[L]ay informants had virtually no knowledge of the policies for global warming actually being debated" and misunderstand the idea of energy efficiency and its ramifications.

Personal actions on the two social problems are similarly lopsided. With the ozone threat, there have been a number of successful consumer boycotts, notably of *McDonalds* and of aerosol cans, and several scholars report that a mobilized public was instrumental in getting European nations to agree to controls. In the case of global warming, U.S. consumers have not made *any* efforts to reduce energy consumption. Rather, they have steadily eroded the conservation measures created in response to the two oil crises. Statistics reveal that people are driving more, using more gas, and getting lower mileage. The last statistic is particularly significant; the fastest growing segment of vehicles sales is in the low mileage vans, sports utility vehicles, and pickup trucks. The top selling American vehicle is the Ford F-series pickup (followed by Chevrolet pickups, and the Camry being a distant third) that gets 16 city and 21 highway miles per gallon. The top selling European vehicle is the Fiat Punto; it gets 42 miles per gallon. Continuous complaints led the U.S. government to rescind the 55 mile-per-hour speed limit. Despite the recycling bandwagon in the late 1980s, energy conservation appears to be a moribund issue at present. While "personal" solutions will not solve the problem, buildings and transport together constitute close to 50 percent of the forecasted carbon emissions for 2010.

Explaining (Some of) the Divergent Outcomes

The preceding discussion suggests that ozone depletion consistently faired better than global warming in international negotiations and in political and public responses in the United States. Hence the obvious question: why? . . .

. . . [T]he present analysis first delineates those conditions common to the two problems. It then considers the possible role of claimsmaking in explaining the differential outcomes obtained in political and public arenas. The paper goes on to examine differences between the two problems that either congealed or failed to congeal into a hot crisis.

Similarities Between the Two Problems

In many respects, ozone depletion and global warming are eminently comparable. Both social problems are portrayed as global environmental threats pertaining to the atmosphere. Both are claimed to result from anthropogenic emissions. Both are "invisible" as such, and can *only* be detected through assembling scientific research and claims. Both are slow-onset problems whose *main* predicted risk is in the future. As well, both portend potentially apocalyptic outcomes. Finally, the two problems intersect, since CFCs are a potent greenhouse gas.

Beyond these common physical and scientific properties are fortuitous overlaps in timing. Starting around 1980 and continuing through the decade, an issue culture builds-up around the atmosphere as a number of issues from this domain rise in tandem or quick succession. Thus the popular theory that climatic change caused the extinction of the dinosaurs was followed by a furor over the threat of nuclear winter. But the Cold War began to wind down after 1985, just in time for the discovery of the ozone hole. But here the timing is remarkable. In its second incarnation as the ozone hole, the ozone problem peaked politically and in the public consciousness between 1985 and 1987. The ozone problem was resolved just in time for its sister issue to be carried along and became a celebrity problem. Global warming peaked in 1988 and 1989. Prior claimsmaking about global warming occasioned only sporadic interest in different public arenas. The issue was put on the map by the greenhouse summer of 1988. The oil industry, which has been a mainstay of opposition to claims about climate change, then took a hit with the *Exxon Valdez* oil spill in early 1989.

The coincident timing of these two global environmental threats has been widely noticed:

> [p]erhaps one reason expectations were so high [for global warming] is the success of negotiating the Montreal Protocols. . . . Environmental NGOs and negotiators moved from ozone to climate change, many of them expecting the second shot to be much like the first one.

Not only were there overlaps in the cast of claimsmakers from the United Nations and environmental organizations, but both social problems peaked during a ripe issue climate when public concern for the environment also crested. . . . Significantly, the peaks of the two problems were so concurrent that changing domestic political opportunities do not afford a good alternative explanation for their differential success. Although public environmental concern started to decline in the 1990s, it held its own until after the 1992 Rio Earth Summit.

* * *

THE ROLE OF CLAIMSMAKING ACTIVITIES

. . . Hence I first ask whether differences in claimsmaking can account for the immense differences in outcomes between the two problems. In other words, were the definitional activities surrounding ozone depletion more viable than those attending global warming—independent of the issues involved? The analysis considers the quantity of claimsmaking in the mass media, the cast of claimsmakers, as well as timing. A separate section examines rhetorical issues.

Over twenty-five years of research on the basic agenda-setting hypothesis demonstrates that the amount of media coverage of an issue is a major determinant of public awareness. More specifically, the media functions better to tell the public what to think about (a salience effect), rather than to tell it how to think about it (a persuasion effect). Events that figure prominently in the media seem to be more "available" or retrievable from memory and are regarded as more "representative" than events that attract less coverage.

Further specifications reveal that the agenda-setting effect is strengthened when prominent media coverage is allied with "obtrusive" real-world cues (as in the case of inflation) that are directly available to members of the public. Agenda-setting also works through a "quantity of coverage" effect, whereby increased coverage not only heightens the salience of the issue but increases fear of and opposition to the specific environmental hazard. . . . [M]edia attention and public opinion are parallel but distinct systems of constructing meaning, the relative absence of direct measures of the latter often leads researchers to employ the amount of media coverage as a surrogate for public concern.

Quantity of coverage is clearly not decisive in the present case. Figure 1 plots the number of magazine stories in the *Reader's Guide to Periodical Literature* and the number of news stories on the three major U.S. television

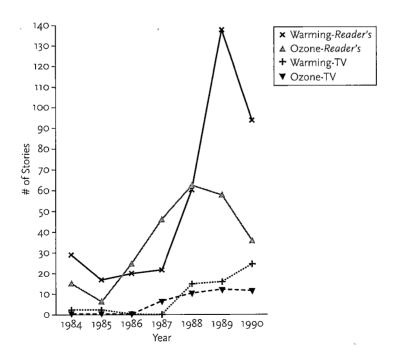

Figure 1

networks devoted to the two problems over the crest of their celebrity issue-attention cycles. Besides revealing the clear temporal overlap between the two problems, Figure 1 shows that at its pinnacle global warming attracts more than twice as many stories in magazines and on TV as did ozone depletion. A separate analysis for the *New York Times* reveals a dead heat, with each problem peaking at about 50 stories (ozone depletion in 1989, global warming in 1990).

Beyond the sheer amount of coverage in the media, the two problems can be compared in terms of the amount of attention they receive in other public arenas and the power and activities of the communities of operatives that formed around them. Short of international negotiations, the most important non-media public arena is arguably the U.S. Congress. With ozone depletion, congressional activity peaked in 1987 with 12 hearings and publications; the two subsequent years averaged about 10 hearings and publications. With global warming, congressional activity peaked in 1989 at 34; the two subsequent years attracted, respectively, about 30 and 25 hearings and publications.

Global warming's quantitative advantage carries through, at least in part, to the claimsmaking activities of the relevant communities of operatives. When it comes to major environmental groups and Non-Governmental Organizations, many followed the practice that had emerged with nuclear issues and first applied themselves to ozone depletion and then shifted to the greenhouse effects. While fewer scientists transferred their activities, several researchers observe that the "level of involvement by scientists in the climate change issue is unprecedented." One indicator of this is the prominence of the scientists and scientific organizations that have come out over this issue. Over 1600 scientists, including a majority of living Nobel laureates, signed the "Global Warning" that took direct aim at climate change. And the Royal Society of London broke 300 years of official silence on public concerns and issued a warning about population growth and climate change. Finally, global warming appears to have thrown up a number of scientific celebrities, notably James Hansen and Stephen Schneider. Ozone depletion did not attract laureates or create media stars.

A further objection can be raised against the claimsmaking argument: the issue of timing. Figure 1 reveals that the highest level of coverage of the ozone problem in magazines occurs in 1988, followed by 1989. Similarly, coverage on television news and the New York Times both peak in 1989. Only congressional activity reached its zenith in the critical 1985 to 1987 period, when the Montreal Protocols were hammered out. But if the surge of media coverage *followed* rather than preceded political and public action on the issue, it casts some doubt on the significance of claimsmaking, at least as it manifests itself in the media. In this instance, it can be suggested that the apparent scientific closure of the issue in 1984 retarded subsequent media interest in the topic. In any case, there is the puzzling result of the substantial domestic success of ozone depletion in a context of relatively limited claimsmaking activities at key points in time. With global warming, in contrast, peak media and congressional activity occur in 1989 and 1990, just after the greenhouse summer and prior to the Rio agreement.

Problem Trajectories and Missed Opportunities

The ensuing discussion pursues the following question: given its advantages in claimsmaking and timing, why did global warming consistently fare so much more poorly than ozone depletion? One possibility is to focus on rhetoric. Perhaps, despite the problem of late-peaking media coverage, the rhetorical strategies designed for ozone depletion did the trick. Thus it is clear that the ozone "hole" was an exaggeration or metaphor and that satellite pictures were doctored and colored to make them more graphic. However, there remains the question of *why* the hole—in Britain it is often referred to as a "crater"—could bear such an explanatory burden?

To give credence to this position, it might be simultaneously maintained that the (more prevalent and timely) rhetoric surrounding global warming missed the boat. Such counterfactual claims, of course, are almost immune to evidence. Commentators would need to know the range of claims that were assayed. More difficult still, they would have to judge which unmade claims were in fact "viable" and hence could have been successfully promoted.

Ongoing perusal of scientific, media, and environmental claims about global warming since 1988 casts doubt on the missed opportunities position. Rather, the reading suggests that claimsmaking pertaining to this issue resembles trial balloons. A multiplicity of metaphors (the "heat trap", "earth fever", "dead heat") and attempted linkages with other congenial issues (ozone depletion, strange weather, emerging diseases, clean air and a "no regret" policy, biodiversity) can be found. Essentially, claimsmakers are continually searching for striking formulations that will be taken up, "resonate," and mobilize actions.

A Darwinian algorithm fits these efforts: entrepreneurs propose, arenas dispose. The disposal of ostensible claimsmaking opportunities can be attributed to the sticky definitional features that arise from and adhere to global warming's scientific trajectory. To return to our earlier example, there were good reasons for this problem to have acquired a future-oriented definitional trajectory. While constructionists could argue that a future-orientation need not be taken as inevitable or immutable, it is likely to remain sticky for some time. In this regard, counterfactual arguments claiming that the problem could have been defined in different ways ought to show, concretely, how and where the scientific trajectory could have been redirected. Both political demands for hard "evidence" to justify spending and oppositional assertions that such a distant threat does not require immediate responses need to be factored into such arguments.

A key consideration here is how the social problem's trajectory meshes with the prevailing institutional formations or arena selection principles. A future-orientation is not a liability as such; it acquires that status when future discounting is embedded in institutional thinking. . . .

A high level of energy consumption is central to the American way of life, and global warming is socially articulated through the fossil fuel economy. The ozone threat, in contrast, is tied to far more secondary chemicals and societal processes. The use of aerosol cans was frivolous (substitutes were always available), and CFCs were otherwise essential for refrigeration, air conditioning, and some medical uses. While substitutes were not immediately available at the peak of the problem's issue-attention cycle, companies were competing for alternatives, and the question may have boiled down to who would win at the lowest cost. Industrial opposition ended as companies realized that substitutes could be readily developed. For example, the increased cost of home refrigerators was pegged at about $100 maximum. When amortized over a minimum 15-year appliance life span, the increase is quite modest. It is also more or less invisible. Whereas strong links were forged in public arenas between spray cans and ozone depletion, few people actually connect the latter with air conditioning and refrigeration. Hence costs did not fetter ozone depletion in the policy arena.

Since global warming is so closely tied to the energy economy, it is related to almost everything people do. Hence the unavoidable question: what are the economic and social consequences of emission reductions? One possibility, which cannot be totally denied, has to do with the fact that the scope or size of global warming as a problem is so much bigger than ozone depletion. Relatively speaking, it could be contended that the ozone problem was easily solved, and hence solutions were found. In contrast, the perception that the challenge of global warming is almost overwhelming can produce a sense of immobility, and even foster the view that action on the issue is, short of a demonstrable crisis, too costly. In effect, the size of the problem may advantage counterclaims who suggest that action is so costly that it is best to wait until more definitive scientific evidence is in. In part, this view simplifies the problem posed by ozone depletion, since it presumes the very solutions that had not yet been found at the time that the key negotiations were taking place. At the same time, global warming need not be regarded as all that intractable, especially if pragmatic steps—these are characteristic of American problem-solving mythologies—are taken.

  While it may seem obvious that reductions will be costly, [there are] . . . good arguments for the more counterintuitive position that many *initial* reductions can be accomplished at a net saving and some subsequent ones at a low cost. First, and most significant, there is a recent precedent for linking energy reductions with cost savings. Specifically, the oil crises in the 1970s resulted in "energy efficiencies" that, in the long run, saved more than they cost. Second, pressure to make changes often yields unexpected innovations and cost-efficiencies (as seems to have occurred with CFCs). Third, the tax system favors fossil fuels (oil depletion allowances, etc.), and a more balanced system should accelerate the penetration of fuel-efficient or alternative energy technologies, which have become more competitive over time. Fourth, many proposed reductions are linked to a "no regrets" policy—for example, cuts in air pollution that should be done for other good reasons and could realize saving in health care, and so on.

  Despite the arguments holding that immediate costs in particular are likely to be low, public debates over the costs and benefits of emission reductions did not materialize. Perusal of the writings found in the public arena yields a lopsided discussion. Excepting a few op-ed articles and technical reports in specialized science and environmental journals, public discourse simply assumes that solutions to the problem will cause personal suffering, job losses, reduced international competitiveness, and possibly a recession. As part of the dominant institutional thinking, the high cost argument functions as a convenient and comfortable assumption, a trusty and almost axiomatic resource that is presented as an indisputable reality. Those who try to present cost efficiency arguments in mainstream arenas mostly encounter silence.

  . . . [T]he high cost argument is so deeply ingrained that it virtually obliterates competing claims. . . . The idea of energy efficiency and its ramifications was clearly "foreign" . . . :

Laypeople tend to interpret energy conservation as decreasing energy services, that is curtailment or sacrifice. This problem was identified a decade ago, and our survey makes clear it is still predominant, even among environmentalists.

Despite the experience of the 1970s, not one of their lay respondents mentioned a more fuel efficient car as a means of dealing with possible rises in energy costs. Altogether, then, the meshing of global warming's energy path with the institutionally embedded high cost argument implies that this social problem will continue to encounter a rough ride in the policy stream.

Hot Crises and the Role of Marketability

This final section reverses tactics and focuses on the ozone puzzle. It argues that the remarkably rapid response to ozone depletion is incomprehensible without taking into account how its trajectory meshed with extant institutional formations. The aim is to go beyond an inventory of differences and show that the greater salability of ozone depletion is not just a matter of this or that advantage but a clustering of factors that redound into a hot crisis. As it turns out, the production of such a crisis owes a great deal to timing and luck, as well as political and media practices.

The concept of hot crisis was developed to explain the reaction to Ebola Zaire:

> Whereas journalists tend to view crises as any kind of trouble at all, hot crises entail dread-inspiring events that are developing in *unpredictable* ways and are seen as having the potential to pose an imminent personal threat to specific populations. Hot crises are startling, as presumed invulnerabilities appear to be challenged. A palpable sense of menace puts the issue "in the air", as unfolding events are watched, discussed and fretted over.

Ebola engendered a hot crisis as a result of its potent dread factor (gruesome and almost certain death with blood oozing from every orifice) coupled with a sense of personal threat due to the much-touted menace of "instant-distant infections." That is, claimsmaking about emerging diseases stresses that boundaries are porous and we are just "a plane ride away" from a "chain of lethal transmission." In what follows, I contend that the trajectory of the ozone problem lent itself to a hot crisis as a result of the "tight coupling" of dread and personal relevance.

The defining moment for the response to ozone depletion is baffling. Just prior to the surprise discovery of the hole, there were abrupt shifts in scientific estimates about likely levels of damage to the ozone layer, culminating in the virtual closure of the issue as a result of the 1984 NRC report. . . . [I]n

1984, "interest among environmental groups was all but dead." With the uncovering of the hole, operatives faced the challenge of managing the recent history of obvious scientific inaccuracies and reviving an issue just a year after it had been declared dead. They also had to deal with the anti-environmental stance of the Reagan administration, which promised "regulatory relief" that effectively stopped research on alternatives to CFCs. The hole itself is not substantial and can only be detected with sophisticated instruments (uncertainty about instrumentation delayed the initial announcement) and then rendered public by the mass media. How, then, did a recycled and unobservable threat in an anti-regulatory atmosphere rebound into consumer boycotts, environmental pressures on industry, industrial reversals, and U.S. leadership on the issue—all in a span of two years? We return to this after a consideration of the rise of its sister problem.

The defining moment for the social birth of global warming is more concrete. The heat and drought of the greenhouse summer were widely felt by the person on the street and, with the generalizing effect of the media, generated a brief scare. While TV pictorials of the pulsating images of the ozone hole were dramatic, it remains to be explained why these were more galvanizing than the felt impacts of the summer of 1988 combined with pictorials of desiccated fields and Yellowstone National Park burning. We first consider why global warming petered out, and then examine why ozone depletion flourished even before the media joined the bandwagon.

While extreme weather events serve as the principal public "sign" of climate change, they present limited opportunities and major difficulties. The problem of attributing specific extreme events to global warming has already been alluded to with James Hansen's "overstatement." U.S. weather is highly variable, and evidence indicates that public weather memory is short-term. Moreover, events become dissociated from their context, so that people quickly forget that the fire in Yellowstone occurred during the greenhouse summer of 1988. Hence as the weather impacts of 1988 petered out, so too did a sense of urgency.

Presumably, the juxtaposition of a number of out-of-the-ordinary impacts in a short time period is required to catalyze a crisis. Evidence consistent with this claim can be drawn from Europe, where chaotic weather from 1987 through 1991 was associated with greater public and political concern over warming than in the U.S. In the latter case, extreme weather impacts have not been as concentrated in time or space. Since U.S. weather (thus far) invariably returns to a "normal" state, it undermines the sense that the problem is pressing, irreversible, or progressive.

Still, impacts capable of catalyzing public or political concern are not simply due to what nature happens to dish out. Rather, they depend on administrative and media practices that render it easier or more difficult to sell the claim that the climate has turned strange. In Europe, but not in the U.S., weather records go back hundreds of years. This provides data that allow claimsmakers to empirically "substantiate" claims about extraordinary impacts. In the U.S., where floods have been particularly prominent, much of the problem is due to population movements into flood plains, based on the belief that engineered systems of dams would thwart future catastrophes. But the dams may well have had the opposite effect and thereby afford alternative explanations for the impacts.

In addition, while extreme weather events virtually "announce" themselves on a regional level, events do not speak for themselves internationally. For the most part, the U.S. media ignore foreign weather events that might confirm the sense that strange weather is a global phenomenon. In short, the problem of selling global warming through the weather depends on a mix of observable conditions, fortuitous events and timing, and social, political and media practices.

The weather connection is even more tenuous when seen in light of the scientific trajectory of global warming. Even a minimally coherent account of why climate change is a threat involves a series of loose postulates that span several scientific fields and transcend both the public's current understanding of science and the information carrying capacity of most of the mass media. To take one disastrous marketing problem, scientific models of climate producing mechanisms lead to predicted increases at both extremes of the climate distribution: summers could be hotter and dryer, winters colder and wetter. But public understandings are limited to warming, not climate change as such. Colder winters are thus thought to belie predictions about global warming, when in fact they are consistent with current models of climate change. One great difficulty in this context is that there are apparently no ready-made social or lay models of reality that mesh with and provide a simple schematic for understanding the science of climate change.

If global warming cannot readily flourish in the context of ever-shortening media sound bites, ozone depletion can. This is illustrated by the previously cited findings that much of the public employs the latter as a template through which they (mis-)interpret the former. Clearly, the chemistry of ozone depletion is no more accessible than the chemistry (or physics) of global warming. But it seems transparent that the "hole" or "crater" is an aberration, something that should not be there. The greenhouse effect, in contrast, is a benign natural phenomenon. Global warming (or climate change) is an extension of this phenomenon, creating the problem of finding the human fingerprint amidst highly variable natural processes.

Unlike global warming, the ozone threat can be rendered into a simple, neat, foreshortened, and tightly coupled schematic as a result of its "Hollywood affinities." Stated succinctly, ozone loss leads to the increased bombardment of the earth by lethal rays. The idea of rays penetrating a "shield" meshes nicely with abiding and resonant cultural motifs. These Hollywood affinities range from the shields on the *Starship Enterprise* to *Star Wars* (the movies and the Strategic Defense Initiative), through a multitude of video games and children's television shows. The penetration model, in other words, is simple and deeply ingrained. When the *gradual* depletion of the ozone layer was supplanted by the unearthing of an unexpected crater, it rendered the progression of the peril unpredictable and ominous. Could the shield disintegrate?

Fortuitously for creating a hot crisis, the principle threat that came to be associated with ozone depletion plays itself out in daily life. That is, leakage through the shield is tied to skin cancer, especially melanoma, its most deadly form. The dread potential of cancer is clear. It has garnered a "war," authorized the Delaney Clause banning all food additives that are found to be carcinogenic in laboratory tests, and is the source of exaggerated fears. Timing again was superb, as President Reagan had skin cancers removed in 1985 and 1987. More important over the long haul, ozone depletion holds everyday relevance for curbing exposure to the sun. Warnings about overexposure became commonplace, particularly in accounts dealing with children. Metaphors about "safe sun" were boosted by the growth of a companion industry encompassing sunscreens, lip gloss, sunglasses, UV-safe hats, clothing, umbrellas, awnings, and so on. The issue was medicalized by reports of increased rates of skin cancer plus the personal need to watch for skin changes. At the worst, people are to avoid the sun between 11:00 a.m. and 4:00 p.m., rendering the outdoors dangerous.

Blunder and luck solidified the personal relevance of this threat. Interior Secretary Donald Hodel misjudged the public mood when he advocated a "personal protection" plan in the place of international action on the issue. Not only was his suggestion immediately mocked (fish don't wear sunglasses), but the gaffe became a sticky resource. That is, his foolish statement is frequently referenced and is an available tool for building a case for protection of the ozone level.

Good positioning of the problem seems to have been effective at the international level. Ozone depletion was narrowly framed in terms of skin cancer, which is most relevant for Caucasians who happen to spend considerable time in the sun. Where skin cancer was a clear asset in selling the threat in the U.S. and Europe, it became a liability and was downplayed as efforts were made to market the threat in other nations. The historical link drawn between the problem and skin cancer was far from inevitable. Scientists concerned with the impact of ozone depletion tend to hold that the most serious issues are the impact of increased ultraviolet radiation on the human immune system, plant life, and aquatic ecosystems.

This last point raises key counterfactual questions. If the current analysis is correct in asserting that it is exceptionally difficult to sell global warming through the weather, one can ask whether other avenues might have resulted in more successful problem formulations? Here it should be reiterated that this problem was launched on the public stage by the greenhouse summer of 1988 and a degree of commitment to weather undoubtedly ensued. As with the weather, extensions of the problem to other domains, including forests, biodiversity, and emerging diseases, are suffused with stated, prominent and, at least for the present, intractable uncertainties. In other words, the most prominent fingerprints of climate change do not include effects that are *unique, direct, individualized* and *indisputable*.

The ozone threat, in contrast, can be encapsulated in a cogent phrase. The importance of this tight coupling is underscored by two points. First, efforts to sell the "other" presumed consequences of ozone depletion have made little headway. Scientists, for example, are particularly concerned about the disappearance of frogs across the globe. But links between this and ozone loss are fraught with the same kinds of difficulties that handicap attempts to link global warming to other issues. As a result, the disappearance of frogs has not engendered much attention in public arenas.

Second, the tightly coupled schematic built around ozone depletion is generally presented in the media without qualifications or caveats; thus many ozone reports are relegated to "news briefs," suggesting that the story is not sufficiently interesting or controversial to warrant an article. This contrasts with linkages to other issues, where one encounters the ever-present qualifications found with global warming. However, the ozone schematic is not immune to criticism. Besides difficulties in measuring levels of ozone loss, the link between it and rates of skin cancer remains unproven. Indeed, ozone depletion does not provide a unique or indisputable explanation for any increases in skin cancer, since these can also be attributed to changes in lifestyle. But problems in measurement and the use of correlations that might be spurious are disregarded. Overall, it seems that the Hollywood affinities with ozone depletion are so simple, lucid, and tangible that they come close to being regarded as an ontological reality. Altogether, then, ozone depletion seemingly fulfilled the conditions for a hot crisis. With global warming, a future orientation, the absence of a ready-made lay model to encapsulate the scientific model, and the high cost argument effectively precluded such a crisis.

* * *

QUESTIONS

1. What evidence does Ungar present to demonstrate that ozone depletion has been more successfully marketed as a problem in need of fixing in the United States than has global warming?

2. What evidence does Ungar provide to document that the more successful marketing of ozone depletion cannot be explained by the amount of claims-making that each issue has received? Answer by discussing the claims-making activities of the news media and the U.S. Congress.

3. What does Ungar mean when he characterizes the American public's unwillingness to reduce fuel consumption as based on "the dominant institutional thinking" concerning fuel efficiency?

4. Why does the construction of global warming as a future-oriented problem pose obstacles for mobilizing the public to find ways to address this problem?

5. What are the "Hollywood affinities" that have led to the considerable public and policy responses to ozone depletion?

Compensating for Deficit versus Enhancing Performance

The Difference Between Steroids and Ritalin Is . . .

KATE ZERNIKE

Some drugs are sold at the corner pharmacy while others are illegal. The vastly different attitudes to different drugs are socially constructed, and indeed what attitudes are assigned to which drugs often has little to do with the drugs themselves. Kate Zernike analyzes the case of performance-enhancing drugs, a subject that has received considerable media attention in the wake of the 2005 congressional investigation of steroid use among Major League Baseball players. Zernike points out that drugs compensating for personal deficit are generally seen as acceptable while drugs that enhance performance are defined as problematic because they give users an unfair advantage. Yet, the distinction between compensating for deficit and enhancing performance is often unclear, indicating that the placement of drugs into these different categories is somewhat arbitrary. Moreover, performance-enhancing drugs are not necessarily defined as problematic; one need only look at the widespread acceptance of caffeine use as a case in point.

At the Congressional hearings last week investigating steroids and baseball, players were scolded not just for taking substances that are unsafe, but for doing something immoral. Those who use performance enhancing substances were called cheaters, cowards, bad examples for the nation's children.

But if baseball players are cheating, is everyone else, too?

After all, Americans are relying more and more on a growing array of performance enhancing drugs. Lawyers take the anti-sleep drug Provigil to finish that all-night brief, in hopes of concentrating better. Classical musicians take beta blockers, which banish jitters, before a big recital. Is the student who swallows a Ritalin before taking the SAT unethical if the pill gives her an unfair advantage over other students? If a golfer pops a beta blocker before a tournament, is he eliminating a crucial part of competition—battling nerves and a chance of choking?

Beyond baseball and steroids, where do you draw the line on the use of performance-enhancing drugs? President Bush said in his 2004 State of the Union speech that steroid use in baseball "sends the wrong message: that there are shortcuts to accomplishment, and that performance is more important than character."

That is easy to say about steroids. After all, the mystique of the major leagues requires that home run records be set without the help of artificial enhancements. And major league players have some responsibility not to encourage teenagers to use a harmful substance.

When it comes to other drugs, and other kinds of endeavors, the lines aren't so clear. Bioethicists, who don't even all agree about whether taking steroids is wrong, are even less clear about everything else.

Some say the use of performance-enhanced drugs simply reflects progress— better living through chemistry—and to be human is to strive to be better.

"We've gotten very used to already assisting ourselves in other ways," said Arthur Caplan, director of the Center for Bioethics at the University of Pennsylvania. "No one's going to say, 'Don't drink coffee before the SAT.' No one's going to say, 'Don't smoke cigarettes before the SAT.' And most of the drugs we're talking about are far less harmful than nicotine."

But others lament that a performance-enhanced society is giving in to a culture that prizes the achievement over the journey. Many Americans already get that message from a young age, said Denise Clark Pope, author of "Doing School: How We Are Creating a Generation of Stressed Out, Materialistic and Miseducated Students."

When surveys ask students which is more important, to be honorable and get a low grade or to cheat and get a high grade, she said, more students choose the A. "The parents will say 'no, no, no,' but the message they're sending says the opposite."

The use of performance enhancing drugs reflects a society where stress and striving have become the national pastime. Ms. Pope calls it the "credentialism society," exemplified in her book through a high school student who describes life as a quest to get the best grades, so you can get into the best college, so you can get into the best graduate school, so you can get the highest-paying job, which brings you happiness.

So where people once took illegal drugs like cocaine to escape or stimulate creativity, they now take legal drugs to focus better and achieve more.

The danger in that, said Carl Elliott, the author of "Better than Well: American Medicine Meets the American Dream," is that not performing well will be seen as a medical condition—one that needs to be treated.

"The lines between treating an illness and enhancing a performance are so blurry," said Dr. Elliott, an associate professor at the center for bioethics at the University of Minnesota. "Most people don't conceptualize it as performance enhancement; most people conceptualize it as a treatment for an illness."

But others think there's no problem. Norman Fost, the director of the medical ethics program at the University of Wisconsin who has long said that the danger of steroids are overstated, similarly sees nothing wrong with taking drugs like Ritalin or Provigil solely to enhance performance.

"We all would like to do better at what we're doing, whether athletic or intellectual or musical," he said. "There's nothing inherently immoral about performance enhancement. It's what everyone does, or would try to do, for their children. We shouldn't be obsessed with the fact that it's a drug, as if it's a drug like cocaine or heroin."

Dr. Caplan mocks the handwringing over self-enhancement drugs. To him, it is all technology: "The lawyer who's taking a pill to stay up is also carrying a computer or P.D.A. to help his brain remember things. Are we going to throw away our calculators?"

Certainly, there is no guarantee that performance enhancement delivers happiness.

As Ms. Pope notes, at the same time stimulants like Ritalin are becoming more popular among high school students, college campuses are reporting a new drug of choice. It used to be marijuana. Now it's Prozac.

1. List the various reasons why the U.S. Congress investigated steroid use in Major League Baseball and why the league recently stiffened its penalties for players who use steroids.

2. Why have prominent claimsmakers, most notably Congress and the national news media, constructed steroid use as problematic because it enhances baseball players' performance yet no such claim has been brought against caffeine, which millions of Americans ingest each morning in order to be alert on the job?

3. How does the increasing emphasis placed on credentialism within American society contribute to the fact that the use of caffeine, No-Doz, Ritalin, and other drugs that help people perform better at school and at work is *not* defined as a social problem?

4. To what extent is American society moving in the direction of defining *not* succeeding at school or work as a medical condition that needs to be treated?

21

The Crimes That Come to Mind

FROM *A Crime by Any Other Name . . .*

JEFFREY REIMAN

Although there is a wide range of behaviors that the law defines as criminal, people tend to view crime as involving only certain kinds of acts committed by particular populations of individuals. This understanding we have of what Jeffrey Reiman calls the "Typical Criminal" comes from how our criminal justice system prosecutes and punishes different kinds of crime. Our images of crime also come from the ways that politicians talk about crime and the kinds of media exposure crimes do or do not receive. Reiman presents data about the pervasiveness of different types of criminal acts that do not ordinarily come to mind when people think of crime, and he argues that the criminal justice system ought to pay more attention to these crimes given the level of human harm they inflict.

* * *

WHAT'S IN A NAME?

If it takes you an hour to read this chapter, by the time you reach the last page, two of your fellow citizens will have been murdered. *During the same time, more than six Americans will die as a result of unhealthy or unsafe conditions in the workplace!* Although these work-related deaths could have been prevented, they are not called murders. Why not? Doesn't a crime by any other name still cause misery and suffering? What's in a name?

The fact is that the label "crime" is not used in America to name all or the worst of the actions that cause misery and suffering to Americans. It is reserved primarily for the dangerous actions of the poor.

In the February 21, 1993, edition of *The New York Times,* an article appears with the headline: "Company in Mine Deaths Set to Pay Big Fine." It describes an agreement by the owners of a Kentucky mine to pay a fine for safety misconduct that may have led to "the worst American mining accident in nearly a decade." Ten workers died in a methane explosion, and the company pleaded guilty to "a pattern of safety misconduct" that included falsifying reports of methane levels and requiring miners to work under unsupported roofs. The company was fined $3.75 million. The acting foreman at the mine was the only individual charged by the federal government, and for his cooperation with the investigation, prosecutors were recommending that he receive the minimum sentence: probation to six months in prison. The company's president expressed regret for the tragedy that occurred, and the U.S. attorney said he hoped the case "sent a clear message that violations of Federal safety and health regulations that endanger the lives of our citizens will not be tolerated."

Compare this with the story of Colin Ferguson, who prompted an editorial in *The New York Times* of December 10, 1993, with the headline: "Mass Murder on the 5:33." A few days earlier, Colin had boarded a commuter train in Garden City, Long Island, and methodically shot passengers with a 9-mm pistol, killing 5 and wounding 18. Colin Ferguson was surely a murderer, maybe a mass murderer. My question is, why wasn't the death of the miners also murder? Why weren't those responsible for subjecting ten miners to deadly conditions also "mass murderers"?

Why do ten dead miners amount to an "accident," a "tragedy," and five dead commuters as "mass murder"? "Murder" suggests a murderer, whereas "accident" and "tragedy" suggest the work of impersonal forces. But the charge against the company that owned the mine said that they "repeatedly exposed the miner's work crews to danger and that such conditions were frequently concealed from Federal inspectors responsible for enforcing the Mine Safety Act." And the acting foreman admitted to falsifying records of methane levels only two months before the fatal blast. Someone was responsible for the conditions that led to the death of ten miners. Is that person not a murderer, perhaps even a *mass murderer?*

* * *

The reality of crime as the target of our criminal justice system and as perceived by the general populace is not a simple objective threat to which the system reacts: *It is a reality that takes shape as it is filtered through a series of human decisions running the full gamut of the criminal justice system*—from the lawmakers who determine what behavior shall be in the province of criminal justice to the law enforcers who decide which individuals will be brought within that province. And it doesn't end with the criminal justice system as such, because the media—particularly television and daily newspapers—contribute as well to the image that people have of crime in our society. Here, too, human decisions are fundamental. The news media do not simply report the facts. There are too many facts out there. A selection must be made. People working in the news media must choose which facts are news, and they must choose how to represent those facts.

Note that by emphasizing the role of "human decisions," I do not mean to suggest that the reality of crime is voluntarily and intentionally "created" by individual "decision makers." Their decisions are themselves shaped by the social system, much as a child's decision to become an engineer rather than a samurai warrior is shaped by the social system in which he or she grows up. Thus, to have a full explanation of how the reality of crime is created, we have to understand how our society is structured in a way that leads people to make the decisions they do. In other words, these decisions are part of the social phenomena to be explained, they are not the explanation.

For the present, however, I emphasize the role of the decisions themselves for the following reasons: First, they are conspicuous points in the social process, easy to spot and verify empirically. Second, because they are decisions aimed at protecting us from the dangers in our midst, we can compare the decisions with the real dangers and determine whether they are responding to the real dangers. Third, because the reality of crime—the real actions labeled crimes, the real individuals identified as criminals, the real faces we watch in the news as they travel from arrest to court to prison—results from these decisions, we can determine whether that reality corresponds to the real dangers in our society. Where that reality does correspond to the real dangers, we can say that the reality of crime simply reflects the real dangers in society. Where the reality of crime does not correspond to the real dangers, we can say that it is a reality *created* by those decisions. Then we can investigate the role played by the social system in encouraging, reinforcing, and otherwise shaping those decisions.

It is to capture this way of looking at the relation between the reality of crime and the real dangers "out there" in society that I refer to the criminal justice system as a "mirror." Whom and what we see in this mirror is a function of the decisions about who and what is criminal. Our poor, young, urban, black male, who is so well represented in arrest records and prison populations, appears not simply because of the threat he poses to the rest of society. As dangerous as he may be, he would not appear in the criminal justice mirror *if* it had not been decided that the acts he performs should be labeled "crimes," *if* it had not been decided that he should be arrested for those crimes, *if* he had had access to a lawyer who could persuade a jury to acquit him and perhaps a judge to expunge his arrest record, and *if* it had not been decided that he is the type of individual and his the type of crime that warrants imprisonment. *The shape of the reality we see in the criminal justice mirror is the outcome of all these decisions.* We want to know how accurately the reality we see in this mirror reflects the real dangers that threaten us in society.

It is not my view that this reality is created out of nothing. The mugger, the rapist, the murderer, the burglar, the robber all pose a definite threat to our well-being, and they ought to be dealt with in ways that effectively reduce that threat to the minimum level possible (without making the criminal justice system itself a threat to our lives and liberties). Of central importance, however, is that the threat posed by the Typical Criminal is not the greatest threat to which we are exposed. The acts of the Typical Criminal are not the only acts that endanger us, nor are they the acts that endanger us the most. As I shall show in this chapter, we have as great and sometimes an even a greater chance of being killed or disabled by an occupational injury or disease, by unnecessary surgery, or by shoddy medical services than by aggravated assault or even homicide! Yet even though these threats to our well-being are graver than that posed by our poor young criminals, they do not show up in the FBI's Index of serious crimes. The individuals responsible for them do not turn up in arrest records or prison statistics. *They never become part of the reality reflected in the criminal justice mirror, although the danger they pose is at least as great and often greater than the danger posed by those who do!*

Similarly, the general public loses more money *by far* (as I show below) from price fixing and monopolistic practices and from consumer deception and embezzlement than from all the property crimes in the FBI's Index combined. Yet these far more costly acts are either not criminal, or, if technically criminal, not prosecuted, or, if prosecuted, not punished, or if punished, only mildly. In any event, although the individuals responsible for these acts take more money out of the ordinary citizen's pocket than our Typical Criminal, they rarely show up in arrest statistics and almost never in prison populations. *Their faces rarely appear in the criminal justice mirror, although the danger they pose is at least as great and often greater than that of those who do.*

The inescapable conclusion is that the criminal justice system does not simply *reflect* the reality of crime; it has a hand in *creating* the reality we see.

* * *

A CRIME BY ANY OTHER NAME . . .

Think of a crime, any crime. Picture the first "crime" that comes into your mind. What do you see? The odds are you are not imagining a mining company executive sitting at his desk, calculating the costs of proper safety precautions and deciding not to invest in them. Probably what you do see with your mind's eye is one person attacking another physically or robbing something from another via the threat of physical attack. Look more closely. What does the attacker look like? It's a safe bet he (and it is a *he*, of course) is not wearing a suit and tie. In fact, my hunch is that you—like me, like almost anyone else in America—picture a young, tough, lower-class male when the thought of crime first pops into your head. You (we) picture someone like the Typical Criminal described above. The crime itself is one in which the Typical Criminal sets out to attack or rob some specific person.

This last point is important. It indicates that we have a mental image not only of the Typical Criminal but also of the *Typical Crime*. If the Typical Criminal is a young, lower-class male, the Typical Crime is *one-on-one harm*— where harm means either physical injury or loss of something valuable or both. If you have any doubts that this is the Typical Crime, look at any random sample of police or private eye shows on television. How often do you see the cops of *NYPD Blue* investigate consumer fraud or failure to remove occupational hazards? When *Law & Order* detectives Briscoe and Green happen to track down a well-heeled criminal, it is almost always for violent crimes such as murder. A study of TV crime shows by The Media Institute in Washington, D.C., indicates that, while the fictional criminals portrayed on television are on average both older and wealthier than the real criminals who figure in the FBI *Uniform Crime Reports,* "TV crimes are almost 12 times as likely to be violent as crimes committed in the real world." A review of several decades of research confirms that violent crimes are overrepresented on TV news and fictional crime shows, and that "young people, black people, and people of low socioeconomic status are underrepresented as offenders or victims in television programs"—exactly opposite from the real world, in which nonviolent property crimes far outnumber violent crimes, and young, poor, and black folks predominate as offenders and victims.

* * *

In addition to the steady diet of fictionalized TV violence and crime, there has been an increase in the graphic display of crime on many TV news programs. Crimes reported on TV news are also far more frequently violent than real crimes are. An article in *The Washington Post* says that the word around two prominent local TV news programs is, "If it bleeds, it leads." The Center for Media and Public Affairs reports a dramatic increase in homicide coverage on evening news programs starting in 1993, just as homicide rates were falling significantly. Other researchers found that news programs were highly selective in the homicides they reported. The murders that were chosen for coverage tended to be committed by strangers in neighborhoods where average household income was over $25,000 a year, while we know that most murders occur between people known to each other, and take place in low-income neighborhoods. The effect is to magnify the risk of lower-class crime to middle-class individuals. Is it any wonder that fear of crime has persisted even as crime rates have gone down sharply?

What's more, a new breed of nonfictional "tabloid" TV show has appeared in which viewers are shown films of actual violent crimes—blood, screams, and all—or reenactments of actual violent crimes, sometimes using the actual victims playing themselves! Among these are *Cops* and *America's Most Wanted. The Wall Street Journal,* reporting on the phenomenon of tabloid TV, informs us that "Television has gone tabloid. The seamy underside of life is being bared in a new rash of true-crime series and contrived-confrontation talk shows." Here, too, the focus is on crimes of one-on-one violence, rather than, say, deadly industrial pollution.

It is important to identify this model of the Typical Crime because it functions like a set of blinders. It keeps us from calling a mine disaster a mass murder even if ten men are killed, even if someone is responsible for the unsafe conditions in which they worked and died. One study of newspaper reporting of a food-processing plant fire, in which 25 workers were killed and criminal charges were ultimately brought, concludes that "the newspapers showed little consciousness that corporate violence might be seen as a crime." I contend that this is due to our fixation on the model of the Typical Crime. This particular piece of mental furniture so blocks our view that it keeps us from using the criminal justice system to protect ourselves from the greatest threats to our persons and possessions.

What keeps a mine disaster from being a mass murder in our eyes is that it is not a one-on-one harm. What is important in one-on-one harm is not the numbers but the *desire of someone (or ones) to harm someone (or ones) else.* An attack by a gang on one or more persons or an attack by one individual on several fits the model of one-on-one harm; that is, for each person harmed there is at least one individual who wanted to harm that person. Once he selects his victim, the rapist, the mugger, the murderer all want this person they have selected to suffer. A mine executive, on the other hand, does not want his employees to be harmed. He would truly prefer that there be no accident, no injured or dead miners. What he does want is something legitimate. It is what he has been hired to get: maximum profits at minimum costs. If he cuts corners to save a buck, he is just doing his job. If ten men die because he cut corners on safety, we may think him crude or callous, but not a murderer. He is, at most, responsible for *indirect harm,* not one-on-one harm. For this, he may even be criminally indictable for violating safety regulations, but not for murder. The ten men are dead as an unwanted consequence of his (perhaps overzealous or undercautious) pursuit of a legitimate goal. So, unlike the Typical Criminal, he has not committed the Typical Crime, or so we generally believe. As a result, ten men are dead who might be alive now if cutting corners of the kind that leads to loss of life, whether suffering is specifically aimed at or not, were treated as murder.

This is my point. Because we accept the belief—encouraged by our politicians' statements about crime and by the media's portrayal of crime—that the model for crime is one person specifically trying to harm another, we accept a legal system that leaves us unprotected against much greater dangers to our lives and well-being than those threatened by the Typical Criminal. Before developing this point further, let us anticipate and deal with some likely objections. Defenders of the present legal order are likely to respond to my argument at this point with irritation. Because this will surely turn to outrage in a few pages, let's talk to them now, while the possibility of rational communication still exists.

The "Defenders of the Present Legal Order" (I'll call them "the Defenders" for short) are neither foolish nor evil people. They are not racists, nor are they oblivious to the need for reform in the criminal justice system to make it more even-handed and for reform in the larger society to make equal opportunity a reality for all Americans. In general, their view is that—given our limited resources, particularly the resource of human altruism—the political and legal institutions we have are the best that can be. What is necessary is to make them work better and to weed out those who are intent on making them work shoddily. Their response to my argument at this point is that the criminal justice system *should* occupy itself primarily with one-on-one harm. Harms of the sort exemplified in the "mine tragedy" are really *not* murders and are better dealt with through stricter government enforcement of safety regulations. The Defenders admit that this enforcement has been rather lax and recommend that it be improved. Basically, though, they think this division of labor is right because it fits our ordinary moral sensibilities.

. The Defenders maintain that, according to our common moral notions, someone who tries to do another harm and does is really more evil than someone who jeopardizes others while pursuing legitimate goals but doesn't aim to harm anyone. The one who jeopardizes others in this way at least doesn't try to hurt them. He or she doesn't have the goal of hurting someone in the way that a mugger or a rapist does. Moreover, being directly and purposely harmed by another person, the Defenders believe, is terrifying in a way that being harmed indirectly and impersonally, say, by a safety hazard, is not, even if the resultant injury is the same in both cases. And we should be tolerant of the one responsible for lax safety measures because he or she is pursuing a legitimate goal—that is, his or her dangerous action occurs as part of a productive activity, something that ultimately adds to social wealth and thus benefits everyone—whereas doers of direct harm benefit no one but themselves. Thus, the latter are rightfully in the province of the criminal justice system with its drastic weapons, and the former are appropriately dealt with by the milder forms of regulation.

Further, the Defenders insist, the crimes identified as such by the criminal justice system are imposed on their victims totally against their will, whereas the victims of occupational hazards chose to accept their risky jobs and thus have, in some degree, consented to subject themselves to the dangers. Where dangers are consented to, the appropriate response is not blame but requiring improved safety, and this is most efficiently done by regulation rather than with the guilt-seeking methods of criminal justice.

In sum, the Defenders make four objections: (1) Someone who purposely tries to harm another is really more evil than someone who harms another without aiming to, even if the degree of harm is the same; (2) being harmed directly by another person is more terrifying than being harmed indirectly and impersonally, as by a safety hazard, even if the degree of harm is the same; (3) someone who harms another in the course of an illegitimate and purely self-interested action is more evil than someone who harms another as a consequence of a legitimate and socially productive endeavor; (4) the harms of typical crimes are imposed on their victims against their wills, whereas harms such as those due to occupational hazards are consented to by workers when they agree to a job; this too is thought to make the harms of typical crimes evil in a way that occupational harms are not.

All four of these objections are said to reflect our common moral beliefs, which are a fair standard for a legal system to match. Together they are said to show that the typical criminal does something worse than the one responsible for an occupational hazard and thus deserves the special treatment provided by the criminal justice system. Some or all of these objections may have already occurred to the reader. Thus, it is important to respond to the Defenders. For the sake of clarity I shall number the paragraphs in which I start to take up each objection in turn.

1. Defenders' First Objection

Someone who purposely tries to harm another is really more evil than someone who harms another without aiming to, even if the degree of harm is the same. Thus, the typical criminal is rightly subject to criminal justice, while the cost-cutting exec who endangers his workers is rightly subject to non-criminal safety regulations.

Response: The Defenders' first objection confuses intention with specific aim or purpose, and it is intention that brings us properly within the reach of the criminal law. It is true that a mugger aims to harm his victim in a way that a corporate executive who maintains an unsafe workplace does not. But the corporate executive acts intentionally nonetheless, and that's what makes his actions appropriately subject to criminal law. What we intend is not just what we try to make happen but what we know is likely to happen as the normal result of our chosen actions. As criminal law theorist Hyman Gross points out: "What really matters here is whether conduct of a particular degree of dangerousness was done intentionally." Whether the actor wants or aims for that conduct to harm someone is a different matter, which is relevant to the actor's *degree* of culpability (not to whether he or she is culpable at all). Here's an example to help understand the legally recognized degrees of culpability: Suppose a construction worker digs a trench in a neighborhood where children regularly play, and leaves the trench uncovered. One rainy day, children are killed while playing in the trench when its walls cave in on them. If the construction worker dug the trench and left it uncovered in order to kill the children, then their deaths were caused *purposely*. But suppose that the trench was dug and left uncovered not in order to harm the children, but knowing that children played in the area. Then, their deaths were brought about *knowingly*. If digging the ditch and leaving it uncovered was done without knowledge that children played in the area, but without making sure that they did not, then their deaths were brought about *recklessly*. Finally, if the trench was dug and left uncovered without knowledge that children played in the area and some, but inadequate, precautions were taken to make sure no children were there, then their deaths were brought about *negligently*.

How does this apply to the executive who imposes dangerous conditions on his workers, conditions that, as in the mine explosion, finally do lead to death? The first thing to note is that the difference between purposely, knowingly, recklessly, or negligently causing death is a difference within the range of intentional (and thus to some degree culpable) action. What is done recklessly or negligently is still done intentionally. Second, culpability decreases as we go from purposely to knowingly to recklessly to negligently killing because, according to Gross, the outcome is increasingly due to chance and not to the actor; that is, the one who kills on purpose leaves less to chance that the killing will occur than the one who kills knowingly (the one who kills on purpose will take precautions against the failure of his killing, while the one who kills knowingly won't), and likewise the one who kills recklessly leaves wholly to chance whether there is a victim at all. And the one who kills negligently reduces this chance, but insufficiently.

Now, we may say that the kernel of truth in the Defenders' objection is that the common street mugger harms on purpose, while the executive harms only knowingly or recklessly or negligently. This does not justify refusing to treat the executive killer as a criminal, however, because we have criminal laws against reckless or even negligent harming. Thus the kid-glove treatment meted out to those responsible for occupational hazards and the like is not simple reflection of our ordinary moral sensibilities, as the Defenders claim. Moreover, don't be confused into thinking that, because all workplaces have some safety measures, all workplace deaths are at most due to negligence. To the extent that precautions are not taken against particular dangers (such as leaking methane), deaths due to those dangers are—by Gross's standard— caused recklessly or even knowingly (because the executive knows that potential victims are in harm's way from the danger he fails to reduce). Nancy Frank concludes from a review of state homicide statutes that "a large number of states recognize unintended deaths caused by extreme recklessness as murder."

* * *

It's worth noting that, in answering the Defenders here, I have portrayed harms from occupational hazards in their best light. They are not, however, all just matters of well-intentioned but excessive risk taking. Consider, for example, the Manville (formerly Johns Manville) asbestos case. It is predicted that 240,000 Americans working now or who previously worked with asbestos will die from asbestos-related cancer in the next 30 years. But documents made public during congressional hearings in 1979 show "that Manville and other companies within the asbestos industry covered up and failed to warn millions of Americans of the dangers associated with the fireproof, inde-structible insulating fiber." An article in the *American Journal of Public Health* attributes thousands of deaths to the cover-up. Later in this chapter I docu-ment similar intentional cover-ups, such as the falsification of reports on coal-dust levels in mines, which leads to crippling and often fatal black lung disease. Surely someone who knowingly subjects others to risks and tries to hide those risks from them is culpable in a high degree.

2. Defenders' Second Objection

Being harmed directly by another person is more terrifying than being harmed indirectly and impersonally, as by a safety hazard, even if the degree of harm is the same.

Response: I think the Defenders are right in believing that direct personal assault is terrifying in a way that indirect impersonal harm is not. This dif-ference is no stranger to the criminal justice system. Prosecutors, judges, and juries constantly have to consider how terrifying an attack is in determining what to charge and what to convict offenders for. This is why we allow gra-dations in charges of homicide or assault and allow particularly grave sen-tences for particularly grave attacks. In short, the difference the Defenders are pointing to here might justify treating a one-on-one murder as graver than murder due to lax safety measures, but it doesn't justify treating one as a grave crime and the other as a mere regulatory (or very minor criminal) matter. After all, although it is worse to be injured with terror than without, it is still the injury that constitutes the worst part of violent crime. Given the choice, seriously injured victims of crime would surely rather have been terrorized and not injured than injured and not terrorized. If that is so, then the worst part of violent crime is still shared by the indirect harms that the Defenders would relegate to regulation.

3. Defenders' Third Objection

Someone who harms another in the course of an illegitimate and purely self-interested action is more evil than someone who harms another as a conse-quence of a legitimate and socially productive endeavor.

Response: There is also something to the Defenders' claim that indirect harms, such as ones that result from lax safety measures, are part of legiti-mate productive activities, whereas one-on-one crimes are not. No doubt we must tolerate the risks that are necessary ingredients of productive activity (unless those risks are so great as to outweigh the gains of the productive activity), but this doesn't imply we shouldn't identify the risks, or levels of danger, that are unnecessary and excessive and use the law to protect innocent people from them. If those risks are great enough, the fact that they may further a productive or otherwise legitimate activity is no reason against making them crimes if that's what's necessary to protect workers. A person can commit a crime to further an otherwise legitimate endeavor and it is still a crime. If, say, I threaten to assault my workers if they don't work faster, this doesn't make my act any less criminal. And, in general, if I do something that by itself ought to be a crime, the fact that I do it as a means to a legitimate aim doesn't change the fact that it ought to be a crime. If acts that intentionally endanger others ought to be crimes, then the fact that the acts are means to legitimate aims doesn't change the fact that they ought to be crimes.

4. Defenders' Fourth Objection

The harms of typical crimes are imposed on their victims against their wills, whereas harms such as those due to occupational hazards are consented to by workers when they agree to a job.

Response: Cases like the Manville asbestos case show that the Defenders overestimate the reality of the "free consent" with which workers take on the risks of their jobs. You can consent to a risk only if you know about it, and often the risks are concealed. Moreover, the Defenders overestimate generally the degree to which workers freely consent to the conditions of their jobs. Although no one is forced at gunpoint to accept a particular job, virtually everyone is forced by the requirements of necessity to take some job. Moreover, workers can choose jobs only where there are openings, which means they cannot simply pick their place of employment at will. At best, workers can choose among the dangers present at various worksites, but rarely can they choose to face no danger at all. For nonwhites and women, the choices are further narrowed by discriminatory hiring and longstanding occupational segregation (funneling women into secretarial, nursing, or teaching jobs and blacks into janitorial and other menial occupations), not to mention subtle and not-so-subtle practices that keep nonwhites and women from advancing within their occupations. Consequently, for all intents and purposes, most workers *must* face the dangers of the jobs that are available to them. What's more, remember that, while here we have been focusing on harms due to occupational hazards, much of the indirect harm that I shall document in what follows is done not to workers but to consumers (of food with dangerous chemicals) and citizens (breathing dangerous concentrations of pollutants).

Finally, recall that the basis of all the Defenders' objections is that the idea that one-on-one harms are more evil than indirect harms is part of our common moral beliefs, and that this makes it appropriate to treat the former with the criminal justice system and the latter with milder regulatory measures. Here I think the Defenders err by overlooking the role of legal institutions in shaping our ordinary moral beliefs. Many who defend the criminal justice system do so precisely because of its function in educating the public about the difference between right and wrong.

* * *

One cannot simply appeal to ordinary moral beliefs to defend the criminal law because the criminal law has already had a hand in shaping ordinary moral beliefs. At least one observer has argued that making narcotics use a crime at the beginning of this century *caused* a change in the public's ordinary moral notions about drug addiction, which prior to that time had been viewed as a medical problem. It is probably safe to say that, in our own time, civil rights legislation has sharpened the public's moral condemnation of racial discrimination. Hence, we might speculate that if the criminal justice system began to prosecute—and if the media began to portray—those who inflict *indirect harm* as serious criminals, our ordinary moral notions would change on this point as well.

* * *

WORK MAY BE DANGEROUS TO YOUR HEALTH

When the *President's Report on Occupational Safety and Health* was published in 1972, the government estimated the number of job-related illnesses at 390,000 per year and the number of annual deaths from industrial disease at 100,000. Since that time, numerous studies have documented the astounding incidence of disease, injury, and death due to hazards in the workplace *and* the fact that much or most of this carnage is the consequence of the refusal of management to pay for safety measures and of government to enforce safety standards, and sometimes of willful defiance of existing law.

For 2000, the U.S. Department of Labor's Bureau of Labor Statistics (BLS) reports 5.7 million workplace injuries and illness, about half of which resulted in lost workdays or restricted duties at work. BLS also reports "362,500 newly reported cases of [nonfatal] illnesses in private industry."

Complete data on occupational fatalities are difficult to come by. BLS says about its data on fatal occupational diseases that

> It is difficult to compile a complete count of fatal occupational diseases because the latency period [the delay between contracting a fatal disease on the job and the appearance of symptoms, and from these to death] for many of these conditions may span years. In addition, there is some difficulty in linking illnesses to work exposures. Data presented are incomplete, therefore, and do not represent all deaths that result from occupational diseases.

Moreover, the Occupational Safety and Health Administration (OSHA) relies on employer reporting for its figures, and there are many incentives for under-reporting. Writing in the journal *Occupational Hazards*, Robert Reid states that:

> OSHA concedes that many factors—including insurance rates and supervisor evaluations based on safety performance—are incentives to under-report. And the agency acknowledges that recordkeeping violations have increased more than 27 percent since 1984, with most of the violations recorded for not maintaining the injuries and illnesses log examined by compliance officers and used for BLS' annual survey.

A study by the National Institute for Occupational Safety and Health (NIOSH) concludes that "there may be several thousand more workplace deaths each year than employers report."

For these reasons, we must look elsewhere for accurate figures. In 1982, then-U.S. Secretary of Health and Human Services Richard Schweiker stated that "current estimates for overall workplace-associated cancer mortality vary within a range of five to fifteen percent." With annual cancer deaths currently running at about 500,000, that translates into about 25,000 to 75,000 job-related cancer deaths per year, but cancer is only part of the picture of death-dealing occupational disease. In testimony before the Senate Committee on Labor and Human Resources, Dr. Philip Landrigan, director of the Division of Environmental and Occupational Medicine at the Mount Sinai School of Medicine in New York City, stated that:

Recent data indicate that occupationally related exposures are responsible each year in New York State for 5,000 to 7,000 deaths and for 35,000 new cases of illness (not including work-related injuries). These deaths due to occupational disease include 3,700 deaths from cancer. . . .

Crude national estimates of the burden of occupational disease in the United States may be developed by multiplying the New York State data by a factor of 10. New York State contains slightly less than 10 percent of the nation's workforce, and it includes a broad mix of employment in the manufacturing, service and agricultural sectors. Thus, it may be calculated that occupational disease is responsible each year in the United States for 50,000 to 70,000 deaths, and for approximately 350,000 new cases of illness.

It is some confirmation of Dr. Landrigan's estimates that they imply work-related cancer deaths of approximately 37,000 a year, a figure that is toward the low end of the range in Secretary Schweiker's statement on this issue.

Landrigan's estimates of deaths from occupational disease are also corroborated by a study reported by the National Safe Workplace Institute, which estimates that the number of occupational disease deaths is between 47,377 and 95,479. Mark Cullen, director of the occupational medicine program at the Yale University School of Medicine, praised this study as "a very balanced, very comprehensive overview of occupational health." In a 1997 article in the AMA journal *Archives of Internal Medicine,* researchers at San Jose State University in California aggregated the national and large regional data sets collected by BLS, the National Council on Compensation Insurance, the National Center for Health Statistics, the Health Care Financing Administration, and other government agencies and private firms and came up with an estimate, for 1992, of 60,300 deaths from occupational illness.

In light of these various estimates, we can hardly be overestimating the actual death toll if we take the conservative route and set it at 50,000 deaths a year resulting from occupational disease, at the low end of Dr. Landrigan's estimates, near the low end of the National Safe Workplace Institute's estimates, and below that of the San Jose State University researchers.

As for nonfatal occupational illness, BLS reports 362,500 new cases for 2000 and the San Jose State University researchers estimate 862,200 cases (based on data from 1992). These illnesses are of varying severity. Because I want to compare these occupational harms with those resulting from aggravated assault, I shall stay on the conservative side here too, as with deaths from occupational diseases, and say that there are annually in the United States approximately 250,000 job-related serious illnesses. This is a conservative figure in light of (1) the San Jose State University researchers' estimate of 862,200 cases, (2) the likelihood of underreporting, and (3) other research suggesting that about one-third of nonfatal occupational illnesses are cases of carpal tunnel syndrome requiring 25 or more days away from work, and so on. These figures are also conservative in that they don't include the effects of workers' exposure to occupational illnesses on the health of their families. Taken together with 50,000 deaths from occupational diseases, how does this compare with the threat posed by crime?

Before jumping to any conclusions, note that the risk of occupational disease and death falls only on members of the labor force, whereas the risk of crime falls on the whole population, from infants to the elderly. Because the labor force (minus the currently unemployed) is about six-tenths (63.2 percent) of the total population (174,035,000 in 2000, of a total population of 275,372,000), to get a true picture of the *relative* threat posed by occupational diseases compared with that posed by crimes, we should multiply the crime statistics by .6 when comparing them with the figures for industrial disease and death. Using the crime figures for 2000 . . . we note that the *comparable* figures would be:

	Occupational Disease	Crime (× .6)
Death	50,000	9,300
Other physical harm	250,000	540,000

If it is argued that this paints an inaccurate picture because so many crimes go unreported, my answer is this: First of all, homicides are by far the most completely reported of crimes. For obvious reasons, the general underreporting of crimes is not equal among crimes. It is easier to avoid reporting a rape or a mugging than a corpse. Second, although not the best, aggravated assaults are among the better-reported crimes. Estimates from the Justice Department's National Crime Victimization Survey indicate that 43 percent of aggravated assaults were reported to the police in 1999, compared with 27 percent of thefts. On the other hand, we should expect more, not less, underreporting of industrial than criminal victims because diseases and deaths are likely to cost firms money in the form of workdays lost and insurance premiums raised, occupational diseases are frequently first seen by company physicians who have every reason to diagnose complaints as either malingering or not job-related, and many occupationally caused diseases do not show symptoms or lead to death until after the employee has left the job.

In sum, both occupational and criminal harms are underreported, though there is reason to believe that the underreporting is worse for occupational than for criminal harms. Finally, I have been extremely conservative in estimating occupational deaths and other harms. However one may quibble with figures presented here, I think it is fair to say that, if anything, they understate the extent of occupational harm compared with criminal harm.

* * *

SUMMARY

The criminal justice system does not protect us against the gravest threats to life, limb, or possessions. Its definitions of crime are not simply a reflection of the objective dangers that threaten us. The workplace, the medical profession, the air we breathe, and the poverty we refuse to rectify lead to far more human suffering, far more death and disability, and take far more dollars from our pockets than the murders, aggravated assaults, and thefts reported annually by the FBI. What is more, this human suffering is preventable. A government really intent on protecting our well-being could enforce work safety regulations, police the medical profession, require that clean-air standards be met, and funnel sufficient money to the poor to alleviate the major disabilities of poverty, but it does not. Instead we hear a lot of cant about law and order and a lot of rant about crime in the streets. It is as if our leaders were not only refusing to protect us from the major threats to our well-being but trying to cover up this refusal by diverting our attention to crime, as if this were the only real threat.

As we have seen, the criminal justice system is a carnival mirror that presents a distorted image of what threatens us. The distortions do not end with the definitions of crime. As we will see in what follows, new distortions enter at every level of the system, so that, in the end, when we look in our prisons to see who really threatens us, all we see are poor people. By that time, virtually all the well-to-do people who endanger us have been discreetly weeded out of the system. As we watch this process unfold * * *, we should bear in mind the conclusion of the present chapter: All the mechanisms by which the criminal justice system comes down more frequently and more harshly on the poor criminal than on the well-off criminal take place *after most of the* *dangerous acts of the well-to-do have been excluded from the definition of crime itself.* The bias against the poor within the criminal justice system is all the more striking when we recognize that the door to that system is shaped in a way that excludes in advance the most dangerous acts of the well-to-do. Demonstrating this has been the purpose of the present chapter.

QUESTIONS

1. Close your eyes for a moment and think of a crime. Now, open your eyes and jot down the images that came to mind: What is the crime? Where is it taking place? Who is committing it?

2. What evidence does Reiman present to indicate that the images that typically come to mind when we think of crime are *not* images of the most harmful type of crime? Which other type of crime does he identify as more harmful? What data does he present in making his case?

3. What are the four justifications Reiman outlines for why many people are inclined to see crimes such as rape and murder, which are intentional efforts to inflict harm on another person, as more evil than crimes like violating worker safety standards, which results from the pursuit of corporate profit?

4. What is Reiman's critique of each of these four justifications?

5. Has this reading changed your view of the ways that the criminal justice system prosecutes and assigns punishments to different types of crime? Why or why not?

22

Babies Having Babies

FROM *Constructing an Epidemic*

KRISTIN LUKER

During the 1970s, '80s, and '90s a number of related issues became the subject of considefable public and policymaking concern: premarital sex, abortion, out-of-wedlock births, and teenage pregnancy. Kristin Luker points out that teenage pregnancy became the most visible of these issues, in spite of the fact that it was not the epidemic that various claimsmakers portrayed it to be. Rather, teenage pregnancy became, in Luker's words, a "lightening rod" issue: it became a powerful, convenient, and shorthand way for the public and for policymakers to make sense of a variety of massive changes taking place in American society. Luker analyzes why teenage pregnancy consequently became identified as a leading explanation for poverty and its related social ills, and she concludes by examining the short-sightedness of this explanation.

By the early 1980s Americans had come to believe that teenagers were becoming pregnant in epidemic numbers, and the issue occupied a prominent place on the national agenda. "Teenage pregnancy," along with crack-addicted mothers, drive-by shootings, and the failing educational system, was beginning to be used as a form of shorthand for the country's social ills. Everyone now agreed that it was a serious problem, and solutions were proposed across the ideological spectrum. Conservatives (members of the New Right, in particular) wanted to give parents more control over their daughters, including the right to determine whether they should have access to sex education and contraception. Liberals, doubting that a "just say no" strategy would do much to curtail sexual activity among teenagers, continued to urge that young men and women be granted the same legal access to abortion and contraception that their elders had. Scholars debated the exact costs of early pregnancy to the individuals involved and to society, foundations targeted it for funding and investigation, government at all levels instituted programs to reduce it, and the media gave it a great deal of scrutiny. In the early 1970s the phrase "teenage pregnancy" was just not part of the public lexicon. By 1978, however, a dozen articles per year were being published on the topic; by the mid-1980s the number had increased to two dozen; and by 1990 there were more than two hundred, including cover stories in both *Time* and *Newsweek*.

Ironically (in view of all this media attention), births to teenagers actually *declined* in the 1970s and 1980s. During the baby boom years (1946–1964), teenagers, like older women, increased their childbearing dramatically: their birthrates almost doubled, reaching a peak in 1957. Subsequently, the rates drifted back to their earlier levels, where they have pretty much stayed since 1975. The real "epidemic" occurred when Dwight Eisenhower was in the White House and poodle skirts were the height of fashion. But although birthrates among teenagers were declining, other aspects of their behavior were changing in ways that many people saw as disturbing. From the vantage point of the 1970s, the relevant statistics could have been used to tell any one of a number of stories. For example, when abortion was legalized in 1973, experts began to refer to a new demographic measure, the "pregnancy rate," which combined the rate of abortion and the rate of live births. In the case of teenagers an increasing abortion rate meant that, despite a declining birthrate, the pregnancy rate was going up, and dramatically so.

Since the rise in the pregnancy rate among teenagers (and among older women as well) was entirely due to the increase in abortions, it is curious that professionals and the public identified pregnancy, rather than abortion, as the problem. It is likewise curious that although the abortion rate increased for all women, most observers limited their attention to teenagers, who have always accounted for fewer than a third of the abortions performed. Teenagers *are* proportionately overrepresented in the ranks of women having abortions. But to pay attention almost exclusively to them, while neglecting the other groups that account for 70 percent of all abortions, does not make sense.

A similar misdirection characterized the issue of illegitimacy. In the 1970s teenagers were having fewer babies overall than in previous decades, but they—like older women—were having more babies out of wedlock. Compared to other women, teenagers have relatively few babies, and a very high proportion of these are born to unmarried parents (about 30 percent in 1970, 50 percent in 1980, and 70 percent in 1995). But although most babies born to teenagers are born out of wedlock, most babies born out of wedlock are *not* born to teens. In 1975 teens accounted for just under a half of all babies born out of wedlock; in 1980 they accounted for 40 percent; and in 1990 they accounted for fewer than a third. Obviously, teens should hardly be the only population of interest.

Thus, in the 1970s and early 1980s the data revealed a number of disquieting trends, and teenagers became the focus of the public's worry about these trends. More single women were having sex, more women were having abortions, more women were having babies out of wedlock, and—contrary to prevailing stereotypes—older women and white women were slowly replacing African Americans and teens as the largest groups within the population of unwed mothers. These trends bespeak a number of social changes worth looking at closely. Sex and pregnancy had been decoupled by the contraception revolution of the 1960s; pregnancy and birth had been decoupled by the legalization of abortion in the 1970s; and more and more children were growing up in "postmodern" families—that is, without their biological mother and father—in part because divorce rates were rising and in part because more children were being born out of wedlock. But these broad demographic changes, which impinged on women and men of all ages, were seen as problems that primarily concerned *teenagers*. The teenage mother—in particular, the black teenage mother—came to personify the social, economic, and sexual trends that in one way or another affected almost everyone in America.

A number of different responses might have been devised to meet the challenge of these new trends. It would have been logical, for example, to focus on the problem of abortion, since more than a million abortions were performed each year despite the fact that people presumably had access to effective contraception. Or the problem might have been defined as the increase in out-of-wedlock births, since more and more couples were starting families without being married. Or policymakers could have responded to the way in which sexual activity and childbearing were, to an ever greater extent, taking place outside marriage (in 1975 about three-fourths of all abortions were performed on single women). Yet American society has never framed the problem in any of these broader terms. The widest perspective was perhaps that of the antiabortion activists, who saw the problem as abortion in general. A careful reading of the specialist and nonspecialist media suggests that, with a few exceptions, professionals and the general public paid scant attention to abortion and out-of-wedlock childbearing among older women, while agreeing that abortion and illegitimate births among teenagers constituted a major social and public-health problem. Why did Americans narrow their vision to such an extent? How did professionals, Congress, and the public come to agree that there was an "epidemic" of pregnancy among teenagers and that teenagers were the main (if not the only) population worth worrying about?

A STORY THAT FITS THE DATA

* * *

Taken together, the data added up to a story that made sense to many people. It convinced Americans that young mothers . . . who gave birth while still in high school and who were not married—were a serious social problem that brought a host of other problems in its wake. It explained why babies . . . were born prematurely, why infant mortality rates in the United States were so high compared to those in other countries, why so many American students were dropping out of high school, and why AFDC costs were skyrocketing. Some people even believed that if teenagers in the United States maintained their high birthrates, the nation would not be able to compete internationally in the coming century. Others argued that distressing racial inequalities in education, income, and social standing were in large part due to the marked difference in the birthrates of white and black teenagers.

Yet this story, which fed both on itself and on diffuse sexual anxiety, was incomplete; the data it was based on were true, but only partial. Evidence that did not fit the argument was left out, or mentioned only in passing. Largely ignored, for example, was the fact that a substantial and growing proportion of all unmarried mothers were not teenagers. And on those rare occasions when older unwed mothers were discussed, they were not seen as a cause for concern. Likewise, although the substantially higher rates of out-of-wedlock childbearing among African Americans were often remarked upon, few observers pointed out that illegitimacy rates among blacks were falling or stable while rates among whites were increasing. Few noted that most of the teenagers giving birth were eighteen- and nineteen-year-olds, or that teens under fifteen had been having babies throughout much of the century.

This story, as it emerged in the media and in policy circles in the 1970s and 1980s, fulfilled the public's need to identify the cause of a spreading social malaise. It led Americans to think that teenagers were the only ones being buffeted by social changes, whereas these changes were in fact pervasive; it led them to think that heedless, promiscuous teenagers were responsible for a great many disturbing social trends; and it led them to think that teenagers were doing these things unwittingly and despite themselves. When people spoke of "children having children" or of "babies having babies," their very choice of words revealed their belief that teenage mothers, because of their youth, should not be held morally responsible for their actions. "Babies" who had babies were themselves victims; they needed protection from their own ungovernable impulses.

In another sense, limiting the issue to teenagers gave it a deceptive air of universality; after all, everyone has been or will be a teen-ager. Yet the large-scale changes that were taking place in American life did not affect all teenagers equally. The types of behavior that led teenagers to get pregnant and become unwed mothers (engaging in premarital sex, and bearing and keeping illegitimate children) were traditionally much more common among African Americans than among whites, and more common among the poor than among the privileged.

* * *

The myriad congressional hearings, newspaper stories, and technical reports on the "epidemic" of pregnancy among teenagers could not have convinced the public to subscribe to this view if other factors in American life had not made the story plausible. The social sciences abound with theories suggesting that the public is subject to "moral panics" which are in large part irrational, but in this case people were responding to a particular account because it helped them make sense of some very real and rapidly changing conditions in their world. It appeared to explain a number of dismaying social phenomena, such as spreading signs of poverty, persistent racial inequalities, illegitimacy, freer sexual mores, and new family structures. It was and continues to be a resonant issue because of the profound changes that have taken place in the meanings and practices associated with sexuality and reproduction, in the relations among sex, marriage, and childbearing, and in the national and global economies. Through the story of "teenage pregnancy," these revolutionary changes acquired a logic and a human face.

THE SEXUAL REVOLUTION

In the 1950s and 1960s (as those who long for the good old days are fond of telling us) sex was a very private matter. Like childbearing, it was sanctioned only within marriage. Respectable women were careful lest their behavior earn them a reputation for being "loose," which would limit their ability to marry a "nice" man. True, in 1958 about four out of ten unmarried women were sexually active before their twentieth birthday, but in those days premarital sex was in a strict sense *premarital,* for the most part occurring within a committed relationship that soon led to marriage. Though the data collected by Alfred Kinsey and his colleagues in the 1940s and 1950s are not nationally representative, they do show that for earlier generations of American women, most premarital sex was in large part "engagement" sex—sex with the man the woman was planning to marry, and then for only a relatively short period before the wedding. In the Kinsey report, almost half of the married women who had engaged in premarital sex had done so only with their fiancés, and for less than two years period to their marriage. More recent and more representative data suggest that this pattern continued for some time: in the 1960s half of all women who engaged in premarital sex did so with their fiancés. By the mid-1980s, this proportion had fallen to less than a fourth.

Many people recall the transformation in sexual behavior that took place in the 1970s, but they may well have forgotten the rapidity of that change. In 1969 the overwhelming majority of Americans—almost 70 percent—agreed that having sex before marriage was wrong; three out of four agreed that magazine photos of nudes were objectionable; and more than four out of five agreed that nudity in a Broadway show (for example, "Hair" or "Oh! Calcutta") was unacceptable. A mere four years later, only traces of these values remained: the percentages of Americans who objected to premarital sex and to nudes in magazines had both dropped an astonishing twenty points, and the percentage of those who objected to nudity on the stage had dropped eighteen points. Similarly, a Roper poll conducted in 1969 found that only 20 percent of the public approved of premarital sex; four years later, the respondents were equally divided on the issue. The General Social Survey conducted by researchers at the University of Chicago asked the question in a slightly different way: in 1972 it found that only 26 percent of the public thought premarital sex was "not wrong at all"; but a decade later this figure had jumped to 40 percent, while the percentage of those who said it was "almost always wrong" had correspondingly declined.

Not surprisingly, as more and more people engaged in premarital sex or extramarital sex (after being divorced, separated, or widowed), it became increasingly difficult to claim that sexual activity should be limited to adults. By what logic could sex be declared taboo for the young? And how young was too young? This created a genuine dilemma. In 1969 the rules about sex were clear, even if they were often ignored in practice. Sex was for married people, and if society sometimes turned a blind eye to sex between unmarried partners, it did so only for those who had attained or were close to attaining legal adulthood. Minors, unless they were deemed mature or emancipated, could not obtain contraception, and in most states "minors" included everyone under twenty-one. Moreover, under the age-of-consent laws that were in force in many states, young women could not legally consent to have sex. In challenging these rules in the courts and in Congress, advocates had been successful in claiming that teenagers had a right to contraception, and therefore a right to have sex. But the new concept of rights for teenagers created a "bright-line" problem. Once adults accepted that unmarried people could have sex and that teenagers had a right to contraception, by what logic was an unmarried thirteen-year-old too young to have sex? What bright line separated the too young from the old enough? The category "teenagers" or "adolescents" included people who were barely out of childhood as well as people who were legal adults. And if teenagers had rights, why not even younger people?

* * *

These changes in the statistics, dramatic though they are, do not begin to capture the extent of the transformation that has actually taken place in teenagers' sexual behavior. For example, we tend to speak of their involvement in "premarital sex," and this is technically correct: today 96 percent of American teenagers have sex before they get married. But this is not the "engagement sex" that young women allowed themselves in the 1950s. Now teenagers are sexually active whether or not they have immediate plans to marry. And for reasons that no one fully understands, Americans of all ages are retreating from marriage. As a result, many of the teenagers who are engaging in sex and having babies are doing exactly what teenagers did in the 1950s, but the nontrivial change is that they are doing so without the benefit of wedlock.

* * *

Public-opinion polls, when read carefully, suggest that adults have complex preferences about the best way to deal with sexual activity among teenagers. Most adults don't want teens to be sexually active, but for a surprisingly long time they have agreed that teenagers who *are* sexually active should have access to birth control information and contraceptives. Most have also long favored providing sex education in the schools, but they are remarkably skeptical about its ability to curtail sexual activity or pregnancy among teenagers. They disapprove of unmarried teenage mothers and consider them a source of social problems, but a majority are strongly in favor of laws that require parental approval before a teenager can have an abortion. In fact, about 40 percent of Americans think that a young woman should not be permitted to have an abortion even if pregnancy would cause her to drop out of school. In short, most adults seem to have a clear first choice—namely, that teens should not have sex. At the same time, a large majority of them support contraceptive and sex education programs for teens, a fact that suggests they doubt they will get their first choice. . . .

* * *

Today's parents want to protect their children from the myriad dangers—seen and unseen, life-threatening and emotionally bruising—that sex entails these days. And they want to set their own timetable, so that they themselves can decide when their children are old enough to have sex. Often parents find it difficult to allow a child to be sexually active while he or she is still living as a dependent under their roof. Yet the point at which many parents consider a child old enough to be sexually active—whether they define it as when the child marries, or moves out of the parental home, or becomes self-supporting—is occurring ever later in American life, due to societal and economic changes over which individuals have minimal control. Except for the relatively few people who think that sex outside marriage is always wrong (and whose problem is chiefly one of finding a way to promulgate their values in an unsympathetic society), Americans have numerous questions relating to teenagers' sexual behavior. Should teens be sexually active? At what age? With whom? How are parents to encourage the use of contraception without seeming to push a teenager into having sex before he or she is ready? How can individuals reconcile their antipathy toward abortion with their desire to see fewer children born out of wedlock? In short, the contradictions inherent in teenagers' sexual activity make it hard for adults to give a clear, precise, and unambiguous message to today's young people.

Teenagers, however, are simply the most visible aspect of a far larger problem. Nowhere has public or private life caught up with the sexual revolution of the 1970s, and most Americans do not yet fully appreciate how far-reaching the changes really were. Now that sex seems to have been permanently disconnected from marriage (or as permanently as anything ever is in social life), private citizens as well as policymakers must grapple with a host of legal, ethical, medical, and social issues. Teenagers are a focus of anxiety because so many of them are participating in the new world of sexual freedom and because most adults are (often rightly) doubtful about the skills and resources these young people possess. The challenge facing parents is to find a way to protect their children and their children's children without making unrealistic or impractical demands, yet still maintain some authority over them. As a consequence, public attitudes toward teenagers' sexual activity are an awkward amalgam of attempts to come to terms with vague fears and a sense that young people are out of control. . . .

* * *

THE REPRODUCTIVE REVOLUTION

Teenagers are not only the most visible exponents of new patterns of sexual behavior but are participating in innovative family structures whose long-term effects are still uncertain. These structures—which have received less attention than the changing sexual mores but which may have even more significance for American society—call into question the relationship between childbearing and marriage. For an increasing number of Americans (and Europeans, for that matter), having and raising a child no longer takes place exclusively within marriage. Demographers have estimated that if present trends continue, an astonishing 50 percent of all American children will spend at least part of their childhood in a single-parent family. In the early 1990s, slightly more than half of these children were being raised by one parent as a result of divorce, but the rest had been born to unmarried mothers.

* * *

That women of all ages are more willing to bear children out of wedlock is usually attributed to the fact that illegitimacy has lost its stigma. This explanation is certainly true. Public attitudes toward what colonial Americans called bastardy have changed dramatically in a relatively short time. In 1970 only about one American in ten thought that childbearing outside marriage should be legal, but four years later that percentage had more than doubled, to 25 percent. By 1985 the figure had risen to 40 percent. Although a majority of Americans still oppose out-of-wedlock childbearing, opinion shifts of this magnitude can truly be called revolutionary.

But these data tell only half the story. It used to be that, for an unmarried woman, becoming pregnant was "a fate worse than death." We can get some idea of what the old days were like, and of how radically society has changed, if we look at media reports from the late 1960s and early 1970s. Neither those who wrote about unmarried mothers nor the unmarried women themselves questioned the belief that having a baby out of wedlock was very wrong. In 1965 *Time* magazine ran a story revealing just how stigmatizing illegitimacy was: a New York Court of Claims had permitted a child to sue for damages resulting from "the mental anguish of being born a bastard." In 1966 a journalist writing in *Ebony,* a magazine aimed at black readers, noted: "In the pecking order of America, unwed mothers are perhaps the most despised minority. They are the targets of abuse from legislators bent on punishing them. They are the scapegoats of moralists decrying an alleged lapse in public morality. They are the butt of jokes by school children and adults." In 1968 a young woman wrote: "I'm a teenager who has made a big mistake. I am pregnant. I'm not proud of what I've done and I hope and pray other teenagers will read my letter, wake up , and start to lead a good, clean life. . . . "

* * *

Social scientists may eventually understand fully why attitudes toward sex and marriage changed so profoundly. Whatever the mechanisms, in less than a decade a shameful condition was transformed into a personal choice. The rise of the women's movement, the sexual revolution, the greater availability of abortion (which made out-of-wedlock childbearing truly a choice), and the increasing fragility of marriage all no doubt contributed to the astonishing shift in the social meaning of illegitimacy.

* * *

THE ECONOMIC TRANSFORMATION
OF AMERICAN LIFE

The fact that the public accepts out-of-wedlock births among older, affluent, white women but deplores them among young, poor, minority women is intimately tied to a third profound change in the lives of Americans—namely, the decline of American economic power and of middle-class affluence.

Today's young Americans are the first generation in living memory who face the prospect of doing less well economically over their lifetimes than did their parents. In recent years the gap between the well-to-do and the poor has grown: the rich are getting richer and the poor are getting poorer. Economists use various measures to estimate the distribution of income, and virtually all of them show that income distribution is "hollowing out," meaning that individuals are more likely to find themselves at the top or bottom of the income distribution and less likely to find themselves in the middle. And inequality among *families* is growing even faster. Poor families are not only getting poorer, but they now tend to be poorer in the United States than elsewhere. When we compare the income of the poorest 20 percent of households in the United States to that of the poorest 20 percent in other industrialized countries, it is clear that Americans are faring very badly. . . .

* * *

But growing disparities in income are not the whole story. As international comparisons reveal, such inequalities have long existed in the United States, and the increases in the 1980s were well within historical trends. In 1969 the richest one-fifth of families earned about $7.25 for each dollar the poorest fifth earned; by the late 1980s the richest fifth were earning $9.60 for each dollar the poorest earned—an increase, to be sure, but one that occurred in the context of an income distribution that was already fairly polarized.

* * *

In the 1970s there were also dramatic changes in the nature of poverty and the structure of families. Once, the poor had been elderly and the elderly had been poor: in 1959 more than a third of all elderly people had been poor. But the program instituted under Lyndon Johnson's Great Society, in particular the indexing of Social Security to inflation, altered the makeup of the poor population. The poverty rates for older people fell by half between 1959 and the mid-1970s, and have continued to decline. Today the poverty rate among the elderly is lower than the national average.

Children, in contrast, are moving in the opposite direction. Although their poverty rates likewise declined as a result of Great Society legislation, during the past fifteen years the risk that an American child will grow up in poverty has increased by about a third. Children, in comparison to adults and the elderly, are now twice as likely to be poor: 20 percent of all children are poor, accounting for fully 40 percent of the poor people in the United States. The fact that poverty among children is growing and that poverty in general is becoming more apparent all across the United States is one cause of the public's concern about pregnancy among teenagers. Looked at from a broad perspective, American families seem to have followed two trajectories. The pattern of traditional families has hollowed out, just like the income distribution.

One large group of Americans has responded to declining real wages by making its family structure more *concentrated*. These people are postponing marriage and childbearing to an ever greater extent, having fewer and fewer children, and forming a growing number of two-career marriages. This trajectory, which we might call the yuppie pattern (after the Young Urban Professionals who adopt it), is the new middle-class norm. Women in particular are investing more time in their education, are training for careers rather than jobs, and are continuing to work even after they have children. This pattern has become so prevalent among the middle class that we often forget what a major shift in behavior it represented when it first appeared. For much of U.S. history, American women married fairly young, had their children fairly early, and retired from the work force until their children were grown. But the new yuppie pattern is available only to the affluent, people who can realistically expect that the market will reward their sacrifices. For people who have fewer resources, there is another shift in the American family: these people *rearrange* the traditional family. They either never get married or start a family at all, or they have children without being married.

* * *

. . . Traditional married couples in which only the husband worked were becoming scarcer, while two-income families and single-parent families were proliferating. In many cases changes in family structure were closely related to—in fact, an adaptation to—changing economic circumstances, and differed according to race. In the 1950s and 1960s virtually all American women married at an early age (especially in comparison to European women), had their first child soon afterward, and completed their childbearing within a few years. But this pattern became less common as fortunes declined and the middle class shrank. The lucky and prosperous were able to invest more in education, obtain a greater return on their investment, and move into the professional upper-middle class. (College-educated people began to receive more of a return on their educational investment than they had in earlier years.) And when men and women invested more in education, they tended to postpone marriage and childbearing, to form two-income families, and to have fewer children. Among people with less money and less cultural capital, this pattern seems to have been less attractive. They may have postponed or forgone marriage, or entered into a partnership that was not a legal marriage, but they did not give up bearing children: poor women continued to do what all American women had done in the postwar era—namely, have babies at an early age—but more and more of them had children out of wedlock. Affluent and successful men and women tended to forsake this older pattern, leaving it mainly to poor women. The new, bifurcated economy, in which good jobs got better and bad jobs got worse, was paralleled by a bifurcated family pattern, in which the affluent postponed their childbearing and had their babies in wedlock while the poor did not.

Consequently, just as the issue of pregnancy among teenagers was being debated in Congress and in the media, many Americans were viewing it from the vantage point of their own restructured lives. People who were affluent and well educated, who had delayed marriage in order to further their schooling, who were members of two-earner couples, and who were postponing and limiting their childbearing had little sympathy for teenage mothers (who were often conflated in the public mind with unwed mothers). The behavior of these young women seemed not only unwise and self-destructive, but unwise and self-destructive in ways that hit particularly close to home. They seemed to be having babies before they were ready, and, worse, to be doing so without a legal husband, at a time when many Americans were becoming keenly aware that it took two or more workers in a family to maintain a middle-class lifestyle. People who had scrimped and saved until they could marry and set up a household, who lived with all of the burdens of the "second shift" (the burdens incurred when wives enter the labor force but are still expected to fulfill their traditional nurturant role), and who were postponing childbearing until they could afford it were particularly unsympathetic: teenagers who had babies seemed to be heedless, irresponsible, and heading for trouble. And those in the middle, the ones whose highly paid blue- and white-collar jobs were becoming scarce and who were having difficulty passing on these middle-class jobs to their children, were no more understanding: young people who had sex and babies too soon seemed to be bringing their troubles on themselves.

In short, pregnant teenagers made a convenient lightning rod for the anxieties and tensions in Americans' lives. Economic fortunes were unstable, a postindustrial economic order was evolving, sexual and reproductive patterns were mutating. Representing such teenagers as the epitome of society's ills seemed one quick way of making sense of these enormous changes. This was particularly true as poverty was becoming ever more visible and being poor appeared to be the direct result of immoral or unwise behavior. Pregnant teenagers seemed to embody the very essence of such behavior. Indeed, the phrase "teenage pregnancy" continues to be a powerful shorthand way of referring to the problem of poverty.

The rhetoric of the 1970s, generated in good faith by advocates who wanted to ensure that young women had access to contraception, created a comforting but unrealistic fantasy to explain the fact that some people were getting poorer in an uncertain economy. By noting that young mothers were poor mothers, advocates persuaded the public that young mothers are poor *because* they had untimely pregnancies and births. This in turn led to the conclusion that if young poor women simply did what young affluent women do, then they, too, would be affluent. It is not surprising that when affluent people dramatically change their attitudes and behavior toward marriage and child-bearing but poor people do not, the well-to-do would try to explain the existence of poverty by saying the poor have failed to adapt. In recent years, both liberals and conservatives have tended to ascribe poverty to the sexual and reproductive decisions that poor women make. What gives this argument resonance is the fact that the affluent are postponing their childbearing and early motherhood is increasingly the province of the "left behind"—poor women who realistically know that postponing their first birth is unlikely to lead to a partnership in a good law firm. But the deep cultural belief that it *might* continues to attract people of every ideological persuasion. Commentators as diverse as Charles Murray and David Ellwood, one a conservative bent on undoing the welfare system and the other a liberal bent on saving it, agree on the foolishness of early pregnancy.

There is no arguing the case that teenagers who bring a child into the world put a strain on public patience, values, and funds. The public assumes that teenagers are unable to support a child financially, and in the overwhelming majority of cases this is true. Moreover, poor mothers tend to have children who will themselves grow up to be poor. Not surprisingly, teenagers and their babies have come to be perceived (to use the words of a *Time* essayist) as "the very hub of the U.S. poverty cycle," often creating up to three generations of poor people who will depend on the public purse. Congress, the media, reports by the National Academy of Sciences, and statements by private voluntary groups all associate poverty with childbearing among teenagers. But this linkage depends on an assumption that reducing pregnancy among teenagers, specifically among unmarried teenagers, can reduce poverty.

In the opinion of many well-meaning middle-class people, the trouble with poor and pregnant teenagers is that they do not do what middle-class people do: invest in an education, establish themselves in a job, marry a sensible and hardworking person, and only then begin to think about having a baby. Many poor people do these things, of course, and so do many poor teenagers. But the deck is stacked against people at the lower levels of a world in which the job distribution has been hollowed out. People who lack an education are less well off than ever before, and thus find it ever harder to maintain a marriage and support a family. Even if they work at one or more of the "lousy jobs" at the bottom of the wage structure, full-time year-round employment is insufficient to keep a family out of poverty. . . . The idea that young people would be better off if they worked harder, were more patient, and postponed their childbearing is simply not true—and is unlikely to become true in the foreseeable future—for a great many people at the bottom of the income scale. Even when poor people obtain more education, for example, they only displace other people at the end of the queue, and the problem of poverty and childbearing among young people continues.

A compelling body of scholarship now shows that although people who become parents as teenagers will eventually be poorer than those who do not, a very large proportion of that difference is explained by preexisting factors. Well over half of all women who give birth as teenagers come from profoundly poor families, and more than one-fourth come from families who are slightly better off but still struggling economically. Taken together, more than 80 percent of teenage mothers were living in poverty or near-poverty long before they became pregnant.Teenage parents are not middle-class people who have become poor simply because they have had a baby; rather, they have become teenage parents because they were poor to begin with. More than two decades of research, summarized in the National Academy of Sciences' report *Risking the Future,* make clear a point not highlighted in the report itself: at every step of the process that leads to early childbearing, social and economic disadvantage plays a powerful role. Poor kids, not rich ones, have babies as teenagers, and their poverty long predates their pregnancy. By the same token, poor kids, not rich ones, have babies without being married. . . .

* * *

But if teenage mothers are poor before they ever become mothers, if in many cases they would be poor and in need of welfare at whatever age they had their first child, and if marriage brings its own set of problems to poor people, much of the easy equation that identifies early pregnancy as a cause of poverty breaks down. If the real problem is poverty, not the age or marital status of young women when they give birth, then it is not surprising that poor women tend to have children and even grandchildren who grow up to be poor. Preventing teenagers from getting pregnant and persuading them to delay their childbearing would merely postpone the problem of poor women and their dependence on welfare. Childbearing among teenagers has relatively little effect on the levels of poverty in the United States. But income disparities have become a pervasive fact of American life, and it is scarcely surprising that when experts in the 1970s labeled "teenage pregnancy" a fundamental cause of poverty, Americans were willing to listen.

1. What evidence does Luker present to indicate that teenage pregnancy was actually on the decline during the 1970s, '80s, and '90s when it was constructed as a problem of epidemic proportions, while premarital sex, abortion, and out-of-wedlock births were on the rise and yet not similarly constructed as epidemics?

2. Among the issues listed in Question 1, why was teenage pregnancy constructed as the key social problem for the public to be alarmed about and for policymakers to address? Answer by discussing how, in Luker's words, the epidemic of teenage pregnancy seemed to "explain a number of dismaying social phenomena, such as spreading signs of poverty, persistent racial inequalities, illegitimacy, freer sexual mores, and new family structures (pp. 361–362)?"

3. How is seeing teenage pregnancy as a leading explanation for poverty consistent with the political ideology that has been prevalent in the United States since the early 1980s?

4. What is the case Luker makes in arguing that the core problem that needs to be addressed is not the problem constructed by claimsmakers—teenage pregnancy—but instead poverty itself?

When Kids Become
Victims of Violence

Monster Hype: How a Few Isolated Tragedies—and Their Supposed Causes—Were Turned into a National Epidemic

JOEL BEST

One of the most publicly visible social problems over the past decade has been school shootings. Joel Best asks readers to carefully consider two critical questions concerning the school shootings problem: First, why has this problem attained such prominence? And second, how often when kids are victimized by violence does this violence actually take place in school? Conventional wisdom would suggest that the visibility of the school shootings problem in news reports, political rhetoric, and public policy stems from irrefutable objective data about the danger of attending school. Best challenges this belief by dissecting how claimsmakers have statistically misrepresented the pervasiveness of shocking events like the massacre that occurred at Columbine High School in 1999. He argues that the framing of these events as part of a national epidemic diverts attention away from the array of contexts outside of school where kids are much more likely to be subjected to violence.

Contemporary discussions about social issues, especially within education, almost always involve statistics. Numbers have become an essential element in policy rhetoric, a form of evidence needed to persuade others. Statistics let us claim that we can measure the size of our problems and the effectiveness of our solutions.

Yet even as we rely on numbers, we are bedeviled by innumeracy, the mathematical equivalent of illiteracy. Too often, we fail to think critically about the statistics we encounter, to ask even the most basic questions. This is important, because accepting numbers uncritically may cause us to badly misunderstand our problems. There are few better examples of this failing than some of the recent figures regarding school violence.

The March 5, 2001, shooting spree at Santana High School in Santee, California, which left 2 dead and 13 injured, revived concerns over the seeming escalation of school violence and its potential links to the age-old schoolyard tradition of bullying. School shootings first became a serious issue in the wake of a series of tragic incidents, the most famous being Dylan Klebold and Eric Harris's April 1999 rampage at Columbine High School, in Littleton, Colorado, during which they murdered 12 students and a teacher before turning their weapons on themselves. Of particular interest was that nearly every shooting was accompanied by reports that the teenagers involved were marginalized in some way; the Santee shooter especially appears to have been a victim of bullying.

Both school shootings and bullying have become subjects of extensive media coverage, featuring the pontification of assorted politicians, activists, and experts. This is how contemporary Americans create new social problems. Typically, the process involves a three-part recipe:

1. Illustrate the problem with an awful example (e.g., the mass murder at Columbine High School).
2. Give the problem a name ("school shootings").
3. Use statistics to suggest the problem's size and importance.

Statistics play a crucial role in this process, because we tend to assume that numbers are factual—that somebody has counted something, that the problem has been measured and therefore is as big as the claims suggest. Coupled with dramatic, headline-grabbing incidents, they have created the impression that both school violence and bullying are on the rise. This may make for compelling television, but the oversaturated media coverage can portray a few isolated incidents as a national trend. Take CBS anchor Dan Rather's post-Santee warning: "School shootings in this country have become an epidemic." Such claims have become commonplace among journalists who haven't thought carefully enough about the evidence. The statistics on violence and bullying that are trucked out by pundits and activists often exaggerate or distort the case. The result is that the public and policymakers tend to overreact as they look for solutions to problems that appear to be out of control. A closer look at the statistics, however, reveals a more complicated and hopeful picture.

A PHANTOM EPIDEMIC

Of course, the phenomenon of adolescents' bringing guns to school and randomly shooting their peers ought to be a source of genuine worry. The 1997–98 school year alone saw tragedy strike West Paducah, Kentucky (3 dead, 5 more wounded); Jonesboro, Arkansas (5 dead, 10 wounded); and Springfield, Oregon (2 deaths and 21 wounded at the school, after the shooter first killed his parents at home). These crimes, along with the Columbine massacre, seemed to be without rational motivation; what could possibly have driven these adolescents to lash out at the world in such bloody fashion? Kids have always divided into cliques and subjected the nonconforming to verbal and physical abuse; only recently, it seemed, had the social drama of high school resulted in mass casualties. It's legitimate to wonder whether these incidents represent a deep-seated change in youth culture.

Nevertheless, these tragic events masked the overall trend: a good deal of evidence indicates that school violence has actually been declining in recent years. When researchers at the National School Safety Center (NSSC) combed media reports from the school years 1992–93 to 2000–01, they identified 321 violent deaths at school. However, not all of these incidents involved student-on-student violence: they included, for example, 16 accidental deaths and 56 suicides, as well as incidents involving nonstudents, such as a teacher killed by her estranged husband, who then shot himself, and a nonstudent killed on a school playground during the weekend. Even if we include all 321 deaths, the average fell from 48 violent deaths per year during the school years 1992–93 through 1996–97 to 32 per year from 1997–98 to 2000–01. If accidental deaths and suicides are eliminated from the data, the decline remains: from an average of 31 deaths per year in the earlier period to 24 per year in the later one. Moreover, the later period includes all of the heavily publicized cases mentioned above. And the later figure may be further inflated by the likelihood that the media were more apt to report school shootings after the topic vaulted to public attention.

This decline is consistent with the evidence suggesting that crime rates were declining nationwide. During the 1990s, the overall crime rate fell, as did the rates of major violent crimes such as homicide, robbery, and aggravated assault. The crime rate, which is the Federal Bureau of Investigation's tally of crimes reported to the police, is only one of two national measures of criminal activity. The second, less familiar measure is the rate of victimization reported in the National Crime Victimization Survey. Researchers with the victimization survey interview a large national sample and ask respondents whether they or anyone in their households have been victims of crime. This survey showed instances of criminal victimization falling during the 1990s. Moreover, reports of teenagers being victimized by violent crimes at school dropped. The data also showed that instances of victimization were less common at school than elsewhere; in other words, teenagers were safer at school.

The federal Centers for Disease Control and Prevention's Youth Risk Behavior Survey also found steadily declining percentages of high-school students who reported fighting or carrying weapons on school property during the 1990s. It is also important to recognize that the risks of school violence are extremely low. For every million children who attend school, there is less than one violent school-related death per year. Moreover, only about 1 percent of children killed by violence are hurt at school, despite the large amount of time they spend there.

None of these data are especially hard to come by; all of them were readily available—and the trends they showed were apparent—before, during, and after the various school-shooting incidents that became subjects of extensive news coverage. All of this evidence flatly contradicted the claims that there was a wave, trend, or epidemic of school violence. In other words, the wave of school shootings was a phantom—that is, a nonexistent trend. What accounts for this misperception? Why did the press and the public assume that school shootings were increasing?

In large part, media coverage promoted this distorted view of the problem. The Columbine killings in particular became a huge story. Columbine involved many victims, and the story unfolded over hours. Because the crime occurred in the suburbs of a major city, there were plenty of reporters nearby, and they had time to arrive on the scene for live coverage. The result was dramatic video footage that would be replayed many times. Furthermore, Columbine was a bastion of suburban privilege; it challenged stereotypes about inner-city violence. It was a story made for television.

The Columbine coverage also reflected recent media transformations. Most Americans now have access to cable or satellite television systems; they are no longer limited to receiving broadcasts from a handful of local stations. Most viewers now can choose among several all-news or public-affairs channels. Those channels need constantly to fill the time with content. In the aftermath of the Columbine shootings, broadcasters like CNN, Fox News, and MSNBC devoted hours, not just to reporting the story and commentary about the violence, but also to live coverage of many funeral and memorial services. Columbine remained a major story for days, and during that period, politicians, activists, and commentators used it as evidence to justify their calls for a wide range of measures, including tougher gun laws, restrictions on adolescents' access to violent popular culture, and so on.

The Columbine killings were a terrible event, but we are accustomed to thinking about such incidents as instances—that is, as examples of some larger problem. The extraordinary level of media coverage reinforced the interpretation that these killings must have had some larger significance. It also gave people the sense that school shootings must be a large and growing problem, regardless of what the available statistics actually showed.

QUESTIONS

1. What is an *epidemic*? Jot down the various meanings that this word can have.
2. How did the news media and other claimsmakers frame the Columbine massacre as just one instance of a much wider school shootings epidemic?
3. How does the epidemic frame statistically misrepresent the school shootings problem?
4. Best reports that "only about 1 percent of children killed by violence are hurt in school, despite the large amount of time they spend there (p. 381)." What do you think accounts for the other 99 percent of children killed by violence? Do some exploratory research to determine whether your hunches are correct.
5. Why do you think other types of violent youth homicide receive so little attention from claimsmakers compared to school shootings?

Homeless, Not Poor

FROM *And We Are Not Seen: Ideological and*
Political Barriers to Understanding Homelessness

GARY BLASI

According to government criteria being poor, or living in poverty, means that a per-
son's income falls below a certain level, which in 2006 was about $20,000 for a
family of four. And even people with higher incomes may face extreme difficulties
making ends meet. Since being homeless means that one does not have a place to
live and since poverty often means being unable to afford housing, the poor and the
homeless are of course intersecting populations. Yet, as Gary Blasi reveals, this fact
is typically made invisible by claimsmaking about social inequality in the United
States. Claimsmakers rarely highlight the intersections between homelessness and
poverty, and instead overwhelmingly draw attention to homelessness in lieu of
poverty. Blasi discusses factors that explain the disparity in attention given to these
two problems and argues that the dominant policy focus on emergency provisions
of food and shelter to the homeless distracts attention away from the underlying
social causes of both homelessness and poverty.

* * *

One of the more dramatic shifts in recent years in public discourse about
poverty in the United States is the degree to which discussions of "the
homeless" have displaced discussions of poverty and the poor. A recent computer search of subject matter indexes of all the articles from *The New York
Times* and *Los Angeles Times* on the NEXIS computer service reveals that since
January 1, 1991, these two newspapers have published more than four times
as many articles (2,146) about the "homeless" as about "poverty" (469). Not
only has "homelessness" attained considerable salience as a public issue in

comparison to "poverty" but the extent to which the two are intricately inter-woven by fact and logic has been glossed.

Although "the other America" seems to be rediscovered by each genera-tion, for the most part the poor in America are "out of sight, out of mind." With the increase in homelessness in the 1980s, however, the poor became increasingly and literally visible. Further, images and issues relating to "the homeless" seemed to have had a power that issues of "poverty" or "housing the poor" did not. Although there has been little systematic investigation, polls and other data suggest that the ways in which the public reacts to these issues has much to do with the differences in the images and schemata they evoke. In the early 1980s, advocates for the poor noticed that there was more pub-lic interest in (and possibly support for) "the homeless" than for "the poor." . . .

* * *

. . . [T]he term "homeless" was virtually unknown in this country before 1980. And, although the number of people lacking homes may have increased in the 1980s, it was not the aggregation of their individual situations that con-stituted the problem of "the homeless." Rather, through the social processes that Edelman describes with great insight, the "problem of the homeless" was constructed over time, as the result of the efforts not only of advocates but also of the unintended consequences of those efforts and of the actions of gov-ernment officials, academics, and popular authors and of the filtering and flam-ing effects in the various channels of the media. Whatever the processes of social problem construction, it is clear that there are important consequences. In particular, there are important "framing effects" (e.g., "homelessness" vs. "poverty") in public discourse. In understanding and acting on concepts like "poverty," "poor people," or "the homeless," people obviously employ the same cognitive apparatus that mediates all understanding and action. There is good evidence that in apprehending and reacting to concepts like these, all of us employ prototypes and schematic knowledge. If asked to describe the char-acteristics of "the homeless," only a few of us will retrieve from memory tables of statistics. Rather, most of us will retrieve from episodic memory an encounter with a particular homeless person or a prototype made of many imagined or real people. . . . After many conversations with academics who have an inti-mate knowledge of the empirical data that belie all stereotypes, I suspect that the prototype effect is very strong indeed. Why should this be so? There are several reasons.

First, the ordinary processes of human cognition lead to the use of "available" prototypes. Virtually everyone in urban America has now encountered people identified (or misidentified) as homeless: the panhandler on the corner, the subway, or freeway onramp (often with a sign that has the word "homeless" somewhere on it) or the disheveled and obviously very disturbed person prowling the alley or walking in the middle of the street. We do not add to our prototype the young couple nursing a cup of coffee at McDonald's, the Vietnam veteran bivouacked in the woods, the elderly woman with a week left in a shelter. These are "the homeless" we either never see or do not identify as homeless. Some people, particularly parents fearful of losing their children, go to extreme lengths to avoid being identified as homeless. Second, most people prefer to cling to prototypes that do not threaten their values and beliefs, even in the face of contrary empirical data or an actual nonprototypical homeless person. The notion that there are among us hungry and homeless people, including children, who seem not to have done anything terribly blameworthy, is hard to accept. Human beings have a strong capacity for denial. These individual processes feed, and are fed by, cultural currents. For hundreds of years in Anglo-American culture, the otherwise troubling fact of the existence of poor, hungry, and homeless people has been made less troubling by the belief that they are, for the most part, reaping the rewards of their own misdeeds and bad character. As suggested earlier, these predispositions and cultural currents have been amplified and nurtured by a consistent conservative ideological campaign. Third, while it is easy enough to blame a hostile, conservative counterattack against the advocacy efforts that began in the early 1980s, those advocacy efforts themselves may have contributed to the development of blind spots and distortions in the public perception of homelessness. For example, it was largely advocates who effectively divided homelessness and poverty into two separate public issues. This division was prompted in part by the realization that the public and politicians reacted quite differently to "the homeless" in comparison to "the poor," even when the people being talked about were precisely the same. For instance, the Community for Creative Non-Violence (CCNV) in Washington, DC had been feeding extremely poor, hungry, and homeless people for many years before the public campaign designed by Mitch Snyder, Mary Ellen Hombs, and others in the early 1980s attracted wide public attention to the issue of homelessness.

To my knowledge, no one has investigated the reasons for the differences in reaction to "homelessness" and "poverty." Perhaps, as a matter of cognition and imagination, it is simply easier for people to identify with the harsh reality of homelessness than with that of mere poverty. Many people have had an array of experiences that can supply details to imagination: being lost, being very far from home, and being between homes, for example. Those who have never been poor, however, likely have more difficulty imagining the myriad minor consequences of being extremely poor, although housed: protecting one's children and possessions from rats, eating macaroni and cheese at 10 meals each week, or walking miles for the simplest errand. Or, perhaps the intrinsically more urgent character of homelessness lifted it to a level of attention simple poverty had not had. This was true both on the level of individuals and of public policy. Although we might not be able to meet all the needs of a given homeless person, surely we could keep him or her from freezing to death. Further, although the poor may always be with us, surely there is a level of degradation we need not countenance. We may not be willing to support the kind of massive restructurings that would end poverty, but surely we could provide to the homeless poor the same kind of shelter we provide to victims of natural disasters. It was thus no accident that the continuing and multifaceted deprivations and degradations that attend extreme poverty—hunger, poor health, educational deprivation, violence and victimization, slum housing conditions, and occasional homelessness—were largely ignored while advocates focused on the "emergency" of homelessness. Advocates were not cynical but merely pragmatic: The focus on homelessness produced some results, whereas a diffuse focus on poverty seemed likely to produce nothing, particularly in the Reagan years. And public officials of all political stripes were more than willing to accept this reconstruction of extreme poverty as a (temporary) emergency in a single dimension of human need. It was thus no surprise that the lead federal agency assigned to deal with the "emergency" of homelessness was neither the Department of Housing and Urban Development nor the Department of Health and Human Services but, rather, the same Federal Emergency Management Agency (FEMA) that provides emergency shelter to the very temporary victims of earthquakes and hurricanes. Moreover, the focus on homelessness as an isolated, emergent situation lessened the attention given to more widespread transformations and increasing inequalities in the American economy. Ironically, one of the most insightful observers of social problem construction sought to explain in 1987 why homelessness had not become a salient social problem on a par with child abuse: "A serious effort to deal with homelessness, by contrast, would entail a reexamination of established economic and social institutions and so might threaten existing power inequalities." As it turned out, of course, the social problem of "the homeless" was constructed and did acquire some prominence—but in a way that did not threaten established institutions. This was a result contrary to the intention of many advocates, but it was an inevitable consequence of the detachment of homelessness from the problems of poverty and growing inequality, and the further oversimplification of homelessness itself.

If advocates oversimplified the relation of poverty to homelessness, they oversimplified even more, often to the point of complete denial, the interplay of economic and housing issues with characteristics that made some people more vulnerable and less able to compete, including mental disorder and substance abuse. . . .

* * *

Although there is only fragmentary evidence at present on this point, it is possible that the final record may suggest that advocacy aimed at ending homelessness actually prolonged it by diverting attention and resources from the wider issues of poverty and inequality. For if we accept the premise that the only way to end homelessness is to eradicate extreme poverty and attend to the various additional decrements that afflict some of the very poor, then the locus on homelessness and the inevitable emergency shelter solution is, indeed, a distraction. Defining the problem as the problem of "the homeless" allows moderately liberal communities to "solve" the problem of extreme poverty and discrimination by reinventing the almshouse in the form of mass shelters. The creation of mass shelters, in turn, inevitably leads to an understandable "not in my backyard" (NIMBY) reaction against these facilities, and equally inevitably, against "the homeless" who will inhabit them. When there are insufficient resources even for mass shelters, government officials may turn to the creation of outdoor camps and "safe zones" into which homeless people—most of them people of color—will be forced to live, perhaps the most ominous development in recent years.

The focus of homelessness also permits local elites to frame the issue around the question of the "rights" of the homeless merely to exist, to do in public those things virtually all of them would prefer to do in the comfort of their own homes. Through the inevitable evolution of this discourse, advocates too often find themselves arguing not about rights to a job or to the economic means to survive but about the right to sleep in the park and to beg in the subway, advocating not for the creation of decent affordable housing but for the placement in neighborhoods of mass shelters that no one (including homeless people) reasonably wants to live in or near. Whatever the outcome of these debates, they have little to do with ending either mass homelessness or extreme poverty and nothing to do with ending inequality and discrimination.

1. What evidence does Blasi present to indicate that claimsmakers tend to focus on homelessness much more than poverty?

2. What are some of the reasons for the discrepancy in attention given to these two problems of social inequality?

3. How does providing emergency food and shelter to the homeless divert attention away from an exploration of the social causes of homelessness and poverty?

4. How does the policy focus on protecting the rights of homeless people to occupy public space distract attention away from the social factors that give rise to homelessness and poverty?

Catastrophes That Count

Flood Tide

HENDRIK HERTZBERG

Disasters are not created equal. Hertzberg cites alarming figures about a variety of tragedies currently taking place around the world that do not receive significant public or policymaking attention in the United States. Yet, when a massive tsunami swelled upon the shores of Eastern Africa and many parts of Asia on December 26, 2004, the charitable response from the United States was overwhelming. Individuals, foundations, and the federal government collectively donated humanitarian relief that contributed to a worldwide response totaling in the billions of dollars. In this selection Hertzberg explores why the tsunami was seen as a matter of greater urgency than other disasters. He urges readers to recognize that our level of concern and response to disasters has little to do with the magnitude of the disaster itself. Instead, it has to do with the capacity for the disaster to be socially constructed as a matter of significant concern; a capacity that stems from factors such as when the disaster takes place, how it occurs, who are its victims, and how visible is the harm.

Nearly four million men, women, and children have died as a consequence of the Congo civil war. Seventy thousand have perished in the genocide in the Darfur region of Sudan. In the year just ended, scores of thousands died in wars and massacres elsewhere in Africa, in Asia, in the archipelagoes of the Pacific, and, of course, in Iraq. Less dramatically, but just as lethally, two million people died of malaria around the world, and another million and a half of diarrhea. Five million children died of hunger. Three million people died of AIDS, mostly in Africa. The suffering of these untimely and terrible deaths—whether inflicted by deliberate violence, the result of human agency, or by avoidable or treatable malady, the result of human neglect—is multiplied by heartbroken parents and spouses, numbed and abandoned children, and, often, ruined survivors vulnerable to disease and predation and dependent, if they are lucky, on the spotty kindness of strangers.

The giant wave that radiated from western Sumatra on the day after Christmas destroyed the lives of at least a hundred and fifty thousand people and the livelihoods of millions more. A hundred and fifty thousand: fifty times the toll of 9/11, but "only" a few per cent of that of the year's slower, more diffuse horrors. The routine disasters of war and pestilence do, of course, call forth a measure of relief from public and private agencies (and to note that this relief is almost always inadequate is merely to highlight the dedication of those who deliver it). But the great tsunami has struck a deeper chord of sympathy.

One can understand why. Partly it's that although the scale of the horror is unimaginable (or so it has been repeatedly described), the horror itself is all too imaginable. A giant wave speaks to a childlike fear that can be apprehended by anyone who has ventured too far out from the beach in a suddenly mounting swell, has felt helpless in the suck of undertow or riptide, has been slammed and spun and choked by a breaker tall enough to block the sky. Partly it's that the reach of the disaster was so vast, far vaster than any hurricane or monsoon or terrestrial earthquake: three thousand miles from end to end. Partly it's that people from all over the world, seeking a holiday in the sun, witnessed the catastrophe. People from more than fifty countries lost their lives in it; among the dead and missing, nearly two weeks later, were more than seven thousand foreign tourists. (Nearly two thousand of them were Swedes; if that number holds, then Sweden's immediate losses, proportionately, will be greater than Thailand's.) Finally, and perhaps most important, it's that this is a drama that has victims and heroes—but no villains. No human ones, anyway.

The terrible arbitrariness of the disaster has troubled clergymen of many persuasions. The Archbishop of Canterbury is among those newly struggling with the old question of how a just and loving God could permit, let alone will, such an undeserved horror. (Of course, there are also preachers, thankfully few, who hold that the horror is not only humanly deserved but divinely intended, on account of this or that sin or depredation.) The tsunami, like the city-size asteroid that, on September 29th [2004], missed the earth by only four times the distance of the moon, is a reminder that, one way or another, this is the way the world ends. Man's laws are proscriptive, nature's merely descriptive.

Yet it is the very "meaninglessness" of the catastrophe—its lack of human agency, its failure to fit into any scheme of human reward and punishment—that has helped make possible the simple solidarity of the global response. President Reagan, to the exasperation of his aides, used to muse that human beings, faced with some mortal threat from beyond the skies, would put aside their differences in common cause. Something like that, on a very modest scale, appears to be happening as the world clamors to help the survivors of the destroyer from beneath the seas. Tsunamis have no politics.

Even so, there were familiar elements in the responses of the Bush Administration. Two days after the disaster, a White House spokesman, asked why President Bush himself had so far remained silent, explained, "He didn't want to make a symbolic statement about 'we feel your pain.'" On the third day, the President finally voiced his condolences in person, and two days later the government's emergency-aid allotment, initially pegged at fifteen million dollars, was raised to three hundred and fifty million, where it remains. On the eighth day, even as Secretary of State Colin Powell, in Thailand, was saying that enough money was at hand, Bush, now back at the White House, appeared side by side with his father, George H.W. Bush (whom he had never before granted such a public role), and his father's successor, Bill Clinton (the object of his spokesman's snideness), to announce that he was appointing them to lead a private fund-raising drive in the United States.

"We're a very generous, kindhearted nation," the President said on December 29th. And so we are. But it is unseemly to boast about it at such a moment. It would be unseemly even if it were not the case that Australia, Germany, and Japan have been considerably more generous in absolute terms and perhaps a dozen other countries have been more so in per-capita terms. "We're showing the compassion of our nation in the swift response," Bush said on January 3rd. "But the greatest source of America's generosity is not our government—it's the good heart of the American people." That is true, too; but it is also true, or should be, that in a democracy a government's generosity is an expression of a people's heart, not something separate from it. There is reason to worry that the Administration regards private relief efforts as a partial replacement for, rather than as a supplement to, the efforts of the United States government; and reason to worry, too, that the funds for tsunami relief will come at the expense of victims of disasters yet to occur. According to the *Times,* the Administration plans to use money from the disaster-and-famine-assistance program of the United States Agency for International Development, whose budget for this year is $384.9 million, and consulted with "senior Republican lawmakers" to try "to cover the costs of this disaster without undermining Mr. Bush's other priorities," such as "making his tax cuts permanent."

A few influential Republicans, however, are beginning to say that America should help the victims of the tsunami without beggaring other assistance programs, and if their view prevails then our aid will indeed be, as the Administration insists, an expression of "American values." But these are American values that, at least for the moment, are also manifestly German values and Japanese values and Norwegian and Swedish and Spanish and British values and Sri Lankan and Indian values—values that are, like the victims of the tsunami, simply human.

QUESTIONS

1. What are some of the monumental human disasters currently taking place around the world that are not getting nearly as much attention in the United States as did the 2004 Indian Ocean tsunami?

2. In what ways was the tsunami more visible than these other disasters?

3. How did the presence of so many foreign tourists among those who died or were injured contribute to the massive attention that the tsunami received?

4. How did the tsunami enable the Bush Administration to gain visibility for the charitable pledge of $350 million made by the United States? Why is this kind of visibility virtually impossible to achieve when the United States supports relief efforts to stave off the many other monumental human disasters currently taking place around the world?

5. Why is there typically lots of claimsmaking attention given to disasters that produce massive suffering in a short period of time (such as the tsunami or an airplane crash) but much less attention given to disasters that produce the same or more suffering gradually, over a longer period of time (such as disease or malnutrition)?

26

Black Men as Criminals
and as Victims

FROM *Black Men*

BARRY GLASSNER

One of the greatest fears pervading white America nowadays is the perceived crim-
inal threat caused by black men. News reports tend to highlight instances of black
men committing violent crimes, feeding public anxieties that these men pose grave
dangers to the rest of society, and fueling political support for tough prison sen-
tencing laws. Barry Glassner questions the "reality" presented in these news reports
by asking why black men are typically constructed as criminals when in truth they
are much more likely to be victimized by American society. His discussion implies
that policymaking could be considerably different if the news media more frequently
focused public attention on the problems afflicting black men.

ournalists, politicians, and other opinion leaders foster fears about particular groups of people both by what they play up and what they play down.
Consider Americans' fears of black men. These are perpetuated by the excessive attention paid to dangers that a small percentage of African-American
men create for other people, and by a relative *lack* of attention to dangers that
a majority of black men face themselves.

The dangers to black men recede from public view whenever people paint
color-blind pictures of hazards that particularly threaten African-American men:
discussions of disease trends that fail to mention that black men are four times
more likely to be infected with the AIDS virus and twice as likely to suffer from
prostate cancer and heart disease than are white men; reports about upturns in
teen suicide rates that neglect to note evidence that the rate for white males
crept up only 22 percent between 1980 and 1995 while the rate for black males
jumped 146 percent; or explorations of the gap between what middle-class

313

Americans earn and the expenses of maintaining a middle-class lifestyle that fail to point out that the problem is more acute for black men. (College-educated black men earn only as much as white men with high school diplomas.)

The most egregious omissions occur in the coverage of crime. Many more black men are casualties of crime than are perpetrators, but their victimization does not attract the media spotlight the way their crimes do. Thanks to profuse coverage of violent crime on local TV news programs, "night after night, black men rob, rape, loot, and pillage in the living room," Caryl Rivers, a journalism instructor at Boston University, has remarked. Scores of studies document that when it comes to *victims* of crime, however, the media pay disproportionately more attention to whites and women.

On occasion the degree of attention becomes so skewed that reporters start seeing patterns where none exist—the massively publicized "wave" of tourist murders in Florida in the early 1990s being a memorable example. By chance alone every decade or two there should be an unusually high number of tourists murdered in Florida, the statistician Arnold Barnett of MIT demonstrated in a journal article. The media uproar was an "overreaction to statistical noise," he wrote. The upturn that so caught reporters' fancy—ten tourists killed in a year—was labeled a crime wave because the media chose to label it as such. Objectively speaking, ten murders out of 41 million visitors did not even constitute a ripple, much less a wave, especially considering that at least 97 percent of all victims of crime in Florida are Floridians. Although the Miami area had the highest crime rate in the nation during this period, it was not tourists who had most cause for worry. One study showed that British, German, and Canadian tourists who flock to Florida each year to avoid winter weather were more than 70 times more likely to be victimized at home. The typical victim of crime in Florida, though largely invisible in the news, was young, local, and black or Hispanic.

So was the typical victim of drug violence in New York City in the late 1980s and early 1990s, when some reporters and social scientists avidly implied otherwise. "The killing of innocent bystanders, particularly in the cross fires of this nation's drug wars, has suddenly become a phenomenon that greatly troubles experts on crime," began a frontpage story in the *New York Times*. It is "the sense that it could happen to anybody, anywhere, like a plane crash" that makes these attacks so scary, the reporter quoted Peter Reuter from the RAND Corporation. According to the *New York Daily News*, "spillover" crime from the drug wars even affected people in "silk-stocking areas." In fact, a *New York* magazine article revealed, thanks to a crack cocaine epidemic, "most neighborhoods in the city by now have been forced to deal with either crack or its foul by-products: if not crack houses and street dealers or users, then crackhead crimes such as purse snatchings, car break-ins, burglaries, knife-point robberies, muggings, and murders." TV newscasts, needless to say, breathlessly reported much the same, with pictures at eleven.

* * *

To suggest that all Americans have a realistic chance of being a victim of homicide is to heighten already elevated anxieties among people who face little risk. In spite of the impression given by stories like the one in *Time* titled "Danger in the Safety Zone: As Violence Spreads into Small Towns, Many Americans Barricade Themselves," which focused on random murders in several hamlets throughout the country, tens of millions of Americans live in places where there hasn't been a murder in years, and most of the rest of us live in towns and neighborhoods where murder is a rare occurrence.

Who *does* stand a realistic chance of being murdered? You guessed it: minority males. A black man is about eighteen times more likely to be murdered than is a white woman. All told, the murder rate for black men is double that of American soldiers in World War II. And for black men between the age of fifteen and thirty, violence is the single leading cause of death.

OF DOGS AND MEN

* * *

Police inattention is one of several factors that journalists accurately cite to account for why white crime victims receive more media attention than black victims. Journalists also cite complaints from African-American leaders about the press paying too much attention to problems and pathologies in black communities. But are crime victims the best candidates to overlook in the service of more positive coverage? A host of studies indicate that by downplaying the suffering of victims and their families the media do a disservice to minority neighborhoods where those victims live. Criminologists have documented that the amount of coverage a crime victim receives affects how much attention police devote to the case and the willingness of prosecutors to accept plea bargains. As a rule, the more coverage, the more likely that an assailant will be kept behind bars, unable to do further harm to the victim or community. In addition, when a neighborhood's crime victims are portrayed *as* victims—sympathetically and without blame, as humans rather than as statistics—people living in other parts of the city are more inclined to support improved social services for the area, which in turn can reduce the crime rate.

Underreporting of black victims also has the effect of making white victims appear more ubiquitous than they are, thereby fueling whites' fears of black criminals, something that benefits neither race. Helen Benedict, a professor of journalism at Columbia University, has documented that rapes of white women by black men—which constitute a tiny proportion of all rapes—receive considerable media attention. In a separate study of women's concerns about crime Esther Madriz, a sociology professor at Hunter College, discovered that stories in the news media "reinforce a vision of society in which black men are foremost among women's fears."

Another explanation journalists and editors give for their relative neglect of black victims might be called the Journalism 101 defense. Those of us who took an introductory journalism course in college remember the teacher pounding into our cerebrums the famous dictate attributed to John Bogart, city editor of the *New York Sun* in the 1880s: "When a dog bites a man that is not news, when a man bites a dog, that is news." Everyone *expects* black crime victims, the argument goes, so their plight isn't newsworthy. Here is how a writer for the *Los Angeles Times,* Scott Harris, characterized the thoughts that go through reporters' and editors' minds as they ponder how much attention, if any, to accord to a city's latest homicide: "Another 15-year-old shot to death? Ho hum. Was he an innocent bystander? What part of town? Any white people involved?"

As heartless and bigoted as this reasoning may sound, actually there would be nothing objectionable about it if news organizations applied the man-bites-dog principle universally. Obviously they do not; otherwise, there would never be stories about crimes committed by black men, since no one considers black perpetrators novel or unexpected.

My friend David Shaw, media critic at the *Los Angeles Times,* offers a simpler explanation for the scant attention to black victims. To stay in business newspapers must cater to the interests of their subscribers, few of whom live in inner-city minority neighborhoods. The same market forces result in paltry coverage of foreign news in most American newspapers, Shaw suggests.

Now *there's* a study someone should do: compare the amount of attention and empathy accorded by the U.S. press during the 1990s to black men shot down in American cities to, say, Bosnians killed in that country's civil war. I wouldn't be surprised if the Bosnians fared better. The tendency to slight black victims extends even to coverage of undeniably newsworthy crimes such as shootings of police by fellow officers. In 1996, after a white New York City police officer, Peter Del-Debbio, was convicted of shooting Desmond Robinson, a black plainclothes transit officer in the back, wounding his kidneys, liver, lungs, and heart, reporters and columnists evidenced great sympathy for Del-Debbio. They characterized him as having made an innocent mistake and suffering overwhelming remorse. The agony of Robinson and his family, by contrast, received more modest attention. Few reporters seriously questioned—and some overtly endorsed—the official spin from the district attorney, mayor, and defense attorneys that the shooting had nothing to do with race and was largely the victim's fault—even though in testimony Del-Debbio recalled having reacted not to seeing just any man with a gun but "a male black with a gun."

While some writers made note of the fact that black officers say their white colleagues are quick to fire at African Americans working undercover because they view them as suspects, no reporter, the best I can determine, investigated the issue. When Richard Goldstein, a media critic for the *Village Voice,* reviewed the coverage of the shooting he found that only the *Daily News*— not the *Times* or *Post*—made note of the fact that, since 1941, twenty black police officers in New York had been shot by white colleagues. During that time not a single white officer had been shot by a black cop. "Imagine," wrote Goldstein, "the shock-horror if 20 female officers had been shot by male cops. But when it comes to race, the more obvious the pattern the more obscure it seems."

* * *

MAKERS OF THE NATION'S MOST HAZARDOUS MUSIC

Fear mongers project onto black men precisely what slavery, poverty, educational deprivation, and discrimination have ensured that they do not have— great power and influence.

After two white boys opened fire on students and teachers at a schoolyard in Jonesboro, Arkansas, in 1998 politicians, teachers, and assorted self-designated experts suggested—with utter seriousness—that black rap musicians had inspired one of them to commit the crime. A fan of rappers such as the late Tupac Shakur, the thirteen-year-old emulated massacrelike killings described in some of their songs, we were told. Never mind that, according to a minister who knew him, the Jonesboro lad also loved religious music and sang for elderly residents at local nursing homes. By the late 1990s the ruinous power of rap was so taken for granted, people could blame rappers for almost any violent or misogynistic act anywhere.

So dangerous were so-called gangsta rappers taken to be, they could be imprisoned for the lyrics on their albums. Free speech and the First Amendment be damned—when Shawn Thomas, a rapper known to his fans as C-Bo, released his sixth album in 1998 he was promptly arrested and put behind bars for violating the terms of his parole for an earlier conviction. The parole condition Thomas had violated required him not to make recordings that "promote the gang lifestyle or are antilaw enforcement."

Thomas's new album, "Til My Casket Drops," contained powerful protest lyrics against California governor Pete Wilson. "Look how he did Polly Klaas/Used her death and her family/So he can gain more votes and political fame/It's a shame that I'm the one they say is a monster." The album also contained misogynistic and antipolice lyrics. Thomas refers to women as whores and bitches, and he recommends if the police "try to pull you over, shoot 'em in the face."

Lyrics like these have been the raw material for campaigns against rappers for more than a decade—campaigns that have resulted not only in the incarceration of individual rappers but also in commitments from leading entertainment conglomerates such as Time Warner and Disney as well as the state of Texas, not to invest in companies that produce gangsta albums. William Bennett and C. Delores Tucker, leaders of the antirap campaigns, have had no trouble finding antipolice and antiwomen lyrics to quote in support of their claim that "nothing less is at stake than civilization" if rappers are not rendered silent. So odious are the lyrics, that rarely do politicians or journalists stop to ask what qualifies Bennett to lead a moralistic crusade on behalf of America's minority youth. Not only has he opposed funding for the nation's leader in quality children's programming (the Public Broadcasting Corporation), he has urged that "illegitimate" babies be taken from their mothers and put in orphanages.

What was Delores Tucker, a longtime Democratic party activist, doing lending her name as coauthor to antirap articles that Bennett used to raise money for his right-wing advocacy group, Empower America? Tucker would have us believe, as she exclaimed in an interview in *Ebony,* that "as a direct result" of dirty rap lyrics, we have "little boys raping little girls." But more reliable critics have rather a different take. For years they have been trying to call attention to the satiric and self-caricaturing side of rap's salacious verses, what Nelson George, the music critic, calls "cartoon machismo."

Back in 1990, following the release of *Nasty As They Wanna Be,* an album by 2 Live Crew, and the band's prosecution in Florida on obscenity charges,

Henry Louis Gates confided in an op-ed in the *New York Times* that when he first heard the album he "bust out laughing." Unlike *Newsweek* columnist George Will, who described the album as "extreme infantilism and menace . . . [a] slide into the sewer," Gates viewed 2 Live Crew as "acting out, to lively dance music, a parodic exaggeration of the age-old stereotypes of the over-sexed black female and male." Gates noted that the album included some hilarious spoofs of blues songs, the black power movement, and familiar advertising slogans of the period ("Tastes great!" "Less filling!"). The rap group's lewd nursery rhymes were best understood, Gates argued, as continuing an age-old Western tradition of bawdy satire.

Not every informed and open-minded follower of rap has been as upbeat as Gates, of course. Some have strongly criticized him, in fact, for seeming to vindicate performers who refer to women as "cunts," "bitches," and "hos," or worse, who appear to justify their rape and murder, as did a track on the 2 Live Crew album that contained the boast, "I'll . . . bust your pussy then break your backbone."

Kimberlé Williams Crenshaw, a professor of law at UCLA, wrote in an essay that she was shocked rather than amused by *Nasty As They Wanna Be*. Black women should not have to tolerate misogyny, Crenshaw argued, whether or not the music is meant to be laughed at or has artistic value—both of which she granted about *Nasty*. But something else also concerned Crenshaw: the singling out of black male performers for vilification. Attacks on rap artists at once reflect and reinforce deep and enduring fears about the sexuality and physical strength of black men, she suggests. How else, Crenshaw asks, can one explain why 2 Live Crew were the first group in the history of the nation to be prosecuted on obscenity charges for a musical recording, and one of only a few ever tried for a live performance? Around this same time, she observes, Madonna acted out simulated group sex and the seduction of a priest on stage and in her music videos, and on Home Box Office programs the comic Andrew Dice Clay was making comments every bit as obscene and misogynistic as any rapper.

The hypocrisy of those who single out rap singers as especially sexist or violent was starkly—and comically—demonstrated in 1995, when presidential candidate Bob Dole denounced various rap albums and movies that he considered obscene and then recommended certain films as wholesome, "friendly to the family" fare. Included among the latter was Arnold Schwarzenegger's *True Lies,* in which every major female character is called a "bitch." While in real life Arnold may be a virtuous Republican, in the movie his wife strips, and he puts her through hell when he thinks she might be cheating on him. In one gratuitous scene she is humiliated and tortured for twenty minutes of screen time. Schwarzenegger's character also kills dozens of people in sequences more graphically violent than a rapper could describe with mere words.

Even within the confines of American popular music, rappers are far from the first violently sexist fictional heroes. Historians have pointed out that in country music there is a long tradition of men doing awful things to women. Johnny Cash, in an adaptation of the frontier ballad "Banks of the Ohio" declares, "I murdered the only woman I loved/Because she would not marry me." In "Attitude Adjustment" Hank Williams Jr. gives a girlfriend "adjustment on the top of her head." Bobby Bare, in "If That Ain't Love," tells a woman, "I called you a name and I gave you a whack/Spit in your eye and gave your wrist a twist/And if that ain't love what is."

Rock music too has had its share of men attacking women, and not only in heavy metal songs. In "Down By the River" amiable Neil Young sings of shooting his "baby." And the song "Run for Your Life," in which a woman is stalked and threatened with death if she is caught with another man, was a Beatles hit.

JUST A THUG

After Tupac Shakur was gunned down in Las Vegas in 1996 at the age of twenty-five much of the coverage suggested he had been a victim of his own raps—even a deserving victim. "Rap Performer Who Personified Violence, Dies," read a headline in the *New York Times*. " 'What Goes 'Round . . . ': Superstar Rapper Tupac Shakur Is Gunned Down in an Ugly Scene Straight Out of His Lyrics," the headline in *Time* declared. In their stories reporters recalled that Shakur's lyrics, which had come under fire intermittently throughout his brief career by the likes of William Bennett, Delores Tucker, and Bob Dole, had been directly implicated in two previous killings. In 1992 Vice President Dan Quayle cited an antipolice song by Shakur as a motivating force behind the shooting of a Texas state trooper. And in 1994 prosecutors in Milwaukee made the same claim after a police officer was murdered.

Why, when white men kill, doesn't anyone do a *J'accuse* of Tennessee Ernie Ford or Johnny Cash, whose oddly violent classics are still played on country music station? In "Sixteen Tons" Ford croons, "If you see me comin'/Better step aside/A lotta men didn't/A lotta men died," and in "Folsom Prison Blues" Cash crows, "I shot a man in Reno just to watch him die." Yet no one has suggested, as journalists and politicians did about Shakur's and 2 Live Crew's lyrics, that these lines overpower all the others in Ford's and Cash's songbooks.

Any young rap fan who heard one of Shakur's antipolice songs almost certainly also heard one or more of his antiviolence raps, in which he recounts the horrors of gangster life and calls for black men to stop killing. "And they say/It's the white man I should fear/But it's my own kind/Doin' all the killin' here," Shakur laments on one of his songs.

Many of Shakur's raps seemed designed to inspire responsibility rather than violence. One of his most popular, "Dear Mama," was part thank-you letter to his mother for raising him on her own, and part explanation of bad choices he had made as an adolescent. "All along I was looking for a father—he was gone/I hung around with the thugs/And even though they sold drugs/They showed a young brother love," Shakur rapped. In another of his hits, "Papa'z Song," he recalled, all the more poignantly, having "had to play catch by myself/what a sorry sight."

Shakur's songs, taken collectively, reveal "a complex and sometimes contradictory figure," as Jon Pereles, a music critic for the *New York Times,* wrote in an obituary. It was a key point missed by much of the media, which ran photos of the huge tattoo across Shakur's belly—"THUG LIFE"—but failed to pass along what he said it stood for: "The Hate You Give Little Infants Fucks Everyone." And while many mentioned that he had attended the High School of Performing Arts in Baltimore, few acknowledged the lasting impact of that education. "It influences all my work. I really like stuff like 'Les Miserables' and 'Gospel at Colonus,'" Shakur told a *Los Angeles Times* interviewer in 1995. He described himself as "the kind of guy who is moved by a song like Don McLean's 'Vincent,' that one about Van Gogh. The lyric on that song is so touching. That's how I want to make my songs feel."

After Tupac Shakur's death a writer in the *Washington Post* characterized him as "stupid" and "misguided" and accused him of having "committed the unpardonable sin of using his immense poetic talents to degrade and debase the very people who needed his positive words most—his fans." To judge by their loving tributes to him in calls to radio stations, prayer vigils, and murals that appeared on walls in inner cities following his death, many of those fans apparently held a different view. Ernest Hardy of the *L.A. Weekly,* an alternative paper, was probably closer to the mark when he wrote of Shakur: "What made him important and forged a bond with so many of his young black (especially black male) fans was that he was a signifier trying to figure out what he signified. He knew he lived in a society that still didn't view him as human, that projected its worst fears onto him; he had to decide whether to battle that or to embrace it."

Readers of the music magazine *Vibe* had seen Shakur himself describe this conflict in an interview not long before his death. "What are you at war with?" the interviewer asked. "Different things at different times," Shakur replied. "My own heart sometimes. There's two niggas inside me. One wants to live in peace, and the other won't die unless he's free."

* * *

QUESTIONS

1. What are the various ways, seldom covered by the news media, in which black men are victimized in American society?

2. Why do the news media exaggerate the likelihood of black men committing violent crimes while underreporting cases of black victimization?

3. Why does Glassner argue that it is hypocritical for claimsmakers to single out rappers for their sexist and violent lyrics?

4. Separately consider each of the problems afflicting black men that you identified in your answer to Question 1: What might be the policy implications if the news media were to give greater coverage to these problems? In other words, what kinds of new initiatives might be undertaken in response to these problems if they received more media exposure?

PART FOUR
POLICYMAKING AND OUTCOMES

Few social problems are monolithic. There are different ways a problem manifests itself and a single problem may have different populations of victims. The various subcategories of a problem are rarely treated equally. Some get more attention from claimsmakers, while others get less. For example, violent crime is typically given much more media coverage when the victim is white than when the victim is a member of a racial minority group, particularly African American (Glassner, 1999; Entman and Rojecki, 2000). Similarly, there is often a class bias when it comes to news coverage about children who have been abducted by strangers. Stories about abducted kids of higher class backgrounds get more coverage than do stories about kids of working-class backgrounds (Liebler, 2004).

Just as media coverage tends to focus on certain dimensions of a problem over others, so too with policymaking. Let's consider the war on terror as an illustration. While President Bush envisioned that this war would "not end until *every* terrorist group of global reach has been found, stopped, and defeated" (quoted in Rothe and Muzzatti, 2004, p. 333; my emphasis), in practice most resources allocated under the war on terror have been directed specifically toward preventing terrorist attacks initiated by Al-Qaeda. Of course, terrorism extends well beyond Al-Qaeda as, for example, so tragically made clear by the grisly 2004 school shooting in the Russian town of Beslan by Chechen extremists.

Looking closely at the war on terror also reveals how policymaking can dramatically shape people's beliefs about which problems are most deserving of attention and how they should be addressed. The very language of "war" and the extensive news coverage given to 9/11 as well as more recent terrorist acts propagated by Al-Qaeda around the world have fueled public fears about the prospect of future acts of terrorism. These fears are instrumental in legitimizing the expansion of government powers at home and abroad, as well as the ongoing allocation of funds to fight a global war on terror (Rothe and Muzzatti, 2004).

Another prominent example of how the policy response to a social problem focuses disproportionately on certain parts of the problem concerns homelessness. Since President Bush appointed Philip Mangano as housing czar in 2002, more than 200 cities from coast to coast have adopted a "housing first" strategy. This strategy provides rent-free apartments to people who are chronically homeless: those who have been homeless for months or years at a time ("Doing the math," 2006). The idea behind this strategy is that providing free housing is a way to enable these people to cease being homeless that is actually cheaper than the decades-old approaches that policymakers have used to address this group of chronically homeless people: treating them like the rest of the homeless by providing shelters, hot meals, and covering emergency medical costs. The consequence of "housing first" is that policymaking resources across U.S. cities are increasingly going to the 10% of the homeless who are chronically homeless rather than to the majority of a city's homeless population. Yet, most cities do not have enough available apartments to help all of their chronically homeless people, and hence some are given apartments while others remain on waiting lists. Therefore, an important implication of this strategy for fighting homelessness is that fixing the problem comes at the expense of violating an age-old principle upon which social policy has traditionally rested: distributing benefits evenly to those who meet certain formal government criteria. It seems that policymakers must choose between fixing the problem and abiding by this principle; they cannot simultaneously do both (Gladwell, 2006).

Another important aspect of policymaking is that the strategies chosen to address a problem reflect what best serves claimsmakers' interests rather than what might do the most to fix the problem. The legalization of gaming on Indian reservations provides a case in point. Contrary to popular wisdom, gaming has done little to help the majority of Native Americans on reservations, who continue to live in concentrated poverty. Only a few select Indian casinos have been very profitable, such as Foxwoods, which is operated by the Mashantuckett Pequots. Yet, for politicians in states where casinos have most benefited local tribes—such as Connecticut, Florida, and California—gaming has become a visible, shorthand way of appearing to address the myriad problems prevalent on reservations. Moreover, this strategy caters to the strong political lobby presented by these tribes. Because gaming remains the most prominent option policymakers pursue in addressing Native American poverty, there is diminished political support for pursuing alternative, and potentially more effective, options (Bartlett and Steele, 2002).

The 1996 welfare reform law (the Personal Responsibility and Work Opportunity Reconciliation Act) offers another illustration of how public policy often wins political support more for its palatability and popularity than for its effectiveness in solving the problem. The impetus for reducing government assistance to poor single mothers gained momentum during the early 1990s, and Bill Clinton was elected to the Oval Office in 1992 in part because he vowed "to end welfare as we know it." Welfare reform created term limits for women on public assistance and established work requirements so that these women could assume greater personal responsibility in caring for themselves and their children. In these ways, the law responded to the primary ways welfare had been framed over the prior couple of decades by the media, researchers, politicians, and pundits: as help that was undeserved because the recipients often used the money to buy drugs or alcohol and had an incentive to have more babies to get more benefits rather than to seek employment. Given the power of this frame, a welfare reform bill that aimed to curtail these abusive practices of recipients stood to carry enormous popular and political support (Katz, 1989).

Yet, how well the 1996 welfare reform legislation has actually addressed the problem is a different matter. If the problem is seen as the rising welfare rolls, then the law has without question proven to be very successful since welfare rolls plummeted during the late 1990s (U.S. Department of Health and Human Services, 2000). But, if we evaluate welfare reform in terms of the underlying social forces that give rise to so many poor single mothers turning to government assistance in the first place, then we have reason to question the effectiveness of this legislation. There is compelling evidence to substantiate that a variety of structural factors explain why women of color are particularly susceptible to being poor, a susceptibility that is compounded by being a single parent as well (Hays, 2003). Indeed, the jobs available to women who have left the welfare rolls—primarily low-wage service-sector jobs—do not offer these women the opportunity to earn much more income than they had gotten while on public assistance (Ehrenreich, 2001). Moreover, a single mother who must work two or three jobs to make ends meet also risks exacerbating family problems at home because she is unable to assume primary childcare responsibilities (Boo, 2001).

This analysis of welfare reform underscores the broader issue at hand—that social problems are constructed in ways that produce particular kinds of policy responses that are invariably partial. Social policy tackles certain dimensions of the problem at the expense of others. What policy alternatives are embraced and with how much vigor depend on which claimsmakers are behind the policy and the degree to which the policy can galvanize public and political support.

REFERENCES

Bartlett, Donald L., and James B. Steele. (2002, December 16). Wheel of misfortune. *Time 164*.

Boo, Katherine. (2001, April 9). After welfare. *New Yorker* 77: 93–107.

Doing the math to reduce homelessness. (2006, June 19). *Christian Science Mon-itor* 99.

Ehrenreich, Barbara. (2001). *Nickle and dimed: On (not) getting by in America.* New York: Metropolitan Books.

Entman, Robert M., and Andrew Rojecki. (2000). *The black image in the white mind: media and race in America.* Chicago: University of Chicago Press.

Gladwell, Malcolm. (2006, February 14 & 20). Why problems like homelessness may be easier to solve than to manage. *New Yorker* 82: 96–107.

Glassner, Barry. (1999). *The culture of fear: Why Americans are afraid of the wrong things.* New York: Basic Books.

Hays, Sharon. (2003). *Flat broke with children: Women in the age of welfare reform.* New York: Oxford University Press.

Katz, Michael B. (1989). *The undeserving poor: From the poor on poverty to the war on welfare.* New York: Pantheon Books.

Liebler, Carol M. (2004). Tales told in two cities: When missing girls are(n't) news. From Don Heider (Ed.), *Class and news.* (pp. 199–212). New York: Rowman & Littlefield.

Rothe, Dawn, and Stephen L. Muzzatti. (2004). Enemies everywhere: Terrorism, moral panic, and US civil society. *Critical Criminology* 12: 327–350.

U.S. Department of Health and Human Services. (2000). www.acf.dhhs.gov/news/stats.6097rf.htm

The War on Terror and a Terrified Public

FROM *Enemies Everywhere: Terrorism, Moral Panic,*
and US Civil Society

DAWN ROTHE AND STEPHEN L. MUZZATTI

Dawn Rothe and Stephen L. Muzzatti illustrate how various claimsmakers' responses to the September 11 terrorist attacks constituted a moral panic—*a period when the threat of a particular type of deviant behavior (in this case terrorism) has been grossly exaggerated. While the authors acknowledge the profound tragedy that 9/11 inflicted on so many families and on the nation as a whole, they urge us not to let this tragedy blind us from critically examining the war on terror. Indeed, seeing the construction of the terrorist threat as a moral panic highlights a number of social consequences of the war on terror. These include the manufacturing of public fears of repeated terrorist attacks and the mobilization of those fears as a key source of legitimacy for the Bush Administration's expansion of its powers both at home and abroad.*

The American public has been inundated with highly mediated images of terrorists and terrorism since September 11, 2001. Perceived threats and heightened security alerts abound in daily media coverage and political speeches, leading to what may be termed a moral panic. The edification of a moral panic among the U.S. population has exacerbated a culture embedded in fear. While the events of September 11, 2001 were indeed tragic, the construction of a moral panic by the media and politicians to support their interests is a greater social tragedy.

* * *

Simply put, a moral panic is an exaggeration or distortion of some perceived deviant behavior or criminal activity. . . . [T]his includes grossly exaggerating the seriousness of the events according to criteria such as the numbers of people taking part, the number involved in violence, and the amount and effects of violence and/or damage. This is, of course, not something that happens spontaneously, but rather is a result of a complex interplay of behaviors and responses involving several actors. For a moral panic to take hold, there need to be in place six sets of actors. These include: (1) folk devils, (2) rule enforcers, (3) the media, (4) politicians, (5) action groups, and, (6) the public. Folk devils are the individuals responsible for the deviant or criminal behavior. Unlike normal deviants or criminals, these folks are "unambiguously unfavorable symbols": the embodiment of evil.

As those responsible for the enforcement of norms, codes of conduct, and law, rule enforcers are a vital part of the moral panic. These groups/organizations, particularly the police, prosecutors, and the judiciary are expected to detect, apprehend and punish the folk devils. These agents . . . present themselves as the "thin blue line", which separates order and civilization from mayhem and anarchy. Depending upon the content and strength of the discourse, it often includes calls for increased numbers of rule enforcers and more extensive authority (i.e., greater power) for them.

The media is likely the single most influential actor in the orchestration and promulgation of a moral panic. Media coverage of certain kinds of deviant/criminal behavior, particularly those involving perpetrators of the aforementioned type is usually distorted. It serves to inflate the seriousness of the incidents, making them appear more heinous and frequent than they truly are. Public anxiety is whipped up through the use of journalistic and linguistic devices. "Special cover story", "in-depth expose" or "investigative report" style coverage employs dramatic photos, video, and sound bites with moralistic rhetoric.

Politicians are also vital actors in a moral panic. As individuals, who must operate in the court of public opinion, it is important that politicians present themselves as purveyors of the moral high ground. As such, they often align themselves with the press and the rule enforcers in a struggle against the evils perpetrated by the folk devils. Self-righteousness and the "politics of rage" characterize the response of politicians in dealing with crime/deviance. Even the most liberal politicians usually take a moralistic, no-nonsense, war on crime stance, advocating reactionary and punitive strategies to deal with this new threat. Common calls include special hearings or sub-committees to deal with the problem, zero tolerance policies, tougher laws and harsher sentences.

The final, and some would argue ultimately the most important, actor in a moral panic is the public. The success of the media, politicians, rule enforcers and moral entrepreneurs in generating and sustaining a moral panic is ultimately contingent upon how successfully they enrage the public and marshal their support against the folk devils. The *vox populi* is enlisted as a front-line agent in the crusade against the designated evil. Members of the public are relied upon to express contempt for the folk devils and support for the rule enforcers, to consume the media coverage, and wait for the latest pronouncements from politicians and/or action groups on how the problem is to be solved.

* * *

Regardless of the lack of consensus in what constitutes terrorism, the definition and imagery put forth by the media and politi is real in its consequences; a socially constructed label that defines someone or something (folk-devils/evil-doers) as a threat to our values or interests. Having said this, the actual fear and impact that victims of random violence and terrorism experience must be acknowledged, and such victimisation should not be minimised. The following sections will address the moral panic that emerged from the tragedy of September 11, 2001. . . .

* * *

STAGE ONE OF A MORAL PANIC: SOMEONE OR SOMETHING DEFINED AS A THREAT TO VALUES OR INTERESTS

The atrocious nature of the attacks of September 11, 2001 was sufficient for the acts to be defined as a threat. . . . [T]he defining of something as a threat to values and interests is the first element in the creation of a moral panic. While the media began this process immediately, the formal definition occurred, when President Bush declared, "America was targeted for attack because we're the brightest beacon for freedom and opportunity in the world. And no one will keep that light from shining" (President Bush, 9/11/2001). The defining of threatened values continued to be re-enforced by the Administration.

Great tragedy has come to us, and we are meeting it with the best that is in our country, with courage and concern for others. Because this is

America. This is who we are. This is what our enemies hate and have attacked. And this is why we will prevail (President Bush 9/15/2001).

* * *

The original identification of the enemy was Bin Laden and the Al-Qaeda network. During the gradient process of constructing and enlarging the folk devils, the enemy became increasingly broadly defined. The Administration began their initial targeting of the enemy with "The al Qaeda organisation is not an organisation of good, an organisation of peace. It's an organisation based upon hate and evil" (President Bush 9/24/2001). The threat to U.S. values and interests grew. A press release by the President's Press Secretary stated, "The al Qaeda organisation is present in, as you've heard from the President, more than 60 countries, and its links are—its links are amorphous" (Fleischer 9/18/2001).

Throughout the following year, those categorised as the enemy continually expanded. The Administration's war on terror began with Al-Qaeda but did not stop there. "It will not end until every terrorist group of global reach has been found, stopped, and defeated" (President Bush 9/23/2001). The State of the Union Address of 2002 set the stage for the "Axis of Evil": Iran, North Korea, and Iraq.

The second actor involved in defining someone or something as a threat to values or interests is the media. The day of September 11, 2001, the media began the first stages of a moral panic by defining the evil. The U.S. populace was presented with a barrage of newspaper headlines that escalated the shock of the attacks. The media are the vehicle of moral condemnation, and propagate a brutal fascination with the terrorist act. The media had become terrorvision; a choreography of violence, fear, revulsion and hatred. The attachment of "unambiguously unfavourable symbols" had begun; the hijackers (and by extension, as we will later illustrate, those who allegedly supported, harboured, or defended them) were the embodiment of evil. The identification of terrorism, terrorists, and war were fed to the press by State information dissemination. Oddly enough, before the State had formally identified the enemy, the media was clued in to prepare the U.S. citizens for the Bush Doctrine that would follow. Already on September 11, 2001, media reports connected Bin Laden with the terrorist attacks, "All eyes look to rich Arab terrorists . . . Bin Laden is the leading candidate said a senior intelligence official" (Billings Gazette 9/11/2001).

These examples were only the first stage in an ongoing process of identifying someone or something as a threat. The depiction of the threat of the folk devil by the media continued as stage two of Cohen's model asserts: threat is depicted in a recognisable form by the media. Throughout the process of creating and maintaining moral panic, the media and politi have continuously re-enforced this identification of terrorists to the embodiment of evil that threaten U.S. values and interests.

STAGE TWO OF A MORAL PANIC: THREAT IS DEPICTED IN A RECOGNISABLE FORM BY THE MEDIA

For months after September 11, 2001, the press was consumed with coverage of the event. Every hosted TV show, newspaper editorials, syndicate columns, panel of pundits, and news stories dwelled on the terrorist attacks. For one year and fifty days,[1] a total of 17,744 stories ran in the *New York Times* regarding terror, 10,761 in the *Washington Post,* and 5,200 in *USA Today.*[2] "Objective journalists" simply relating the facts informed us. A *NY Times* analysis stated, "The perpetrators acted out of hatred for the values cherished in the West as freedom, tolerance, prosperity, religious pluralism and universal suffrage." . . . The media is the principle vehicle for popular views, ideology, and information. Societal foci are committed by media accounts of events and political dictates. The rigorous adherence to coverage of the events of September 11, 2001, and the war on terrorism as doctrinal truths and imminent threats, repeated day after day, succeeds in its purpose of establishing a sacrosanct doctrine. The absence of alternative coverage helped instill beliefs and a consensus of concern. As consumers of this coverage, the average American was transformed into a "factotum" of State discourse, organising agent of hegemony, and proactive resonator of terrorology.

. . . "[M]edia spasms of a seismic scale" and "hyper production" was clearly evidenced by the abundance of books written about terrorism in response to the event. Similarly, following a brief respite from its standard fare of exploding buildings and vehicles, Hollywood aired weekly drama shows with themes of terrorism and terrorists, always depicting the evil and horrors of the folk devil (*The Shield, Third Watch, 24,* and *Law and Order*). Conversely, movie reviewers wrote that this or that film was a welcome antidote to the events of

[1]The 50 days was added to encompass the coverage of the one-year anniversary of 9/11 and the following days.
[2]The three newspapers used in the content analysis were searched via the computer database LexisNexis.

September 11, 2001. Travel agents encouraged domestic vacations as a healing experience and often, not so subtly, suggested that they were a patriotic way to aid a sagging economy.

Everywhere the U.S. populace turned, a reminder of the terrorists and their evil doings was present. . . . The terrorist and terrorism had been reified to a new reality. It had become a necessary truth, requiring no further evidence: the terrorists sought the violent transformation of all the things "we" stand for while they only stand for "apocalyptic nihilism." The production and reproduction of such pieties are an important discursive practice insofar as they serve to re-establish order and meaning by reinforcing State hegemony.

The interests of the media and entrepreneurs reflect self-interest (economic interests), but also the narrow conformism of the media to the State. The media has two competing and contradictory roles. They control the flow of information (guided by the dissemination of information by the State) while making the news entertaining to sell. The media serve their function by defining the range of expressible views, framing the news reporting within assumptions laid down by the State, and excluding coverage deemed inappropriate. In a dark parody of the general narrowness of debate on a host of social, political and economic issues in the U.S. media, over 75 percent of terrorist stories come from State sources. This is in part a response to the State propaganda system, to wit guarantees the effectiveness of the State to ensure a moral panic, thereby serving the political interests of the Administration.

The restrictions imposed on the media's coverage included maintaining control over media access to information about the investigation into the hijackings and Counterterrorism operations. The media were not only limited by the political reigns, but high level executives, fearing State reprisals (i.e., being "cut out of the loop") ordered correspondents to remind viewers that the Taliban were evil and harboured terrorists that killed thousands of Americans whenever they broadcast reports or footage of civilian deaths, hunger, or devastation in Afghanistan as a result of the U.S. war on terrorism. Such media subservience and the unquestioning reproduction of the State's political economy of terrorology exemplify its role as an ideological State apparatus. The outcome of these restrictions has ensured that the media would feed the consuming audience the propaganda necessary to create a moral panic. Creating a generalised fearfulness gives State leaders greater freedom of action to advance and justify exceptional legislation, encroach on civil liberty rights, and accomplish their geopolitical agendas.

STAGE THREE OF A MORAL PANIC: A RAPID BUILD-UP OF PUBLIC CONCERN GENERATING HOSTILITY

Public concern about terrorism and terrorists escalated after September 11, 2001, taking many forms. Patriotic jingoism was evidenced by the abundant sale and display of American flags, bumper stickers, lapel pins, and patriotic clothing all aimed at publicly signifying concern and unity. Rage, anger, and confusion proliferated. Attacks on Mosques were conducted, graffiti saying, "bomb the terrorists" was etched on vehicles; hate crimes escalated targeting the terrorist boogeyman image.[3] The media portrayed images of the united flag waving country: indeed, it was reactionism guised in a narrow, highly suspect, and problematic "patriotism" while simultaneously reminding the consuming audience of the evil that lurked around the corner.

The Bush Administration not only built on the public concern but also fed it with political jargon that would pave the way for the State to ensure its interests. The dichotomous, "Either you are with us or you are with the terrorists" speech by President Bush became typical. Any public dissent that contradicted the propaganda for a moral panic was met with political repression. John Ashcroft addressed the Senate Judiciary Committee by saying,

> To those who scare peace loving people with phantoms of lost liberty, my message is this: Your tactics only aid terrorists, for they erode our national unity and diminish our resolve. They give ammunition to America's enemies.

As the Administration's narrow war on terrorism took hold, the rallying for public concern and support continued. The *New Republic* ran an editorial criticising "dissidents" for speaking out against military action, "This nation is at war. And in such an environment, domestic political dissent is immoral." Public concern turned to public support for getting the evil that threatened our values and interests. Rooted in the sense of individual vulnerability and loss of national impunity, sentiments such as, "If we go after Bin Laden, my family or I will be safe", become prominent.

As the political schema enlarged to include geo-political agendas of imperialism, the level of public consensus and concern was even more relevant. It

---

[3]The social changes that occurred will include a detailed look at the effects of social concern in the form of hate crimes.

was necessary to make the U.S. populace acutely sensitive to the threat from "a thousand cuts", so as to ensure their malleability and concessions to the demands of the political elite. Fear was continuously instilled in the public with escalations of terror alerts. Notifications of things to be weary [sic] of included household products (bottles, suspicious mail, boxes). Air travel and public transportation (particularly subways) became less popular as the Administration warned that retaliatory attacks could occur due to the "righteous" decisions of this Administration to rid the world of this terror. Smallpox vaccinations were suggested as protection against a biological attack. The Anthrax scare was immediately associated with terrorists, aiding the heightened level of public concern. Similarly, media speculation about possible terrorism immediately arose surrounding other acts of violent crime, and was quickly discarded when the violence was linked to traditional street criminals (the Washington Beltway snipers) or determined to be "tragic accidents" (e.g., the corporate and State-corporate criminality behind the Chicago nightclub stampede and the disintegration of the Space shuttle Columbia respectively). The assertion that "there is no evidence of terrorist involvement" accompanying "newsworthy violence" became a strangely banal component of the media lexicon.

Despite the "ever-present threat of terrorism", and ongoing speculation of "possible terrorist involvement" which abounded, the nation was not to be "paralysed by fear". Entrepreneurs opened stores targeting the existing fears (Safe At Home Store).[4] The media continued to grip America with stories of "how to be prepared". Whether it was updates about the status of the availability of plastic sheeting and duct tape at the local hardware store or the appearance of the Homeland Security Director Tom Ridge on NBC's Today Show showing the ration of canned goods, bottled water, and a first aid kit they keep in a cardboard box in their home, the media continued to feed the consuming public safety tips generated by the Administration.

The general public is one of the key actors in a moral panic. The success of the politicians and media in generating and sustaining a moral panic is contingent on how successfully they enrage the public and marshal their support against the evil-doers. The crusade against evil requires the public to express contempt for the folk devil and support for the decisions from politicians on how the problem is best solved.

* * *

[4] Just blocks from "ground zero" this store opened to sell survival goods (e.g. gas masks).

STAGE FOUR OF A MORAL PANIC: RESPONSE FROM AUTHORITIES, POLITICIANS, AND MORAL ENTREPRENEURS: DISPROPORTIONATE REACTIONS

* * *

The initial response from the State took the form of a massive mobilisation of military, strategic, and diplomatic power: a call to war. The media had made this connection for the State prior to the formal announcement as headlines read "War at Home" (The Dallas Morning News 9/11/2001), "ITS WAR" (Daily News, 9/11/2001), and "ACTS OF WAR" (The Day 9/11/2001). Early coverage of the event by TV Anchor Tom Brokaw declared, "This is a war zone, we are at war". The initial war on terrorism was portrayed to the public as the means to capture those responsible for the events of September 11, 2001; however, the folk devil, terrorist, quickly grew to tens of thousands of terrorists that remained at large, threatening our very way of life and our fundamental values and interests. Bush stated, "Tens of thousands of trained terrorists are still at large. These enemies view the entire world as a battlefield, and we must pursue them wherever they are" (Bush 9/24/2001).

September 11, 2001 was identified by President Bush as an "attack of all the civilised nations". The need to legitimise the war on terror was a concern for the Administration, and hence it felt the need to escalate public fear at home, muster pseudo-international support, and increase threat levels to mask the global war that was under way.

The first official response to the crisis of September 11, 2001 was on September 13, when the Senate and House of Representatives voted to approve the Administration's "Authorization for Use of Military Force". The bill gave President Bush a virtually unlimited mandate,

> To use all necessary and appropriate force against those nations, organizations, or persons he determines planned, authorized, committed, or aided terrorist attacks that occurred on September 11, 2001, or harboured such organizations or persons in order to prevent any future acts of international terrorism against the United States.

This opened the doors for the utilisation of a moral panic to aid the Administration in expanding its doctrine. Terrorology was employed to neutralise those who might pose an impediment to the Administration's agenda by raising constitutional questions. When read, it becomes clear why the connection of Iraq to Bin Laden was essential. Without the acquiescence of the public and the legislative branches regarding the connection between Hussein and Bin Laden, the President must have Congress make the "Call to War" according to the U.S. Constitution.

On September 12, 2001 the US called the UN Security Council (UNSC) into special session. The outcome was Resolution 1368 which called on nations/states to work together to bring to justice the perpetrators and sponsors of the terrorist attacks. This was not an authorisation for war, nor did it invoke Article 51 of the UN Charter (self-defence clause). On September 28th, 2001, Resolution 1373 was passed and although it did not condone military force, it did provide economic measures to cut terrorists' access to funds. However, the disproportionate reactions by politicians and the rush to declare war on unknown enemies overpowered the international "legalities" of war. The Bush Doctrine of war was begun in a cloud of illegalities and will continue on that course throughout the duration of the Administration's ability to induce fear and inoculate the public from the realities of its underlying political interests. A pre-emptive, unilateral first strike would set a terrible international precedent.

Along with the change of course doctrine comes the understanding that history is irrelevant, the lessons of the past no longer matter and conventional tactics can be disposed of. As a nation, we no longer need to adhere to previous studies and advice provided by the Pentagon's Defence Science Board that showed a strong correlation between U.S. involvement in international situations and an increase in terrorist attacks against the U.S. Instead, the U.S. must take preventative measures against the imminent threat that terror, terrorism, and terrorists pose. The Axis of Evil must be contained. Especially the one posing the greatest threat: Iraq.

Regardless of reality, the rhetoric of propaganda assured the U.S. public that Iraq was among the existential terrorist threat. It would have been difficult to convince the public that Saddam Hussein really was a threat to the U.S. had Iraq not been included in the Evil Empire that was poised to attack: amongst the evil doers—the terrorists. Administration officials seemed to think that simply repeating the phrase "Iraq is a threat to America" would somehow validate a war. Sadly, as Benjamin's sociological inquiry into demagoguery illustrated, saying something frequently and loudly through the conduit of political power does often make it so.

During November 2002, British and U.S. warplanes attacked Iraq's defences daily, and made practice runs on other targets, and U.S. Special Forces were deployed in Western and Northern Iraq. In many ways, the war on Iraq had already begun well before 19 March 2003. To induce fear, the propaganda system was utilised to conjure up the new "Hitler/Satan". The inducement of fear to obtain the acquiescence of the public to policies it may oppose was continually attempted by the Administration through the use of inflammatory rhetorical strategies.

Other disproportionate reactions by the polity included the creation of a large bureaucracy to ensure domestic security: the Office of Homeland Security. The Bush Administration also instituted an alert system to keep the public informed as to what level or how much fear "we" should be experiencing: The Homeland Security Advisory System. The official purpose of the Homeland Security Advisory System is a means to disseminate information regarding the risk of terrorist acts to federal, state, and local authorities and to the American people. However, the vague information (i.e., an unspecified threat) given about changes in the alert is not adequate enough for other agencies or the U.S. populace to know what to look for or expect. It is however, an effective tool for maintaining fear and suppression of its citizens.

Still other reactions included the legislation of the Uniting and Strengthening America by Providing Appropriate Tools Required to Intercept and Obstruct Terrorism Act (USA Patriot Act) and the Homeland Security Act. Both of these legislative documents were a direct response to the terrorist attacks of September 11, 2001.

* * *

The aforementioned examples of legislation and disproportionate responses by the State to September 11, 2001 are not exhaustive. However, they do provide examples of the State's use of terrorism to: (1) ensue alternative political interests (the war on Iraq), (2) maintain "legitimacy" for public concern, and (3) continue the generation of a moral panic through intimidation, coercion, and induced fear. Just as the Communist Boogeyman role aided US imperialism and military supremacy (and while generating tremendous profit for military contractors, did little to enhance national security) during the Reagan administrations, the Terrorist Boogeyman is aiding the Bush, Cheney, Rumsfeld, and Wolfowitz Doctrine of Imperialism and military supremacy.

STAGE FIVE OF A MORAL PANIC: PANIC RESULTS IN SOCIAL CHANGES

The final stage [of a] moral panic [is] that [after] the panic . . . passes and is forgotten, it has serious and long lasting repercussions. This moral panic was created in such a way that its diffusion is impossible. There are, undoubtedly, serious social ramifications hitherto comprehended.

One of the earliest signs of negative social changes was reflected in the Uniform Crime Report (UCR)—figures . . . [on] hate crimes. Prior to 2001, the fewest number of hate crimes incidents resulted from ethnic or national origin bias. Crime incidents motivated by bias against this group became the second largest reported bias in 2001, more than doubling the number of incidents. The anti-other ethnicity/national origin category quadrupled in incidents, victims, offences, and known offenders. Anti-Islamic incidents (once the second lowest) became the second highest reported among religious bias incidents: a growth of more than 1,600 Percent over the 2000 volume. The FBI Foreword stated, "The distribution changed in 2001, presumably as a result of the heinous incidents that occurred on September 11".

Controversy over antiterrorist legislation surfaces whenever a State reacts to terrorism with the implementation of new laws. The laws give rise to concerns about the infringement of civil liberties. Critics maintain that antiterrorist legislation is based on a political schema versus an objective evaluation of the real threat. Americans have been filled with terrorist anxiety, fear, and panic, which is conducive to the overregulation of society without opposition. Suffice it to say, " . . . the price of freedom is high when hysteria is the norm and morality has gone on holiday".

* * *

The USA Patriot Act has many potential long-term negative social impacts. The implications for the 20 million immigrants, non-citizens, and short-term visa holders include potential subjection to military tribunals, expedited deportation, and detention (for an undetermined time) if they are suspected of having something to do with terrorism. It is not only the non-US citizen that is at risk, but US citizens now face the potential to be classified as enemy combatants and or stripped of citizenship. The power given to the State to "snoop" on citizens overturns some previous restrictions placed on the State from previous abuses of such powers. As Nancy Chang, attorney for the Center of Constitutional Rights, has stated, "the Bush Administration's actions since September 11th portend a wholesale suspension of civil liberties that will reach far beyond those who are involved in terrorist activities". Legitimate political dissent may qualify for criminal proceedings.

* * *

Perhaps the most significant social change that has and will occur is the U.S. expansion of American hegemony and imperialism. The events of

September 11, 2001 (as horrific as they were) provided the Administration with the excuse to act on its simmering geo-political agenda. The orchestration of the Administration's intentions had begun prior to the terrorist attacks. Prior to his appointment as Secretary of Defense Rumsfeld told President Bush that US military power was needed "to discipline the world". Then came the terrorist attacks. The time was perfect, an excuse had been given to them, and the ease of creating and enhancing a moral panic to ensure public conformity was ripe. Overlooked by many, the intentions of the Administration were slightly captured when Bush himself made reference to the attacks of September 11, 2001 as "an opportunity to strengthen America". The media also hinted at the opportune time given to this administration claiming Bush should "take advantage of the unique political climate and to assert his leadership not just on security and foreign policy but across the board".

* * *

CONCLUSION

* * *

In lieu of the detrimental and traumatic effects a moral panic can have on policy and levels of societal fear, the images, definitions, and projections of terrorism should be presented in an integrated and multipositioned frame. The current use of terrorism by the polity and media is one-dimensional: them or us. It is not until the media apply multilevel factual coverage to terrorism and the potential threat [that] the U.S. populace [will] be able to make a broad assessment and to voice a knowledgeable position on the reactions by social agents of control. Terrorology must be replaced by cultural readings of retail-terrorism which situates it historically and geo-politically, and must involve " . . . not only an inquiry into the State's archival accretions but also into its most sensitive secretions". People's efforts should be directed toward deconstructing political propaganda and demystifying jargon rather than supporting with blind faith unsubstantiated threats about evildoers.

* * *

The September 11th crisis was seen as "a great gift" for President Bush. It enabled him to strengthen his faltering credibility and to implement the long-standing right wing agenda. September 11th brought the opportunity to vastly enhance Senate power, erode civil liberties, undermine environmental defences, reject and ignore foreign policy imposed on the rest of the world, and establish an empire. The responses of the Administration were not solely about bringing anyone to justice for the terrorist attacks. It was also about expanding U.S. global power and conquest all in the name of righteousness. Yet, the rhetoric gushed at the American people serves to mask this reality:

> America will always stand firm for the non-negotiable demands of human dignity: the rule of law; limits on the power of the state; respect for women; private property; free speech; equal justice; and religious tolerance. America will take the side of the brave men and women who advocate these values around the world, including the Islamic world, because [we] have a greater objective than eliminating threats and containing resentment. We seek a just and peaceful world beyond the war on terror (State of the Union Address, 2002).

Between the lines of propaganda and rhetoric, the generation of public fear stands to suppress opposition to the legitimacy of a war against enemies that have been so broadly defined, the end is not in sight. Today, the moral panic continues: the Olympics of terror. Regrettably, future research on negative latent and manifest social implications may well abound with information.

QUESTIONS

1. Since 9/11, how have the Bush Administration, the news media, and a variety of other claimsmakers collectively constructed public fears of repeated terrorist attacks?

2. Of the six sets of actors that are necessary for a moral panic to arise, why do the authors claim that the public is the most important? Answer by discussing how the public has been instrumental in giving legitimacy to the war on terror.

3. How do the authors support their contention that the various measures and reforms instituted under the war on terror are disproportionate to the magnitude of the terrorist threat?

4. How has the rhetoric of the war on terror masked the Bush Administration's efforts to use the September 11 terrorist attacks as a justification for expanding its influence both at home and abroad?

5. What consequences has the war on terror had in eroding the civil rights of people who are, or appear to be, of Middle Eastern descent? How does the Bush Administration justify these civil rights infringements?

6. What do the authors mean when they argue, "In lieu of the detrimental and traumatic effects a moral panic can have on policy and levels of societal fear, the images, definitions, and projections of terrorism should be presented in an integrated and multipositioned frame (p. 430)." How would the kind of frame the authors are proposing be different from the frames that have been predominant during the war on terror?

7. Even for those who politically support the Bush Administration's agendas at home and abroad, how can the authors' analysis still be useful in probing the consequences of the war on terror?

28

Fostering Personal Responsibility among Women on Welfare

Pyramids of Inequality

SHARON HAYS

Perhaps the most significant piece of social policy legislation enacted in the past forty years was welfare reform in 1996. Sharon Hays begins this selection by highlighting the array of widely held stereotypes that provided the foundation for this law (the Personal Responsibility and Work Opportunity Reconciliation Act). These include seeing welfare mothers as lazy, abusive of the system, and wanting to have more babies to get more benefits; in short, viewing the hardships these women experience as the result of their own deviant behaviors. Hays then explores the implications of the welfare reform law's attributing these hardships to personal irresponsibility on the part of those receiving welfare. She argues that this construction of the welfare problem by policymakers has left the chief social causes of single parenthood unexamined and consequently unaddressed.

Among all major industrialized nations, the United States now holds the noteworthy position of being the country with the greatest gap between rich and poor. According to the Congressional Budget Office, the wealthiest 1 percent of American households made an average annual income of $1,016,900 in 1997, and the entire top one-fifth were also doing quite well with an average of $167,500. The bottom fifth, on the other hand—representing about 57 million people—earned an average of just $11,400 that year. Thirty-one million people lived in poverty in 2000; over 12 million lived in dire poverty. Welfare mothers and their children are situated at the very bottom of that hierarchy.

The mere mention of welfare, for many people, brings to mind not just poverty but a whole series of daunting social problems: teenage pregnancy, unwed parenting, divorce, abortion, drug abuse, unsafe streets, volatile race relations. This is clearly dangerous ground. And it is, in fact, the ground upon which most welfare mothers walk.

This connection between welfare and widespread social problems provides the foundation for the cultural demonization of welfare mothers. The image of these women as deviant and dangerous people, suffering from forms of immorality that seem almost contagious, is so ubiquitous that it tends to seep into one's consciousness almost unnoticed. Opinion polls show that the majority of Americans believe, for instance, that welfare mothers are lazy, abuse the welfare system, commit fraud, are sexually promiscuous, and are afflicted with the parasitic condition of "dependency." These stereotypes are so powerful that many welfare recipients share them with the American public and, as I've suggested, readily accuse other welfare mothers of immorality and sloth.

The widespread image of welfare recipients as perverse nonconformists was one of the central assumptions underlying the Personal Responsibility Act. And the debate over welfare reform acted to rekindle long-held stereotypes of welfare mothers as "wolves," reckless breeders, and cheating "welfare queens," caught in the "trap" of welfare, and failing to seek a way back into the American mainstream. This process of cultural distortion, this use of negative stereotypes and simplistic slogans to categorize welfare mothers as deviant outsiders, has been fueled by multiple sources. In all cases, it hides a different story about the values of welfare mothers and about the broader basis of the social problems that welfare reform accused them of creating.

Part of the process of distortion is elucidated by Sheila, a 30-year-old welfare mother from Sunbelt City. Referring to the crack cocaine dealers who work the sidewalk in front of her housing-project apartment, she said, "See, I think this is the reason why we have such a bad reputation. We've got a couple of bad apples in the apple cart and then the next thing you know, everybody says, 'All welfare recipients are drug users, all welfare mothers are lazy, all welfare mothers are bad.' Most of us are not bad." Welfare mothers are simply thrown into the cart of "ghetto culture" along with all poor people (whether they live in inner-city conditions or not, whether they are men or women or children, good or bad), and left there, only to have their image spoiled by a few bad apples.

Demonizing welfare mothers, labeling their values and behavior as deviant and therefore distinct from the American "mainstream," is also an understandable cultural phenomenon in that it implicitly allows us to wash our hands of this population. It is to claim that their values, beliefs, and practices bear no relation to our own. The problems they face are therefore not our responsibility. After all, if we can say that all the difficulties they encounter are simply a result of their bad behavior and immorality then we don't even have to look their way, or see their lives. The fact that the welfare system has been judged by some to be inadequate, and even harsh, is similarly washed clean by the implicit claim that the people it serves are hardly worth our time and attention. And, if all the social problems faced by welfare mothers are confined to this group, then we don't have to reexamine our culture, or the structure of our economic and political systems.

These are not the only reasons that politicians and members of the American public might easily be convinced to think ill of welfare recipients. The purpose of this chapter is to provide a further rendering of the cultural processes by which welfare mothers came to have such a negative reputation, to examine the central arguments and social problems that motivated it, and to offer the beginnings of a more comprehensive and clear-headed vision. . . .

Just as welfare policy can provide a window onto our nation's values, just as the operations of welfare offices can illuminate the economic and cultural difficulties involved in achieving independence and familial stability, so a look at the basis of the demonization of welfare mothers says a lot about contemporary American society. The Personal Responsibility Act was propelled, in large measure, by the dramatic simultaneous rise of welfare receipt and single parenting that occurred between 1960 and 1994. The proportion of single-mother families more than tripled between 1960 and 2000, rising from 8 percent to 26 percent of American families with children and translating into the fact that one in three children today lives with a single parent. The number of welfare recipients rose even more dramatically, from 3 million in 1960 to 14 million in 1994 (when it reached its peak). An examination of the story that lies behind these increases in single parenting and familial poverty ultimately offers a vivid picture of the massive changes in work and family life that have left us all a bit disoriented and searching for someone to blame.

In this context, it is certainly fair enough to hold individual welfare mothers responsible for their *own* choices (to the extent they actually have a reasonable array of options). But the social changes that led so many women and children to need the help of welfare cannot be blamed on today's welfare recipients, nor were they the result of a spontaneous eruption of individual immorality or the overly generous provision of public aid. The changes in work and family life that propelled the contemporary attack on welfare mothers have impacted many more people than the population of welfare recipients. And these problems cannot be solved by simply reforming poor mothers or the system that has served them.

CARICATURING THE POOR

The notion that the poor themselves, through their deviance, are responsible for the problem of poverty has a long history. In one form or another, it has been a part of the rhetoric of politicians and social reformers ever since the first poor laws were instituted in this country. And in the last 30 years, one particularly powerful version has been very effectively disseminated by a group of influential conservative scholars, including Charles Murray, Lawrence Mead, and George Gilder. These scholars all argue that poverty is the result of giving money to the poor. That is, welfare policy causes welfare deviance and thereby causes welfare poverty. One cannot help but notice the circular nature of this argument—the poor are deviant because we give them money because they are poor; as long as we give them money, they will be deviant, they will be poor, the more money they will need, and the more they will arrive at our doorstep to claim it. It is surely true that the elegant simplicity of this analysis is part of its allure. Underlying this logic, however, are more serious and haunting questions: Does the offer of financial aid actually cause people to eschew work? Does it serve as an incentive to choose single parenting over marriage?

Although these thinkers arrive at their answers from different angles, they agree that past welfare policies actively encouraged immorality and sloth. The more attractive welfare became, they say, the more people were invited to become nonworking single parents. Murray, for instance, imagines the poor as a group of "rational actors" who carefully weigh the costs and benefits of marriage and work against single parenting and welfare, and realistically, but dangerously and unethically, choose welfare as the more lucrative option. Mead focuses on the immoral "culture" of the poor that is encouraged by the availability of welfare—a culture of illegitimacy, incompetence, and immaturity marked by a lack of discipline and a lack of commitment. Together, they claim that our nation's welfare laws bred promiscuity, a declining commitment to family, financial and emotional "dependence," and a belief that one is "entitled" to support without any obligations to the community or the nation. It was the generosity of our former welfare system, these theorists agree, that not only supported the immorality of the poor and reproduced poor people with bad values but actually caused the number of such people to proliferate. Their solution—stiffer rules and the end of entitlement to welfare benefits—is the solution the nation enacted with welfare reform.

These arguments resonate perfectly with a widespread sense that our nation suffers from deepening social problems and overall moral decline. This analysis also fits well with one central piece of social science evidence—the historical coincidence of the disturbing rise in welfare usage and rates of single parenting. Hence, the arguments of such scholars are not only charming in their simplicity but they also seem to make sense of alarming social changes and offer to reclaim the nation's moral principles, putting an end to poverty, single parenting, immorality, and indolence by simply dismantling the welfare system. As an added benefit, the solution they offer promises to safe taxpayers a good deal of money.

It also makes sense that the demonization of welfare mothers would find a strong foothold in American culture in that it follows smoothly from the ethos of individualism. If people become poor, if they find themselves seeking aid at the welfare office, we say, it must be because of something they, as individuals, did or did not do. The cultural power of this analysis cannot be overestimated. The relatively comfortable American middle class tends to ask three questions about welfare mothers. How did this woman wind up on welfare in the first place? How did she become a single parent? And once she became a welfare recipient, why didn't she just find a job or get married and get off of welfare?

I know these questions and their variations quite well. Not only did I hear them asked time and again by people with whom I discussed my research but I found myself asking them over and over with each new welfare mother I met. The impulse to seek individual-level answers to what are often social-level questions is so strong in American culture that despite all my training as a sociologist this framework would draw me in again and again. The trouble is, given that all the women we ask these questions are, in fact, single mothers on welfare, no matter how many harsh circumstances they might recount, the implicit standards behind the questions mean that the poor women thus interrogated always end up looking individually culpable for the problems of single parenting and welfare usage. In other words, the questions themselves are set up in such a way as to produce a circular logic. When we ask, "Why did *you* become a single parent? Why did *you* go on welfare?" we are not seeking social causes; we are looking for an individual-level response. Therefore, no form of answer can be provided that won't make the respondent look guilty and ultimately responsible for all the larger social problems associated with welfare and single parenting.

The Personal Responsibility Act captures perfectly the spirit of this individualistic logic. It also explicitly relies on the claim that past welfare policy encouraged bad behavior. And there is no question that this reasoning is extremely alluring. The trouble is, from a sociological point of view, it is simply wrong. It is wrong for three central reasons.

First, the wholesale demonization of welfare mothers is wrong because there is actually wide variation in the values, beliefs, and practices of welfare mothers. Having spent time with scores of these women, I can tell you . . . that the majority of welfare mothers are not wolves, reckless breeders, and cheats, nor are they primarily calculating profit-maximizers, passive dependents, or lazy couch potatoes without any sense of obligation to their communities or the nation. It is also true that welfare mothers are not all noble victims and self-sacrificing heroes. They are ordinary people. Their moral characters are as varied as those of the people who live in my neighborhood, the consumers who share my grocery store, or the college students who attend my classes. Some are lovable, some are not; some are heroic, most are not.

When attempting to measure the morality of welfare mothers, however, two small caveats are in order. As a group, most of the welfare mothers I met tended to be a bit more tolerant of individual failings than most of my neighbors, fellow consumers, and college students. This, I would argue, is precisely because they have hit the bottom, and they know what it feels like. And morally speaking, most of the welfare recipients I encountered had one leg up on most of my college students—precisely because they are mothers. Their mothering tends to teach them a moral lesson about taking care of others and sacrificing for the ones we love. That is a lesson the depth and reality of which most of my students have not yet fully grasped. But, of course, welfare mothers' position at the bottom and welfare mothers' mothering are two of the things that the American public is worried about.

Second, arguments that demonize welfare mothers, laying the blame for widespread social ills at their doorstep, completely ignore the broader social and historical bases of poverty, single parenting, and welfare use. All welfare mothers, like all individuals, are embedded in, and socialized by, social institutions; all are shaped and constrained by the structures of our economic, cultural, and political systems. When we make use of the "personal responsibility" framework and find them guilty, we are simply allowing the proverbial "trees" to obscure our view of the larger forest.

Finally, although the argument that our nation's welfare policy corrupts welfare recipients' values is more theoretically sophisticated than the individualistic framework in that it recognizes the institutional shaping process, this analysis remains profoundly nearsighted. It operates on the faulty assumption that welfare institutions *alone* impact the values and behavior of poor people. The form of cultural distortion taking place in this case is akin to allowing a single species of trees to cloud our awareness of the multiple layers of life in the forest. From a scientific point of view, analyses that blame the welfare system for the creation of welfare recipients requires us to believe that the rise of welfare usage and single parenting took place in a social vacuum. It is as if the rest of the world stood still while the nation increased the availability and attractiveness of welfare.

The clearest indication of the faulty logic of this analysis is the fact that, as it turns out, there is little causal connection between the attractiveness of welfare benefits and the size of the welfare rolls or the rate of single parenting. These phenomena did, at first, appear to be linked: in the 1960s the value of welfare benefits, rates of single parenting, and the welfare rolls all went up together. Since then, however, the value of welfare benefits in the United States has decreased dramatically (in constant dollars), yet single parenting and welfare usage have continued to rise steadily. In fact, the most rapid and historically unprecedented rise in single parenting and welfare receipt occurred between 1970 and 1995—yet, during that same period, the value of welfare benefits decreased by 50 percent. Studies comparing welfare benefits over time, across states, and across nations have repeatedly demonstrated this point. Miserly states (e.g., Alabama) have spawned just as many single-parent households as the more generous ones (e.g., Connecticut). And industrialized nations that offer higher welfare payments do not face any higher growth rates of single parenting than nations that spend little (and sometimes, as is the case with the United States, the reverse is true).

The historical rise in the welfare rolls had little to do with economic calculations of the "benefits" of nonwork and single parenting. The rise in welfare receipt followed, in part, from the 1960s' revolution in civil rights that allowed equal access to welfare benefits for *all* desperately poor families, no matter what their race, residence, or state-determined moral virtue. Beyond this, the primary fuel that kept those rolls rising well beyond the 1960s was the simple fact that increasing numbers of single mothers and children were living in dire poverty.

Thus, the story behind the rising welfare rolls over the last 40 years ultimately boils down to this: growing economic inequalities met up with revolution in family life. More specifically, the participation of women in the labor force, the decline of the breadwinner wage, and changing norms regarding marriage, sex, and family life led to rising rates of divorce and unwed childrearing and confronted, in turn, inequalities of gender, race, and income, and the continued privatization and implicit devaluation of the care of children. Together, these factors led many families to the welfare office. They also led all of us to a difficult situation that the reform of welfare alone cannot repair.

THE LINKAGE OF SINGLE PARENTHOOD, GENDER, RACE, AND POVERTY

Welfare reform affects very specific sets of people. They are predominantly women and children, disproportionately nonwhite, and overwhelmingly single parents. As I've noted, most welfare recipients are children, most of these children are cared for by their mothers, and black and Hispanic Americans are overrepresented on the welfare rolls.

That these particular groups of people are so deeply poor as to be eligible for welfare benefits is no accident, no mere historical footnote. Their membership in these social groups is, at this historical juncture, the primary basis of their poverty. The backdrop for their poverty is persistent gender and race inequalities. The new additions to this scene are the growing number of mothers who raise their children alone and the declining number of people who make a wage sufficient to support a family.

One-half of all marriages in the United States today will end in divorce. One-third of all children born will be born outside of marriage. In 1900, less than 5 percent of children lived in households headed by a single mother. By the 1970s, that number had more than doubled, reaching 13 percent, and the public was already expressing serious concern. Yet, by today's standards, that 13 percent is a paltry figure. One-third of children are now living in single-parent households, and nearly half will live in such a home at one time or another during their lives. Almost no one thinks this is good news.

The vast majority of these single-parent households are headed by women, one-third of all single-parent households are poor, and one-half the young children living in these families are poor. This is the basis for what has come to be called the "feminization of poverty." The connection between single parenting and poverty is not hard to figure out. Once you become a single parent, no matter who you are or where you start out, no matter if it is divorce or unwed parenting that brought you there, your financial resources are stretched and, simultaneously, your ability to make money is diminished by the added pressure of caring for children without the help of a spouse. These difficulties are exacerbated if you are a woman or if you are nonwhite, since women and nonwhites systematically make less money than men and whites. The average woman with a high school diploma, for example, earns 55 cents on every dollar earned by her male counterpart; a woman with a college education earns just 64 cents on every dollar earned by a college-educated man. Earnings among nonwhites follow the same pattern. The average black woman, for instance, makes 85 cents to each dollar earned by a white woman, the average black man makes 78 cents relative to his white counterpart. Black Americans are also consistently less likely than whites to have the economic assets to see them through hard times. As is true for women, these income differentials are also indicators of other forms of disadvantage in their working lives, including more inflexible schedules, less room for advancement, and fewer fringe benefits. In short, women and nonwhites are simply more easily pushed below the poverty line in cases of single parenthood, and their disadvantaged circumstances make it all the more difficult for them to climb out of that position.

Women, the economically disadvantaged, and nonwhites are not only more likely to suffer dire poverty if they become single parents but they are also more likely than their white, male, wealthier counterparts to become single parents in the first place. Women are more likely than men to be single parents because our culture has long seen women as the proper persons to carry out the job of rearing children. They are more likely than men to become the sole caregivers for children born out of wedlock; they are more likely to have custody of the children in cases of divorce. The poor are more likely than the rich to become single parents in part because their position at the bottom means that they are less likely to encounter viable, financially stable, marriage partners. Research also suggests that working-class and working-poor people, relative to their wealthier counterparts, are more likely to value their family over their paid work, following largely from the fact that raising children can offer a great deal more satisfaction, fulfillment, and social status than a job in fast foods, cleaning bedpans, or manufacturing widgets. Hence, the idea of foregoing the chance to establish a family is virtually unfathomable at the same time that being financially "ready" to have children is that much more unlikely. This simultaneously makes divorce more common and increases the chances of having children without a marriageable partner.

Middle-class blacks with comparable income, economic assets, and education have marriage rates that are nearly the same as their white counterparts. But blacks in general are at greater risk for single parenting than whites, largely because the history of discrimination means that they are more likely to have low incomes and therefore don't have the same reasons to focus on family life and worry about viable marriage partners as do similarly positioned whites. Following the logic of William Julius Wilson's well-known account of the lack of suitable mates for black women, recent research suggests that for every three unmarried black women in their 20s, there is only one unmarried black man with earnings above the poverty level. Yet black Americans are in an even more difficult situation than such statistics on earnings can capture. Relative to white Americans, they are much more likely to suffer discrimination in housing, health care, and loan availability. More than that, they are much less likely to have economic assets to back them up in trying to establish or sustain stable families. (In 1995, for instance, the average net worth of white families was $49,030; for black families it was $7,073.) When all these factors are taken together, it is not surprising that low-income black men and women are likely to "wait" longer to find the right mate.

It is important, at this point in the argument, that one not fall into the trap that Congress fell into in composing the Personal Responsibility Act. To say that single parenting is systematically linked to poverty is not the same thing as naming single parenting as the *cause* of poverty. Poverty existed long before single parenting became prevalent, and without major changes in social policy or a reconfiguration of our economic system, we have every reason to believe that it will continue to exist even if all single-parent households disappear. The faces of the people at the bottom of the economic pyramid have changed over time, yet the relative number of positions at the bottom has remained fairly stable. Waves of European immigrants once filled this category, but most are now dispersed throughout the class structure. Our most recent historical example of the changing face of poverty is the changing position of older, retired Americans who once held the "leading" role as the largest group of people living in poverty. They have now been "replaced" in that role by women and children living in single-parent households.

With this logic in place, we have come halfway toward understanding the social basis of the rising welfare rolls in the second half of the twentieth century. Women, children, and nonwhites have long been at greater risk for poverty than males, adults, and whites. If they become members of single-parent households, their risk is greater still, and a larger proportion of them will need to seek out the help of the welfare office. Although there are certainly questions of justice involved in this portrait, we can nonetheless make sense of the central social forces operating to increase the usage of welfare without resorting to any argument regarding the immorality of individual welfare recipients. If we stop at this point in the argument, however, we might still be tempted to imagine that single parenting itself is the root of all our problems and thereby ignore the processes that led to its rise.

THE REVOLUTION IN FAMILY LIFE

The dramatic rise in the number of single-parent households has occurred in every Western industrialized nation in the world. Hence, we have good reason to believe that there is a close connection between the processes of advanced capitalism and the rise in single parenting. This connection is certainly worth pondering in its own terms, but like the conservative attack on welfare recipients and the old welfare system, it leaps too swiftly over the multiple intermediary processes involved.

First, it is important to note that the rise in single parenting does not represent a historical increase in the number of children women are having. That is, it is not as if unmarried people are having "extra" children just to get a welfare check (or just to pass the time). Rather, people who (by historical standards) would have been raising children anyway are now simply more likely to do so outside of marriage. Couples today are having children later and having fewer of them, but they are also getting married later and getting divorced a lot more often. Thus, everyone is spending more of their adult years outside of marriage. Looking at the trends in single parenting from this angle, one could argue that there is actually a culturally induced, age-graded "urge" to produce (at least some) children, and men and women are simply "unwilling" (or unable) to put it off until they have found a suitable mate or until they are absolutely certain that their marriages will last for life.

There are four primary social trends impacting people's cultural "willingness" and "need" to become single parents:

- The rise in women's paid labor force participation
- The decline of the family (breadwinner) wage
- A "revolution" in sexual practices
- And a corresponding (ambivalent) cultural acceptance of these changes

These social trends—not the availability of welfare or some mysterious rise in individual immorality—ultimately brought us higher rates of divorce, out-of-marriage childbearing, the feminization of poverty, and the rising number of families who must seek out the aid of welfare.

Nearly all scholars of family life agree that these trends played a central role in changing marriage and childrearing patterns. Most also agree that the primary factors are the increasing number of employed women and the declining availability of wages sufficient to support a family. These two changes reinforce one another in their effects: at the same time women's work offers them more choices regarding marriage and childrearing, men's declining ability to be financial "heads" of households influences their marital behavior. Both changes create fewer incentives to get married and stay married, more problems in finding suitable partners, and an increase in the potential for conflict within marriage. To the extent that women's struggle for equality is a crucial factor in these trends, the outcomes relative to welfare mothers are all the more (darkly) ironic.

In the crudest terms (for the sake of simplicity) the story runs as follows. The historical rise of single parenting follows close on the heels of the rising number of wives and mothers who go out to work for pay. These women enter the labor force because they live in a society that values independence as one of its highest goals and marks the achievement of this goal by one's ability to make money. These wives and mothers also enter the paid labor force because changing labor market conditions offer them an opportunity to do so and because the changing economy makes it increasingly necessary for women to work to maintain familial standards of living. Hence, while only 28 percent of mothers worked for pay in 1950, today 73 percent do. While just 31 percent of mothers with infants were employed in 1976, today these mothers are in the majority at 59 percent.

The decline of the family wage occurred right alongside the rise in women's labor force participation. Working people fought hard throughout the twentieth century to gain wages sufficient to support a family, and though they were never fully successful, by the 1950s, more men than ever before were making a breadwinner's income. Yet the more that women went to work for pay, the less employers felt pressure to provide a wage large enough to support a family. This has been good news for American business, since lower wages generally translate into higher profits. Of course, workers at the top of the income pyramid can still command a family wage, but those in the middle and at the bottom are not so lucky. The increasingly tough position for those at the lower levels is apparent in the exponential growth of the income gap between ordinary workers and high-level managers, and the fact that no one in the bottom fifth of American households today (averaging $11,400 a year) makes a wage high enough to support a family.

The decline of the family wage and rise in women's paid work have obviously had significant consequences for men. These social changes mean that men feel less able, and less compelled, to take the role of the primary breadwinner. In 1973, a full 60 percent of marriage-age men earned a wage high enough to support a family of four above the poverty line. By 1995, the majority of male workers were without the means to support their families on a single salary. The situation at the bottom of the hierarchy is dire: only 25 percent of men with less than a high school diploma earn a wage sufficient to support a family; only one-third of all black men do. There is every reason to believe that for these men their sense of identity has suffered right along with their pocketbooks. And there are indications that men's interest in taking on the breadwinner role has diminished as well. In the 1950s, two-thirds of families had a breadwinning husband and a stay-at-home wife, and we might guess that at least some men in the remaining one-third wished that they could also be successful breadwinners. Today, according to a study by sociologist Kathleen Gerson, only about one-third of marriage-age men are strongly committed to the breadwinner role; of the others, about one-third hope to have a dual-earner household, and one-third distance themselves from family life.

The so-called sexual revolution, although not as central as the massive changes in gender roles, likely played some part in the rise of single parenting. And this cultural phenomenon, which had many sources and quite mixed consequences, was clearly connected to changing gender roles. It gave women and men the right to fulfill their individual sexual desires and, simultaneously (and unintentionally), created the assumption that women could be held individually responsible for their own fertility. At the same time, in breaking the culturally prescribed linkage of sex, marriage, and childbearing, the sexual revolution meant that controlling fertility became that much more crucial. Today, over three-quarters of unmarried women in their 20s are sexually active. The chances of a contraceptive failure run from 2 to 14 percent depending on the method, and three-quarters of pregnancies to unmarried women are unintended. A number of these women are left to raise their children alone.

In all cases, these processes lead to higher rates of divorce as well as higher rates of childbearing outside of marriage. It's not just that marriages become more economically unstable for those in the bottom ranks of the income pyramid. Couples at all income levels increasingly face a double shift of work and family responsibilities. This creates a time crunch at home, and one that disproportionately impacts women (who are most likely to be faced with the bulk of domestic duties). Issues of breadwinning, housework, and childcare thus become central sources of conflict in marriage, as sociologist Arlie Hochschild so powerfully illustrates in *The Second Shift*. At the same time, given that both men and women are independent wage earners, both have less reason to feel committed to the marital bond. All these factors are sources of marital strain; all ultimately lead to a higher incidence of divorce.

Of course this story of the revolution in family life is far too simple, and there are many secondary processes involved. One could easily, for instance, focus on the interests of employers and consider how they capitalized on women's desire for independence to create a situation where labor would be cheaper and more readily available. One could also argue, as Barbara Ehrenreich does in *The Hearts of Men,* that men had grown quite tired of their responsibility for breadwinning and therefore dropped the ball, went off to pursue their individual dreams, and left women scrambling for jobs just to save themselves. Similarly, the sexual revolution's message that women are individually responsible for their own fertility could be interpreted as useful to both men and capitalism—no more worries about breadwinning (or finding sexual partners), no more worries about the family wage. If women want to make babies, then they can support them.

These are not, of course, self-conscious conspiracies; they are slow social processes with interconnected cultural, economic, and political feedback loops that nudge one another forward. All these processes have had unintended consequences. The central point is that multiple—and highly significant— wider social changes all played a part in establishing the dramatic rise in single parenting. By these standards, the system of welfare support was a miniscule player on the historical stage—and its primary impact was to provide minimal support for those most adversely affected.

Taken together, these changes add up to a revolution in family life. This social transformation means that more people are having sex outside of marriage more often. It means that more people are feeling less willing to commit to marriage in general, since it is no longer an absolute cultural or economic requirement that women and men take up prescribed positions of domestic wife and breadwinning husband. It means that the idea of a family wage has virtually disappeared, the minimum wage has declined, and the earnings of ordinary workers are increasingly insufficient to support a family. At the same time, this transformation has meant that more women are economically independent than ever before.

The more these changes take place, the more socially acceptable they become, and the more they come closer to being the norm. The trouble is, in the end, alongside the very real social benefits of some of these changes, there is also a large number of very real social costs. And no one has yet figured out exactly what to do about them.

WHO'S TO BLAME?

All of us, our parents, and our grandparents, collectively participated in these changes, wittingly or unwittingly, for good or ill. If we're looking for someone to blame, that is one direction in which to turn our attention. But in doing so we would make that same mistake of blaming individuals for what are, in fact, social processes that no single individual, or even group of individuals, has orchestrated or controlled. To blame women, the poor, and nonwhites for these problems is simply to blame those for whom the consequences have been most negative and most dramatic.

There is one final point that should not be missed. The outcomes of the family revolution would have been very different if the rise in women's employment and the decline of the breadwinner wage had resulted in a society where everyone considered children just too expensive and too much trouble, and no one bothered to have them any more. If this were the case, we wouldn't have seen the rise in the double shift of family and work responsibilities, the rise in single parenting, and the rise in welfare receipt. Yet, despite all the changes in work and family life that occurred in the second half of the twentieth century, neither men nor women have given up on their desire to have children and their certainty that children are our future. Opinion polls show that the vast majority of Americans agree that having children is a central life goal, an important route to adulthood, and a valued protection against loneliness.

What we have today, therefore, is a striking mismatch between the private valuation of children and the lack of public support for the work of raising them. As much as children are highly prized, there is little institutionalized support for their care: employers don't pay for it, politicians provide little more than lip service to it, and women get almost no cultural or economic "bonuses" for being the primary persons to carry it out (and, in fact, often receive quite the opposite).

Putting it all together, what we are seeing when we look at the welfare rolls is the interaction of the revolution in family life with inequalities of income, gender, and race and the privatized value of children. This is what brought us large numbers of single-parent households, headed primarily by women, overrepresenting nonwhites, at a high risk for poverty and welfare use. It is as simple (and formidable) as that.

The primary point I want to drive home is that all the welfare mothers I have and will describe are not the *causes* of the rise in single parenting or the rising number of women and children living in poverty. They are its *consequences*. If we want to change the number of people who are forced to go on welfare, if we want to change the rate of single parenting, if we want to change the color of welfare, if we want to undo the feminization of poverty, then we must squarely address those larger phenomena. If we approach these social problems only by attempting to "fix" all the individual women currently using welfare, our efforts will fail. The social system that created their plight will simply spawn a whole new generation to take their place.

Although it may sound contradictory at this point, it is for precisely these reasons that understanding the lives of individual welfare mothers is so important. It is not so much because their life stories can answer those particular questions about why this or that woman ended up on welfare—why she wasn't smarter and more conscientious about birth control, why she didn't have an abortion, why she was so naive as to think that pregnancy would lead to a happy marriage, why she failed to get married, why she was divorced, why she didn't get better grades in school, why she didn't go on to college, why she didn't get a job, why she didn't get it faster, and why she didn't get a better job. The answers to these questions are meaningless if the focus is solely on changing this or that woman. Welfare mothers' lives are significant because they follow social patterns, and those patterns are significant because they can provide a useful angle of vision for viewing the more extreme consequences of the social transformation we are all experiencing. They offer us, in this sense, an exaggerated image of difficulties faced by all Americans today—difficulties that have taken an especially dramatic toll on women, on children, and on the most vulnerable among us.

QUESTIONS

1. What does Sharon Hays mean when she argues that "the social changes that led so many women and children to need the help of welfare cannot be blamed on today's welfare recipients"?

2. Identify and discuss the three sociological critiques the author gives of the 1996 welfare reform law's construction of poor single women as personally responsible for their own problems.

3. What are the various changes in work and family life that have taken place over the last several decades that, according to the author, have played a

pivotal role in creating the various hardships experienced by women on welfare?

4. Think of another problem that, like single parenthood, policymakers attribute largely to personal irresponsibility. Then jot down what you think might be some of the social causes of this problem that do not get much policymaking attention. Why do policymakers tend not to focus on these causes?

Providing Free Housing
to the Homeless

Why Problems Like Homelessness May
Be Easier to Solve Than to Manage

MALCOLM GLADWELL

How policymakers address a social problem reflects the way they construct the harm.
In this selection, Malcolm Gladwell describes a recent and growing trend in how
policymakers across U.S. cities are thinking about and responding to the homeless:
by allocating resources disproportionately to the roughly 10 percent of this popula-
tion who are chronically homeless rather than distributing resources more equitably
among all homeless people. In practice, this means that providing rent-free apart-
ments to the chronically homeless is gaining favor over making shelters and soup
kitchens available to anyone who happens to be homeless on a given day. Gladwell
discusses the economic rationale for the rising popularity of this "power-law theory
of homelessness" and explores the moral implications of focusing social policy on the
chronically homeless instead of addressing homelessness as a whole.

Murray Barr was a bear of a man, an ex-marine, six feet tall and heavy-set, and when he fell down—which he did nearly every day—it could take two or three grown men to pick him up. He had straight black hair and olive skin. On the street, they called him Smokey. He was missing most of his teeth. He had a wonderful smile. People loved Murray.

His chosen drink was vodka. Beer he called "horse piss." On the streets of downtown Reno, where he lived, he could buy a two-hundred-and-fifty-millilitre bottle of cheap vodka for a dollar-fifty. If he was flush, he could go for the seven-hundred-and-fifty-millilitre bottle, and if he was broke he could always do what many of the other homeless people of Reno did, which is to walk through the casinos and finish off the half-empty glasses of liquor left at the gaming tables.

"If he was on a runner, we could pick him up several times a day," Patrick O'Bryan, who is a bicycle cop in downtown Reno, said. "And he's gone on some amazing runners. He would get picked up, get detoxed, then get back out a couple of hours later and start up again. A lot of the guys on the streets who've been drinking, they get so angry. They are so incredibly abrasive, so violent, so abusive. Murray was such a character and had such a great sense of humor that we somehow got past that. Even when he was abusive, we'd say, 'Murray, you know you love us,' and he'd say, 'I know'—and go back to swearing at us."

"I've been a police officer for fifteen years," O'Bryan's partner, Steve Johns, said. "I picked up Murray my whole career. Literally."

Johns and O'Bryan pleaded with Murray to quit drinking. A few years ago, he was assigned to a treatment program in which he was under the equivalent of house arrest, and he thrived. He got a job and worked hard. But then the program ended. "Once he graduated out, he had no one to report to, and he needed that," O'Bryan said. "I don't know whether it was his military background. I suspect that it was. He was a good cook. One time, he accumulated savings of over six thousand dollars. Showed up for work religiously. Did everything he was supposed to do. They said, 'Congratulations,' and put him back on the street. He spent that six thousand in a week or so."

Often, he was too intoxicated for the drunk tank at the jail, and he'd get sent to the emergency room at either Saint Mary's or Washoe Medical Center. Marla Johns, who was a social worker in the emergency room at Saint Mary's, saw him several times a week. "The ambulance would bring him in. We would sober him up, so he would be sober enough to go to jail. And we would call the police to pick him up. In fact, that's how I met my husband." Marla Johns is married to Steve Johns.

"He [Murray] was like the one constant in an environment that was ever changing," she went on. "In he would come. He would grin that half-toothless grin. He called me 'my angel.' I would walk in the room, and he would smile and say, 'Oh, my angel, I'm so happy to see you.' We would joke back and forth, and I would beg him to quit drinking and he would laugh it off. And when time went by and he didn't come in I would get worried and call the coroner's office. When he was sober, we would find out, oh, he's working someplace, and my husband and I would go and have dinner where he was working. When my husband and I were dating, and we were going to get married, he said, 'Can I come to the wedding?' And I almost felt like he should. My joke was 'If you are sober you can come, because I can't afford your bar bill.' When we started a family, he would lay a hand on my pregnant belly and bless the child. He really was this kind of light."

In the fall of 2003, the Reno Police Department started an initiative designed to limit panhandling in the downtown core. There were articles in the newspapers, and the police department came under harsh criticism on local talk radio. The crackdown on panhandling amounted to harassment, the critics said. The homeless weren't an imposition on the city; they were just trying to get by. "One morning, I'm listening to one of the talk shows, and they're just trashing the police department and going on about how unfair it is," O'Bryan said. "And I thought, Wow, I've never seen any of these critics in one of the alleyways in the middle of the winter looking for bodies." O'Bryan was angry. In downtown Reno, food for the homeless was plentiful: there was a Gospel kitchen and Catholic Services, and even the local McDonald's fed the hungry. The panhandling was for liquor, and the liquor was anything but harmless. He and Johns spent at least half their time dealing with people like Murray; they were as much caseworkers as police officers. And they knew they weren't the only ones involved. When someone passed out on the street, there was a "One down" call to the paramedics. There were four people in an ambulance, and the patient sometimes stayed at the hospital for days, because living on the streets in a state of almost constant intoxication was a reliable way of getting sick. None of that, surely, could be cheap.

O'Bryan and Johns called someone they knew at an ambulance service and then contacted the local hospitals. "We came up with three names that were some of our chronic inebriates in the downtown area, that got arrested the most often," O'Bryan said. "We tracked those three individuals through just one of our two hospitals. One of the guys had been in jail previously, so he'd only been on the streets for six months. In those six months, he had accumulated a bill of a hundred thousand dollars—and that's at the smaller of the two hospitals near downtown Reno. It's pretty reasonable to assume that the other hospital had an even larger bill. Another individual came from Portland and had been in Reno for three months. In those three months, he had accumulated a bill for sixty-five thousand dollars. The third individual actually had some periods of being sober, and had accumulated a bill of fifty thousand."

The first of those people was Murray Barr, and Johns and O'Bryan realized that if you totted up all his hospital bills for the ten years that he had been on the streets—as well as substance-abuse-treatment costs, doctors' fees, and other expenses—Murray Barr probably ran up a medical bill as large as anyone in the state of Nevada.

"It cost us one million dollars not to do something about Murray," O'Bryan said.

In the nineteen-eighties, when homelessness first surfaced as a national issue, the assumption was that the problem fit a normal distribution: that the vast majority of the homeless were in the same state of semi-permanent distress. It was an assumption that bred despair: if there were so many homeless, with so many problems, what could be done to help them? Then, fifteen years ago, a young Boston College graduate student named Dennis Culhane lived in a shelter in Philadelphia for seven weeks as part of the research for his dissertation. A few months later he went back, and was surprised to discover that he couldn't find any of the people he had recently spent so much time with. "It made me realize that most of these people were getting on with their own lives," he said.

Culhane then put together a database—the first of its kind—to track who was coming in and out of the shelter system. What he discovered profoundly changed the way homelessness is understood. Homelessness doesn't have a normal distribution, it turned out. It has a power-law distribution. "We found that eighty per cent of the homeless were in and out really quickly," he said. "In Philadelphia, the most common length of time that someone is homeless is one day. And the second most common length is two days. And they never come back. Anyone who ever has to stay in a shelter involuntarily knows that all you think about is how to make sure you never come back."

The next ten per cent were what Culhane calls episodic users. They would come for three weeks at a time, and return periodically, particularly in the winter. They were quite young, and they were often heavy drug users. It was the last ten per cent—the group at the farthest edge of the curve—that interested Culhane the most. They were the chronically homeless, who lived in the shelters, sometimes for years at a time. They were older. Many were mentally ill or physically disabled, and when we think about homelessness as a social problem—the people sleeping on the sidewalk, aggressively panhandling, lying drunk in doorways, huddled on subway grates and under bridges—it's this group that we have in mind. In the early nineteen-nineties, Culhane's database suggested that New York City had a quarter of a million people who were homeless at some point in the previous half decade—which was a surprisingly high number. But only about twenty-five hundred were *chronically* homeless.

It turns out, furthermore, that this group costs the health-care and social-services systems far more than anyone had ever anticipated. Culhane estimates that in New York at least sixty-two million dollars was being spent annually to shelter just those twenty-five hundred hard-core homeless. "It costs twenty-four thousand dollars a year for one of these shelter beds," Culhane said. "We're talking about a cot eighteen inches away from the next cot." Boston Health Care for the Homeless Program, a leading service group for the homeless in Boston, recently tracked the medical expenses of a hundred and nineteen chronically homeless people. In the course of five years, thirty-three people died and seven more were sent to nursing homes, and the group still accounted for 18,834 emergency-room visits—at a minimum cost of a thousand dollars a visit. The University of California, San Diego Medical Center followed fifteen chronically homeless inebriates and found that over eighteen months those fifteen people were treated at the hospital's emergency room four hundred and seventeen times, and ran up bills that averaged a hundred thousand dollars each. One person—San Diego's counterpart to Murray Barr—came to the emergency room eighty-seven times.

"If it's a medical admission, it's likely to be the guys with the really complex pneumonia," James Dunford, the city of San Diego's emergency medical director and the author of the observational study, said. "They are drunk and they aspirate and get vomit in their lungs and develop a lung abscess, and they get hypothermia on top of that, because they're out in the rain. They end up in the intensive-care unit with these very complicated medical infections. These are the guys who typically get hit by cars and buses and trucks. They often have a neurosurgical catastrophe as well. So they are very prone to just falling down and cracking their head and getting a subdural hematoma, which, if not drained, could kill them, and it's the guy who falls down and hits his head who ends up costing you at least fifty thousand dollars. Meanwhile, they are going through alcoholic withdrawal and have devastating liver disease that only adds to their inability to fight infections. There is no end to the issues. We do this huge drill. We run up big lab fees, and the nurses want to quit, because they see the same guys come in over and over, and all we're doing is making them capable of walking down the block."

The homelessness problem is like the L.A.P.D.'s bad-cop problem. It's a matter of a few hard cases, and that's good news, because when a problem is that concentrated you can wrap your arms around it and think about solving it. The bad news is that those few hard cases are *hard*. They are falling-down drunks with liver disease and complex infections and mental illness. They need time and attention and lots of money. But enormous sums of money are already being spent on the chronically homeless, and Culhane saw that the kind of money it would take to solve the homeless problem could well be less than the kind of money it took to ignore it. Murray Barr used more healthcare dollars, after all, than almost anyone in the state of Nevada. It would probably have been cheaper to give him a full-time nurse and his own apartment.

The leading exponent for the power-law theory of homelessness is Philip Mangano, who, since he was appointed by President Bush in 2002, has been the executive director of the U.S. Interagency Council on Homelessness, a group that oversees the programs of twenty federal agencies. Mangano is a slender man, with a mane of white hair and a magnetic presence, who got his start as an advocate for the homeless in Massachusetts. In the past two years, he has crisscrossed the United States, educating local mayors and city councils about the real shape of the homelessness curve. Simply running soup kitchens and shelters, he argues, allows the chronically homeless to remain chronically homeless. You build a shelter and a soup kitchen if you think that homelessness is a problem with a broad and unmanageable middle. But if it's a problem at the fringe it can be solved. So far, Mangano has convinced more than two hundred cities to radically reevaluate their policy for dealing with the homeless.

"I was in St. Louis recently," Mangano said, back in June, when he dropped by New York on his way to Boise, Idaho. "I spoke with people doing services there. They had a very difficult group of people they couldn't reach no matter what they offered. So I said, Take some of your money and rent some apartments and go out to those people, and literally go out there with the key and say to them, 'This is the key to an apartment. If you come with me right now I am going to give it to you, and you are going to have that apartment.' And so they did. And one by one those people were coming in. Our intent is to take homeless policy from the old idea of funding programs that serve homeless people endlessly and invest in results that actually end homelessness."

Mangano is a history buff, a man who sometimes falls asleep listening to old Malcolm X speeches, and who peppers his remarks with references to the civil-rights movement and the Berlin Wall and, most of all, the fight against slavery. "I am an abolitionist," he says. "My office in Boston was opposite the monument to the 54th Regiment on the Boston Common, up the street from the Park Street Church, where William Lloyd Garrison called for immediate abolition, and around the corner from where Frederick Douglass gave that famous speech at the Tremont Temple. It is very much ingrained in me that you do not manage a social wrong. You should be ending it."

The old Y.M.C.A. in downtown Denver is on Sixteenth Street, just east of the central business district. The main building is a handsome six-story stone structure that was erected in 1906, and next door is an annex that was added in the nineteen-fifties. On the ground floor there is a gym and exercise rooms. On the upper floors there are several hundred apartments—brightly painted one-bedrooms, efficiencies, and S.R.O.-style rooms with microwaves and refrigerators and central air-conditioning—and for the past several years those apartments have been owned and managed by the Colorado Coalition for the Homeless.

Even by big-city standards, Denver has a serious homelessness problem. The winters are relatively mild, and the summers aren't nearly as hot as those of neighboring New Mexico or Utah, which has made the city a magnet for the indigent. By the city's estimates, it has roughly a thousand chronically homeless people, of whom three hundred spend their time downtown, along the central Sixteenth Street shopping corridor or in nearby Civic Center Park. Many of the merchants downtown worry that the presence of the homeless is scaring away customers. A few blocks north, near the hospital, a modest, low-slung detox center handles twenty-eight thousand admissions a year, many of them homeless people who have passed out on the streets, either from liquor or—as is increasingly the case—from mouthwash. "Dr. Tichenor's—Dr. Tich, they call it—is the brand of mouthwash they use," says Roxane White, the manager of the city's social services. "You can imagine what that does to your gut."

Eighteen months ago, the city signed up with Mangano. With a mixture of federal and local funds, the C.C.H. inaugurated a new program that has so far enrolled a hundred and six people. It is aimed at the Murray Barrs of Denver, the people costing the system the most. C.C.H. went after the people who had been on the streets the longest, who had a criminal record, who had a problem with substance abuse or mental illness. "We have one individual in her early sixties, but looking at her you'd think she's eighty," Rachel Post, the director of substance treatment at the C.C.H., said. (Post changed some details about her clients in order to protect their identity.) "She's a chronic alcoholic. A typical day for her is she gets up and tries to find whatever she's going to drink that day. She falls down a lot. There's another person who came in during the first week. He was on methadone maintenance. He'd had psychiatric treatment. He was incarcerated for eleven years, and lived on the streets for three years after that, and, if that's not enough, he had a hole in his heart."

The recruitment strategy was as simple as the one that Mangano had laid out in St. Louis: Would you like a free apartment? The enrollees got either an efficiency at the Y.M.C.A or an apartment rented for them in a building somewhere else in the city, provided they agreed to work within the rules of the program. In the basement of the Y, where the racquetball courts used to be, the coalition built a command center, staffed with ten caseworkers. Five days a week, between eight-thirty and ten in the morning, the caseworkers meet and painstakingly review the status of everyone in the program. On the wall around the conference table are several large white boards, with lists of doctor's appointments and court dates and medication schedules. "We need a staffing ratio of one to ten to make it work," Post said. "You go out there and you find people and assess how they're doing in their residence. Sometimes we're in contact with someone every day. Ideally, we want to be in contact every couple of days. We've got about fifteen people we're really worried about now."

The cost of services comes to about ten thousand dollars per homeless client per year. An efficiency apartment in Denver averages $379 a month, or just over forty-five hundred a year, which means that you can house and care for a chronically homeless person for at most fifteen thousand dollars, or about a third of what he or she would cost on the street. The idea is that once the people in the program get stabilized they will find jobs, and start to pick up more and more of their own rent, which would bring someone's annual cost to the program closer to six thousand dollars. As of today, seventy-five supportive housing slots have already been added, and the city's homeless plan calls for eight hundred more over the next ten years.

The reality, of course, is hardly that neat and tidy. The idea that the very sickest and most troubled of the homeless can be stabilized and eventually employed is only a hope. Some of them plainly won't be able to get there: these are, after all, hard cases. "We've got one man, he's in his twenties," Post said. "Already, he has cirrhosis of the liver. One time he blew a blood alcohol of .49, which is enough to kill most people. The first place we had he brought over all his friends, and they partied and trashed the place and broke a window. Then we gave him another apartment, and he did the same thing."

Post said that the man had been sober for several months. But he could relapse at some point and perhaps trash another apartment, and they'd have to figure out what to do with him next. Post had just been on a conference call with some people in New York City who run a similar program, and they talked about whether giving clients so many chances simply encourages them to behave irresponsibly. For some people, it probably does. But what was the alternative? If this young man was put back on the streets, he would cost the system even more money. The current philosophy of welfare holds that government assistance should be temporary and conditional, to avoid creating dependency. But someone who blows .49 on a Breathalyzer and has cirrhosis of the liver at the age of twenty-seven doesn't respond to incentives and sanctions in the usual way. "The most complicated people to work with are those who have been homeless for so long that going back to the streets just isn't scary to them," Post said. "The summer comes along and they say, 'I don't need to follow your rules.'" Power-law homelessness policy has to do the opposite of normal-distribution social policy. It *should* create dependency: you want people who have been outside the system to come inside and rebuild their lives under the supervision of those ten caseworkers in the basement of the Y.M.C.A.

That is what is so perplexing about power-law homeless policy. From an economic perspective the approach makes perfect sense. But from a moral perspective it doesn't seem fair. Thousands of people in the Denver area no doubt live day to day, work two or three jobs, and are eminently deserving of a helping hand—and no one offers them the key to a new apartment. Yet that's just what the guy screaming obscenities and swigging Dr. Tich gets. When the welfare mom's time on public assistance runs out, we cut her off. Yet when the homeless man trashes his apartment we give him another. Social benefits are supposed to have some kind of moral justification. We give them to widows and disabled veterans and poor mothers with small children. Giving the homeless guy passed out on the sidewalk an apartment has a different rationale. It's simply about efficiency.

We also believe that the distribution of social benefits should not be arbitrary. We don't give only to some poor mothers, or to a random handful of disabled veterans. We give to everyone who meets a formal criterion, and the moral credibility of government assistance derives, in part, from this universality. But the Denver homelessness program doesn't help every chronically homeless person in Denver. There is a waiting list of six hundred for the supportive-housing program; it will be years before all those people get apartments, and some may never get one. There isn't enough money to go around, and to try to help everyone a little bit—to observe the principle of universality—isn't as cost-effective as helping a few people a lot. Being fair, in this case, means providing shelters and soup kitchens, and shelters and soup kitchens don't solve the problem of homelessness. Our usual moral intuitions are little use, then, when it comes to a few hard cases. Power-law problems leave us with an unpleasant choice. We can be true to our principles or we can fix the problem. We cannot do both.

1. What are policymakers' rationales for conceiving homelessness policy primarily in terms of those who are chronically homeless?

2. Bush Administration housing czar Philip Mangano and other proponents of the power-law theory of homelessness hail the provision of rent-free apartments as a way to solve homelessness because people will now have a place they can call home rather than having to sleep in doorways or on subway grates. To what extent does this policy offer a meaningful solution to the array of problems associated with chronic homelessness?

3. What are the implications of politicians' reducing funding for shelters and soup kitchens, the likely consequence as homelessness policy shifts increasingly toward providing housing for the chronically homeless?

4. Why does Gladwell argue that providing rent-free apartments to the chronically homeless is unfair?

5. Do a Web search and identify three cities that are embracing the power-law theory of homelessness. What do the results look like so far? Is homelessness being reduced? If so, to what degree?

The Politics of Disaster

Disaster Aid: The Mix of Mercy and Politics

DAVID E. ROSENBAUM

Disasters seem all too frequent nowadays. We hear of natural disasters such as Hurricane Katrina, technological disasters such as system malfunctions in the space shuttle, and terrorist disasters like 9/11. We are inclined to think we know a disaster when we see one because of the level of destruction that has taken place. Yet, David Rosenbaum points out that disasters are not that simple. They often have as much to do with politics as with the devastating event itself, since presidential declarations of disaster automatically make affected populations eligible for various kinds of assistance and can thereby elevate the president's image among those populations. Indeed, U.S. presidents tend to declare more disasters during an election season than at other times. Rosenbaum's discussion is useful in enabling us to think about the implications of declaring certain calamitous events disasters while other kinds of harms do not garner the same kind of government assistance.

President Bush's declaration last week that the wildfires in Southern California were a "major disaster" was the 50th such declaration he has issued this year.

That is more than one disaster a week, double the average annual figure in the 1980s. At the rate he is going, Mr. Bush's total for the year could approach the record of 75 disasters declared by President Clinton in 1996, his re-election year.

When a president declares a region a disaster zone, like the four counties in California hit by fires, millions, even in a few cases billions, of federal dollars become available overnight. The residents can be eligible for assistance ranging from unemployment benefits to temporary housing to low-interest loans, and the communities receive grants to cover expenses like debris removal, repairs to damaged buildings and emergency public services.

No one seriously believes there are more floods, fires and pestilence than there used to be. What has happened, in the view of students of the subject, is that presidents have discovered the political utility of the Federal Emergency Management Agency's disaster program.

Without question, the fires last week left a terrible trail of devastation, destroying more than 3,100 houses and other structures. But in a comprehensive analysis of disaster declarations over the years, two economists, Thomas A. Garrett of the Federal Reserve Bank of St. Louis and Russell S. Sobel of West Virginia University, found this year that "nearly half of all disaster relief is motivated politically rather than by need."

They used as the takeoff point for their paper this quotation from Congressional testimony in 1996 by James Lee Witt, then the director of the emergency management agency: "Disasters are very political events."

Mr. Witt declined to be interviewed for this article. Several other politicians and officials said they agreed with Mr. Witt's description, but they said it only after being promised their names would not be used.

"It's so awkward to talk about," said Representative Earl Blumenauer, Democrat of Oregon. "You don't want to appear mean-spirited."

The reluctance of politicians to speak out leaves criticism of the disaster programs primarily to an odd alliance of free-market conservative economists and avid environmentalists.

Even the most ardent libertarians do not hold that the federal government should offer no help when communities are devastated—by a big earthquake, say, or a powerful storm.

"There are national emergencies in which there is clearly a legitimate role for the government," said John Frydenlund, a senior fellow at Citizens Against Government Waste, a conservative research and lobbying organization. "But what's happening in agriculture, for instance, is that some part of the country has a little too much or too little rain, and there is pressure to declare a disaster area."

When assistance is too freely available, Mr. Frydenlund and some other economists say, it can result in more harm than good.

They hold that private disaster insurance is more expensive and less widely available than it should be because federal relief programs reduce the demand for private coverage. They also argue that the programs induce risky behavior, allowing Californians whose homes are destroyed by fire, for instance, to rebuild on fire-prone hillsides.

Other economists are more concerned about what they see as the inequity in requiring struggling taxpayers in, say, North Dakota, to pay taxes to cover the expenses every time a hurricane strikes affluent taxpayers in South Florida. In many parts of the country, statistics show, the farther people live from the coastline, where the property is most vulnerable to storms and flooding, the less well off the people are likely to be.

The case against the relief programs that environmentalists make is that natural disasters are part of the normal ecological cycle.

Federal flood insurance, to take one example, has often resulted in people building or rebuilding on high-risk flood plains that are "some of the richest and most important ecological areas in the country," said David Conrad, a water resources specialist at the National Wildlife Federation.

But these arguments carry little weight with the politicians. Rarely does any lawmaker take issue with offering money to regions where disasters have occurred. One reason, some suggest, is that the day may come when their states or districts will be seeking relief.

The disaster relief law is vague on how it should be applied, so presidents have great latitude. The General Accounting Office, the auditing arm of Congress, has recommended more specific guidelines and standards for years, but Congress has never seen fit to enact them.

Mr. Clinton was a master at showing compassion and spreading the wealth. Time and again at countless fires, floods and blizzards, he showed up to hug victims and offer the government's largess. The television correspondent Brit Hume once called him "almost the national chaplain to those in distress."

Mr. Bush has picked up where his predecessor left off. People are likely to remember the California fires and Hurricane Isabel for years to come. But how many remember even now the ice storm that struck South Carolina last January, the winter storm in upstate New York in April or the heavy rains in New Hampshire and Vermont in July, all belonging to the president's list of 50?

Still, even the president's staunchest political opponents in Congress are not complaining. To the bill providing $87 billion for military operations and reconstruction in Iraq, Congressional negotiators last week added $500 million for "disaster relief activities associated with recently declared disasters, such as Hurricane Isabel and the California wildfires."

The words "such as" were added at the end of the negotiations to appease lawmakers whose states and districts were not affected by the fires or the storm, but perhaps had some other emergency.

1. In what sense are disasters not merely devastating events but also social and political constructions?

2. Identify specific ways that a president can benefit from declarations of disaster.

3. Think about the September 11 terrorist attacks. How has the Bush Administration benefited politically from the construction of this event as a national disaster?

4. Look up the word "disaster" in the dictionary. Then think of an event that seems to you to fit this definition yet was not declared as such by the president? Based on Rosenbaum's analysis, why do you think this event was not declared a disaster?

5. Compare the government's allocations of funds to address the harms caused by an event declared by the president a "disaster" with government funding for everyday harms that people endure. There is typically much more political debate over the justification for the latter than for the former. Why do you think this is the case? Why is there much greater political support—and considerable bipartisan support—for the view that the government should lend a helping hand to people in the wake of a disaster than for the view that government should assist those who experience everyday hardships such as unemployment and poverty?

Labor Strife Produces
Disgruntled Consumers

FROM *Framed! Labor and the Corporate Media*
CHRISTOPHER R. MARTIN

Christopher Martin illustrates how frames monumentally influence the kinds of knowledge that audiences have, or do not have, about a social problem. Martin traces mainstream news coverage of the 1993 American Airlines flight attendants' strike, which took place during the busy Thanksgiving travel period. In documenting the focus of news reports on the various inconveniences that the strike imposed upon stranded airline passengers, Martin highlights how key dimensions of the labor strife between flight attendants and management went undocumented. Because of journalistic inattention to the broader issues behind flight attendants' decision to strike at a time of year that would be devastating to travelers, audiences blamed the strikers for the inconveniences they had caused and were precluded from possibly sympathizing with the labor injustices that flight attendants had been experiencing.

* * *

I f we recall James Carey's statement that "news is not information but drama," then we can remind ourselves that national news stories of a strike will not necessarily provide a comprehensive account of the events. Instead, the news delivers just enough information to frame a compelling drama—one that both stirs the audience with familiar narratives and fits within the journalistic value of objectivity. Most typically, the news dramatizes a strike by pitting labor against management, with the economy's mighty consumer as the jilted third party.

The story of the 1993 flight attendant strike against American Airlines is a perfect example of such a strategically framed drama. . . . [T]he news media largely framed this strike as a story of consumer inconvenience and expense, precluding rational-critical debate of class and compensation issues in the airline industry or of the ways in which the airline industry had been managed since its deregulation in 1978. With "impact on the airline passenger" as the central organizing theme, the news media left out of the story a number of important details that could have helped their readers/viewers make an informed judgment about the strike. Instead, the national news media whipped up a story of an intractable airline conflict that left consumers waiting in the wings.

THE TRAVELERS' ADVOCATE

The timing of the strike by the American Airlines flight attendants—just before Thanksgiving—fit the news media's consumer-based view of labor-management conflict. About 95 percent of the 21,000 flight attendants walked out on Thursday, November 18, 1993, exactly a week before the Thanksgiving holiday, and one of the busiest air travel seasons of the year. The Association of Professional Flight Attendants planned the strike to last no longer than eleven days, with the knowledge that should American try to employ replacement workers, minimum Federal Aviation Administration standards required at least a ten-day safety training program for them.

With the travel plans of American's usual 200,000 passengers a day disrupted, finding an upset passenger was not difficult for the news media. ABC, CBS, and NBC broadcast a total of eighteen news packages during their evening newscasts, but limited coverage to the immediate strike period of November 18 (when the flight attendants walked out) to 23 (when they returned to work). The two mainstream national newspapers offered more extensive coverage over a longer period of time, with *USA Today* filing a total of thirty-three stories between October 21 and December 2, and the *New York Times* publishing thirty stories between October 14 and December 12.

For the three major news networks, the difficulties between the nation's top airline and its flight attendants didn't even merit a package report until November 18, when the threatened walkout began and peeved consumers were in great supply. For the television networks, stories of traveler woe were more important than trying to explain the factors behind the strike, as illustrated in a report by ABC's Bob Jamieson on November 19:

JAMIESON [over VIDEO of flight attendants on a picket line]: While American and its striking flight attendants argued over who was winning the labor dispute, [cut to VIDEO of long lines in an airline terminal] angry passengers declared both losers.

JAMIESON [over VIDEO of customer in terminal with American Airlines representative]: Many blamed American for stranding thousands at airports like Chicago's O'Hare by promising flights would operate when they did not.

FEMALE CUSTOMER #1: I've been on the phone for two days, rescheduling. They tell me one thing, then they lie to us.

FEMALE CUSTOMER #2: For people that have international flights booked months in advance, trips that come once in a lifetime, it's pathetic.

JAMIESON [over VIDEO of picket lines with flight attendants chanting "American's lying, we're not flying"]: Others lashed out at the attendants for striking in the days before Thanksgiving.

MALE CUSTOMER #1: I blame it on the people who are striking. I don't think they are hurting the airlines as much as the passengers.

MALE CUSTOMER #2: I hope they replace all their flight attendants.

On November 20, NBC's Gary Matsumoto trumped Jamieson's story of anonymous traveler misfortune with a dramatic package focusing on the odyssey of the Seffren family of Illinois as they tried to meet their Princess Cruise in San Juan, Puerto Rico before it left port for a Caribbean tour. In his on-camera stand-up in O'Hare, Matsumoto explains "This one family of 26 holiday travelers has lugged hundreds of pounds of suitcases through three different airports, several different terminals, and has spent nearly a hundred extra dollars in skycap fees." Matsumoto later noted that the cruise line, not American, finally made the arrangements for the Seffrens to fly to San Juan via several connecting flights and still meet their cruise ship on time. Still, he said, it wasn't clear how the extended family would return from the Caribbean once the cruise ended seven days later.

USA Today and the New York Times also joined the abandoned traveler narrative. A November 22 story by USA Today began: "Misery reigned over U.S. airports Sunday as a strike by American Airlines flight attendants hobbled the carrier, leaving passengers stranded and tempers frayed." The report then cited reactions from immobile passengers at six airports across the country:

Miami International Airport: Newlywed Joanie Smith of Newtown Square, Pa., sat in a chair while her husband, David, slept at her feet. The Smiths planned to spend their honeymoon in the Caribbean.

When the strike canceled their flight from Philadelphia, they managed to book a USAir flight to Miami. There, they learned the American flight to Aruba had been canceled three days straight.

"I feel so angry, I feel like . . . yelling at (the strikers)," Smith said. "It's my honeymoon. I've had no sleep, no rest."

The *New York Times* used a similar narrative approach in a November 20 report:

Like a coast-to-coast blizzard, the strike by flight attendants has hamstrung travel throughout the nation, upending plans for business meetings, family reunions, vacations, even weddings.

"We've been planning this vacation forever," said Sue Karnes, whose flight to San Juan, P.R., had been delayed for five hours and counting, as fellow would-be passengers slept in chairs. "We're supposed to be on a cruise that leaves tomorrow. We paid $2,600, and it's nonrefundable."

The *New York Times'* simile of "a coast-to-coast" blizzard to describe the consequences of the strike on customers is not surprising. The sound bites and quotes from the frustrated, angry passengers could almost be lifted from the stories the news media routinely do when bad weather shuts down airports. Although the resulting canceled flights and missed connections are similar outcomes, the causes of bad weather and strikes are different: One is an act of Mother Nature; the other is an act of people. Yet, coverage of airline industry labor conflict puts consumers in the same state of powerlessness that bad weather does. Like the case of a bad winter blizzard or summer thunderstorms, the news reports seem to be communicating that there's no use in trying to make sense of a strike—we're all helpless in its wake. Thus, the passenger sound bites and quotes are rarely about what those people understand about the strike, but only how they feel about their immediate situation.

Even after the strike had ended, *NBC Nightly News* apparently felt that the story of the worried and angry traveler merited top billing in its newscast. On November 23, the day after the strike ended, anchor Tom Brokaw led off the newscast this way:

BROKAW: Good evening. Thanksgiving travel is underway tonight—the busiest travel time of the year in this country. And it is a little chaotic at this time, but it would have been much worse if American Airlines were still on strike. NBC's David Bloom now takes us through the travel prospects for the next few days.

Bloom's report was a compendium of bad things that could happen to holiday travelers—such as the already-ended American Airlines flight attendant strike, a possible work slowdown at United Airlines, crowded air terminals, cranky children, and bad weather. His voice-over narration began "American's planes are flying but many of the passengers are still grumbling." Later he alerted the viewer that "travel experts predict Thanksgiving weekend blues." A source from a travel magazine warned in a soundbite to "expect crowds . . . a lot of angry and frustrated people, and lots of crying babies." Next, Bloom noted that a potential work slowdown by United Airlines machinist and pilots union members could result in delays. Bloom concluded (over video of a weather satellite image, a man shoveling snow, and an icy freeway pileup) with "the last bit of bad news, the weather—a storm heading east across the Plains."

Thus, strikes and work slowdowns are equated with nasty winter weather, angry strangers with suitcases, and someone else's incessantly crying baby—all bad things that give us the blues. These are unpredictable events, NBC seems to say, that weigh against our holiday happiness and render us powerless. We cannot understand or prevent such situations, we must only try to avoid them and hope they don't happen to us.

So, what the mainstream news media gave their audience in this time of crisis was mobilizing information of a consumer sort. For example, USA Today (which is heavily dependent on the travel industry, with about 20 percent of its circulation supported by bulk sales to hotels and airlines) provided three stories in a five-day period that directly addressed airline fliers with advice. A November 19 report, entitled "What to Do If You're Flying During the Strike" provided a question-and-answer list and was followed by "Advice, Refunds, Options," on November 22 and by "Playing It Smart with Your Ticket" after the strike on November 23. Even the New York Times took the consumer hotline approach with its own November 19 question-and-answer report on tickets and flight availability, aptly titled "Advice for Travelers During the Strike."

THE TRAVELER'S ADVOCATE, ERGO THE BUSINESS ADVOCATE

It is an attractive and enduring myth that the news media in the United States operate in a free market, presenting all possible views, thus allowing truth to prevail with an informed citizenry in the marketplace of ideas. As Michael Schudson has noted, the utopian model of the active, informed citizen operating in a free marketplace of ideas has given way to the contemporary reality of what Schudson calls the *monitorial citizen*—the citizen who keeps an eye on the sociopolitical scene, but only acts when necessary. For the monitorial citizens of today, more private but always scanning the informational environment and "poised for action" when needed, the news media seem to be crucial. Schudson writes: "All that is required to criticize the present state of affairs is to know that some serious injustices persist, that some remediable conditions that limit human possibility lie before us, and that resources for reconstituting ourselves can be found."

Schudson's concept of the monitorial citizen is useful in explaining the state of civic activity in the United States. I would agree that most Americans are still willing to act on serious injustices, given adequate explanatory and mobilizing information. Yet, to use the example of labor in the United States, I would suggest that the monitorial citizen who informally scans the mainstream news media on a regular basis comes up woefully short on sufficient information to know the injustices that persist in U.S. labor relations and to discover the resources to remedy the situation.

In the case of the flight attendants' strike against American Airlines, the news media gave the anxious airline passenger mobilizing information on how to get from point A to point B, but treated the monitorial citizen to a superficial tit-for-tat that presented some of the competing claims of the union and company but never investigated the truth of the claims. The final product is a journalism of stenography, not of inquiry or analysis. Even the *New York Times*, generally lauded for the insight and analysis it provides for readers, threw its hands up at trying to sort out the information. An October 24, 1993, story by Barbara Presley Noble had one of the most indeterminate leads ever to begin a story in the "newspaper of record":

> Objective reality is the uninvited guest to virtually any labor-management negotiation, but rarely more so than in the current lengthy dispute between American Airlines and one of its unions, the 21,000-member Association of Professional Flight Attendants. Perhaps Srinivasa Ramanujan, the late Indian mathematical genius, could untangle the airline industry's wizardly compensation formulas and arrive at a kernel of pure truth.
>
> Mere mortals wait in vain for any fact, factoid, or fact-ette to stand up and bark. Are flight attendants still getting the shaft a decade after they made concessions, including allowing the company to impose its two-tier wage system, to save jobs and, supposedly, the airline? Or is

American a benevolent employer, simply seeking flexibility to allow it
to compete in what every American man, woman, child and kitty cat by
now agrees is a killer industry?

Unfortunately, the mere mortals reading the story would also wait in vain for
any kind of journalism investigating and weighing the competing claims. The
article's lead paragraphs quickly define the situation as a story of competing
compensation claims and declare any further understanding of the situation
to be impossible. Thus, the mere mortal reader is quickly discouraged from
ever knowing the inequities between labor and management in this case. If
the New York Times can't evaluate the principles of each side's stance, a reader
might conclude, how can anyone else?

Given the limited mainstream news coverage of the strike's issues and the
lack of assistance in sorting through the ethical merits of the airline's and
union's claims, the news audience is left to evaluate the strike from a consumer perspective. The consumer is therefore directed only to ask which side
is most concerned about keeping the planes flying and keeping ticket prices
low. The easy answer from this perspective is American Airlines.

The New York Times' nonevaluative framing of the strike was generally consistent with the approaches taken by ABC, CBS, NBC, and USA Today. The
conflict, these news outlets seem to agree, was between an airline that wants
to cut costs via reduced staffing, changes in work rules, and increased flight
attendant health care contributions and flight attendants who feel squeezed
after years of concessions and comparatively low wages. As with the story of
General Motors' Willow Run Assembly Plant shutdown, the news media
reports approved of the post-Fordist logic of flexibility. Thus, the news characterized American Airlines' "hard-nosed" dealings with its flight attendants
as the only possible path for American and the rest of the airline industry.
For American to survive in the contemporary economy, the report generally
concluded, workers needed to flexibly accommodate management's strategies
to control labor costs.

A November 22 USA Today article even explicitly linked the cost-cutting
and consumer ticket prices issues:

The strike may even be an image winner for American if it succeeds in
cutting costs and lowering fares, says James O'Donnell, a consultant and
former Continental Airlines marketing executive.

"American's frequent fliers are business people who know how to add
and subtract," O'Donnell says.

Thus, from a journalistic standpoint, advocating a cost-cutting strategy that undermines labor is not necessarily a probusiness bias (although it is) but an acceptable objective, neutral, proconsumer position. In other words, the consumer-oriented ends justify the antilabor means.

* * *

QUESTIONS

1. Which details did news reports highlight in portraying the strike as a story about consumer inconvenience?

2. What types of alternative framings of the strike did the reporting not make visible to audiences?

3. How would being made aware of these alternative frames have deepened, and perhaps changed, audiences' understanding of the social problems highlighted by the strike?

4. Why do you think that people who follow the news would prefer to hear stories about how a strike might inconvenience them than about the events leading up to the strike?

32

The Colored Stigma of Imprisonment

Blacks and Ex-Cons Need Not Apply

DEVAH PAGER

This selection illustrates the implications that social problems construction can have upon a particular group of people. Devah Pager examines the consequences of employers believing that black workers are in general less desirable than white workers and black workers with criminal backgrounds are unemployable altogether. After sending black and white students of hers to apply for jobs, Pager found that both race and whether or not the applicant had a criminal background powerfully influenced employers' level of interest in hiring the person. Not only did race and criminal history each adversely affect black applicants, but black applicants with a clean criminal record were less likely to be hired than white ex-cons. Pager briefly explores the psychological effects that these biases may have on people of different races seeking employment. Her study suggests that the socially constructed link between blackness and criminality contributes toward blacks' ongoing difficulties in the labor market. The study, therefore, has important implications for how our society ought to prepare people disadvantaged by employer racism to become more employable, and consequently less motivated to commit crime.

Jerome entered the local branch of a national restaurant chain in suburban Milwaukee. He immediately noticed that he was the only black person in the restaurant. An employee hurried over to him, "Can I help you with something?" "I'm here about the job you advertised," he replied. The employee hesitantly nodded and went off to produce an application form. Jerome carefully filled out the forms, which included checking the box marked "yes" in answer to the question, "Have you ever been convicted of a crime?" He was given a math test and a personality test and then instructed to wait for the manager. The manager came out after about 10 minutes, looked over Jerome's application, and frowned when he noticed the criminal history information. Without asking any questions about the conviction, the manager started to lecture: "You can't be screwing up like this at your age. A kid like you can ruin his whole life like this." Jerome began to explain that he had made a mistake and had learned his lesson, but the manager cut him off: "I'll look over your application and call if we have a position for you." The expression on his face made it clear that he would not be calling any time soon.

Jerome could have been any one of the hundreds of thousands of young black men released from prison each year who face bleak employment prospects as a result of their race and criminal record. Except in this case, Jerome happened to be working for me. He was one of four college students I had hired as "auditors" for a study of employment discrimination. His assignment was to apply for entry-level job openings throughout the Milwaukee metropolitan area, presenting himself as an ex-offender some of the times. For each job opening, a second black auditor also submitted an application, presenting equal educational qualifications, work experience and interpersonal skills. Everything was the same in the two cases except for the criminal record, which Jerome and the other auditor alternated presenting weekly. This one detail made a decisive difference.

After those applications in which Jerome reported a criminal record, Jerome was about one-third as likely to receive a call-back for an interview as was his equally qualified partner who presented no criminal record. Based on these results, a black ex-offender would have to apply for an average of 20 job openings to receive just one call-back—and that's just for an interview. Getting to a job offer would require still more effort and good fortune.

At the same time, I had a second pair of auditors—white students—applying to a separate set of job openings. The contrast between their outcomes and those of Jerome and his partner was striking. A white auditor who reported no criminal record was more than twice as likely to receive a call-back than a black auditor with no record. Indeed, the white applicant with a criminal record was more likely to receive a call-back than a black applicant without any criminal background. I was shocked that race could present a barrier to employment as large or larger than that of a criminal record, especially in light of the widespread belief that discrimination is a thing of the past. . . .

I was not the only one dismayed by these findings. Though I did not discuss the study's results with the audit teams, they were well aware of how their reception varied by race and how it changed when they rotated into the criminal record condition. One of the auditors reported early on feeling discouraged and frustrated that he had received very few responses from employers. As a successful, bright, African-American college student, "becoming" a young black criminal was an extreme change, and the difference in treatment he received seemed to take a toll. With experience he (and the others) grew more comfortable with their assigned roles and became better at playing their parts, but it was clear from these initial responses how much even impersonal rejections can undermine self-confidence and motivation.

The white auditors were also sensitive to the treatment they received when they played an ex-offender, though in different ways. For John, it was the first time he had experienced direct discrimination. He was surprised that one characteristic could make such a big difference in how employers viewed him, and his reactions contained a mixture of disappointment and disbelief. Though for the most part John moved easily through the application process, he once mentioned that he felt "irrationally bad about [him]self" when he checked off the conviction question. He knew what employers were thinking of him, and he could not help but blame himself at the moment.

In all of my planning for this project, I had not appreciated how taxing these daily exposures would be for the auditors. I had expected to find that a conviction record and race made a difference, but I didn't anticipate how the dismissive glances, the curt responses, and the invidious comparisons with peers made the discrimination so blatant. Beyond inequalities in employment outcomes, I saw that seeking work itself demanded differing amounts of effort and stamina depending on one's profile.

Seeing the way these interactions undermined the self-confidence of my testers made me wonder what this experience must feel like for actual job seekers with disadvantages. Unlike my auditors, these people do not get paid to endure discouraging encounters and fruitless job searches, they do not get to share their frustration and seek support in daily briefings, and their experience is not limited to a six-month project. The psychological toll this can take on a job seeker, I came to understand, is dishearteningly heavy. For my testers, it was something they wrestled with and learned from. For real disadvantaged job seekers, it presents yet another obstacle to employment that they must overcome.

QUESTIONS

1. Why do you think the various biases exist that Pager uncovered in her study of the impacts of race and criminal background on employers' per-

ceptions of potential workers? Pager does not delve into an analysis of this specifically, so you will need to spend a bit of time thinking through possible answers to the following:

a. Why are employers in general more inclined to hire a white worker than a black worker? What kinds of assumptions and stereotypes may play into employers' thinking?

b. Why do employers tend to regard having a criminal record as a substantially greater liability for black workers than for white workers?

c. Why would employers want to hire a white person with a criminal record over a black person with a clean criminal history?

2. How do the biases that Pager describes get under job applicants' skin? In other words, what kinds of effects might these biases have on people's self-esteem and motivations to work hard? Draw on Pager's discussion of the college students she hired to conduct her study as a way of inferring what goes on in the minds of people seeking jobs within a biased labor market.

3. Given that the deck is stacked against black job seekers and particularly against those with a criminal record, what can be done to prevent employer biases from creating a self-fulfilling prophesy, making black workers with criminal histories unemployable and hence more likely to commit a crime?

33

Gaming on Native American Reservations

Wheel of Misfortune

DONALD L. BARTLETT AND JAMES B. STEELE

Investigative journalists Donald Bartlett and James Steele look at the consequences of the federal government's efforts since the 1980s to promote gaming as a viable strategy for tackling the monumental problems afflicting Native Americans living on reservations. The authors point out that these efforts have indeed enormously benefited some tribes, such as the Mashantuckett Pequots who operate the Foxwoods Casino in Connecticut. However, the majority of Native Americans on reservations have not been aided by gaming, and they continue to live in destitute conditions. This disparity is especially significant given that the political popularity of gaming diminishes the impetus for the federal government to devise alternative, more broad-based strategies for addressing the myriad problems afflicting Native Americans living on reservations.

Imagine, if you will, Congress passing a bill to make Indian tribes more self-sufficient that gives billions of dollars to the white backers of Indian businesses—and nothing to hundreds of thousands of Native Americans living in poverty. Or a bill that gives hundreds of millions of dollars to one Indian tribe with a few dozen members—and not a penny to a tribe with hundreds of thousands of members. Or a bill that allows select Indian tribes to create businesses that reap millions of dollars in profits and pay no federal income tax—at the same time that the tribes collect millions in aid from American taxpayers. Can't imagine Congress passing such a bill? It did. Here's how it happened—and what it means.

Maryann Martin presides over America's smallest tribe. Raised in Los Angeles in an African-American family, she knew little of her Indian ancestry

387

until 1986, when at age 22 she learned that her mother had been the last surviving member of the Augustine Band of Cahuilla Mission Indians. In 1991, the Bureau of Indian Affairs (BIA) certified Martin and her two younger brothers as members of the tribe. Federal recognition of tribal status opened the door for Martin and her siblings to qualify for certain types of government aid. And with it, a far more lucrative lure beckoned: the right to operate casinos on an Indian reservation.

As Indian casinos popped up like new housing developments across Southern California, Martin moved a trailer onto the long-abandoned Augustine reservation in Coachella, a 500-acre desert tract then littered with garbage, discarded household appliances and junk cars, about 25 miles southeast of Palm Springs. There she lived with her three children and African-American husband William Ray Vance. In 1994, membership in the tiny tribe dwindled from three adults to one when Martin's two brothers were killed during separate street shootings in Banning, Calif. Police said both men were involved in drug deals and were members of a violent Los Angeles street gang.

Subsequently, Martin negotiated a deal with Paragon Gaming, a Las Vegas company, to develop and manage a casino. Paragon is headed by Diana Bennett, a gaming executive and daughter of Vegas veteran and co-founder of the Circus Circus Casino William Bennett. Martin's Augustine Casino opened last July. With 349 slot machines and 10 gaming tables, it's the fifth and by far the most modest casino in the Palm Springs area. But it stands to make a lot of non-Indian investors—and one Indian adult—rich.

And get this: Martin still qualifies for federal aid, in amounts far greater than what many needy Native Americans could even dream of getting. In 1999 and 2000 alone, government audit reports show, she pulled in more than $1 million from Washington—$476,000 for housing, $400,000 for tribal government and $146,000 for environmental programs.

It wasn't supposed to be this way. At the end of the 1980s, in a frenzy of cost cutting and privatization, Washington perceived gaming on reservations as a cheap way to wean tribes from government handouts, encourage economic development and promote tribal self-sufficiency. After policy initiatives by the Reagan Administration and two U.S. Supreme Court rulings that approved gambling on Indian reservations, Congress enacted the Indian Gaming Regulatory Act in 1988. It was so riddled with loopholes, so poorly written, so discriminatory and subject to such conflicting interpretations that 14 years later, armies of high-priced lawyers are still debating the definition of a slot machine.

Instead of regulating Indian gambling, the act has created chaos and a system tailor-made for abuse. It set up a powerless and underfunded watchdog and dispersed oversight responsibilities among a hopelessly conflicting hierarchy of local, state and federal agencies. It created a system so skewed—only a few small tribes and their backers are getting rich—that it has changed the face of Indian country. Some long-dispersed tribes, aided by new, non-Indian financial godfathers, are regrouping to benefit from the gaming windfall. Others are seeking new reservations—some in areas where they never lived, occasionally even in other states—solely to build a casino. And leaders of small, newly wealthy tribes now have so much unregulated cash and political clout that they can ride roughshod over neighboring communities, poorer tribes and even their own members.

The amount of money involved is staggering. Last year 290 Indian casinos in 28 states pulled in at least $12.7 billion in revenue. Of that sum, *Time* estimates, the casinos kept more than $5 billion as profit. That would place overall Indian gaming among *Fortune* magazine's 20 most profitable U.S. corporations, with earnings exceeding those of J.P. Morgan Chase & Co., Merrill Lynch, American Express and Lehman Bros. Holdings combined.

But who, exactly, is benefiting? Certainly Indians in a few tribes have prospered. In California, Christmas came early this year for the 100 members of the Table Mountain Rancheria, who over Thanksgiving picked up bonus checks of $200,000 each as their share of the Table Mountain Casino's profits. That was in addition to the monthly stipend of $15,000 each member receives. But even those amounts pale beside the fortunes made by the behind-the-scenes investors who bankroll the gaming palaces. They walk away with up to hundreds of millions of dollars.

Meanwhile, the overwhelming majority of Indians get nothing. Only half of all tribes—which have a total of 1.8 million members—have casinos. Some large tribes like the Navajo oppose gambling for religious reasons. Dozens of casinos do little better than break even because they are too small or located too far from population centers. The upshot is that a small number of gaming operations are making most of the money. Last year just 39 casinos generated $8.4 billion. In short, 13% of the casinos accounted for 66% of the take. All of which helps explain why Indian gaming has failed to raise most Native Americans out of poverty. What has happened instead is this:

A LOSING HAND

Revenue from gaming is so lopsided that Indian casinos in five states with almost half the Native American population—Montana, Nevada, North Dakota, Oklahoma and South Dakota—account for less than 3% of all casino proceeds. On average, they produce the equivalent of about $400 in revenue per Indian. Meanwhile, casinos in California, Connecticut and Florida—states with only 3% of the Indian population—haul in 44% of all revenue, an average of $100,000 per Indian. In California, the casino run by the San Manuel Band of Mission Indians pulls in well over $100 million a year. That's about $900,000 per member.

THE RICH GET RICHER

While federal recognition entitles tribes to a broad range of government benefits, there is no means testing. In 2001, aid to Indians amounted to $9.4 billion, but in many cases more money went to wealthy members of tribes with lucrative casinos than to destitute Indians. From 1995 to 2001, the Indian Health Service, the agency responsible for looking after the medical needs of Native Americans, spent an average of $2,100 a year on each of the 2,800 members of the Seminole tribe in Florida. The Seminoles' multiple casinos generated $216 million in profits last year, and each tribe member collected $35,000 in casino dividends. During the same six years, the health service spent an annual average of just $470 on each of the 52,000 members of the Muscogee (Creek) Nation in Oklahoma, whose tiny casinos do little more than break even.

BUYING POLITICIANS

Wealthy Indian gaming tribes suddenly are pouring millions of dollars into political campaigns at both state and federal levels. They are also influencing gaming and other policies affecting Native Americans by handing out large sums to influential lobbying firms. In 2000 alone, tribes spent $9.5 million on Washington lobbying. Altogether they spend more to influence legislation than such longtime heavyweights as General Motors, Boeing, AT&T—or even Enron in its heyday.

GAMING TRIBES AS EXCLUSIVE CLUBS

Tribal leaders are free to set their own whimsical rules for admission, without regard to Indian heritage. They may exclude rivals, potential whistleblowers and other legitimate claimants. The fewer tribe members, the larger the cut for the rest. Some tribes are booting out members, while others are limiting membership. Among them: the Pechanga Band of Mission Indians in Riverside County, Calif., whose new Las Vegas-style gaming palace, the Pechanga Resort & Casino, is expected to produce well over $100 million in revenue.

GOLD RUSH

Since only a federally recognized tribe can open a casino, scores of groups—including long-defunct tribes and extended families—have flocked to the BIA or Congress seeking certification. Since 1979, as gambling has boomed, the number of recognized tribes on the U.S. mainland has spiked 23%, to a total of 337. About 200 additional groups have petitioned the bureau for recognition. Perhaps the most notorious example of tribal resurrection: the Mashantucket Pequots of Connecticut, proud owners of the world's largest casino, Foxwoods. The now billion-dollar tribe had ceased to exist until Congress re-created it in 1983. The current tribe members had never lived together on a reservation. Many of them would not even qualify for government assistance as Indians.

THE IMPOTENT ENFORCER

Congress created the National Indian Gaming Commission (NIGC) to be the Federal Government's principal oversight-and-enforcement agency for Indian gaming—and then guaranteed that it could do neither. With a budget capped at $8 million, the agency has 63 employees to monitor the $12.7 billion all-cash business in more than 300 casinos and small gaming establishments nationwide. The New Jersey Casino Control Commission, by contrast, has a $59 million budget and a staff of 720 to monitor 12 casinos in Atlantic City that produce one-third the revenue. The NIGC has yet to discover a single major case of corruption—despite numerous complaints from tribe members.

THE WHITE MAN WINS AGAIN

While most Indians continue to live in poverty, many non-Indian investors are extracting hundreds of millions of dollars—sometimes in violation of legal limits—from casinos they helped establish, either by taking advantage of regulatory loopholes or cutting backroom deals. More than 90% of the contracts between tribes and outside gaming-management companies operate with no oversight. That means investors' identities are often secret, as are their financial arrangements and their share of the revenue. Whatever else Congress had in mind when it passed the regulatory act, presumably the idea was not to line the pockets of a Malaysian gambling magnate, a South African millionaire or a Minnesota leather-apparel king.

FRAUD, CORRUPTION, INTIMIDATION

The tribes' secrecy about financial affairs—and the complicity of government oversight agencies—has guaranteed that abuses in Indian country growing out of the surge in gaming riches go undetected, unreported and unprosecuted. Tribal leaders sometimes rule with an iron fist. Dissent is crushed. Cronyism flourishes. Those who question how much the casinos really make, where the money goes or even tribal operations in general may be banished. Indians who challenge the system are often intimidated, harassed and threatened with reprisals or physical harm. They risk the loss of their jobs, homes and income. Margarite Faras, a member of the San Carlos Apache tribe, which owns the Apache Gold Casino in San Carlos, Ariz., was ousted from the tribal council after exposing corruption that led to the imprisonment of a former tribal leader. For three years, Faras says, those in control mounted nighttime demonstrations at her home, complete with loudspeakers. They initiated a boycott of her taco business, telling everyone she used cat meat. They telephoned her with death threats. Says Faras: "I don't know what else to say, other than it's been a nightmare."

QUESTIONS

1. In paving the way for casinos to operate on reservations, which problems prevalent among Native Americans did the federal government intend to mitigate? Although the authors allude to some of these problems, it would be helpful to do a Web search to get a fuller sense of them.

2. What kinds of inequalities has gaming created among tribes? Discuss the gap between those who have profited enormously versus those who have not?

3. The authors suggest that the legalization of gaming on reservations in 1979 may explain why the number of federally recognized tribes has grown con-

siderably since then. The authors indicate that the Mashantuckett Pequots were recreated by Congress in 1983. Use the Web to research examples of other Native Americans whose efforts in recent years to gain legal tribal status may have been motivated by the prospect of profiting from gaming.

4. Take the perspective of a member of Congress who represents a state where reservation gaming has been enormously profitable, such as Connecticut, Florida, and California.

    a. Why would you be inclined to continue to support gaming? How would you be influenced by the lobbying efforts of tribes in your home state that have profited from gaming?

    b. How might your continued support of gaming cause you to neglect giving consideration to other policy options that might offer more broad-based strategies for addressing the myriad problems afflicting Native Americans living on reservations?

Acknowledgments

Donald L Bartlett and James B. Steele, "Wheel of Misfortune," *Time*, December 16, 2002. Copyright © 2002 Time, Inc. Reprinted by permission. Time is a registered trademark of Time, Inc. All rights reserved.

Mitch Berbrier and Elaine Pruett, "When Is Inequality a Problem?" *Journal of Contemporary Ethnography* 35, no. 3 (2006): 257–58, 263–75, 278–84. Copyright © 2006 by Sage Publications. Reprinted by permission of Sage Publications, Inc.

Joel Best, "Chapter 1: Random Violence," from *Random Violence: How We Talk about New Crimes and New Victims.* Copyright © 1999 by the University of California Press. Reprinted with permission.

Joel Best, "Monster Hype: How a Few Isolated Tragedies—and Their Supposed Causes—Were Turned Into a National Epidemic," *Education Next* (Summer 2002). Excerpted from pp. 51–53. Reprinted with permission of Education Next.

Amy Binder, "Constructing Racial Rhetoric: Media Depictions of Harm in Heavy Metal and Rap Music," *American Sociological Review* 58, no. 6 (December 1993): 753–67. Reprinted with permission of the American Sociological Association.

Gary Blasi, "And We Are Not Seen: Ideological and Political Barriers to Understanding Homelessness," *American Behavioral Scientist* 37, no. 4 (1994): 563–86, Copyright © 1994 by Sage Publications. Reprinted by permission of Sage Publications, Inc.

Frank Bruni, "Behind Police Brutality: Public Assent," *The New York Times*, February 21, 1999. Copyright © 1999, The New York Times. Reprinted with permission.

The Center for Consumer Freedom, excerpts from "Introduction," in *An Epidemic of Obesity Myths.* Reprinted by permission of The Center for Consumer Freedom.

Martin Gilens, "Race and Poverty in America: Public Misperceptions and the American News Media," *Public Opinion Quarterly* 60 (1996): 515–41. Reprinted by permission of Oxford University Press.

Malcolm Gladwell, "Million Dollar Murray: Why Problems Like Homelessness May Be Easier to Solve Than to Manage." Originally published in *The New Yorker*, February 13, 2006 & February 20, 2006. Reprinted by permission of the author.

Malcolm Gladwell, "Talk of the Town: Drunk Drivers and Other Dangers," *The New Yorker*, March 8, 1999. Copyright © 1999 Conde Nast Publications. All rights reserved. Originally published in *The New Yorker*. Reprinted by permission.

Barry Glassner, *Culture of Fear*. Copyright © 1999 by Barry Glassner. Reprinted by permission of Basic Books, a member of the Perseus Books Group.

Sharon Hays, "Chapter 5: Pyramids of Inequality," from *Flat Broke With Children: Women in the Age of Welfare Reform*, pp. 121–37. Copyright © 2003 by Sharon Hays. Reprinted by permission of Oxford University Press.

Hendrik Hertzberg, "Talk of the Town: Flood Tide," *The New Yorker*, January 17, 2005. Copyright © 2005 Conde Nast Publications. All rights reserved. Originally published in *The New Yorker*. Reprinted by permission.

Derrick Jackson, "Why Do Stereotypes and Lies Persist?," *Nieman Reports* 51 (Spring 1997): 44–45. Reprinted by permission of the author and Nieman Reports.

Philip Jenkins, *Using Murder: The Social Construction of Serial Homicide*. Copyright © 1994 by Aldine Publishers. Reprinted by permission of AldineTransaction, a division of Aldine Publishers.

John M. Johnson, "Horror Stories and the Construction of Child Abuse," from *Images of Issues: Typifying Contemporary Social Problems*. Copyright © 1995 by Aldine Publishers. Reprinted by permission of AldineTransaction, a division of Aldine Publishers.

Eric Klinenberg, "Chapter 5: The Spectacular City," from *Heat Wave: A Social Autopsy of Disaster in Chicago*. Copyright © 2002 by The University of Chicago. All rights reserved. Reprinted with permission.

Michael Lipsky and Steven Rathgeb Smith, "When Social Problems Are Treated as Emergencies," *Social Science Review* (March 1989). Copyright © 1989 by The University of Chicago. All rights reserved. Reprinted by permission.

Kathleen S. Lowney and Joel Best, "Stalking Strangers and Lovers," from *Images of Issues: Typifying Contemporary Social Problems*. Copyright © 1995 by Aldine Publishers. Reprinted by permission of AldineTransaction, a division of Aldine Publishers.

Kristin Luker, Reprinted by permission of the publisher from "Constructing an Epidemic" from *Dubious Conceptions: The Politics of Teenage Pregnancy*, pp. 81–90, 92–97, 100–108, Cambridge, Mass.: Harvard University Press, Copyright © 1996 by the President and Fellows of Harvard College.

Christopher R. Martin, Reprinted from *Framed! Labor and the Corporate Media*. Copyright © 2004 by Cornell University. Used by permission of the publisher, Cornell University Press.

Devah Pagar, "Blacks and Ex-Cons Need Not Apply" from *Contexts*, Vol. 2, No. 4, pp. 58–59. Copyright © 2003 University of California Press. Reprinted with permission.

Jeffrey Reiman, *The Rich Get Richer and the Poor Get Prison: Ideology, Class and Criminal Justice*, 7/e. Published by Allyn and Bacon, Boston, MA. Copyright © 2004 by Pearson Education. Excerpted by permission of the publisher.

Craig Reinarman and Harry G. Levine, "Chapter Two: The Crack Attack," from *Crack in America: Demon Drugs and Social Justice*, pp. 1–28. Copyright © 1997 by The University of California Press. Reprinted with permission.

David E. Rosenbaum, "Disaster Aid: The Mix of Mercy and Politics," *The New York Times*, November 2, 2003. Copyright © 2003, The New York Times. Reprinted with permission.

Dawn Rothe and Stephen L. Muzzatti, "Enemies Everywhere: Terrorism, Moral Panic and US Civil Society," *Critical Criminology* 12, no. 3 (2004): 327–50. Copyright © 2004. Reprinted with kind permission from Springer Science and Business Media.